CHOCTAW TALES

CHOCTAW TALES

Stories from the Firekeepers

Tom Mould and Rae Nell Vaughn

University Press of Mississippi / Jackson

The University Press of Mississippi is the scholarly publishing agency of
the Mississippi Institutions of Higher Learning: Alcorn State University,
Delta State University, Jackson State University, Mississippi State University,
Mississippi University for Women, Mississippi Valley State University,
University of Mississippi, and University of Southern Mississippi.

www.upress.state.ms.us

The University Press of Mississippi is a member
of the Association of University Presses.

Copyright © 2025 by University Press of Mississippi
All rights reserved
Manufactured in the United States of America

∞

Publisher: University Press of Mississippi, Jackson, USA
Authorised GPSR Safety Representative: Easy Access System Europe -
Mustamäe tee 50, 10621 Tallinn, Estonia, *gpsr.requests@easproject.com*

Library of Congress Control Number: 2025935047

Hardback ISBN 978-1-4968-5707-1 | Paperback ISBN 978-1-4968-5708-8
Epub single ISBN 978-1-4968-5709-5 | Epub institutional ISBN 978-1-4968-5710-1
PDF single ISBN 978-1-4968-5711-8 | PDF institutional ISBN 978-1-4968-5712-5

British Library Cataloging-in-Publication Data available

In memory of Gladys Willis
and all the storytellers who have gone before .-.-. and come after

CONTENTS

Foreword by Chief Phillip Martin xv
Preface to the Second Edition. xvii
Preface to the First Edition xxv
Introduction 3

THE STORYTELLERS 29

THE GENRES OF CHOCTAW STORYTELLING 79

Native Terms 80
Commentary and Context 84
Patterns of Performance. 89
Synthesis: Supernatural Stories 91
A Note on the Texts 93

CREATION STORIES AND MYTHS 96

The Choctaw Creation Legend 98
Nané Chaha. 99
Men and Grasshoppers 99
Creation of the Tribes 100
Origin of the Crawfish Band 100
A Short Story of the Creation of the First Man 101
The Creation of the Choctaw 101
The Migration Legend. 103
Migration 104
Tradition of the Flood 105
The Flood 106
Lightning and Thunder 107

Thunder and Lightning 107
Fani Losa and the Sun 107
Dark Sun 110
The Origin of Corn 110
Corn-Finding Myth 111
Wild Geese and the Origin of Corn 111
The Geese, the Ducks, and Water. 111
The Life of Dogs 112
How the Snakes Acquired Their Poison 113
The Owl 113
Tashka and Walo 114
The Hunter of the Sun 115
Yallofalaiya 116
Nameless Choctaw 118
The Hunter and the Alligator 120

SUPERNATURAL LEGENDS AND ENCOUNTERS 122

The Girl and the Devil 124
The Eagle Story 125
Skate'ne 126
Hoklonote'she 127
A Story of Kashikanchak 127
Kashikanchak 128
The Spectre and the Hunter 129
The Hunter Who Became a Deer 131
The Man Who Became a Snake 132
Horse Man 134
Half Horse, Half Human 135
Kashehotapalo 136
Na Losa Falaya 136
Manlike Creature 137
Okwa Nahollo—White People of the Water 137
Big Pond 138
The Water Choctaw 139
The Mermaid 139
Voices on the Mound 140
The Long-Haired Lady 140
Pąš Falaya 141
Nishkin Chafa—One-Eye 143
Headless Man 144

The Inhuman *Na Losa Chito* 145
The Demon *Na Losa Chito* 146
A Big Hog. 146
Big, Black, Hairy Monster. 147
Black Dog. 148
Choctaw Bigfoot 148
Na Losa Chito's Lair 149
The Black Stump 150
The Choctaw Robin Goodfellow 151
The Little People in Nanih Waiya Cave 152
Doors in Nanih Waiya Cave 153
Watcher in the Woods. 153
Throwing Rocks 153
Throwing Competition 154
No Playing after Dark 155
The Floating Light 155
Lights 157
Kowi Anukasha 157
Medicine Woman 158
The Little Man 159
Pile of Rocks 161
A Witch 163
Choctaw Doctors. 163
Shape Changer 164
The Baseball Game. 164
Dancing Lights 165
Hashok Okwa Hui'ga—Dew Drop (Will-o'-the-Wisp) 166
The Blue Light 166
Disappearing Lights 167
Lingering Spirit. 167
The Ghost. 168
Spirit of the Dead 169
Two Brothers 169

HISTORICAL TALES 170

The Coming of Christianity. 171
Helping the New Immigrants. 171
White Men Bring Alcohol. 172
Fighting the Muskogees 172
Crossing the Line. 173

Pushmataha	175
Death of Pushmataha	176
Pushmataha's Suspicious Death	176
Removal	177
Hiding to Avoid Removal	177
Second Removal and Return	178
Sneaking Back from Oklahoma	179
Land Swindling	179
Grandfather's Land	180
Burning Sticks	181
Escaping Slavery	181
Sinking Ship	182
German Surrender	183
Army Volunteer	184
Patriots	185
Go Back to Europe	185
Poll Tax	186
Segregation in the Fields and at the Movies	187
Injustice at the Laundromat	187
Discrimination	188
Murder of Civil Rights Workers	189
Mississippi Burning	190
Banned	190
Troubling Times	191
Treated like a Dog	192
Framed for Murder	193
Whites-Only Water Fountain	194
Shortchanged	195
Overcharged	196
Some Bad, Some Good	196
No Trust and No Choctaw	197
Served in the Back in High School	197
Eat in the Back	198
A Simple Hello	198
Believe It When You See It	199
Segregation Then and Now	199
Housing Discrimination	200

PROPHECY 202

Changing Landscape and Intermarriage. 203
Invention of the Airplane 203
Planes, Roads, and Culture 204
Intermarriage, Roads, and Changing Seasons. 205
Changing World 205
Electricity, Plumbing, and Social Dancing 206
Cars, Roads, and Changing Values 208
Gender Roles, Roads, and Housing 209
A Fearful Future 210
A Great Illness 211
Prophecies of Disease 212
Snatched from Above 212
The Third Removal. 212
War 214
Land Getting Old 215
Extinction. 216
Snake Returns 216
End of the World. 217
Big Fire 217

JOKES AND TALL STORIES 218

The Car 219
Running Water 220
Whatyousay. 220
Time to Kill Hogs 221
The Horse's Egg. 221
The Funeral 222
The White Cat 223
The Man and the Turkey 224
Talking Frogs 225
A Praying Bear 226
The Dog Who Spoke Choctaw 226
The Trip to Arkansas. 227
Tall Stories 228
The Lucky Shot 229
Help from Above. 229

ANIMAL STORIES... 231

The Ball Game 232
Race between the Hummingbird and the Crane 233
The Hummingbird 234
The Dove Story 234
How the *Biskantak* Got Water for the Birds 234
Why the Buzzard Has More Offspring than the Owl 235
Why the Guinea Hen Is Speckled 235
Boatmaker 235
The Hunters and the Bears 236
Rabbit and the Bears 237
How the Bear Lost His Tail 238
How the Rabbit Got a Short Tail 238
How the Bullfrog Lost His Horns 239
How the Alligator Got His Back 239
Rabbit and Turtle Race 240
Race between the Turkey and the Terrapin 241
Turtle and Turkey 242
Why Terrapins Never Get Fat 242
Turtle, Turkey, and the Ants 243
Why There Are Seams in the Terrapin's Shell 244
Why the Turtle's Shell Is Sewed Up 244
How the Terrapin Lost the Ability to Climb Trees 244
Possum's Tail 245
Possum and Coon 246
The Panther and the Opossum 247
How the Possum Tricked the Wolves 249
Possum and the Fox 250
Possum and the Woodpecker 250
Why the Rabbit's Skin Is Loose 251
Bear and Rabbit 252
How the Rabbit Fooled the Turkeys 252
Rabbit and Fox Farm Together 253
Rabbit Rides Wolf 253
Rabbit Gains a Wife 254
How Rabbit Made the Animals Angry 255
Rabbit and the Garden 255
The Cat Tricks the Mouse 257
Mouse, Rooster, and Cat 257

STORIES IN CHOCTAW 259

The Choctaw Creation Legend 259
Lightning and Thunder 260
Corn-Finding Myth 260
A Story of Kashikanchak 260
Kashikanchak 261
The Man Who Became a Snake 262
The Big Pond 265
Pąš Falaya 265
The Inhuman *Na Losa Chito* 268
The Black Stump 269
Cars, Roads, and Changing Values 269
The Funeral 270
The Dog Who Spoke Choctaw 271
Help from Above 272
The Dove Story 273
How the *Biskantak* Got Water for the Birds 273
How the Possum Tricked the Wolves 273
The Cat Tricks the Mouse 274
Mouse, Rooster, and Cat 274

Annotations to the Stories 276
Notes 309
Sources Cited 317
Index 325

FOREWORD

Choctaw Tales is a book that needed to be written. For centuries, the Choctaw people in Mississippi have retold the age-old stories, keeping alive the history and legends and traditions that have shaped who we are as a tribe and what we value. Like the tribal elders before them, today's storytellers continue this tradition, telling the old stories and creating new ones to fit a changing world. Part of that changing world is a world of television, computers, the internet, cell phones, airplanes, and books. These modern conveniences are also part of Choctaw life, just like the oral tales still told on front porches, around campfires, and around family dinner tables.

The storytellers are still here with us, but so are new audiences who have become accustomed to reading, not just listening, to learn. Sadly, there are relatively few books about our tribe available to our youth to guide their learning. The history books have tended to either ignore our unique Choctaw culture, including us with other Indians from across the continent who differ greatly from us, or mention us marginally in the context of the story of White America and stop there. Our Choctaw views, our history, and our people have too often been ignored. This book will not remedy this oversight altogether, but it does join a growing number of recently published books as an important start.

When Tom Mould first visited our tribe in the winter of 1995, he was an earnest young man interested in helping us collect and record our tribal stories. He saw the possibility of fulfilling his own interests in learning about our culture with our interests in gathering the stories for the Choctaw people. Tom met Rae Nell Vaughn, the tribal archivist at the time, who brought him to meet me. I was pleased at the prospect of producing a book to honor the tribal elders and our Choctaw culture. I have had a long-standing interest in such a publication, even since the late 1950s, when I first became involved in tribal government leadership.

Back then, our tribe was strong, but suffering. Just as in many other American Indian communities across the country, unemployment was high and social problems rampant. With the support of the Choctaw people and the wisdom and guidance of the Tribal Council, we built an industrial park to begin creating jobs, and hope, for all tribal members. Today, the tribe ranks as Mississippi's third-largest employer. Throughout the process of our growth, we have never lost sight of our culture and its importance in guiding us as a people. In 1981, we established both the Choctaw Heritage Council and the Choctaw Museum of the Southern Indian to ensure the preservation and development of our culture. We have continued to develop new programs such as the Choctaw Language Preservation Program and the Cultural Affairs Program, both of which have been active in continuing our oral traditions.

I introduce this book, *Choctaw Tales*, with great pleasure, and I am happy that it is being added to our efforts to preserve and invigorate our culture. My hope is that this publication will serve as inspiration to young tribal members to take up the vital job of becoming our future storytellers.

—Chief Phillip Martin

Mississippi Band of Choctaw Indians

PREFACE TO THE SECOND EDITION

Things change. In some ways, the justification for a second edition of *Choctaw Tales* is as simple as that. But of course, things are never really that simple.

This new, fully revised edition has a new title, a new coauthor, and more than fifty new stories. That would seem to indicate significant change since 2004, when the book was first published. Yet many of these revisions are indications of greater collaboration and awareness more than outright change.

The addition of the subtitle was developed collaboratively with some of the storytellers in this book, most notably Eddie Johnson, Jay Wesley, and Rae Nell Vaughn, who brought not only their perspectives immersed in Choctaw culture, but also a savviness of what would appeal to a general audience.

The addition of Rae Nell Vaughn as coauthor was a recognition that authorship is not solely about who drafts the words on the page. The work that Rae Nell contributed to the first edition between 1995 and 2004, and the second edition more recently, involved every step in the process in producing this manuscript except the writing. She helped develop the idea for the book, introduced Tom to storytellers in the community, helped develop a collaborative research model with Choctaw high school students through the Youth Opportunity Program (YOP), discussed what should and should not be included in the book, and helped Tom answer every question raised by this rich storytelling tradition by pointing him to an elder in the community, directing him to an archival source, or referencing her own lived experience growing up in the Pearl River community. For the second edition, she became even more involved in the writing process: brainstorming the updates a second edition would require and suggesting revisions to the stories to make them more approachable to a general audience. Beyond this preface, however, we have continued to use *I* to indicate Tom since the fieldwork he describes is shared from his perspective; shifting to third person seemed both disingenuous and unnecessarily distant.

Finally, virtually all of the new stories added were being told back in 2004 as well. It is impossible to record all the stories from all the storytellers in a community where the oral tradition continues to serve such a central role. This edition adds some important stories missed the first time around, and while it is fairly comprehensive, it cannot presume to be exhaustive.

These revisions, therefore, are less about change than about collaboration, recognition, and awareness of what has been present from the start. Of course, things have also changed since 2004, and this edition attempts to account for those changes as well. The most glaring and devastating of these changes is the loss of so many of the storytellers from the first edition. Most of those deaths were long before COVID-19, but the pandemic's impact on the community was severe.

Many of the changes on the reservation are easy to spot. In Pearl River, where the tribal government is headquartered, there are new government office buildings; a new shopping center; a new health center; a new justice complex; a new museum, archive, and cultural center; a new business complex with the Choctaw TechParc; a new lake recreation area; and a new sportsplex. The completion of both the Golden Moon Hotel & Casino and the Geyser Falls Water Theme Park occurred after this book was written but before it was published. New housing communities, facility buildings, and schools have been built in many of the communities, including a new casino in Bogue Homa. The fairgrounds sport a new historic village, dance pavilion, and cultural-events area, as well as new staging areas. After twenty-eight years in office, Chief Phillip Martin was followed by Miko (Chief) Beasley Denson, then Chief Phyliss Anderson, and now Chief Cyrus Ben. Tribal Council seats similarly changed hands, while old businesses were replaced with new ones.

The changes that impact the storytelling tradition, however, are less obvious. Storytelling continues to be a critical form of communication for the elders, sharing tribal, familial, and personal histories and knowledge with their children and grandchildren. It also continues to face competition from a myriad of new technologies that offer quick entertainment at the touch of a button or the swipe of a screen. Despite perennial concerns that with the passing of every elder comes the loss of crucial information, new storytellers continue to step into the shoes of past ones. Further, tribal initiatives continue to be developed to ensure that stories and storytelling are not left solely to individuals in private settings. Storytelling presentations continue to be part of the lineup at the annual fair, and staff at the Department of Chahta Immi continue to field requests for storytellers to local and regional festivals and events.

One change since 2004, however, is a direct result of the publication of *Choctaw Tales*. Exactly as Chief Martin hoped, the book has become a resource in the tribal school system as part of their cultural heritage curriculum, for public presentations to non-Choctaw audiences, and for community members filling in gaps in their own knowledge both for their own edification as well as that of their children and grandchildren. Part of the reason for the book's usefulness is that it offers Choctaw storytellers an easily accessible and searchable cache of stories recorded as they were told, in the voices and idioms of the Choctaw elders themselves. When Director of the Department of Chahta Immi Jay Wesley needs to share stories with groups on or off the reservation, he often consults *Choctaw Tales* in addition to combing through his own repertoire of stories he heard growing up. Talking one afternoon in 2021 with Tom Mould and the YOP students working on a future book of Choctaw narratives, Dan Isaac put it bluntly. It wasn't the writing *about* Choctaw storytelling that was so powerful, it was the stories shared just as they were told.

> I love it because you keep it the way they said it. You don't try to edit. If Jake York said, "The wolf and the dog and the dogs sat on the wolf . . ." or "the rabbit sat on the wolf," or whatever, you say it the way he said it. Exactly how he said it. That's the way when I read them, I can just hear Jake. I knew Jake. I worked with him before. I knew Gus, Gus Comby. He was just awesome, man. He was full of humor. I used to drive for the hospital, and I would take him to VA. On the way, he would just talk the whole way. And I would just eat it up.

More than once in our more recent interviews with Choctaw elders, a person would point out that one of the stories they were about to tell was similar to one in *Choctaw Tales*. The stories recorded in *Choctaw Tales* serve not only as resources but also as memory prompts and dialogue partners.

Scholars and authors have found the book useful too, many for the analysis of the storytelling genre system, but others solely for the elders' stories, often including whole narratives in their own work.[1] And yet, other scholars have not picked up the study of Mississippi Choctaw oral traditions, which is no doubt partially why, during a casual phone call in 2017, Rae Nell told Tom it was time to come back and write another book. As usual, she was right, and Tom did write that book with Choctaw storytellers and cultural preservationists Eddie Johnson and Jay Wesley. The book is *Choctaw Traditions: Stories of the Life and Customs of the Mississippi Choctaw*. But it was also time to update *Choctaw Tales*. New storytellers, new and newfound stories, and new opportunities for storytelling beyond the reservation required addition and revision to the first edition.

The genre system of storytelling has similarly remained fairly stable, but our understanding of it has shifted, prompted by new linguistic developments. The most obvious change is that the tribe is using a new orthography. The Choctaw word for hog, *shukha*, is now written as *shokha*, and the word for talk, *anumpa*, is *annǫpa*. What was once known as *shukha anumpa* is now written as a single word: *shokhannǫpa*. *Chitto* is now spelled *chito*, which means previous terms such as the supernatural being *na losa chitto* is now *na losa chito*.

More impactful than new spellings are the addition of new words. With no native term in use in 2004 for the category of stories that sits opposite *shokhannǫpa*, Tom coined the term *talk of the elders*. Since then, the tribal language program has developed new terms, including *hopáki ikhąna*, defined as "legends, old stories, history." The new term offered a more emic term for *talk of the elders*, but it also required us to reevaluate the entire system. In doing so, we realized that contemporary stories of supernatural encounters did not fit comfortably in either the new umbrella term or the old one. Further, although Tom noted that people continued to create animal tales, he did not include their contemporary appearance on the chart. All three of these issues have been addressed in the "Genres of Choctaw Storytelling" as well as in a revised chart.

For all these shifts, revisions, and evolutions, however, it is the addition of more than fifty new stories that most clearly justifies the publication of a second edition. All six of the chapters acquired new stories, some chapters more than others. "Creation Stories and Legends" remain fairly stable. People are not creating wholly new stories about how the world began, though they are continuing to adapt, revise, and personalize the two main stories of migration and emergence. Similarly, while people continue to share the old prophecies from the past, new predictions are less common.

Stories of the supernatural continue to be the most widespread narrative tradition in the community, but this section was already twice as long as any of the others, so we chose to only add a few more that represented new developments in the tradition, including the increasing use of "Bigfoot" as a way of interpreting *na losa chito*.

The humorous stories, tall tales, comic anecdotes, and animal tales of *shokhannǫpa* continue to be shared, though the additions are fairly evenly divided among older stories ignored in the first edition and new ones created and shared since. In the first edition, Tom noted that storytellers continue to create new *shokhannǫpa* stories about animals. However, he omitted any story with a clear, individual authorship, ignoring the dynamism of the storytelling tradition, where oral and written stories move back and forth across media. This edition corrects that omission and includes a handful of written stories, all created under the auspices of the tribal language program. Accordingly, we not only have a few new animal tales in English, but in the Choctaw language as well. Although Possum had already emerged alongside Rabbit as a central trickster figure in the 2004 edition, the new additions here make it clear just how dominant Possum's role is in both fooling and being fooled. Further, legendary "funny man" Ashman is revealed here as a real person, living just down the road from some of the storytellers who told tall tales about his side-splitting behavior.

By far the largest additions, however, appear in the "Historical Tales" chapter. Focused on passed-on stories tied to major cultural belief systems or events, Tom recognized the importance of including stories of first-person encounters with the supernatural but missed the importance of first-person stories of historical events. Accordingly, the first edition included stories of the distant historical past that described intertribal warfare, early encounters with White colonists, removal to Indian Territory in Oklahoma and its aftermath, and the attack on cultural traditions by misguided missionaries. It did not, however, include the vast body of stories of growing up in a segregated South where aggressive discrimination was the norm. Nor did it include stories about relocation efforts in the mid-twentieth century or war stories from World Wars I and II. Inexplicably, the first edition also skimped on stories of historical encounters with Whites, removal, and famous chiefs, offering only one or two stories rather than sampling more broadly. This edition remedies those omissions, but only to a point. Stories of more personal histories that, taken collectively, offer a picture of Mississippi life, customs, and traditions are so numerous that they require their own book. *Choctaw Traditions: Stories of the Life and Customs of the Mississippi Choctaw* captures many of those stories, rooted in a past as recent as last week and as long ago as the creation of the Choctaw from the Nanih Waiya Mound. Many of the stories included there could be included in this chapter, and vice versa, particularly the stories of Cameron Wesley's infamous murder trial in 1940, which got moved back and forth between the two books until finally settling in the "Rituals and Laws" section of *Choctaw Traditions*. One account of the trial, however, is included here as a nod to the story's relevance for both books.

The stories themselves continue to be verbatim, maintaining the distinct ways of speaking so that the voices of Jake and Gus and the many other storytellers remain recognizable to those who knew them. However, based on conversations with storytellers still living, teachers who use the book, and recognition of how best to reach our intended audiences and ensure that the storytellers could communicate as effectively in writing as they did in speaking, we have done some very slight editing, removing false starts when they added no new information and omitting some but not all of the verbal fillers such as "you know" and "well" that are ignored by the ear in oral performance but can trip up the eye when reading.

A final note. In the chapters that follow, Tom often describes his fieldwork, meeting and working with people who helped create this book. But we wanted to include an opportunity for Rae to also offer some thoughts specific to her position and role, in her own voice. And so we did. Here.

INTRODUCTION

In January 1996, I was introduced to two grad students, Guy Hardy and Tom Mould, who were here to record tribal members singing church hymns in the Choctaw language. One of the grad students, Tom, stopped by the Tribal Archives to chat. I spoke with him about what I did, and he shared the work he was hoping to do to record stories. Tom was a folklorist. I was intrigued. As he spoke of his work, I thought, "Isn't this what we do? Share stories; talk about the things that have been passed down?" At that point, all of the history and stories I had read were written by non-Indians, which in some cases were inaccurate, superficial, or written with a touch of romanticism of Native Americans. Here was someone who wanted to record the stories as *we* told them.

As tribal archivist, my charge was to capture the history, oral traditions, and collections of work and stories in all their forms. During our conversation, I shared that one of my goals was to develop material for a curriculum of Choctaw stories and history that would be available to the school system.

FRIED CATFISH, BLACK-EYED PEAS, CORNBREAD, AND SWEET TEA

On one of Tom's first visits to Choctaw, I invited him to dinner at my house to meet my then-husband, Harley Vaughn, and my mother, Caroline Morris. Harley and I cooked dinner and invited my mother over to meet Tom and let him share what he would be doing while at Choctaw. Our daughters, Hillary, Mahlih, and Breanna, were planning to spend the night with my mother. Our dinner was filled with my mother telling what I call "Rae stories"—stories of me growing up and the mischief I would get into. Of course, I would protest, but to no avail, so I was resigned to listen again to stories like the "Rubber Ducky" and the "Emergency Broadcasting System Test."

WILLIS ROAD

Tom was introduced to my grandmother, Gladys Willis, and that was it. He became family. She invited him to dinner. They would sit on the porch and talk even during the hot summer evenings with the mosquitoes buzzing in his ear. Grandma shared with him that when her grandpa and dad would share scary stories by the fireplace, she would try not to listen because they scared her, so she didn't remember any scary stories. It was at one of the dinners that

Tom met my Uncle Hulon and Aunt Marybell (Mary). My Uncle Hulon was the jokester, the storyteller and the one who made you laugh . . . loudly! One afternoon, while sitting at Hulon's carport, he said, "Tom, I'm not a storyteller, but I can tell you a story." That was in 1996.

LOSING VOICES

In 1999, we lost Grandma Willis. We lost Mom in 2010; we lost Harley in 2022; we lost Hulon and my brother Greg in 2023. During the COVID-19 pandemic, we lost several family members, grandparents, aunts, uncles, cousins, sons, daughters, mothers, and fathers. It was losing a generation. It was losing our history.

SEVEN GENERATIONS

The three little girls Tom met who were two, four, and six are now in their thirties and have started families of their own. To my grandchildren, Tom is their Uncle "Guy" . . . Why that name? Something to do with a movie and a hip young man. After the grandchildren met Tom, they asked, "What does he do?" We told them, "He is here to record Choctaw stories and tales." Too young to understand, they said, "Okay." During his visits Tom would join us for meals and celebrate birthdays and special family events. At birthday dinners, we would end the evening sharing childhood stories of the birthday person. Pointing at each other, saying, "That was you," "No that was you!" and laughing until our sides hurt. I'm sure if you asked my daughters about the "Rubber Ducky" story, they could probably share the tale.

Tom has also been with our family during sad times as he sat with the firekeepers during family members' wakes. He has walked with us in family procession and recession. He has stood with us, prayed with us, and cried with us. He was not Tom Mould the Researcher. He was Tom Mould our family.

Stories are important. They "document" the road map; they provide understanding of who we are as a family and as people. We are the descendants of Choctaw people who refused to go on the Trail of Tears. We have survived poverty, racism, discrimination, oppression. As a people, we have relied on what we were taught and what we were told.

TWENTY-FIRST CENTURY

From sitting around a fire and sharing stories, to downloading apps to learn the Choctaw language, it's important to collect and document as much as possible, but it's a priority to share the information with both the next generation of tribal members and the public. My grandchildren will never know my mother, their great-grandmother, but they see her picture on my mantel, and we talk about her and her stories.

Choctaw Tales is a key for the future to unlock the past. The past is the foundation for their future. It is a fragile balance. Ebb and flow.

PREFACE TO THE FIRST EDITION

She turns the pages in the book slowly, scanning each one until her eye alights on the information she is searching for. With a precise hand, Estelline Tubby folds the small spiral notebook open to the spot and silently reads what she has written. After a minute or two, she looks up and begins speaking. The book remains open on her lap, but she does not consult it again.

She tells the old stories—of Nanih Waiya, the Third Removal, and the supernatural beings in the woods. These are the stories that have been passed along from generation to generation.

The words in her notebook are from her own hand, but they reflect the words of her grandmother and her grandmother before that. They are brief notes to remind her of what she heard both as a child and as an adult; they are too important to risk losing to a faulty memory. At over seventy, such concerns are not idle to Estelline Tubby.

"Long time ago, we didn't have it written in books or anywhere," she says. "They just handed it down from generation to generation. "We had a workshop in Nevada, and I went there. A lot of Indians met together. And the last session was how can we let our language, our culture, our heritage and all—be alive. And one got up and said, 'In books.'"

Estelline has her notebook. Her grandchildren are the beneficiaries. Whenever they visit, Estelline tells them the old stories. She sees it as her duty.

Many people have grandparents who still remember the old stories. But many others do not. Here was the chance for a communal notebook.

The contents of this book are the product of storytellers throughout the Mississippi Choctaw community who have remembered, retold, and created the stories that have been theirs for longer than human memory can prove. If this book is a resource of the oral narratives of the Choctaw, it stands only as a pale reflection of the actual resource of this material—the individual storytellers who continue to entertain, enlighten, debate, and instruct. They are thanked in their way in the chapter titled "The Storytellers," but even this list is pale and partial compared to the number of storytellers that can be counted in the community. As important, even heroic, are the people who have spurred and encouraged the creation of this collection out of their own recognition of the importance of these stories.

ACKNOWLEDGMENTS FROM TOM MOULD

First and foremost is the coauthor of this book: Rae Nell Vaughn. As coauthor, she has her own acknowledgments below, but my debt to her is deep as she has served as guide, mentor, consultant, creator, and friend for almost thirty years. Her concern for the oral traditions of her community led to many of the stories in this book. She began by introducing me to her family—her grandmother Gladys Willis, her uncle Hulon Willis—and slowly branched out to others, in Pearl River as well as other communities. Rae Nell also involved high school students working through the tribal Youth Opportunity Program during the summer of 1997. All of them—Liasha Alex, Danielle Dan, Lionel Dan, and Curtis "Buck" Willis—accompanied me separately on interviews, sometimes sitting quietly and listening, other times asking their own questions and adding their own perspectives. Their interest encouraged the speakers; the stories would be for a book, but they were also being heard by the youth of the community, the way it was supposed to be.

The enthusiasm and facilitation that Rae Nell Vaughn provided in Pearl River was mirrored by sisters-in-law Meriva Williamson and Glenda Williamson in the Conehatta community. Piling into the car together, we drove around the community, stopping off at the homes of their friends and neighbors, people they knew could tell stories. The people in Conehatta pride themselves on retaining their culture; while virtually everyone speaks English, many of the older people prefer to talk in Choctaw. Meriva and Glenda Williamson not only introduced me to the storytellers in Conehatta; they translated my questions and asked many of their own. They were as much fieldworkers as I. Their help was invaluable; their friendship even more so. Melford Farve, Henry Williams, and Billy Amos have extended similar trust and similar friendship. They, too, are responsible for the creation of this book.

Along the way, many others throughout Mississippi have helped, through their words, actions, friendship, and expertise: Robert Ben, Deborah Boykin, Charlie Denson, Lena Denson, Bob and Martha Ferguson, Berdie John, Leigh Jordan, Harry and Geri Harm, Frank Henry, Norma Hickman, Ricky and Cathy Irons, Calvin Isaac, Roy and Alvina Mitch, Sonja Monk, Roseanna Nickey, Pam and Roy Smith, Creda Stewart, Doyle Tubby, Henderson Williams, and Ken York. In the very beginning, Guy Hardy, a fellow folklorist and ethnomusicologist, invited me to help record a hymn sing in Mississippi back in December 1995, giving me my first introduction, and glimpse, into the Choctaw community. It was obviously an introduction that has changed the course of my life. I will always have him to thank for his generous invitation.

Maggie Chitto, Pam Smith, Jesse Ben, and Roseanna Nickey transcribed and translated the interviews conducted in Choctaw, making it possible to hear some of these stories in the language so many are trying so hard to keep alive. Few who have not attempted such work can appreciate their hard work and patience as they listened to tapes over and over, straining toward exact translations. One group who does is the Jacobs Research Fund, who generously provided the money to pay these talented translators, as well as additional funds years later in 2021 to return to Mississippi to continue this work.

As a collection of stories past and present, this book contains the contributions of many fieldworkers. Those from the past are recorded in the introduction, but there are others, more recent collectors who have provided me with their notes, transcripts, and insights. In the mid-1980s, Geri Harm recorded the stories of Inez Henry among others. Geri Harm's linguistic training has made the stories she collected particularly rigorous and particularly invaluable. She also lent her expertise to Inez Henry's daughter, Pam Smith, as she translated stories I collected more recently in the community. All three have not only been invaluable with regard to the work in this book but have opened their doors to me when I was just beginning my work in Mississippi. They offered meals, lodging, and friendship to someone they knew only by a friend's introduction.

In 1990, Greg Keyes, then a student at the University of Georgia, and Ken Carleton, the tribal archeologist, recorded the stories of Gus Comby, who has since passed away. Informal conversations with them both have been as useful in understanding Choctaw storytelling as the stories they collected. And finally, though their work began and ended long before I ever heard of the Choctaw, tribal high school students in the 1970s and 1980s published *Nanih Waiya*, a student publication of interviews with community members modeled after the Foxfire project in Appalachia. They created a resource of cultural material that is unparalleled in the community in its scope, covering a host of cultural traditions including cooking, politics, beadwork, and storytelling. Their work has been particularly useful to this book, adding narratives as well as more general insight into Choctaw culture.

Also, as a collection incorporating material of the past, this book benefited greatly from the help of Robert Leopold, Daisy Njoku, and Vyrtus

Thomas at the Smithsonian Institute, who guided me through the collections and helped secure photos of some of the storytellers of the past. Thanks are also due the Alabama Department of Archives and History for permission to publish parts of Henry Halbert's manuscript "Choctaw Indians East of the Mississippi River," housed in their collection. I am also indebted to a grant from the American Philosophical Society in 1996 to conduct preliminary research in Mississippi.

The book as a textual and visual entity owes much to the incredible staff at University Press of Mississippi, Alana Dunn at Butler University, and friends and colleagues across the US. In 1997, friend and photographer Allyson Whyte took time out from her job in New York City to come to Mississippi at her own expense and take photos of some of the storytellers. Her pictures are exquisite. I only wish she had had time to take photos of all the storytellers rather than a few. In 2023, Ken Calhoun similarly carved out weekends and after-hours time from his job as assistant provost and professor of design at Lasell University to help design the cover for the second edition, handling our dozens of suggestions with grace and patience.

Finally, there are debts I owe that cannot be paid with small thanks in a book, though I will include them here anyway. Rae Nell and Harley Vaughn took me into their home and fed and housed me like a member of their family. The rest of their family has done the same. Caroline Morris and Gladys Willis, Rae Nell's mother and grandmother respectively, have welcomed me to their dinner tables countless times. The children and grandchildren, nieces, nephews, sisters and brothers, and cousins who have gathered with us have been as generous and welcoming as any relative. They have made this work feasible, not just by allowing me into their homes and lives, making sure I understood them as they attempted the same with me, but also by providing friendship in a place where I initially knew so few.

As integral as anyone to this project is Henry Glassie, my advisor and friend. From my first trip to Mississippi back in the winter of 1995, Henry has listened to my exhilarations and disappointments, dilemmas and successes, offering good advice and a kind ear. Along with Henry Glassie, Sandy Dolby and Greg Schrempp took the time to read the original manuscript and offer both broad and specific suggestions; their help can be found throughout these pages.

I have also relied greatly on the support of my family. My parents, Bill and Lucille Mould; my brother, Rob, and his family Laura, Caroline, and Charlie; my extended family; and my many in-laws. Most of all, I thank my wife, Brooke, and my children, Lily and Jack, all of whom continue to support me, in research and in life. Thank you. Yakokih.

ACKNOWLEDGMENTS FROM RAE NELL VAUGHN

There are many people to acknowledge. To begin I would like to say a personal thank you to all the people who participated in sharing their stories for this book. They knew the assignment and took on the challenge. We have lost many storytellers from the first edition to the second. To the families, I say, "Yakọki." Their words will forever be memorialized in this book and will be shared for generations to come.

Second, I would like to thank my siblings, Billie and Christina, and daughters, Hillary, Mahlih, and Breanna. You got to sit in and listen to stories, share stories, and sometimes create stories. Billie and Christina, thank you for being there with me. To my daughters, you have always been my inspiration because I wanted stories to be put to pen and paper. They will be here for you to share with your children and their children to learn about oral stories and traditions of the Choctaw people.

Most important, I want to acknowledge those our family has lost along our journey. Losing Jenny Roa, Michah Tubby, Shannon Willis, Marcus Willis, Marybell Willis, Harley Vaughn, Hulon Willis, and Gregory Morris has been a devastating blow to our family. We miss them every day.

My grandmother Gladys Mae Tubby Willis and my mother, Caroline Willis Morris—these two women have meant so much to me. Raising me, caring for me, disciplining me (Mom, not Grandma), teaching me, but most importantly loving me. As a child, I saw their strength and courage when we were living at a time when life was difficult. We were poor, but we were loved. As an adult, they were my inspiration and my heroes. Losing them was painful, but I know they are with me always.

To our readers, thank you for reading *Choctaw Tales*. Hash mọma kat yakókih.

CHOCTAW TALES

INTRODUCTION

"Stop by," he said. We had set no day, no time for arrival. "Just stop by, and we'll talk," Hulon Willis told me. "I'm not a storyteller," he said, "but I can tell you a story."

It is the spring of 1996, and stories are what I have come to Mississippi to hear. So when he told me to stop by, I accepted the invitation. "We'll talk about stories," he said. "I'll try to remember some of them for you. Stop by."

That's just what I was doing. Perhaps he would be home, perhaps not. If so, perhaps we would talk. This was not a business appointment or formal event. Even had it been, such occasions are almost never set to the minute. Events begin when the audience is there and the speaker is ready, birthday parties when the food is done. To get impatient is foolish.

Following the directions I scrawled on a piece of paper towel from the family dinner that Hulon hosted the week before, I drive north from Philadelphia, Mississippi. Ahead of me lies Pearl River, home of the Mississippi Band of Choctaw Indians. One of eight Choctaw communities scattered throughout Mississippi, Pearl River is both the geographic and tribal center, home to the tribe's offices, high school, museum, industries, and casino. In the past forty years, it has become a very visible example of the synthesis of traditional American Indian life and modern American comfort—comforts like paved roads, luxury cars, washing machines, and air conditioning. It is that last thing I am most thankful for now as the summer sun beats down on my car.

Ahead of me, I spot the neon of the Silver Star Hotel & Casino. Today it is mirrored by the Golden Moon Hotel & Casino across the road and has become only one small part of a series of massive construction projects to turn Pearl River into a vacation resort. But back in 1996, the Silver Star shone bright and lonely in the middle of the Mississippi woodlands. After only two years, the Silver Star had already paid for itself as well as for new elementary schools and various community-improvement programs.

The casino appears to the traveler as a dazzling, glittering, blinking emblem of the progress the Choctaws have made in the past four decades. Yet this emblem is misleading; the guaranteed revenue of gambling is only the latest financial achievement for a people who have built their success through the development of an industrial empire, thanks in great part to the efforts of Chief Phillip Martin. Since 1959, when he was first elected as tribal leader, Phillip Martin has developed over a dozen tribal businesses, some affiliated with major corporations, others, wholly independent.

Yet for all the glitter of the casino and the asphalt and aluminum siding of the industrial park, Pearl River remains mainly a woodland. Tall southern pines dominate the earthly landscape, just as the burning Mississippi sun dominates the sky.

I turn off the highway and drive down Willis Road, named for Hulon's family. Small brick homes, many with satellite dishes and expensive cars in their driveways, appear among the tall pines. I am on Choctaw land, though I know this only from experience. No gate or sign greets me. Land owned by the tribe is too scattered—a plot here, an acre there—for formal delineation. Hulon's home is not far, and I soon spot him in the front yard, mowing the few blades of grass that have managed to push their way through the dry, red dirt. It hasn't rained in a month, a fact neither the land nor the people can ignore.

He greets me as he abandons the mower and leads me to the shade of his carport. An assortment of chairs, stools, and coolers awaits us. I alight upon a cooler, Hulon in a kitchen chair. It is obvious that I am not the first person he has entertained in this makeshift living room. I soon learn that, in fact, this is a permanent arrangement for the many guests who stop by on a regular basis to talk with and listen to Hulon Willis.

We sit and talk. I mention the weather. It seems too hot for mowing the grass, I say. Hulon nods. He tells me he'll be leaving soon. Now I nod, remembering that soon Hulon will be returning to work down in Louisiana. He supervises a barge that travels the Mississippi River through the Gulf of Mexico. He works continuously for a couple of months, then gets a month off. The work is hard, long, and far from home. Hulon divides his time between Louisiana and Mississippi, between the ship and home, between coworkers and family.

But Hulon doesn't mind the work, and he loves the month-long breaks he can take in between. When he's home, he can devote himself to his family and friends and to relaxing—except for the lawn that needs mowing, of course.

"But it's too hot for mowing," I say again. "Yeah," Hulon agrees. "Yeah."

Eventually, I ask him about his childhood. He tells me about growing up in Mississippi, on this very land. That was before they got indoor plumbing and electricity in their home. And when travel was "a thing we hardly ever did."

If we went anywhere, it was usually to the hospital, and going to the hospital meant getting a shot, as far as I knew, growing up. If they dressed you up, told you to get ready to go to town, you were going to go get a shot.

They'd cover it up by telling you you was going to get some Coke, you know, which was a treat because we never had Cokes before. "We're going to take you to town," but they're not taking the rest of the kids to town, so you knew right then and there you were going to the hospital.

He laughs, and I laugh with him. We continue to talk. Time passes. I begin to feel like just another of the people who has come to listen to Hulon Willis, though I know that with my tape recorder and my white skin, I am not. But he tells me a joke, and I tell him one in return. We banter back and forth, falling in and out of conversation with jokes and stories—about his work on the boats on the Mississippi River or the golf course being built behind his house, or of Bear and Rabbit serving each other dinner.

"This is a story that was told to me by Alexander Tubby," Hulon explains, preparing to tell one of the stories he learned as a child. "He's passed on, about twenty years or so."

"Is this a relative?" I wonder aloud.

"Yeah. He was my—he was something on my mother's side. I really can't remember," he says, laughing apologetically. "But they used to come around."

And this is a story about the Bear and the Rabbit.

On these certain occasions, on this certain occasion, the Bear asked the Rabbit to come over to his bear den, have supper with him. So the Rabbit went along, went over to his house that Sunday. And the Bear was sitting there, talking away. Finally got time, he said—the Bear said to the Rabbit—"Well, I'll just go in and cook up some steaks."

He said, "Steaks?"

He said, "Yeah, steaks."

So the Bear goes into the back, got him a knife, and starts sharpening it up a little bit.

Rabbit's sitting there just idling his thumb. And after a little while, he look back in there.

Well, the Bear was standing there, got his knife out, and cut out two slices of steak out of his side—out of his side like, you know, out of his side. So he sews himself back up, and then he gets a frying pan and fries the steak. And then they both ate.

Rabbit says—when he got ready to leave—he said, "Well, next Sunday, you come over to my house, and we'll do the same thing."

He said, "All right." The Bear said, "All right."

And the next thing you know, it's that Sunday, and here comes the Bear. And the Rabbit's getting ready for him and everything. And he said, "Sit down."

So the Bear sat down and got ready.

And the Rabbit finally got around to going inside and said, "You ready to eat?"

He said, "Yeah."

He said, "Well, let me cook up some steaks, and we'll have some steak."

And the Bear's just sitting there. And pretty soon he look behind him, and there's the Rabbit with the knife.

And he started—he started sticking himself. But you know how rabbits are, they're real lean.

So when he started sticking himself, he started bleeding, you know. And bleeding to death he was.

And the Bear got ready, had himself some rabbit steak.

Hulon and I both begin laughing.

"And that's the end of that," he says, still grinning.

We move on to other topics, about work and life and the changing world. He talks about the creek behind his house, their only source for water while he was growing up. His arm swings and gestures around his land, pointing out landmarks from his past, each carrying with it a story. He tells me about the race between the turtle and the hare, another story he learned from Alexander Tubby. We trade stories back and forth. He tells me a story about spending Thanksgiving on his barge; I tell him about the Thanksgivings I spent away from my family while living in Missouri. He tells me a joke about a farmer's wife and a minister; I tell him one about a one-eyed bartender and a parrot.

"I like to sit just like this," he says,

with maybe two or three other people. Because at times I will draw a blank, and then I'll ask, "Don't you remember a story?" And then they'll tell me something, and then we'll relate, going back and forth.

And we keep the little thing going for a while. I've sat here almost six or seven hours at one time, actually. Just tell jokes, tell stories, back and forth.

As Hulon hopes, others join us to help carry the burden of entertaining. Mary Willis, Hulon's wife, grabs a spot on a cooler in between errands to tell a few jokes and stories of her own, as does his sister Marilyn Tubby. Another sister, Sandra Weaver, also stops by, though only for a few minutes at a time. Sandra lives across the road, and today she has agreed to watch some of the children of her brothers and sisters in addition to her own two sons. Tomorrow, another of the mothers or a grandparent will volunteer, or be asked, to do the same.

Weekends and holidays are times when friends often come by to talk and pass the time under Hulon's carport. Today is Memorial Day, but no other friends stop by except for me. Today it is just family. Passing in and out, tending to the daily tasks that occupy their time, they join to hear a joke or a story or to tell one, on their way back to the neck-bone soup simmering in the kitchen, or the baseball game on television inside, or the child who has just woken up from her nap.

The laughter that punctuates our talk is not incidental. With television and movies and VCRs, entertainment can be had more quickly and with less thought or effort than storytelling demands. But people need human interaction, and television is no substitute. So there are days like today when family members and friends stop by, sit awhile, and talk. They talk of the weather, of children, of jobs and each other. They tell jokes, and they tell stories, and they laugh.

The cool shade of Hulon's carport, where his family surrounds him, is not so different from the setting for storytelling held in the memories of many of the community, of the elders as well as younger adults like Hulon, who at the time was only thirty-nine. The memories of the elders—as some call them; elderlies, say others—reach as far back as eighty years, but the things they remember from their parents and grandparents extend this timeline even further. The stories they remember lead them into the past, not a chronological one of dates and historic events, but a tribal past of thought and religion and culture, connecting them just as personal memories and genealogy do.

If storytelling leads them into the past, then it is the family that locates them. And while the setting for storytelling shifts, the closely knit family audience remains. It is not by accident. The people here continue to nurture close familial relations. Many live as neighbors. Visits back and forth may even now entail a shortcut through a pine stand or a step across the road, just as they did fifty years ago, when the heat and the need for entertainment drove them to the porches of their kin.

INTO THE PAST

It is nine-thirty at night. An hour ago, the sun mercifully disappeared behind the silhouettes of pine trees, but only now does the night begin to cool off. Inside the small log home, a mud-brick fireplace glows faintly after heating the black-eyed peas and hominy that fed the family. But the fire dies slowly, too slowly on this sweltering night, and once again, the family is forced outside on the porch to seek air and respite from the heat. The one or two windows in the home do little to disperse the heat. The porch becomes a haven, a cool, open oasis. It is uncluttered and unadorned, allowing the mind to wander easily, unfettered by the duties that await inside.

Soon aunts and uncles, cousins and neighbors show up on the front porch, driven from their own homes by the heat and drawn to the homes of their family in the desire for human contact. The crickets drone, creating a silence more oppressive than no sound at all. But there are children here; prolonged silence poses no threat. While the young race around the yard, and babies squirm on their mothers' laps, adults sit and talk—about the weather, or the crops, or each other. Eventually, the children join their parents on the porch to listen.

On those rare nights when a breeze whispers in the air, the evening is almost comfortable. The mind leaves the labor of the cotton fields and follows the breeze into the woods, into the night.

But this is Mississippi in August. More often, the humidity stifles any movement in the air, cementing hair to foreheads, shirts to backs. There is a need for entertainment, for something to break the monotony of the heat. People talk. Sometimes the casual conversation sparks a memory, a story from the past. The story is told. Others follow.

Other times, nature provides the inspiration. An owl hoots or a light flickers in the distance. An animal snorts. For the children lying on the planks of the porch or on mattresses dragged from the bedroom, such sounds spark imagination and fuel fears. For the adults sitting with them in cane chairs and wood rockers, the mind recalls the tales of their grandparents and their grandparents before them. Of the spirits and creatures that roam the Mississippi woods. Of *na losa chito* and *bohpoli* and *nishkin chafa*. They are reminded of the land, their origins in Mississippi. Of the brothers Chahta and Chikasa who traveled to this land from the West. And of the leaders who have brought them through time to the present, leaders such as Mushulatubbee, Pushmataha, and Cameron Wesley.[1] Minds wander to the past but remain in the present. They tell stories to teach, stories to frighten, stories to excite, stories to question—but all of them, stories to entertain.

These memories of hot summer nights and cool front porches are shared throughout the community. For many people, these memories are their only ties to the stories once told by their elders. Fragments of an animal tale, a recollection of a creation story, faint memories of how corn was introduced to the Choctaws. Bits of stories pepper the mind, refusing to be fully remembered or fully forgotten.

Other memories conjure similar settings for storytelling in the winter when the crops were harvested and life slowed. Gathered outside around fires or inside by chimneys, families and neighbors nestled in for conversation.

Sitting on a wooden bench under her carport, her eyesight failing but her mind as sharp as the needles she uses to crochet blankets, Gladys Willis remembers these times when her father told stories.

"When daddy and his uncle I think it was, used to sit around in the wintertime or in the summertime, when they used to sit outside and talk. In the wintertime they used to sit by the fire and they'd talk. They had their mouths full of snuff and they used to spit into the fire until the fire goes out."

We laugh. Gladys Willis is Hulon Willis's mother, and it is easy to see where he gets his sense of humor.

"They would sit there and talk and start telling ghost stories. And that's one thing I used to get afraid of, and I didn't hear much. I'd go to sleep. I used to enjoy hearing tales about something like Rabbit's and Turtle's race."

I nod, recognizing perhaps a similar story about a race between a rabbit and a turtle that I was told as a child.

"When they'd sit around and talk, lots of times they just tell stories. They didn't have radio, TV, or anything."

Gladys Willis once listened to her grandparents and elders talk of the old days. Now she is the grandparent, and great-grandparent, with children clustered around her at family dinners. But trampolines, movies, and video games are hard to compete with; her memories of the past lie dormant in her mind, recalled for her family only by request. When she does tell stories, they are reflective and entertaining, with a casual, self-effacing humor. She talks of walking down to the nearby creek to get water, of seeing snakes in the water where they used to fish, and of singeing squirrel over a fire. One story leads to another, topics suggesting connections between past and present.

"We was playing in the water. And one of the little kids said, 'There's a snake.' I ran; I was going to get out of the water. But the snake was right after me. I thought it was after me. But when I got out and run, the snake got out and ran the other way," she laughs. "It really did scare me."

I remind her of a story she told me the day before about a prank her grandkids pulled on her some time ago with a rubber snake. She graciously retells the story, reminding me that she was so scared "she jumped twice."

As Gladys Willis says, telling stories was not limited to front porches in the summer heat. Nor was family interaction confined to nocturnal visits. There were other times for storytelling, even when time was scarce and work plentiful. Family gatherings on the weekends also inspired stories, both communal and personal. Sundays were special, as were birthdays, and the ends of seasons such as harvest time. Any excuse to get together was a good one.

Such times were always breaks from the rigorous labor of the week or season. Back in the early decades of the twentieth century, most members of the community were farmers, a life that demanded hard work for much of the year.

Terry Ben explains,

> During that time period, most of the Choctaw families were self-sufficient farming families. From sunup to sundown, they would plant crops, work the fields, maybe cotton and so forth. If they had their own fields, they tended that; or they went over to maybe the White man who had maybe a cotton area, which they would help out, maybe sharecropper or whatever, probably to make their living. Of course, during that time period, there was hardly no business around here, no factories. So that's how basically, whatever little money they had, they got by farming and bartering and so forth. Maybe if they had cotton fields, they sold cotton, maybe in October, November, and got a little money.

Terry Ben leans back in his chair at Pearl River High School where he serves as superintendent of the entire tribal school system. He is a history teacher, knowledgeable about what the books written by non-Native people say about the Choctaws as well as what the people themselves—himself and his grandfather included—understand about their past.

> And so, once harvest season is over, they would go hunting. You know, like maybe October, November, December—they would go hunting. I guess to make up for all the days they didn't go hunting, and to get away from the hard work. Once that real hard work is done, they would go hunting.
> My granddad, during that time period, he would get together with some of his friends around Standing Pine, not only Choctaw friends, but White friends, and they would go into the woods, maybe the Pearl River swamp here or elsewhere for a whole weekend or a whole week at a time.
> A group of men might, at nighttime, after they finished eating, sit around and talk about the day's events, or talk about women or whatever.

"Whatever," as Terry Ben goes on to explain, were stories about the animals and spirits in the woods. These were stories that would scare as much as entertain and teach as much as scare. The woods were filled with animals, both familiar and unfamiliar, that were dangerous. There were water moccasins and alligators and wild boar; but there were also *na losa chito, nishkin chafa*, and *bohpoli*. These beings are part of the spiritual world of the Choctaws, actual creatures with supernatural powers and forms: small, wizened men; half men, half animals; creatures that can change form and size at will. The origin of such beings cannot be traced; they have lived in these woods as long as the people remember. Only as more and more of the woods are cleared for housing and business have the beings begun to diminish.

Yet stories that can be traced to the past are not ruled out as history, sterilized by time; rather, such stories hold power today, helping to explain the world then as now. Stories of creation and origin are important, not only because they serve as reminders of a communal past, but because they reflect upon the views and values of the present.

IN THE BEGINNING

Settled around the kitchen table, we wipe crumbs of fried catfish, buttered cabbage, cornbread, black-eyed peas, and hominy from our faces and laps. I turn the tape recorder on. Harley Vaughn sits across from me, his mother-in-law, Caroline Morris, beside him. Playing around us, racing from living room to dining room, chair to sofa and back again are Harley and Rae Nell Vaughn's children, Hillary, Mahlih, and Breanna, ages six, four, and two. From time to time, they get too loud or too rowdy, and they are quieted by one of the adults. They are all three spirited girls. All three understand Choctaw but generally speak English. The youngest, Breanna, can chant the war dance when asked, and once begun, is hard to stop. Mahlih dances traditional Choctaw dances, dressed in the long, hand-embroidered dresses worn daily by many older women but only for special occasions by the young. Hillary has begun to learn beadwork and won first place at the Choctaw Indian Fair that year for a beaded collar she made. Right now, however, their attention has been captured by a videotape of Disney's *The Lion King* that their mother has put in the VCR to give some peace to the adults who are recording stories at the table.

Harley cooked the catfish, so Rae Nell gets the chore of cleaning up, leaving Harley, Caroline, and me to talk at the table. It is after-dinner talk, casual and unhurried, but more focused than usual considering my interests and my tape recorder. My questions lead the discussion, but it hops around from topic to topic without a need to stick to one subject or another. We talk a lot about the past, and they tell family stories, many about Rae Nell as a little girl. We laugh when Rae Nell hollers from the kitchen, telling me not to listen to a word of it. Other stories are about stickball and the importance of remembering the language. All the while, Hillary, Mahlih, and Breanna bombard us with their own questions, comments, and stories.

At one point, Harley and I are alone at the table, discussing the upcoming wedding of a mutual friend. Someone taps me on the shoulder. Before I look, I know it's Mahlih. She has her coat on.

"Goodnight, Mahlih. You taking off?"

"Yep. That's my coat."

"You got a load of stuff there. Baby dolls, dresses," I say.

"Because I'm going to spend the night with my grandma."
"Cool."
She giggles. "I haven't heard that."
"Cool?"
"I haven't heard that," echoes Breanna nearby.
"Hi, Breanna." I smile, waving.
"I haven't heard that one," Mahlih repeats.
"I haven't heard that one," echoes Breanna.
"Speaking of Nanih Waiya," Harley says, interrupting the verbal stalemate Mahlih and Breanna and I seem to be headed toward.
"Yeah?" I nod, waving bye to the girls.
"You know there's a hole in the ground, like a cave?"
"Um-hm. Yeah." About an hour earlier, I had asked Caroline about the Nanih Waiya Mound. Our conversation had veered from the topic, and we had never returned to it. Caroline was gone now, but Harley brought us back to the subject.

> The way I've heard it is that, well my dad told me, it's like, when God made man, you know? And God dig this hole, where he would get three kind of races. And the longer he waited, the darker the man got.
>
> That's where this whole cave thing comes in. The way my dad told me was that God would dig the hole in this ground. And he was going to take out three men. About three different colors.
>
> The first one he took out, out of the ground, sooner than he wanted to and set him out in the sun. That man turned white. And he went to the second one, and he waited a little longer and took him out and set him outside, and he turned brown. And the third one, he waited too long, took him out and set him aside, and he turned black.
>
> That's where mankind started from—a cave.

Harley begins laughing. This version of creation is one often told in the community, told as a humorous story rather than a sacred myth. Yet as Harley understands, this story is similar to a more strongly held belief in the community of the origin of the Choctaws.

"There's a story behind that Nanih Waiya, but I never heard of it. My dad knows; I think he knows. He usually tells it every now and then. But I really never paid attention to it except for that cave part."

Harley knows there are other stories about Nanih Waiya, but he enjoys the humorous version of the story. Others in the community, depending on their memories and reasons for telling the story, tell other myths, other versions of the origin of the Choctaw people. Estelline Tubby, for example, describes the migration of the Choctaws from the West. In this origin myth, the people once lived to the west but were led east by two brothers, Chahta and Chikasa. Each night they planted a sacred pole in the ground, and each morning it would be found leaning in the direction they were to travel. One morning, they woke to find the pole standing upright, a sign they had reached their home.

Melford Farve, past councilman for the Tucker community and now editor of the *Choctaw Community News* monthly newspaper, remembers this version but also tells another, similar to Harley Vaughn's but involving the creation of the southeastern tribes. In this story of creation, the Creator makes men out of mud. They emerge from the Nanih Waiya Mound and sun themselves on its ramparts until dry. The southeastern tribes come out, one after another, and move eastward until finally the Choctaws emerge and settle nearby, where they remain today.

These two bare-bones summaries can only hint at the multitude, beauty, and complexity of the variations and versions told from community to community, family to family. The richness and wealth of the oral tradition of the tribe extends as far back as written records and certainly beyond that. Even now that the content of these stories has been fixed upon the page in both native and foreign languages, authority remains with the teller. There is room for adjustment, room for change.

The first to record narratives of the Choctaws was probably the French traveler Antoine S. Le Page du Pratz. In his book *Histoire de la Louisiane* published in 1758, he refers to a version of the origin of the Choctaws that actually embodies both myths: "According to the tradition of the natives this nation passed so rapidly from one land to another and arrived so suddenly in the country which it occupies that, when I asked them from whence the Chaktas came, to express the suddenness of their appearance they replied that they had come out from under the earth." Du Pratz suggests that the Choctaws were describing their migration to the area, and through metaphor, they suggested an emergence out of the earth.[2]

Yet du Pratz may have been rationalizing the stories himself, for a story of emergence from the earth was recorded again thirteen years later by another scholar and explorer, Bernard Romans. Then came William Bartram in 1791. The primary mission of Romans and Bartram was not to understand the people living in the southeastern United States but to study the land. Both were trained botanists and spent much of their energy detailing the flora and fauna of the uncharted lands of the southeastern United States. Romans was also a surveyor and is best remembered for his early maps of the area. The people they encountered on their travels were incidental to their primary research but captured their interest nonetheless, and each writer attempted to decipher these communities for the outside world. When they did record information about the Choctaws, it was general ethnographic material, summarized to facilitate the understanding of native culture rather than to preserve the narratives themselves. Stories were viewed as modes of conveying cultural data, not artistic performances.

Accordingly, the myths of creation and migration recorded by many of the early travelers and scholars are summaries and compilations, perhaps faithful to the plot and structure of the tale but void of the teller's name, style of narration, or suggestion of meaning. These brief summaries only hint at the complexity, prosody, and beauty of the actual stories themselves.[3]

It is perhaps ironic, if not surprising, that some of the first non-Native people to deem the wealth of oral narratives of the Choctaws worthy of record are more accurately described as adventurers, reporters, and travel writers than as academics. One was George Catlin, whose self-professed goal was to rescue "from oblivion the looks and customs of the vanishing races of native men in America."[4] The task was immense; too big, in fact, to allow the depth such study demanded, which may explain why Catlin is better remembered for his paintings. However, he did manage to capture an assortment of dances, battles, initiation rites, religious ceremonies, and various other cultural traditions that had never before been recorded, and some never since. Included in this ethnographic grab bag of material recorded in the first few decades of the nineteenth century are some stories told by Peter Pitchlynn, who would later provide many subsequent researchers with tales and traditions of his people.

One of these subsequent researchers, and the other notable travel writer to appreciate early on the oral narratives of the Choctaws as worthy of more than brief summaries, was Charles Lanman. An unabashed romantic, Lanman recognized the legends and myths of the American Indian communities he encountered on his travels as wonderful fodder for the popular audience for which he wrote. With little or no explanation, he tacked a scattered sampling of "Indian legends" to the end of his book *Records of a Tourist* published in 1850. The stories are overwrought with florid language, Victorian turns of phrase, and romantic descriptions that belie the cultures to which Lanman credits them. He seems to recognize this discrepancy when he notes in his brief introduction to the stories that what follows are "romantic but authentic legends."

In his defense, such editing and overblown turns of phrase were common in Lanman's time, and criticism has been leveled against scholars of his era as well as against the travel writers who were presumably more prone to such transgressions. Where Du Pratz, Romans, and Bartram err by providing too little information—selected material reduced to minimal summaries void of native narrative style or structure—Lanman overcompensates and errs by providing too much, believing he must impose the style currently in vogue among his audience, rather than allow the aesthetic of the narrator to show through.

Lanman claims to have received the approval to edit the stories from the narrator himself, Peter P. Pitchlynn. Although the nature and duration of their relationship remains unclear, Lanman was certainly in written contact with the Choctaw statesman and must have met him face-to-face at least once on his travels. Further, as a university-educated man, Pitchlynn would have been familiar with the writing style of the time and may in fact have encouraged Lanman to "alter an occasional phrase in the text." Either way, the stories remain literary constructs, different from the oral narratives captured just over a century later with the aid of the tape recorder.[5]

While still not attending to the oral aspects of storytelling, Horatio B. Cushman did manage to add important contextual information about storytelling while minimally expanding the recorded collection of Choctaw narratives. His most useful asset in this endeavor was his own upbringing.

As one of twin sons of missionary parents located in Mayhew and then Hebron, two missionary stations established in Mississippi for the Choctaws, Horatio Cushman grew up among the Choctaws he wrote about. In his book *History of the Choctaw, Chickasaw and Natchez Indians* published in 1899, he reminisces frequently about his childhood when he played with Choctaw children. He was there, too, during the removals of the 1830s—a watershed moment that instilled anger and sadness in the adult Cushman that he would carry throughout his life as well as in his writing.

It is Cushman's writing that is the most problematic for us today. When he borrowed Lanman's already flowery legends, he proceeded to add his own flourishes. While the stories are obviously derivative, identical in structure, plot, and some verbatim passages, Cushman has added more description. In the story "The Unknown Woman," Cushman adds a lengthy description of the swamps in Mississippi, which he knows from "long personal experience." Like Lanman, Cushman is not embarrassed by this tendency to sentimentality. "I oft sat among the Choctaws and Chickasaws in youth and early manhood and listened with romantic emotions to the narrations of the aged."[6]

While not a missionary himself, but nonetheless devoutly religious, Cushman signals the influence of a long line of religious men who, in working to convert the Choctaws to Christianity, became close friends with many in their congregations and well versed in the local culture. Accordingly, these missionaries were some of the first participant-observers in the area, though they acted in a religious role first and were scholars second. Some of these men offered the public more than others. C. C. Copeland provided a version of "The Hunter of the Sun" in a brief article published in 1853 but not much else. The Reverend Alfred Wright lived and worked with the Choctaws as a Presbyterian missionary for thirty-three years; his tenure with the community is reflected in his work. Wright learned the Choctaw language, working with

Cyrus Byington, a fellow missionary, to translate the New Testament. He also translated several religious tracts for his congregation.

While his work with the language was extensive, he dabbled only occasionally in scholarly publication. Certainly, part of the reason for this was his religious background and focus. As an active and dedicated missionary, Wright's interest in the Choctaws seems to have revolved around conversion. When he published an article on the Choctaws for the *Missionary Herald* in 1828, it was appropriately titled "Religious Opinions, Traditions, &c. of the Choctaws." Like Du Pratz, Romans, and Bartram, Wright was interested in the oral traditions of the Choctaws only as sources of cultural information, in this case, specifically of a religious nature.

And as it was with his predecessors, Wright's focus is narrow: ideas of creation, supreme beings, powerful forces that govern the earth, sea, and sky, and values governing human relations permeate virtually all of the narratives that follow in this collection. But for Wright, who was concerned with shifting a community's views to Christianity, only obvious religious stories of creation seemed important to his mission. Information on human relations and specific cultural practices such as burial customs were more easily attained from observation and direct questioning. Stories were too complicated, too far removed from life to be useful. Creation stories were accepted for study because there was nothing else to examine; one could not watch the creation of the world as part of daily life. Cosmological belief was bound into narratives and expressed artfully.

Religious mission does not seem to have stifled Father Adrien Emmanuel Rouquette, however. Working in the St. Tammany Parish community of Louisiana in the middle of the nineteenth century, Rouquette was the first to record a number of the hunting and animal stories characteristic of the southeastern tribes. Though the stories are written by Walt Whitman, as told by Rouquette, who recalled them from Choctaw storytellers, they nonetheless bear a remarkable similarity to those collected a few decades later by David I. Bushnell Jr., who attributes his versions to specific members of the community—Heleema, Pisatuntema, and Ahojeobe.

Bushnell, a trained ethnologist and archeologist, lived in St. Tammany Parish from 1908 through 1909, when he collected his material. His work is important not only because it covers a corpus of stories generally neglected until this point, but also because he credits the majority of these narratives to individuals. Whether it is because these stories are individual creations as opposed to communal summaries, or because of Bushnell's own style, the stories avoid the florid passages and turns of phrase that contaminate those provided by Lanman and Cushman.

This attention to hunting and animal tales must also be credited to Henry Sale Halbert, who acts temporally and theoretically as a link between H. B. Cushman from the nineteenth century and John R. Swanton of the twentieth, both his friends and peers.

Henry S. Halbert presents a representative profile of the Choctaw scholar of the nineteenth century: he was devoutly religious, lived and worked among the Choctaws for a number of years, and focused primarily on historical and cultural aspects of the Choctaws when he wrote about them. Like Rouquette and Wright, Halbert learned the Choctaw language. He also reflected the shifting trends in scholarship that have already been noted in some of his predecessors and peers because he recognized the value of narratives as more than vessels for other data, and he attributed the information in his work to specific individuals.

After graduating from Union University in Murfreesboro, Tennessee, in 1856, he joined the Texas State Troops and fought against the Kiowa and Comanche. He also fought in the Civil War until a severe wound forced him out of the service. After a few brief teaching stints throughout the South, he took a job as the first teacher at the Holy Rosary Catholic Mission school in 1884. In this role, he educated the Choctaws in formal elements of reading, mathematics, and history, as well as in spiritual matters, helping to convert many to Christianity. Eventually, he went on to become superintendent of the Choctaw school system from 1894 to 1899. Then from 1900 to 1903, he became the colonization agent for the second major removal of the Choctaws to Oklahoma. Presumably Halbert would have been able to act on the Choctaws' behalf, being well versed in both their culture and their language. Yet like many of the missionaries and men of Christian faith at the time, he deemed much of Choctaw culture sinful. On hearing that many of the people living in the Bogue Chitto community resisted removal, Halbert called them "the most barbarous and non-progressive of all our Choctaws." Yet while the biennial reports he wrote as superintendent of the school system contain occasional disparaging remarks, the narratives that Halbert recorded and the historical articles he wrote appear neutral in their opinion. Halbert seems to have been able to separate his scholarship from any severe cultural or religious bias, and he produced a wealth of information about the Choctaws that remains useful in style and rigor as well as content.

Such rigor helps us understand the possible sources for stories previously collected yet unattributed. The first version of the migration story that Halbert collected, for example, was "taken down from the lips of Mr. Jack Henry, an old citizen of Okitibbeha County, he stating that he had received it in early life from an Irishman, who had once lived among the Choctaws, and had heard the legend from an old Choctaw woman."

It is unfortunate, however, that not all of the narratives he collected are equally well documented. Living in Mississippi, Halbert interacted with many people in the area, Choctaw and White alike. His sources reflect this exchange between communities.

Halbert did credit a version of the corn-finding myth to Ilaishtubbee from the Six Towns community, who apparently wrote the version out in Choctaw, which Halbert then translated. One finds other names sprinkled throughout his work—Hopahkitubbe and Charly Hoentubbee—suggesting people who may be responsible for some of the stories in his collection. Many of the narratives he amassed in his unpublished manuscript titled "History of the Choctaw Indians East of the Mississippi" are written in Choctaw and then translated into English, suggesting that the narratives came directly from Choctaw storytellers. Such bilingual translations are invaluable and help assure the reader that the stories do not follow the circuitous path that Halbert's first migration story took.[7]

By the 1920s, heavily influenced by Franz Boas, the field of ethnology became even more rigorous and mindful of the individual artistry behind verbal traditions to the point of establishing an informal methodology for fieldwork. Halbert was part of this shift for he worked with John R. Swanton of the Bureau of American Ethnology.

If Halbert has a competitor for most prolific scholar on the Choctaws, Swanton is it. His landmark compilation of writings on the Choctaws, titled *Source Material for the Social and Ceremonial Life of the Choctaw Indians*, remains the most comprehensive introduction to the community's past. In it, we find Bartram, Romans, Du Pratz, Lanman, Catlin, Cushman, Bushnell, Halbert, and an assortment of other travelers and scholars who met and wrote about the Choctaws. We also find the scattered voices of the Choctaws themselves, whenever they were recorded directly and named, which was rare.

Yet even more important than this convenient compilation is Swanton's own fieldwork with the Choctaws. Student of Boas and member of the Bureau of American Ethnology for over forty years, Swanton carried a new agenda for ethnological research into the field. The result was a body of research that spanned ethnology, linguistics, archeology, and folklore. It is in terms of the last of these fields that this book is most indebted to Swanton for he recorded a large corpus of narratives and attributed them to their storytellers: Olman Comby and Simpson Tubby.

Although Swanton himself was not following a particular religious agenda, as did many of the men who recorded narratives before him, the influence of Christian missionaries on the storytellers he recorded was undeniable. Henry Halbert suggests that not until the 1880s did Christianity gain a substantial foothold among the Mississippi Choctaws.[8] Yet when we review the collectors of these narratives, we find religious men, often missionaries, and their informants, who were devout converts. Even if Halbert is correct that the majority of the Mississippi Choctaws were not Christian by the 1880s, many of the storytellers then recorded were.

By the time Swanton began visiting Mississippi in the early twentieth century, this influence was widespread. Simpson Tubby, one of Swanton's main storytellers, was a Baptist minister, even publishing a booklet on his religious conversion. This influence is made explicit in Simpson Tubby's version of the great flood, a story that had been recorded among the Choctaws almost a century earlier but never before naming Noah as the sole survivor, as Tubby does. In time, the community seems to have caught up with the Christian influence so prevalent in the early storytellers: today, the majority of the Mississippi Band of Choctaw Indians identify themselves with some Christian faith.

In tracing the scholars who have written about the Choctaws, we begin to see outside influences reflected in the stories themselves. With different agendas and an evolving opinion of which stories were worth recording and in what form, the people who recorded the stories seem to have influenced the form and style of the narratives. The early focus solely on myths of origin that could be traced historically, the artificial aesthetic of the travel writer, the religious doctrine of the recorders, and the anonymity of many of the stories all limit the ability of the reader to understand the texts.

But there were other influences shaping these narratives, ones potentially far more important to the form and function of the texts. These influences could be traced to the tumultuous period in history when European contact changed the lives of American Indians profoundly.

THE CHANGING FACE OF THE STORYTELLER

Perhaps the most common misconception about the moment when Europeans and American Indians first came into contact is that native culture was a static, harmonious entity that had not changed in millennia. Beliefs, customs, rituals, modes of sustenance, and stories were all imagined to be permanently fixed, as though they had been passed down through the years with amazing stability. Once the first Europeans began exploring the continent, bringing with them weapons, disease, manufactured goods, and Christianity, it was believed that all this was forever destroyed.

True, much did change with the European invasion, but life had been changing before then, too. The changes that occurred before the fifteenth century may not have been as dramatic as after, but it is important to note that there *was* change. Culture is dynamic. Its survival depends on its perpetual capacity to change.

Stories, like all aspects of culture, are always changing too. Their oral nature makes them all the more dynamic. So when we look at the stories in this collection, even the first ones recorded in the middle of the eighteenth century, we do not find the original story—there is rarely such a thing. And conversely, stories that include obvious reference to the Bible are not inauthentic; they merely highlight the influences that have shaped that version. Despite the bias of collectors and the obvious influences of outside cultures, all of the stories in this book are authentic. And when different versions contrast or seem to conflict, we see evidence both of the breadth of the tradition and of the individual storytellers behind each narrative, even though they exist as part of a larger, collective tradition of storytelling.

All that said, we cannot ignore the fact that the changes wrought by European contact were, in fact, tremendous. And while the face of storytelling had been changing as part of inevitable cultural processes, the arrival of the Europeans marked a drastic leap that is notable not only for its intensity but also for the fact that it was recorded in writing. Since American Indians were preliterate people, we must document previous cultural shifts primarily through archeology, a difficult task to perform with any certainty. Yet with the written words of the Europeans, the memories of older members of the community could be recorded, documenting the shifts they saw happening in their lifetimes, shifts in belief, shifts in economic structures, shifts in storytelling.

Though the early recorded accounts are hazy, storytelling seems to have once been a sacred and vital part of a Choctaw youth's education. Without a written language, history was passed down orally, crafted into stories that would instruct, inspire, provoke, question, challenge, and entertain. Children were gathered together to listen to the elders of the tribe as they related the sacred knowledge once entrusted to them when they were children. Such storytelling sessions were perhaps casual by today's standards of schooling, where the sound of a bell and the hands of a clock impose a structure on learning; yet these older sessions also appear to have happened regularly. In 1828, for example, Alfred Wright notes:

> It is said to have been formerly the practice for old men, especially those who were considered as the "ancients" of the people, frequently to assemble the youth and children of their respective towns, and rehearse to them those fabulous stories which embodied all their traditional knowledge, and which had in like manner been communicated to them. In this way was their traditional knowledge, depending alone on the memory for its preservation, transmitted from generation to generation. Since their acquaintance with the whites, this practice has gone into disuse.[9]

Horatio Cushman provides a slightly different yet equally formal picture of oral instruction:

> In their ancient councils and great national assemblies the Choctaws ... all sat on the ground in a circle around a blazing fire called "The Council Fire." The aged, who from decrepitude had long retired from the scenes of active life, the warpath and the chase, formed the inner circle; the middle-aged warriors, the next; and the young warriors, the outer circle. The women and children were always excluded from all their national assemblies. The old men, beginning with the oldest patriarch, would then in regular succession state to the attentive audience all that had been told them by their fathers, and what they themselves had learned in the experience of an eventful life—the past history of their nation; their vicissitudes and changes; what difficulties they had encountered, and how overcome; their various successes in war and their defeats; the character and kind of enemies whom they had defeated and by whom they had been defeated, the mighty deeds of their renowned chiefs and famous warriors in days past, together with their own achievements both in war and the chase; their nation's days of prosperity and adversity; in short, all of their traditions and legends handed down to them through the successive generations of ages past; and when those old seers and patriarchs, oracles of the past, had in their turn gone to dwell with their fathers in the Spirit Land, and their voices were no longer heard in wise counsel, the next oldest occupied the chairs of state, and in turn rehearsed to their young braves the traditions of the past as related to them by the former sages of their tribe, together with their own knowledge; and thus were handed down through a long line of successive generations, and with much accuracy and truth, the events of their past history.[10]

Yet by the beginning of the nineteenth century, the landscape of the American Indian was changing dramatically. Increased contact with White settlers and a United States government policy of cultural extermination had begun to erode the education of young Choctaws in their tribal past. If instruction by the elders of the tribe was ever as organized as Wright and Cushman suggest, it had disappeared by the time of sustained contact with Europeans, when concerns with new lifestyles and the problems inherent in them began to infuse themselves into Choctaw life. The years between 1830 and 1833 were irreparable. The removal to the West rightly earned its name, the Trail of Tears. Once again, promises would be broken and land claims revoked as the Choctaws began their journey to a new home in Oklahoma.

Not all the Choctaws left, however. According to the Treaty of Dancing Rabbit Creek signed on September 27, 1830, Choctaw people could remain in Mississippi, but they would have to forfeit their tribal citizenship for that of the United States. As compensation, they would receive 640 acres on which to farm and live. Or so they had been told. Colonel William Ward, the US agent for the Mississippi Choctaws at the time, was an alcoholic, a racist, and a malcontent, refusing or ignoring his responsibilities of allowing the Choctaws to register in Mississippi. Those who did receive their 640 acres were often bilked out of their land by scurrilous White opportunists even before they moved onto it.

The majority of the Choctaws who stayed in Mississippi were forced into anonymity, scattered in the backwoods of Mississippi, trying to eke out a living by farming. Without their own land, many of the Choctaw men became sharecroppers to White farmers. Choctaw women continued in the arts they had learned from their mothers—weaving baskets, sewing dresses, and making blankets. These they traded with the White women in town for staples such as meal, cloth, and sugar.

No longer able to support themselves independently, many families were forced to move to find work. The remaining elders could no longer gather the tribe's youth together for group lessons in tribal history and lore. Education, once a tribal task, fell to individual families, and in many families, knowledge of this rich oral history was incomplete.

During this tumultuous time between the second half of the nineteenth century and the first half of the twentieth, many stories were forgotten or abbreviated. Creation myths and legends recorded less than thirty years earlier by ethnographers such as Henry S. Halbert, H. B. Cushman, and David Bushnell Jr. were no longer being told. Further, the lives of the Choctaws who remained in Mississippi had changed, strengthening the need and desire to hear and tell certain stories, while lessening the need for others.

Removal of family and friends to the West and persistent efforts by the US government to eradicate their culture weakened Choctaw unity for a time, but to assume such efforts permanently destroyed this unity, or Choctaw culture more generally is—at the least—presumptuous. The Choctaws living in Mississippi had endured intense hardships in order to remain in the land of their birth, the land that their oral history tells them was theirs by divine decree. Tales as vital as these would not be forgotten. Just as the red clay hills of Mississippi were important, so too were the legends and myths that established this land as that of the Choctaws. The storytellers were not gone; rather, they had become the men and women, grandmothers and grandfathers, who sat on the porches of their log homes with their extended family around them and told stories into the night air.

These stories, too, were told to educate. The world could be a confusing and dangerous place—it was important to prepare one's children, to instruct them in the moral codes of the community, as well as in the practical dangers of the woods. The woods were, after all, an integral part of life until recently. Hunting and fishing trips were necessary to supplement the meager income sharecropping afforded. Groups of men, even whole families, went into the woods for days at a time to procure food such as fish, squirrel, possum, deer, turkey, and small birds. Gathered around fires, singeing the fur off squirrels or rabbits or frying the fish caught earlier in the day, people told stories—humorous ones that detailed the day's exploits or scary ones about the creatures that inevitably lurked nearby. The flames of the fire cast strange shadows that slid and slipped along the faces of the storytellers and then vanished into the deep wooded swamps. It was a dangerous place, not only because of the spirits and beings that roamed there; a person could get lost or fall into the water or get bit by the water moccasins that infest the area. One had to be careful.

Terry Ben's grandfather warned him of these dangers, of the dangers of creatures who roamed the woods looking for food.

> He always told me, that, you know, when you go hunting in the woods, and so forth, never go by yourself. When you go fishing in the deep woods, never go by yourself. Simply because safety factor and because of creatures like that, that lived in the woods. And because of these small creatures that lived in the woods that might do a person harm, as such.
>
> So that's one of those lessons that I guess in telling you all these things, he told me. As far as me going camping or hunting or whatever along that line—never go by yourself. I still remember that.
>
> Sound practice. Maybe in part there was a little fear too, you know—make sure it's sound and safe practice too.

As stories are told, meaning is sought, even by the storytellers themselves. The unknown can be frightening, for adults as well as children. The *bohpoli*—also called *kwanokasha*, *kowi anukasha*, or the Little People—stand three feet tall and resemble children, except for their wizened features. Powerful tricksters, the *bohpoli* are mischievous, throwing rocks at houses and pine trees. They are also endowed with the power to train people to become doctors. Many people in the community have seen the *bohpoli*, and those who have not seen them know someone who has. A few have welcomed contact with them, hoping to become a medicine woman or man; but most people are naturally afraid, and all question themselves as to why they saw what they saw. "Maybe I was supposed to be a Choctaw doctor, I don't know," one woman said. Her sentiments are repeated time and time again by people who have seen the *bohpoli*. They question their life choices, and in telling these stories, they cause their listeners to question, too—not the validity of the tale or the belief in the supernatural, but the connection of the spirit world to the modern world they inhabit.

A CULTURE IN BALANCE

The contemporary world poses dilemmas for us all, Choctaw or not. We inevitably straddle the past and the future, the traditional and the modern, trying to accommodate the two without sacrificing either. Just over forty years ago, the majority of the Choctaws in Mississippi were living in poverty, trapped in a cycle of dependency thanks in great part to the temperamental policies of the US government. But in 1954, the Choctaws adopted a policy of self-determination and have since built a thriving, economically stable, and prosperous community.

But with this prosperity comes the need for balance, balance between two cultures. One is the mainstream American culture to which the Choctaws, as well as other American Indians throughout North America, have been forced to adjust. The other is a traditional culture, one that continues to persist and change. Only after a full day at the harness plant, school, tribal office, or greeting-card company do men and women gather to practice their dancing or play stickball or learn beadwork. And when they return home to their air conditioning, washing machines, and cable television, they can choose to throw a chicken pot pie in the microwave or serve up the hominy that has been simmering on the stove all day. One is not considered more natural than the other, though the word *traditional* is understood by all. Rather, the two overlap in daily life so that traditional culture and modern culture intertwine to form Choctaw culture.

Just as the stories of Heleema, Pisatuntema, Ahojeobe, Pistonatubbee, Olman Comby, and Simpson Tubby have evolved into the tales told by Hulon Willis, Gladys Willis, Terry Ben, Melford Farve, and Estelline Tubby, so too has the face of storytelling changed to accommodate new needs, new roles, and new challenges. Tribal myth keepers have become high school teachers and principals, particularly those like Terry Ben who continue to teach traditional Choctaw history to their students. No longer sitting beside the banks of the Pearl River, the Choctaw students sit in classrooms, in cultural enrichment courses that have become part of every school day. Students learn to bead sashes and necklaces, make stickball sticks, and bake *banaha*. They learn in the classroom as well as the living room, where life still centers around the family.

New education systems have created new needs. With modern forms of education developing alongside the oral forms that have existed far longer, there is a growing need for written texts. Cultural preservation has become a major concern in the community. Video and audio archives are growing. And with the need to record and preserve one's culture comes the wish to share it with others. This book is an attempt to answer these needs, to bridge the traditional and the modern by fitting traditional material to a modern form. The result is a book designed for both members of the community and interested outsiders, fulfilling the need for reflection as well as education.

The people here have been doing just this for at least fifty years.

Since 1947, the Mississippi Band of Choctaw Indians has been holding the annual Choctaw Indian Fair during the middle of July. It is a time to gather together as a community, a chance for the Choctaws to celebrate their heritage in dance, song, and art. It is a chance to display the beautiful cane baskets, beadwork, stickball sticks, blankets, and handsewn shirts and dresses that old and young hands alike have struggled and puzzled over, delighted and excelled in. It is a time for the townspeople of Philadelphia, Mississippi, to see a side of their coworkers, friends, and neighbors that they may have been blind to before. For visitors outside Philadelphia, the fair provides a chance to witness a culture perhaps surprisingly similar to their own and yet amazing in its variation. But most important, the fair is a good time for the Choctaws themselves.

Prior to its official conception in 1950, the fair seems to have evolved from informal gatherings to dance, eat, and play stickball. Some have suggested an origin in the annual Green Corn Ceremony familiar among many southeastern tribes; others remember more frequent and less ceremonial events. Either way, the event and the purpose were the same.

Word was passed around that a stickball game would be held on a certain date at a certain place. Sometimes the trip took over two days, but that seems to have deterred few. Communities gathered; extended families reunited. The feasting and playing that ensued might last a weekend, might last a week, but it was always well attended. Then, as today, the celebration was a chance to come together not as individuals but as a tribe. And now, the net is cast even wider, incorporating non-Choctaw visitors as well.

One of the highlights is the World Series of Stickball championship. The other is the crowning of the year's Choctaw Indian Princess. From the first night when she is crowned, the young woman presides over various events of the fair, giving speeches between dances and receiving public congratulations periodically throughout the day. One of her duties is to read the history of the Choctaws to the crowds at the fair. For some, it will be the first time they hear the story—for others, the hundredth.

At the forty-seventh annual fair, in 1996, the princess was Summer Saunders. Wearing a traditional Choctaw dress and beadwork crafted by family members, she took her place in front of the microphone. She began with the beginning.

Good afternoon, ladies and gentlemen. Here is a story describing the settlement of the Choctaw people in Mississippi centuries ago.

Many years ago, the ancestors of the Choctaws lived in the Northwest. In time, the population became so large that life there was difficult. The tribal wise men announced that a land of fertile soil and abundant game lay in the Southeast. The people could live there in peace and prosperity forever.

Under the leadership of two brothers, Chahta and Chikasa, our people set forth. At the end of each day's journey, a sacred pole was planted erect in front of the camp. The next morning, the pole would be found leaning one way or another. The tribesmen would travel in that direction for the day.

For months our people followed the sacred staff until they crossed the Mississippi River and reached what is now Winston County, where they stopped during a heavy rain. The band that became the Chickasaws moved away from the main group, which was led by Chahta.

We found our home. We'll call this place "Nanih Waiya." Here we'll build our homes and a mound as the sacred burial spot for the bones of our ancestors.

As she speaks, she consults her notes, carefully making sure to read each word on the pages accurately and clearly.

Once our people arrived here, they developed into one of the largest and most prosperous Indian nations east of the Mississippi River, with a population of twenty-five to thirty thousand people. In the early 1500s, the Choctaw nation controlled almost twenty-six million acres of land.

Our ancestors were a powerful people and supported a sound agricultural economy. Women shared in the work; they tended, planted, and harvested the crops. The men built the houses and cleared the land. They hunted, made stone and wood tools, and gathered cane from the swamps, which the women wove into baskets. The men usually hunted with the bow and arrow while the little boys hunted with a blowgun.

As farmers, our people were superior. They were so successful that they often sold surplus goods at a profit to their neighbors. Corn was our principal crop. Many legends grew up to account for its origin. One story says that corn was the gift of a beautiful woman to a couple of Choctaw hunters who shared their last meal with her. Another legend tells of a child playing in a field when a crow flew over and dropped a single grain of corn. The child planted the grain, and a crop began to grow for us.

Summer Saunders continued to read, describing the Choctaws when they lived unmolested in Mississippi, farming and dancing and living peacefully with their neighbors. But that time soon disappeared.

> By 1801, our tribe's self-reliance and traditional way of life had been undermined. In 1803, we'd ceded almost a million acres of land to the United States; in 1805 over four million acres of fertile south Mississippi land was ceded to the government. Again and again our tribal leaders were asked to sign treaties, which took land.
> In 1820, amid increasing federal and state pressure for Choctaw land and only three years after Mississippi was admitted to the Union, Andrew Jackson and other American commissioners tried to convince us that we would be better off west of the Mississippi River. They told us wonderful stories of how good the land was and how happy we'd be there, but the tales fooled no one.

She read about the treaties that forced many to move to Oklahoma. But then she reminded us that many stayed, the ancestors of the people here today.

> Today's Mississippi Choctaws are the great-great-grandchildren of nearly one thousand Choctaws who retreated into the swamplands of east-central Mississippi, where they wandered homeless in a country once their own. For them, there was no fixed home; home was a paradise they dreamed of but did not enjoy. They camped near the school and within the sound of the church bell, but their children were never taught.
> We the Choctaw Nation of Mississippi, descendants of these strong people, are proud of the legacy of their courage, and we welcome you to our nation with the Choctaw warrior's proudest boast: Chahta siyah hoke. I am Choctaw.[11]

The ending was triumphant. The crowd applauded, some in recognition, all in appreciation, of the young woman and the story she shares.

Her care to read the material exactly is partly explained by the purpose of her speech. For the visitor, it is an explanation of an unfamiliar history. Fixed to the page and read verbatim, the stories serve primarily a pedagogical rather than expressive function to the first-time hearer. The visitor from nearby Canton or Tuscaloosa or as far away as Seattle or Boston or across the ocean listens to the stories and attempts to understand a different view of the world. The Choctaw Indian Princess becomes an instructor and guide for the visitor as she reads.

For the Choctaws, however, the brief summaries serve as a touchstone to a common heritage, to a recognizable past. The stories each knows are different; Harley Vaughn may tell a version unknown to Estelline Tubby, who may tell a version unknown to Hulon Willis. But the stories are familiar, the history collective. Each recognizes the other's story, if not explicitly then at least by feel and character.

The same could be said of the stories that follow in this book. Written, they are cemented in form, inflexible, unable to shift to meet the needs of a changing world. Spoken, they live, from person to person, grandmother to grandchild, father to daughter. But just as writing does not eliminate the need to speak, speaking cannot ensure the preservation of history.

And so this book. Written to preserve and educate, it celebrates not only the stories themselves in their complexity and variety, but also the people who have created, narrated, and passed them on. For in the end, it is they who must continue to preserve these tales, not by reading them, but by telling them.

THE STORYTELLERS

Ahojeobe—Emil John

BAYOU LACOMB, LOUISIANA. BORN 1890s.

Ahojeobe was the son of Heleema and was part of the Choctaw community living in Bayou Lacomb, Louisiana. It remains unclear whether this group was once part of the Acolapissa tribe that shared a language with the Choctaw, but by the time Adrien Rouquette arrived in 1845, the community considered themselves fully Choctaw.

Just after 1900, when Ahojeobe was a young boy, his father, Emil John Sr., left for Oklahoma as part of the removal process, taking one son, Jewell (Joel) with him. His mother, Heleema, refused to go and kept her other son, Emil Jr., with her. (As was the case with many Native Americans at that time, particularly those who had been converted to Christianity, Ahojeobe had a Choctaw name and an anglicized name—Emil John.) As well as being one of Bushnell's three major collaborators and thus knowledgeable and willing to talk about his community's customs, Ahojeobe was an excellent artisan, making pipes and drums that can be seen in Bulletin 48 of the Bureau of American Ethnology.[1]

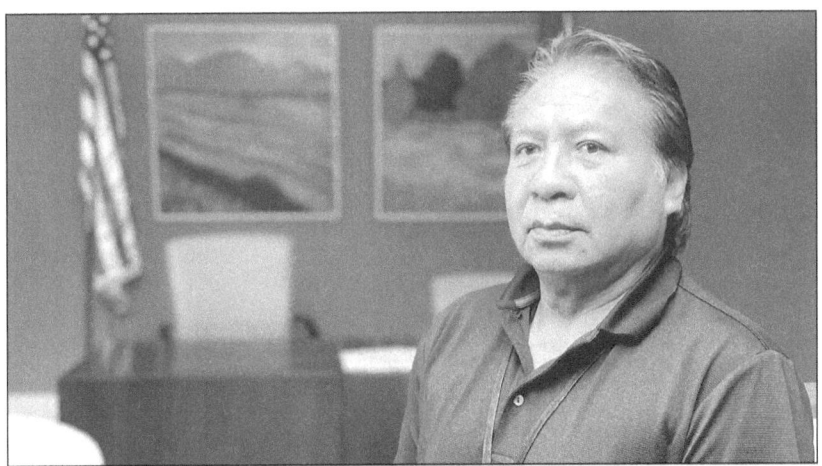

Bradley Alex

BOGUE HOMA / PEARL RIVER. BORN 1955.

Bradley Alex grew up speaking Choctaw in a traditional Choctaw home, where parents and grandparents looked out for one another's kids and disciplined them if they got out of line. "You never got away with anything," he laughs. That spirit of traditional, community-based ways of maintaining good relations and a healthy society carries over into his work as a traditional peacemaker or *itikana ikbi* for the Choctaw judicial system. His openness, warmth, and easy laugh make it clear why he is so good at his job, restoring peace and balance through trust and conversation. Bradley's interest in documenting Choctaw cultural traditions dates back to at least high school, when he and a group of fellow students, including his future wife, Linda, and storyteller Hulon Willis helped start the *Nanih Waiya* magazine, modeled on the Foxfire project in Georgia, where students interviewed their family and community members about traditional practices. His interests seem to be genetic; his son Liasha Alex helped conduct similar interviews with elders for this book in 1997, and his granddaughter Makaylin Alex did the same in 2021 for *Choctaw Traditions: Stories of the Customs and Life of the Mississippi Choctaw*. Today, Bradley has shifted from recording stories to telling them, all of them infused with insight and humor.

Billy Amos

BOGUE CHITTO. BORN 1940.

Billy Amos was one of my closest collaborators and closest friends. From the beginning, I was awed by his energy and passion about all things Choctaw. Officially, Billy's job years had been spent as a custodian for the elementary and middle school in Bogue Chitto. Unofficially, he had been one of the leaders at the school in training the young people how to chant, drum, and dance the traditional Choctaw social dances. He regularly chanted for various dance groups at the Choctaw Indian Fair and was constantly learning new chants and experimenting with new ways to sound out the rhythm. Billy's importance in the community lay in many places, but in terms of the culture, it lay here, in combining knowledge and skill with the desire to keep these traditions relevant and active in the community. While some tribal members attempt to freeze the old traditions in an imagined past, Billy treated them as they should be treated: as vibrant, meaningful, usable, and useful modes of understanding the world. Billy was as warm and personable as he was knowledgeable and passionate. He passed away on November 20, 2006.

Wagoner Amos

BOGUE CHITTO. BORN 1908.

Wagoner Amos has been memorialized as a renowned fiddle player in the large photos that hang in the tribal museum as well as in the song "Choctaw Saturday Night" by Bob Ferguson, reflecting the community's veneration of this extraordinary man. His artistic talents were not confined to his music; he was also a famed storyteller. Both talents—music and narrative—have been recorded on cassette tapes that have been circulating around the community since they were recorded back in the 1980s. Most contain various songs and performances of Wagoner's fiddling, but almost all contain the story of Nanih Waiya he tells. Above all else, even his fiddling, Wagoner Amos was a devout Christian and a devout Choctaw, and the two intermingled as one to create a devoutly spiritual man. His son, Billy Amos, continued in his father's musical footsteps as a chanter for dances. (Note: Like many of his peers, the spelling of his name varied in different published sources; the spellings included Wagner, Waggoner, and Wagonner.)

Odie Mae Anderson

CONEHATTA. BORN 1933.

Glenda Williamson and her sister-in-law Meriva Williamson had been taking me around the community of Conehatta to speak to some of the elders there when we stopped at the middle school to talk to her mother, Odie Anderson. She and two of her coworkers told stories in Choctaw as Glenda and Meriva asked them questions. A few weeks later, we sat down together again, this time with her sister Jeffie Solomon and a tape recorder. Casually snapping peas, the two women told stories back and forth, reminding each other of tales they had heard when they were younger. Occasionally, Odie Anderson would sing a song she remembered from her childhood. Most of the stories she remembered she attributed to her mother and father. Odie passed away on October 25, 2005.

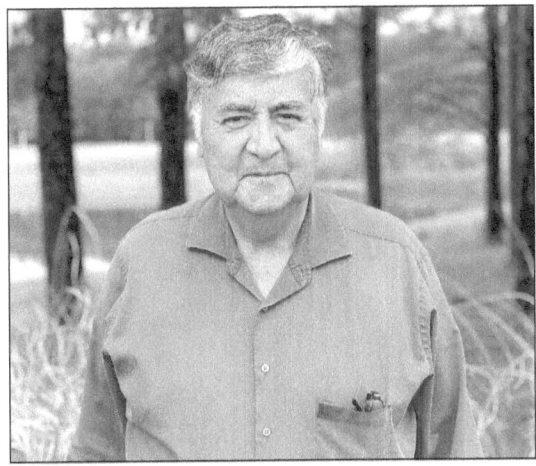

Terry Ben

STANDING PINE. BORN 1957.

When I first met Terry Ben, he was acting superintendent of the Choctaw school system, a system that includes Head Start programs, elementary/middle schools in six of the communities, and a high school at Pearl River. He has since been confirmed as the permanent superintendent and can now be seen handing out diplomas during graduation, presiding over teacher-appreciation assemblies, and bustling around the various schools, attending to the problems that arise during the course of a day. And that, of course, is only his outwardly visible work, which does not include the variety of other jobs, such as hiring new staff and reviewing curricula, that come with the job.

It was my luck to have caught him during the summer, when these jobs are a little less pressing, a little less overwhelming. Rae Nell Vaughn, who was then the tribal archivist, had been introducing me around the community and led me to Terry Ben's office, where he was waiting for us with a warm handshake and an invitation to sit awhile. I began by asking questions, but soon Terry Ben slipped into the comfortable role of history teacher and storyteller, roles he has adopted periodically in his life, officially and otherwise. When the only history lessons that young Choctaw boys and girls were getting in school were from dusty, canonized books written by White men, Terry Ben taught Choctaw history that incorporated ethnographic texts and oral history. The stories he told me continue in this vein, part written, part oral. He attributes some of his stories to books but more of them to his grandfather, who helped raise him.

Judy Billie

PEARL RIVER. BORN 1946.

Judy Billie worked at the Choctaw Health Department as an alcohol and drug counselor. The job was difficult and often depressing, yet Judy understood how important her job was and worked diligently to help the members of her community overcome their addictions. It is perhaps not surprising then that she found herself one day with coworkers Sally Allen and Regina Shoemake discussing the stories imbued with moral values and beliefs that they heard while growing up. They were concerned that these stories were not getting passed down to younger generations, particularly the young men and women who appeared in their offices. Complaints about the younger generation are common in any community but seem especially dire in this one. For many, loss of respect is a sign of loss of culture, an unacceptable development.

When I arrived to record these three women, I was far less an interviewer than a facilitator, someone to record the material that they felt should be remembered. As the women talked, they helped each other remember, adding a story here, another perspective there. They all agreed that what seemed to be the most important thing missing today, that could help explain the loss of the language and the stories and the increase of problems they saw every day, was respect: for one's elders, one's family, even oneself.

Judy Billie had given this topic a lot of thought. The stories that she told expressed her effort to understand and interpret the material, not merely recount it. It is this effort to translate the past into a viable present that Judy Billie hoped would help guide the youth today. She passed away on January 9, 2008.

Nellie Billy

RED WATER. BORN 1943.

Nellie Billy was one of a number of counselors for the summer language camp organized by the tribe in an effort to teach and maintain the Choctaw language among the youngest generations. During the break after lunch, she joined the other counselors in telling stories to the young campers. She began with songs sung in Choctaw meant not only to engage the children but also to strengthen their command of the language. The stories were aimed to do the same, though with the children as listeners rather than participants. This did not keep them from participating anyway, pleading to hear a ghost story before every narrative and commenting freely during the storytelling. Despite Nellie Billy's calm, kind demeanor, she acquiesced, attempting to scare the children as they so demanded. She was, of course, familiar with the supernatural spirits and beings that roam the nearby woods, and so she drew upon them for her story. However, the penchant for horror is not hers, and the story she tells is a catch tale where a benign tree stump is found to be the presumed monster (see "The Black Stump"), much to the dismay of the children, but much to the relief, she told me later, of herself and her family.

Cynthia Clegg

TUCKER. BORN 1964.

Like virtually all of the storytellers in the community, Cynthia Clegg learned her stories from relatives, particularly her aunt and her father. But attribution is important, and she is careful to trace the stories back, many of which lead to her father's father. Cynthia also worked at the language camp held during the summer to teach or reinforce the Choctaw language among the children of the community. After lunch, the children lay on blankets to "rest" while Cynthia or one of the other counselors told them stories. Inevitably, the children clamored for "scary stories." Cynthia was not one to disappoint. Using dramatic gestures and rolling her eyes back into her head until only the whites showed, the stories became far more than crafted words; they were animated performances. The children loved it.

Gus Comby

PEARL RIVER. BORN 1924.

On a cold day a few days after Christmas, Gus Comby invited Greg Keyes and Ken Carleton into his home to talk. With *The Price Is Right* blaring in the background, the wood stove blasting hot air, an old friend beside him, and three or four nephews or grandchildren nearby, Gus Comby told some of the stories he heard growing up. Some of these stories were humorous animal tales; others were more serious, about the supernatural beings that roamed the nearby woods and roads.

Gus Comby was not a stranger to the tape recorder when he sat down with Greg Keyes and Ken Carleton. Earlier, in the 1980s, he worked extensively with George Aaron Broadwell, who was working on his master's thesis, "Extending the Binding Theory: A Muskogean Case Study." Gus Comby, along with Josephine Wade, provided Broadwell with the majority of the linguistic material he used in his study. His openness to friends and strangers alike was remarkable. A regular attendee of the Elderly Nutrition Program, Comby was always quick with a smile, and often a joke, for anyone he met.

Harold Comby

PEARL RIVER. BORN 1955.

Harold Comby was a historian, not by formal training but by natural inclination and passionate interest. He poured over John Swanton's Sourcebook countless times and frequently asked his mother what she knew about past and present traditions, which is a lot. Part of this desire seemed to stem from a natural curiosity and a desire to understand his past; part from his interaction with other American Indians at powwows, strengthening a need to understand Choctaw culture as distinct from Chippewa or Sioux or Blackfeet; and stemming from this, part from pride in his heritage. That heritage is familial as well as tribal; Olman Comby was his great-grandfather.

Harold Comby served in a number of roles in the tribal justice system, including captain of police. His duties were intensely time consuming. Yet he nonetheless found time for what was most important to him: dancing, stickball, and learning ever more about Choctaw culture, not only as a reader, but also as a participant, whether in weekend rabbit hunts near Conehatta or intertribal powwows across the country. Harold was a peer in scholarship and a true collaborator. When I had a question, my first impulse was to call Harold. Harold passed away on March 10, 2022.

Olman Comby

STANDING PINE. BORN 1878.

Olman Comby was a leader in the Standing Pine community in the 1920s when John Swanton interviewed him. He would have been about thirty-five years old then. Five years later in 1933, Frances Densmore interviewed him about music and tribal customs, which she later published in Bulletin 136 of the Bureau of American Ethnology. She notes that he was a policeman at the Choctaw Agency and acted as a translator for her in her interviews, though he, too, recorded some dance songs.

Swanton notes that although Olman Comby (far right) was not formally educated and could not write, he was fluent in the traditions of his people. From the collection of stories he recounted, Comby was especially fluent in *shokhannopa*—animal tales and humorous stories. Many of the stories have close analogs with stories told within the African American community and found in Joel Chandler Harris's Uncle Remus books. In one of Comby's stories, he even mentions Uncle Remus by name. Virtually all of the stories Olman Comby knew he attributed to hearing from his aunt.

Carmen Denson

STANDING PINE. BORN 1956.

I met Carmen Denson at a hymn sing organized by local Baptist leaders whose goal was to record the Choctaw music that accompanied the hymns sung in churches every Sunday. Much of this music was being forgotten, so community members, old and young, were called upon to sing what they could remember to preserve it. One of the principal singers was Charlie Denson, who was accompanied every one of the five nights of the hymn sing by his son Carmen. In time, I got to know them both. Though he always deferred to his father during our interviews, Carmen spoke passionately about the need to preserve the Choctaw language and the importance of the Bible as a means of organizing one's life. He spoke, too, about respect and about educating the youth so they would not be lost in the world. Stories he had heard from his father helped do this. Many of these stories were funny. Through them, Carmen expressed a wonderful sense of humor that is belied by his reserved manner.

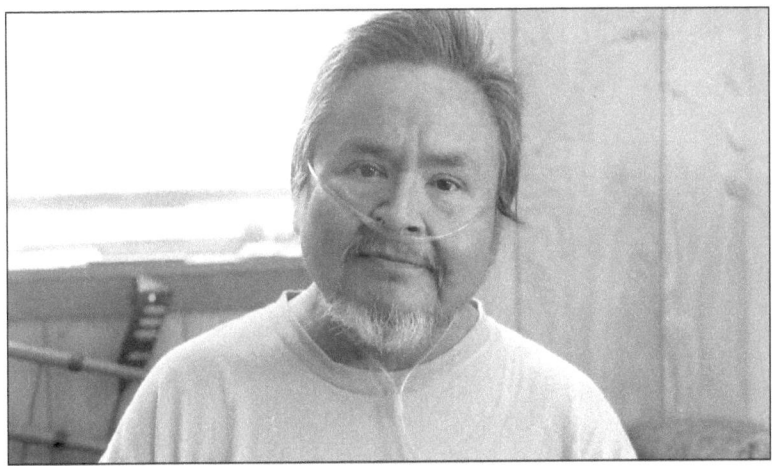

Theron "Duke" Denson

PEARL RIVER. BORN 1956.

Theron "Duke" Denson was born in 1956 and grew up in Dallas, Texas, before moving to Pearl River at the age of twelve. He received mixed signals about speaking Choctaw when he was growing up. On the one hand, his parents wanted him to learn English to be able to succeed in the schools he was attending. On the other, he was occasionally punished for not being able to speak Choctaw fluently. Duke attended college and played in the marching band, but he disagreed with some of the teachers and ultimately transferred to Haskell Indian Junior College, where he says he got a good education. A guitar player and singer, he was a member of a number of bands. He was also an excellent artist, illustrating many of the storybooks for the Tribal Language program with images that inspired the COVID-19 cutouts planted around the reservation warning people to mask up, stay at home, and stay safe. Duke was particularly interested in *na losa chito*, believing it might be the Choctaw version of Bigfoot, and appeared briefly in local media when Bigfoot hunter Tom Biscardi came to town in 2012. He was also a member of the Church of Jesus Christ of Latter-Day Saints. He lost his cousin and one of his closest friends to COVID-19 and almost died from it himself, only partially recovering. He passed away on April 12, 2023.

Melford Farve

TUCKER. BORN 1961.

Melford Farve is a natural storyteller. Perhaps it stems from his love of movies—both watching and making—or perhaps the reverse is true. Either way, a conversation with Melford is an entertaining tour de force of personal experiences, tribal lore, race issues, local politics, and humorous anecdotes. Such breadth in narrative is not surprising considering his many and varied interests. Melford is a man of many talents. He has served as councilman for the Tucker community, following in his father's footsteps. Before becoming a councilman, Melford worked across the road at the local television station, learning to interview, conduct newscasts, and make videos. It is the last that most intrigued him. While a student, he made a video that pits a medicine man from the past against contemporary high school students. Drawing upon a belief system of the supernatural embedded in his culture, and adding his avid interest in horror movies, Melford created a video that combines the traditional culture of the Choctaw and the contemporary culture of the United States. It is a feat he is familiar with, having to balance these two cultures in his daily life, as do most people in the community. Today, Melford is one of the editors of the *Choctaw Community News*, combining his talent in the media with his knowledge of the tribal system.

Some of Melford's most penetrating and most humorous stories describe moments when these cultures clash. When he worked at the tribal museum, he guided guests around the reservation, explaining the business, culture, and daily life of the community to people whose conceptions of the Indian could vary widely but almost always entailed some sort of stereotype, whether romantic or derogatory. One woman planning a visit asked Melford if there were things her group should or should not do when they came to the reservation. "Yes," he replied solemnly. "Don't wear purple."

Israel Folsom

BORN 1802.

Israel Folsom was born in Mississippi in 1802 to Nathaniel Folsom, a White trader, and Aiahnichih Ohoyoh, a Choctaw woman and descendant of a long line of Choctaw chiefs. The Folsoms, along with a few other prominent Anglo families, such as the LeFlores and Pitchlynns, helped form a multiracial elite in the Choctaw community in the late eighteenth and nineteenth centuries that dominated the political arena both in Mississippi and later in Oklahoma.

Like many of his mixed-blood peers, Israel Folsom had the benefit of a formal education. Further, he adopted the Christian religion of his teachers and soon became a missionary to the Choctaw in Oklahoma. With his brother David Folsom, Israel Folsom was also a secular leader, serving frequently as a delegate of the Choctaw Nation in Oklahoma.

Before he moved to Oklahoma, however, Israel Folsom wrote a manuscript about the Choctaw and their traditions, which Horatio B. Cushman quoted from extensively in his book *History of the Choctaw, Chickasaw and Natchez Indians*. The manuscript is heavily biased toward his religious training, and he often condemns his community for their views that do not align with Christian doctrine.

Peter Folsom

BORN 1814.

According to a letter written by fellow missionary Joseph S. Murrow at Peter Folsom's death, Folsom was the first Choctaw to become Baptist in 1829. Soon after, he became a Baptist missionary in Oklahoma, where he worked so diligently that Murrow wrote that Folsom "might appropriately be termed 'the father of the Baptist mission work in the Choctaw Nation.'" In 1879, at the age of seventy-seven, he was invited back to Mississippi to continue his missionary work and soon established the Mount Zion Baptist Church before returning to Oklahoma.[2] In the meantime, Folsom served as a delegate to Washington, DC, for the Choctaw Nation in Oklahoma and frequently engaged in local politics.

It appears that even Folsom's early years were less typical than those of the average Choctaw boy. He attended the Choctaw Academy that had recently been established in Kentucky to educate the youth of the tribe's elite. At that time, many White and Choctaw people alike believed good education could only be obtained outside of Indian communities. It does seem clear that Peter Folsom was not fully enculturated into Choctaw culture. In prefacing the migration legend Folsom told him, Henry Halbert comments: "Mr. Folsom stated that soon after finishing his education in Kentucky, one day in 1833, he visited Nanih Waiya with his father and while at the mound his father related to him the migration legend of his people."[3] Folsom seems to suggest that this was the first time he had heard the story.

Eddie Gibson

CONEHATTA. BORN 1953.

Eddie Gibson was born in 1953 to Lillie Kate Farmer Gibson and Homer Gibson. He grew up in Conehatta but has lived much of his life off the reservation in between Tucker and Pearl River. His community identity, however, is clear: "I think I'll always be Conehatian," he told us, laughing. Storyteller Lilly Gibson is Eddie's mom; Calvin Gibson is his brother; and Jaeden Wesley, who worked on this book through YOP, is his granddaughter. Eddie grew up speaking Choctaw in the home but going to a non-Choctaw Baptist church. His father became a preacher later in life. Their devout faith meant that he didn't participate in many Choctaw traditions as a child because they were told their culture was antithetical to Christianity. Eventually, he played stickball, often with Henry Williams, another storyteller from Conehatta. He also joined a dance troupe that his cousin started. He describes growing up as sharecroppers in a frame house without running water. Although neither of his parents was able to complete high school, Eddie graduated from Mississippi State University and has remained a diehard fan, greeting us with the popular rallying cry "Hail State!" Although he grew up with an "English" name, his wife has many nieces and nephews with Choctaw names, and his grandson is Tashka, or "Warrior," a name he says has grown in popularity in recent years.

Esbie Gibson

CONEHATTA. BORN 1910.

Esbie Gibson was a well-known and well-respected basket weaver in Conehatta, though you would not know it from glancing around her living room, where there was not a basket in sight. She could not keep up with demand and sold her baskets faster than she could make them. I arrived at Esbie Gibson's home with YOP student Lionel Dan, brought there by Meriva Williamson and Glenda Williamson, also from Conehatta, who had been taking me around the community to talk to the elders. If Esbie Gibson thought our entourage was a bit overwhelming, she did not let on. She was a slight woman with a disarming smile and a deadpan delivery that made her jokes all the funnier for being unexpected. Though I did not understand the words she spoke as she told her stories in Choctaw, I could not help noting, and joining, the frequent laughter she sparked in the others who had come to listen. She passed away on September 7, 2007.

Lillie Gibson

CONEHATTA. BORN 1919.

Lillie Gibson was an artist, as were many of the women in Conehatta who used what little spare time they had to sew dresses, bead, weave baskets, or quilt. Lillie Gibson learned the last two from her mother. Her bed was covered with a double wedding ring quilt that she made when she was younger. The rest of her home was filled with her children's and grandchildren's art and crafts, from dream catchers to birdhouses. An American Indian doll collection that sat in rows on shelves in her living room also attested to her admiration for objects that reflect not only beauty and handcrafted skill but identity as well.

Like many of her peers born in the first few decades of the twentieth century, Lillie Gibson grew up the daughter of a sharecropper. Her stories reflect the transition she made from a rural farming life to one in an extended and more modern community. That transition in geography, as well as in time, involved new technology such as electricity and running water, amenities that appear in the humorous stories she told. Subtle and reserved, her wit imbued her stories of the past with self-effacing humility. She passed away on November 11, 2007, at the age of eighty-eight.

Heleema—Louise Celestine

BAYOU LACOMB, LOUISIANA. BORN 1862.

Heleema was one of David Bushnell Jr.'s primary informants when he visited the Choctaw community of Bayou Lacomb in Louisiana between 1909 and 1910. She was originally married to Emil John Sr. and had two children with him, Joel and Emil Jr. (the latter of whom was another of Bushnell's contacts, also known as Ahojeobe). However, when the government was encouraging removal again in the early 1900s, Emil John Sr. left, leaving behind Emil Jr. and Heleema, who would not leave her home. Eventually, she married again, this time to Joe Celestine, another Bayou Lacomb resident.

When Heleema was a child, she was baptized into the Catholic Church by Father Adrien Rouquette, a well-liked missionary to the community who had collected some of the stories of the Choctaw when he worked among them. When Roquette died in 1887, Heleema joined the crowds, some of them Choctaw, who followed the body through the streets of New Orleans.

Inez Henry

BOGUE CHITTO. BORN 1926.

In an interview for the *Nanih Waiya* magazine, Inez Henry was heralded throughout the Choctaw country as one of the best cooks of *banaha*—a traditional Choctaw food made with cornmeal and beans or peas. Her fame as a storyteller was perhaps not as widespread but not for being any less talented at it. Geri Harm, a Mennonite missionary who worked with her husband, Harry Harm, to translate the Bible into modern Choctaw, met Inez Henry in the course of her work studying the language and recorded some of Inez Henry's recollections of the past. Some of her stories are humorous animal tales, others far grimmer, dealing with painful memories of removal and broken treaties.

Like many of the storytellers in this book, Inez Henry was an artist in many media, not only the verbal arts. She is pictured here with some of the reed baskets she made. She passed away on August 23, 1992.

Ilaishtubbee

SIX TOWNS.

A brief reference to Ilaishtubbee comes from Henry Halbert, who translated his story of the origin of corn, saying: "The version here given is a translation by the writer of a version which was written down for him in the Choctaw language by Ilaishtubbee (Ilaishtobi) a Six Towns Indian."[4] As the brief comment notes, Ilaishtubbee was literate and could write in Choctaw, an unusual skill at that time. Six Towns was a Choctaw community in the southwestern part of Mississippi.

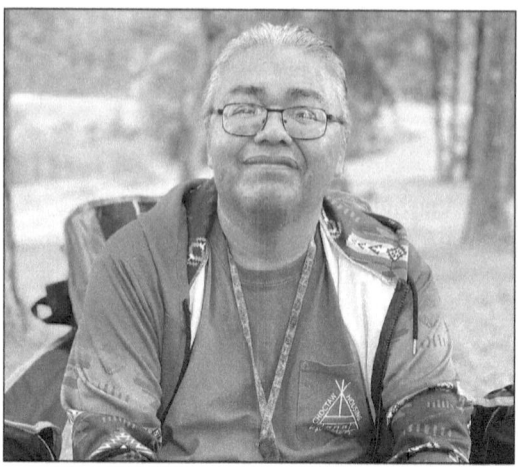

William "Dan" Isaac

PEARL RIVER. BORN 1968.

When I returned to Mississippi in 2018 after a long time away and asked people if there were any new storytellers I should meet, Dan was one of the first names people mentioned. But it wasn't until 2021 that we finally met in person, under the pine trees outside the Choctaw Cultural Center, masked out of an overabundance of caution since COVID-19 remained a very real threat. Dan greeted me and each of the YOP students with warmth and a huge smile. Dan has never met a stranger. Before I knew it, I was joining him and his drum group at stickball practices, community picnics, political rallies, and wakes. Like Harold Comby, Dan is an avid scholar of both Choctaw and intertribal traditions. Where Harold fell in love with powwow dancing, eventually becoming an emcee for powwows around the country, Dan fell in love with powwow drumming, forming the Southern Pine Drum Group with his brother Ralph and friends Donald Cotton and his son Jake Kirk, among others. Deeply spiritual, Dan is a firm believer in reviving and creating ceremonies to heal community members and the community from generational trauma as well as contemporary challenges.

Bobby Joe

BOGUE CHITTO. BORN 1953.

I met Bobby Joe late one afternoon behind his home in Bogue Chitto. He was raising hunting dogs and had a new litter he was trying to train. The task was hard; the idea of telling stories somewhat less so. So we headed indoors to the cool darkness and began to talk, a routine we fell into whenever I was in town.

Bobby was a philosopher, though he would not claim the title himself. An avid follower of the news and popular media, Bobby constantly sorted through contemporary events, weighing them against the knowledge and values he had grown accustomed to in Bogue Chitto, one of the most traditional of the various Mississippi Choctaw communities. He spoke eloquently and deeply about his life and the world around him, making even casual conversations with him intensely thought-provoking. Bobby passed away on March 3, 2019.

Grady John

PEARL RIVER/HENNING, TENNESSEE. BORN 1934.

Grady John was perhaps best known as the only contemporary Choctaw potter. It was a title that Grady had been trying to change; he wanted to train younger boys and girls to make the pots that he learned to make from and with his uncle, L. D. John. Unlike the stories he told, the art of making pottery was not a continuous tradition being passed down through generation after generation until the present. Before Grady and his uncle, the art had died out completely. Yet by studying the pottery shards dug up by archeologists—carefully analyzing the materials used as well as the designs and forms employed—the two men had resurrected the art. Grady did not want it to die again.

    I visited Grady regularly, both in his home in Henning, Tennessee—where a small but viable Choctaw community has established itself, having moved there to find work just after removal and during the lean sharecropping years of the turn of the century—and at Chucalissa, a reconstructed fifteenth-century Indian village in Memphis, where Grady worked as an exhibit interpreter and local artisan. Even after he retired, he still dug his clay nearby. He loved the public and their enthusiasm for his culture and people and could not seem to keep from shaking hands and greeting visitors even when he was just back for a visit or more clay. Not surprisingly, he was a popular guest at area festivals, telling stories and making pottery. The two artistic traditions seem to work well together, his stories creating in words what his hands created in clay. Grady John passed away on December 16, 2001.

Jessica Miller

CRYSTAL RIDGE. BORN 1984.

Jessica Miller has lived all her life in the Crystal Ridge community, a community that her great-great-grandfather Cameron Wesley once led as chief. She grew up hearing stories of his abilities to heal family and friends with the herbs he collected in the woods. As a child, she picked peas in the fields during summer days and entertained her elders at night by dancing with the other children in the family to the "Rabbit in the Garden" song her mother sang. It was a song that Frances Densmore had recorded from her great-grandfather Sidney Wesley in the 1940s (1943:179). Those family nights also included storytelling, including stories about the supernatural beings on land and in the water—stories that she remembered when she herself encountered a *shilop* or ghost out by Nanih Waiya Mound.

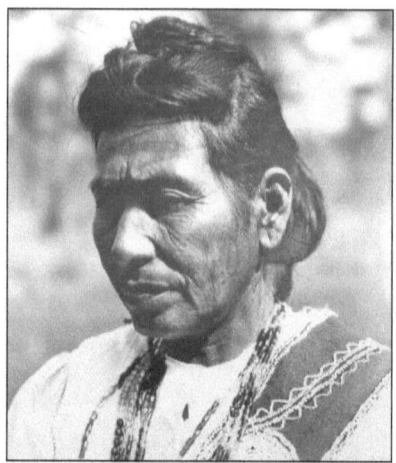

Pisatuntema—Emma

BAYOU LACOMB, LOUISIANA.

Along with Heleema and Ahojeobe, Pisatuntema provided David Bushnell Jr. with many of the myths and legends he collected from the community at Bayou Lacomb in Louisiana. Apparently, she was Bushnell's primary informant. He describes her as the oldest member of the community (about fifty years old) and the daughter of one of the previous leaders of the community who was generally regarded as a chief. She attributed the stories she knew to him. Bushnell also adds that while she was telling the stories, others would add or suggest other parts of the story although none of the essential parts differed.

Pisatuntema was a basket maker as well as a storyteller, and she made at least one of the baskets pictured in Bureau of American Ethnology Bulletin 48. And like Heleema, she was baptized into the Catholic church as a young girl by Father Roquette. Bushnell suggests that the biblical influence on her story of the flood can be understood by this Catholic instruction.

Isaac Pistonatubbee

CONEHATTA.

According to Henry Halbert's brief mention of Isaac Pistonatubbee, he was born sometime in the 1820s and died in his eighties in Newton County, Mississippi, just before 1900. Halbert recorded a version of the emergence myth from Pistonatubbee in Choctaw, stating that he recorded it word for word as it was spoken. Pistonatubbee told Halbert that as a boy, he often heard this story from the old chiefs.

Peter P. Pitchlynn

NOXUBEE COUNTY, MISSISSIPPI. BORN 1806.

Perhaps the most frequently recorded historical person who told stories of the Choctaw was Peter P. Pitchlynn. In 1841, George Catlin may have been the first to record him when he described Pitchlynn as "a very intelligent and influential man in the tribe" and "a distinguished and very gentlemanly man, who has been very well educated, and who gave me much curious and valuable information, of the history and traditions of his tribe." Charles Lanman and Horatio B. Cushman also found him to be a willing and knowledgeable informant. While Cushman considered him a good friend and lauded his intelligence and character, Lanman's respect and admiration bordered on hyperbole, often referring to Pitchlynn as a hero and calling him the leading intellect among his people. More recently, David Baird provided a less starry-eyed and less favorable picture of Pitchlynn in his book *Peter Pitchlynn: Chief of the Choctaws*. The title is somewhat ironic since Pitchlynn was never an officially elected chief, though he often adopted the role.

Like his brother-in-law Israel Folsom, Peter Pitchlynn was born to a White trader and a half Choctaw, half White woman, and was raised as one of the educated elite. Throughout his life, he seems to have struggled with his identity as both White and Choctaw. Torn in allegiance socially and politically, it seems Pitchlynn often deferred to his own self-interests, which helps explain the contradictory stances he took with regard to Choctaw land rights. Scandal plagued him throughout his career, beginning with accusations of mismanagement of the Choctaw Academy to claims of misappropriated funds in his frequent role as delegate to Washington, DC. Nonetheless, it does seem obvious that Pitchlynn was both interested and knowledgeable about the narrative traditions of the Choctaw. His tendency to rearrange history to fit his needs in his personal life (such as claiming college degrees he did not have) may have carried into his accounts of Choctaw mythic history, but such alterations would not be unique to Pitchlynn. Further, considering his education and social circles, the flowery language that Charles Lanman employs in recounting Pitchlynn's narratives may have been encouraged by Pitchlynn.

Harry Polk

RED WATER. BORN 1937.

I met Harry Polk at the summer language camp organized by the community to help Choctaw children retain their language. Harry was certainly a good role model, much more comfortable speaking Choctaw than English, which is slowly dominating the everyday parlance of the community. While Harry's official role was to teach the young campers how to make blowguns and rabbit sticks, he was also one of the storytellers who entertained the children during their break after lunch.

For Harry, this was a natural extension of a pastime he shared with his family, particularly his brothers and sisters. Gathered together at one or the other's home in the community of Red Water, they took turns telling the stories they learned as children and have continued to learn as adults. He attributed most of his stories to his grandfather. "My grandfather used to build a fire, and we all sat around," he remembered. "And my grandfather tell all kind of stories, used to be." Like most who remember these sessions, he was young, and he spent more time playing with his cousins than listening to the stories. Despite this, Harry remembered lots of stories and the practice he received telling them—among his brothers and sisters, to the children at camp, and to his own grandchildren—kept them vivid in his memory. He passed away on June 26, 2012.

Regina Shoemake

CONEHATTA. BORN 1948.

Regina Shoemake, like Judy Billie and Sally Allen, has devoted her life to helping others. When these three women gather to discuss the traditions they believe need to be passed down and remembered, they find that in talking and listening, each remembers more that she thought, and each hears more than she alone knew. The conversations have become learning experiences for all of them.

Regina Shoemake's concern for the younger generation is as obvious in her comments as it is in the line of work she has chosen. Part of this concern, it seems, stems from memories of her own childhood, encountering things such as *nishkin chafa* that, without knowing what they were or how to respect them, could have been harmful. The stories she told were meant to teach not only respect through admiration and understanding of the old ways but also that respect is often the key to very practical living.

Jeffie Solomon

CONEHATTA. BORN 1919.

Meriva Williamson and Glenda Williamson had been generously taking me around Conehatta to record the stories of the elders in the community when we stopped at Jeffie Solomon's home. She and her sister Odie Anderson (Glenda's mother) were expecting us. I had not met Jeffie Solomon before, and she kindly welcomed me into her home. Like many of the older women in some of the more traditional communities such as Conehatta, Jeffie Solomon was wearing a traditional Choctaw dress replete with white apron. It was her daily attire and so had none of the beaded medallions and collar necklaces worn for formal occasions. I remembered that I had seen her before, in pictures in the tribal museum, cutting swamp cane and making baskets for which she was well known and well respected.

As we walked in, both Meriva and Glenda were handed an empty bowl and a bag of peas to shell. Perhaps because I was the guest, or perhaps because I was male, I was exempt from the work. So as the four women snapped peas, I settled back into an overstuffed sofa and listened. Jeffie Solomon and Odie Anderson traded stories back and forth, prodding each other when memories stalled. Meriva and Glenda also encouraged them with their questions. None of the women seemed to notice the work their hands were performing. They spoke in Choctaw, so I listened without truly understanding, catching a word or two here and there. Only after we were back in the car and Meriva and Glenda could casually translate the stories for me did I get to enjoy the stories as narratives, not just as poetic performances. That's the way stories are supposed to be told, Harley Vaughn told me later when I described the scene: sitting around, shelling peas. Jeffie passed away on February 27, 2004.

Rosalee Steve

TUCKER. BORN 1922.

Anyone familiar with contemporary Choctaw storytelling knows the name Rosalee Steve. A frequent guest at local schools, festivals, conferences, even Boy Scout National Jamborees, Rosalee Steve was as close to the full-time storytellers of old as one might expect to find. Rosalee learned her stories the way people have been learning them for centuries—by listening to the elders, even though she was an elder herself by the time she actively searched out community storytellers in 1993. She found them at the Elderly Nutrition Program, a chance for elderly community members to meet in Pearl River for a nutritional meal and a chance to socialize. She told stories ever since.

Telling stories was only one of Rosalee Steve's many talents, however. She painted, drew, sewed traditional dresses, did beadwork, was teaching herself German and Spanish, albeit slowly, and baked arguably the best biscuit around. She was a devout Catholic, a medicine woman, a certified nurse, and a fiercely independent woman. Her legacy lives on in more great-grandchildren than she could count. She told stories freely but was reluctant to record them since she made part of her living by telling them to groups that hired her. From the letters she received thanking her for past performances and asking her back again, there seemed to be no worry that her services would lack demand. She was justly proud of these acknowledgments and accomplishments, but she continually strived to do more. As she said, God does not want you to waste your talents. There seemed to be no fear of that for Rosalee Steve. She passed away on June 10, 2010.

John Hunter Thompson

BOGUE CHITTO. BORN 1891.

Since he died in 1985 at the age of ninety-four, his granddaughter Louise Wilson calculates that John Hunter Thompson must have been born around 1891, which means he was a young boy during the second removal to Oklahoma in 1903. She remembers that he had carved his birth year into the wooden walls of his house, but the house no longer stands, and the image has faded from her memory.

What has not faded are the stories he told her as a young girl: about stickball games and picnics, making homebrew, the importance of adhering to marriage laws, and even older stories that he had heard such as those about intertribal wars. He was entertaining as well as knowledgeable, she remembers. He taught himself the harmonica and sang and told stories, all while she and her cousins gathered around him. "Now this was kind of funny, and he said it in a funny way too, so I don't know whether to believe him or not," Louise says, describing how John Hunter Thompson married his brother's widow, her grandmother, when his brother died. "He said that when his brother died, he said here he saw this woman with all these little kids. And he said that, in the family, they believe in helping other family members. And he said, 'Since this is my brother's kids,' he said that 'I felt like I should step in and help raise those kids.' And that's why he married her. He said, 'But I think she really wanted to marry me first anyway.'"

Estelline Tubby

PEARL RIVER. BORN 1928.

Estelline Tubby was famous in Pearl River for her knowledge about Choctaw culture, whether stories, blankets, or gardening. This interested, interesting, gracious woman spent much of her life raising her own children and helping to raise countless grandchildren. She had a full career in the Choctaw school system, nursed a husband whose failing health dominated her time, and managed to learn to quilt, make dolls, do beadwork, sew traditional shirts and dresses, and garden. "I only wish I was younger. You know, about fifty, fifty-five. Then I could do all the things I want to do."

Her blankets, or quilts, regularly won prizes at the annual Choctaw Indian Fair, but they were rarely for sale, instead going to her family as gifts. Her artistic talent has been passed down to at least one of her sons, Carl Tubby, whose paintings hang in the Tribal Archives as well as in various homes in the community including, of course, that of his proud mother.

Her artistry was prevalent in her stories as well. She crafted the narratives with attention to attribute faithfully what she had heard to her parents and grandparents and their grandparents before them. This storytelling legacy is deep, connected to her father-in-law, Simpson Tubby, another of the storytellers in this book. She was also an intensely thoughtful person and added her own interpretation to the stories to make sense of them in the world in which she lived. Much of this interpretation was guided by her religion. Originally raised Baptist, she became a Mormon when one of her sons encouraged her to go to church with him and his family. Her narrative about the third removal is tied closely with the idea of the second coming of Jesus Christ. Estelline passed away on October 4, 2006.

Simpson Tubby

PEARL RIVER. BORN 1867.

The Reverend Simpson Tubby was born in Neshoba County, Mississippi, on April 1, 1867, "a child of the forest," as he says in his pamphlet titled "Early Struggles," an account of his conversion to Christianity. In this passionate autobiographical sketch, Tubby disassociates himself from the "savages" that were his people, praising instead the White Methodist missionaries who had shown him the light and the error of his and his people's ways. He eventually became an avid missionary to his people in Mississippi, establishing the first Methodist church for the Choctaw. This disassociation in writing, however, was not one in reality. Baxter York remembers that "old man Simpson Tubby" was on the temporary Tribal Council with him in the 1930s and 1940s when they drew up a constitution declaring self-government.

Considering his conversion, it is perhaps not surprising that many of the stories Simpson Tubby recounted to John Swanton were heavily tinged with biblical references and third-person language such as "they," "the Choctaw," and "Indians," instead of "we" and "us." Nonetheless, as is obvious from his "Early Struggles," Tubby grew up a Choctaw and was enculturated with the stories of his community, to whom he attributed them. He, like Swanton's other major collaborator, Olman Comby, was well versed in animal stories of Possum, Rabbit, and Fox. He told these stories, and many others, to his children and grandchildren, too. Although she never heard them from him, his daughter-in-law Estelline Tubby—another of the storytellers in this book—carried on Simpson Tubby's storytelling legacy.

Rae Nell Vaughn

PEARL RIVER. BORN 1964.

As her formal bio on the jacket of this book attests, Rae Nell has worn many hats. But her role as storyteller moves her from outside the book to the pages inside. Most of her stories are recorded in the book *Choctaw Traditions: Stories of the Customs and Traditions of the Mississippi Choctaw*, capturing the customs and traditions she grew up with and continues to share with her own children and grandchildren. But since working on this book, she has begun adding tribal stories to her repertoire of family ones, particularly when entertaining her six grandchildren at all hours of the day and night. One of those stories is included here: the story of the squirrel who ate the sun, which she first encountered on a Facebook post from a member of the Choctaw Nation in Oklahoma. She then told her grandchildren the story and, in doing so, brought the story back to Mississippi oral traditions where it began.

Henry Williams

CONEHATTA. BORN 1945.

In the memories of many in the community, there were men who, when gathered around family and friends at meals, festivals, or community events, entertained themselves and others with humorous stories and jokes. The truly great storytellers could take a story and work in a friend's name, even adapt the plot to fit present circumstances, all for the good-natured fun of the group. Henry did this regularly. Like Hulon Willis, who described himself as an ad-lib man, Henry Williams was always quick with a joke, especially if it was aimed playfully at a nearby friend. But Henry could also be deeply thoughtful. He frequently hosted sweat lodges in his backyard to express a spiritual side one might otherwise miss. He passed away on September 25, 2011.

Gladys Willis

PEARL RIVER. BORN 1926.

Gladys Willis was the matriarch of a family that extends throughout the Pearl River community and includes Hulon Willis, her son and neighbor and another prodigious storyteller. Perhaps because of this role, or perhaps because she was by nature a kind and generous woman, she welcomed me into her home and made me feel as comfortable there as anywhere I have been. When she was feeling well, she sat on her front porch and waved to the cars that honked hello. With failing eyesight, she could no longer tell just who she was waving to, but that did not bother her. She joked that if she did not know a person from their voice, she just brazenly asked, "Who are you?"

And when her eyes no longer allowed her to do the beadwork she once taught her daughters, and for which she was featured in the student publication *Nanih Waiya*, she continued to knit blankets for friends and family. Her fingers had learned the well-traveled routes, and she no longer needed her sight to guide her needles. Her mind traveled the past well, too, and though she admitted she could hardly remember any of the stories she was told as a young girl, the stories she did remember were honed into beautiful, pithy narratives such as those about Ashman, the community's scapegoat and helplessly naive buffoon. When Gladys Willis told these tales, it was clear that we were supposed to identify with Ashman, not ridicule him. Life is humorous and ironic, and it must be dealt with accordingly. Her ability to accept her loss of eyesight with humor suggests she had taken these narratives to heart.

Gladys Willis died on April 25, 1999. This book is dedicated to her for her spirit, her warmth, and her deep appreciation for her culture.

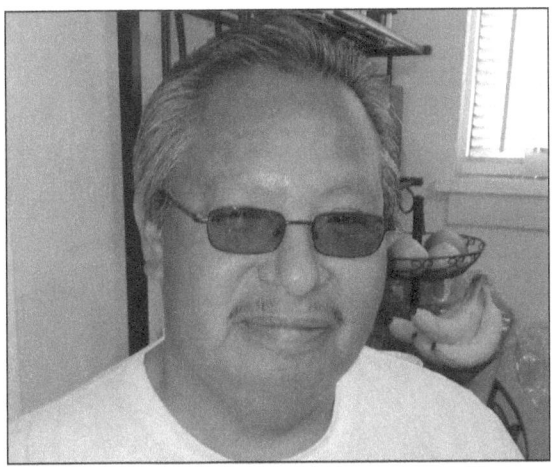

Hulon Willis

PEARL RIVER. BORN 1956.

A self-professed ad-lib man, Hulon Willis was the consummate contemporary storyteller. Mixing stories from the past with stories of the present, he was able to entertain his peers with culturally and socially relevant stories, making them all the funnier. The introduction to this book attempts to more fully describe Hulon and his art of storytelling and joke telling. One thing not mentioned in the introduction, however, is his proficiency in the written word as well as the spoken. In high school, Hulon published poems in the *Nanih Waiya*, the same magazine that provided some of the stories in this collection. He dealt with issues of land rights and identity that suggested a fierce pride in his heritage and a simmering anger at the injustices perpetrated against Native Americans. He passed away on September 18, 2023.

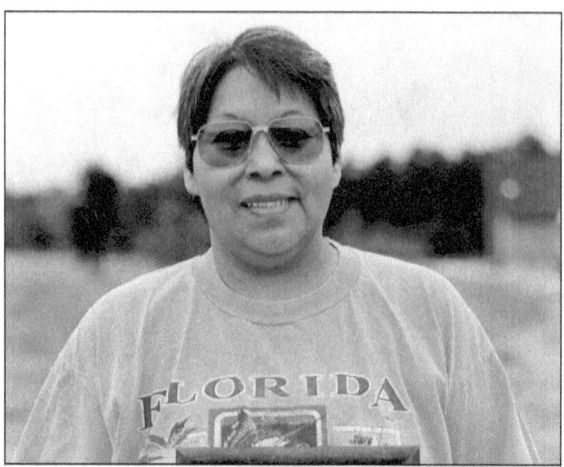

Linda Willis

CRYSTAL RIDGE. BORN 1953.

Cameron Wesley is a name known by all in the community. Many herald him as the last traditional chief of the Choctaw. Linda Willis called him something else—Grandpa. As storytelling has traditionally been conducted among the Choctaw, it was the grandchildren who most often heard the old stories, and Linda listened carefully as a child. The stories Linda told she attributed to him. His values of the importance of maintaining a clear Choctaw identity, of being able to produce the necessities of life, and of the land, were all imparted in his stories. When I met Linda, she was recovering from chronic health problems. Sadly, those problems claimed her life far too soon on July 20, 2002. Happily, she spent a lot of time with her own grandchildren. A few of the stories are preserved here; many others are continuing to be told among family members.

Travis Willis

PEARL RIVER. BORN 1958.

Travis Willis was born in Pearl River to Gladys Mae Willis and Claude Yates Willis, one of eleven children, including Caroline Morris and Hulon Willis. One of his main chores growing up was to feed the cows, which meant getting up at four o'clock in the morning and then heading off to school when he was done. On weekends, it was fishing and hunting. Travis is a Baptist minister who has led a number of churches in the area and regularly offers prayers and eulogies for friends and community members. At a family wake, his brother Hulon Willis dropped Travis into a set joke, in classic *shokhannǫpa* style, of the preacher who asked who was ready to go home to the Lord. Everyone had their hand up except Travis. The preacher asked Travis whether he didn't want to go home to the Lord. "I do," he replied.

"Then why didn't you raise your hand?"

"Because my daddy said I needed to come home right after church, so I better go on and go."

Everyone laughed, Travis most of all. Travis's first wife was Navajo, and his children, grandchildren, and great-grandchildren are multiracial, spread out across the southern United States. Today he still lives in Pearl River, married to Frannie Willis. He was the last family member to see his mother before she passed away and mourns the loss of the regular family dinners she hosted that kept his family so close.

Louise Wilson

BOGUE CHITTO. BORN 1950.

Louise Wilson heads up the Youth Opportunity Program, which places high-school-aged boys and girls into jobs throughout the community to give them work experience and an idea of some of the job options the tribe has to offer. Liasha Alex, Lionel Dan, Danielle Dan, and Curtis "Buck" Willis were all members of the program that I worked with at the archives, and they often came with me to interview members of the community. Danielle Dan accompanied me to talk to Louise Wilson the first time we spoke. We have talked regularly since, with Louise generously sharing stories of the past and present.

Louise Wilson comes by her storytelling naturally. When her grandfather died, his brother married his brother's widow to help care for both her and her young children. Louise Wilson says he used to joke that she really wanted to marry him all along. Her new grandfather, the only one she ever knew and the one who used to gather her and her cousins together to hear stories, was John Hunter Thompson, another storyteller in this collection. The stories Louise tells she attributes to him.

Baxter York

PEARL RIVER. BORN 1907.

Baxter York was a leader in the community, both formally and informally, throughout the twentieth century. In the 1930s and 1940s, he was a member of the first temporary Tribal Council set up in Mississippi after removal along with Simpson Tubby, another storyteller in this collection. He helped develop the constitution and bylaws that were adopted in 1945, establishing the Mississippi Band of Choctaw Indians as a self-governing nation. Such leadership was a family affair. His brother, Emmett York, was eventually elected the first tribal chairman and worked with Phillip Martin to train him in the role of chief, a role Martin held for twenty-eight years. Baxter York, however, dropped out of formal politics, though he continued to stand as a leader in the community. He was perhaps an obvious subject for interview by the high school students in the 1970s working for *Nanih Waiya*. He was interviewed twice for the magazine, once about politics, the other about culture. His legacy lives on in his son, Jake York, who continues to tell the stories he once did. In one of his interviews, Baxter York notes a concern that continues to be repeated throughout the community today: "I still believe in my old ways of thinking and the Creator. The Creator equally set things on the earth. I think that we, Choctaws, ought to keep our culture and language. Live like you should, use what God, the Creator, gave you." He passed away on October 27, 1975.

Jake York

PEARL RIVER/CONEHATTA. BORN 1950.

I met Jake York at the summer language camp organized by the tribe. He, like Harry Polk, Nellie Billy, and Cynthia Clegg, also told stories to the children during their rest after lunch. An entertaining storyteller, Jake was as comfortable retelling an old story he remembered from his father, Baxter York, as he was using his knowledge of such narratives to create new ones. Listening to him one day, I noticed that he seemed to create a story on the spot for the children at camp. Working for the language camp, Jake was supposed to be encouraging the campers to learn, speak, and revere the Choctaw language. His story "The Dog Who Spoke Choctaw" did just that, with a moral at the end that if dogs can learn Choctaw, so can they. Jake also told stories among his peers for less didactic reasons. His stories about the legendary Jim Dixon, as told to him from his father and from Jim Dixon himself, were outrageous and hilarious. Such stories seemed to reflect well Jake's own sense of humor. Jake passed away on December 14, 2014.

THE GENRES OF CHOCTAW STORYTELLING

One of the perennial dilemmas of story collections such as this is how to organize the various stories. Shifts in theoretical approaches to folklore have led to shifts in how stories are arranged and presented. One of the greatest shifts in the field has been a move from folklore as thing to folklore as process. Stories, for example, do not get handed down like heirloom jewelry but rather are created anew in each telling. Different storytellers and audiences, with different goals and contexts, result in different stories. It is the process of storytelling more than a static notion of the story that is crucial for constructing meaning.

Coupled with this shift is the recognition of the importance of discovering native or emic categories. This is preferable to categorically applying more universal or etic terms agreed upon in scholarship but not necessarily agreed upon or used by the people who actually tell the stories. These shared etic terms for stories are quickly recognizable: myths, legends, folktales, fairy tales, tall tales, and jokes. Other less recognizable terms have been added in the study of narrative, such as memorates to describe personal encounters with the supernatural. A number of scholars have spent careers discussing generic categories, trying to delineate their boundaries. The task is far from trivial. Imagine the following: A person is wary of how quickly people are becoming dependent on new technology. It does not dominate her every thought but nags her periodically. This fear can be expressed in action, by throwing away the newfangled telephone, or nonaction, by refusing to buy it in the first place. It can also be enacted verbally. The person can choose to denounce technology every chance she gets in the form of soapbox sermons; she can recount urban legends about rats in fried chicken and microwaved pets; she can choose to tell jokes about the ignorant city slicker and his much wiser rural cousin; she can even tell personal experience narratives about instance after instance where technology failed, and people were not equipped literally or mentally to deal with the breakdown. Each of these forms provides an outlet for the narrator, but each is vastly different in the kind of message it conveys and the way in which that message is meant to be interpreted.

This last part is worth notice. What is often missing or shuffled to the side in so many definitions of genre and generic systems is the power of that system not just for creation but also for interpretation. The genre as a tool facilitates communication not only by providing the speaker with a form to use to convey her sentiment but also by providing the audience with similar tools to recognize those forms, and hence interpret the distinct message, symbol, emotion, or belief that accompanies them.

With such power, generic divisions cannot be applied lightly. Further, if the goal is to understand how a particular oral tradition operates within the specific community in which it is told, then to apply broad, academically agreed-upon etic terms rather than culturally specific emic ones is misleading.

The task for the folklorist, then, is to combine the two mandates: that of addressing process and not just product and native emic categories rather than academic etic ones. More specifically, we must uncover the native system that storytellers draw upon to construct the various types of stories they tell.

Easily stated, less easily done.

After a great deal of struggle, a three-part approach to the study of the generic system of Choctaw storytelling seemed to adhere to these demands: (1) begin with native terms that signify genres; (2) move to commentary and context that frames the story; and (3) end with patterns evident from analysis of the performance.[1]

NATIVE TERMS

Native genres in Choctaw storytelling are few if judged by the existence of specific terms. *Shokhannǫpa* is the only native-language term used today. *Shokha* means "hog," *annǫpa* "talk"—literally, "hog talk," though the English term "hogwash" may provide a better translation. *Shokhannǫpa* couples two seemingly disparate groups of stories within one category: humorous stories and animal tales.

Sitting in his office, Henry Williams talks about stickball, the army, and life growing up. Eventually, I ask Henry some form of the question "Do you know any stories?" He thinks for a moment. "There's lots of stories that talk about—hog story. But I don't know nothing about that. Except I guess Raccoon is part of that story. Grandma used to tell us. Possum and Raccoon used to be buddies, you know."

Possum used to have tail, had furs on it, you know. Raccoon had that striped tail, you know. So Possum asked Raccoon how did he get a striped tail. And the Raccoon told him to gather the woods and get it real hot and put the tail in that fire, and it will become striped.

So Possum decided to do that. But instead of it striped, it took all the fur off it. So the reason why the Possum don't have fur—it burned.

That's the story they used to tell us. Possum decided to get his tail striped. His tail in the fire, put that tail in the fire, it burned all his hair. [*laughter*]

I like that one, so I used to have him tell about Possum and Raccoon. There's a few more, but I don't know how it goes.

Indian, seems like they're dumb, to me. The way they tell us the story; it's not real, but when you try to make it read about it, it sounds stupid. But it's funny. It's a make-up stories. They're good at it, like comedians. I guess they're Indian comedians.

Henry identifies the genre clearly, though he uses an English translation for the category since he knows I do not speak Choctaw. Here are the animal stories of Possum and Raccoon, Rabbit and Bear. Many storytellers specifically name this subgenre. Harry Polk, for example, notes that his grandfather "used to tell all kind of story. When he built a fire, he said he going to tell a story. Just sitting around, tell a story. All kind of story. He tell me about animal story too. And the possum and the fox."

But animal stories are only one part of *shokhannopa*. When Henry Williams finishes his tale, and the laughter has died down, he goes on to describe the genre. He makes two observations of critical importance. The first is that he identifies *shokhannopa* as "make-up stories." There is double meaning here: as an adjective—fictional—as well as a verb—making up stories. There is no belief that Henry Williams or any of his ancestors could have wandered through the woods and stumbled across talking animals burning their tails. *Shokhannopa* are made-up stories, not literally true.

But *shokhannopa* are also made-up stories in the sense that they are constantly being created. These are the humorous stories and jokes people like Henry Williams regularly make up. The second type of *shokhannopa* is referred to in Henry Williams's second observation, those stories that are the product of the "Indian comedian." The Indian comedian is always ready with a story, a joke, or some sly, witty, obscene, raucous, but always humorous observation. Sometimes these "jokes" are ones the comedian has heard before and performs himself, altering as much or as little as he sees fit. Other times, these performances are better described as situational joking, such as good-natured ribbing and teasing.[2] Henry Williams combines both in his story "The Man and the Turkey," printed in its entirety later in this collection. In the story, an incompetent young man tries to impress a girl and her family by hauling the same turkey past their house every day as if he has killed a different turkey each day. His ruse is discovered, and he presumably loses the girl's hand in marriage. A few days later, I pass by Henry Williams talking with fellow Conehatta councilman Billy Chickaway out in front of the tribal offices. I wave hello, and Henry shouts after me, "Hey, you remember that guy with the turkey? This is him!" Billy Chickaway can perhaps guess that he is the butt of the joke and smiles good-naturedly. He knows Henry too well to take offense.

In these performances, Henry Williams employs the joke not only as a performance in and of itself, but also as a resource with which to make other jokes. The first is a self-deprecating comment on his own luck with women when he comments after the joke: "If this was the same today, I'd die; they'd probably take their time finding me a woman." The second is the situational joke he creates to tease Billy Chickaway. These performances suggest at least a few of the variations of *shokhannopa*.

Both narratives and situational jokes may derive not from passed-down narratives but also from experience. Here, the misstep, the human error that can occur daily, is exploited by the comedian. Real incidences are taken by the narrator and exaggerated and contorted to make them ludicrous and subsequently hilarious. Hulon Willis is a master of such teasing and joking, so proficient he does not always require an actual event as source material but finds resources in stereotypes and general bawdiness. These are the kinds of jokes that are generally effective only in the moment and would embarrass both the narrator and the butt of the joke in print, so they are not included in this collection. Such jokes are not categorically different from the general sort of teasing and ribbing common among friends of many cultures.

The demand of *shokhannopa* is, above all else, to be funny, and consequently to provoke the audience to laughter. Narrators are expected to adapt the stories creatively, to invent not merely recite. When Glenda Williamson asked Esbie Gibson to tell a humorous story for the group gathered in her home, she replied, "If you want to hear a funny story, go make one up!" We all laughed, but she was exactly right. Such a task is a responsibility as well as a license.

This license applies to all *shokhannopa*, not only the jokes. Animal stories, too, may be made up on the spot. As with Esbie Gibson's declaration of this freedom for any humorous tale, Roseanna Nickey claims the same freedom for animal stories. During an in-service day for school employees, Roseanna and her Choctaw Language Program staff hosted a session on the state of affairs of the Choctaw language and the importance of incorporating native-language materials into the classroom. One woman in the audience asked Roseanna about stories that she could tell to her class since she did not know any. Roseanna told her to make them up. She laughed, as did the others, but Roseanna was serious.

While Roseanna Nickey does not face the same problems as the woman in the audience—not knowing any stories—she herself makes them up when teaching children the Choctaw language. During story time at the language immersion camp her program runs each summer, Roseanna donned a furry puppet on each hand and made up a story about an opossum and a raccoon, all in flawless Choctaw. Other storytellers during the summer created their own animal stories too, including Maggie Chitto, who adapted a story about Rabbit losing his tail that she heard from some American Indian but non-Choctaw friends when she lived out West.[3]

When discussing *shokhannọpa*, many refer to animal stories, others to jokes. Another subgenre is noted by Jake York when he introduces the story he heard from his father about legendary funny man Jim Dixon: "My dad had a friend that he used to talk about, and his name was Jim Dixon. And I guess Jim had a knack for telling tall stories." Tall stories, like animal stories, comprise a recognizable genre outside Choctaw culture, and the etic definition seems to apply here: "Humorous narrative, usually short, based on exaggeration . . . usually told as factual accounts of real happenings . . . while listeners make that 'willing suspension of disbelief' necessary to a successful session."[4] The category of the tall story or tall tale can help to refine the more general term of *joke* that Henry Williams used for his story of the hunter and the turkey, clearly a tall story itself. *Joke* encompasses both this kind of story and the less explicitly narrative subgenre of situational joking that does not depend on a narrative structure to facilitate the humorous jab.

So, based on native terms, frequently used as introductions to the stories themselves, a model of the genre of *shokhannọpa* emerges. The stories are above all else humorous. They are also made up—either exaggerated or outright fictional. And they are either passed on or continuously created. While the subgenres of the animal story and joke can be divided by content, temporal attributes, involvement of narrator, literal versus metaphorical or allegorical application, and variation in social function, these differences are secondary to those that unite both groups into one category.

The personal joke is the only part of the genre that is not explicitly named by storytellers. Its validity as a genre is based not on emic terms but rather on patterns and structures uncovered during the course of studying emic genres.

At first glance, the lack of a specific term may not seem surprising. Genres are not always distinctly laid out by name. Yet as we move through the rest of Choctaw storytelling, an explanation rises to the surface, a culturally salient reason that such personal jokes are not explicitly named as "stories," even though storytellers clearly recognize them as *shokhannǫpa*.

COMMENTARY AND CONTEXT

The generic systems developed so far have been based on terms expressly recognized in the community as genres. The Choctaw have relatively few such terms, yet storytellers distinguish between stories further, as their performances indicate. By examining the introductory material storytellers have employed to preface and contextualize their narratives, these divisions begin to emerge.

The system underlying *shokhannǫpa* is one based on tone. *Shokhannǫpa* comprises stories that are funny. The rest of the stories, then, might be expected to be not funny. These "not-funny" or serious stories need not be bereft of the humorous turn, confined to the dark and macabre or stonily didactic. Harold Comby says the ability to tell a "not-funny" story with humor is one of the hallmarks of "Indian humor." "Like my mom, when she used to tell stories in a funny way. The stories wouldn't be funny, but she would tell it in a funny way where people would laugh. And they say that's good medicine."[5] Consider a Navajo comment by Yellowman, a Navajo elder, who noted that coyote stories are not funny stories, but things that Coyote does are funny.[6] The same applies here. The dog in Jake York's story "The Dog Who Spoke Choctaw" is funny. So are the unsuspecting animals in the story of how snakes became poisonous. But they are not funny stories. There is a sense that the stories outside *shokhannǫpa*, that we can tentatively place in this other section, demand more attention and require the audience to move more consciously beyond entertainment. While *shokhannǫpa* certainly operates on deeper levels of behavior modification, instruction, and negotiation of social relations of character types as well as very real neighbors and friends, it does not need to. The only requirement of *shokhannǫpa* is that it be humorous. The responsibility and expectation extend to the audience as well, who needs only to appreciate the performance as funny.

These other stories require more. But there is no clear, universally recognized native term to guide us here. Henry Williams, however, clearly recognizes the division and even suggests there is such a term when he introduces the story about the inept hunter: "Grandpa wasn't that old, so he didn't tell us stories. He would tell us jokes." Henry then follows with one of these jokes that has a clear narrative structure, and so, one might assume, could be labeled a story. But Henry tells us his father never told him stories. For Henry Williams, *shokhannǫpa* are not "stories." "Stories" are narratives that older people tell. There is a responsibility in the words of the elders, and Henry avers that though the narrator was his grandfather, he "was not yet that old," and so did not yet fill the role of elder. Instead, he remained in Henry's words "the Indian comedian."

The category that sits opposite *shokhannǫpa*, then, is not particularly "serious stories," but rather "elders' stories." Such a name seems apt since, like these stories, the term *elder* suggests not merely a role but an element of authority, respect, power, tradition, and, perhaps most obviously, the past. These stories are important, carrying with them information about creation, the past, and the future. They are stories that reflect on the state of the world, where it has been and where it is headed. They are stories told by the elders of long ago as well as those of elders today.

However, in 2021, the tribal dictionary committee added the term *hopáki ikhąna* defined as "legends, old stories, history," a combination of *hopákih*: to be far in distance or time, and *ikhanah*: learn. Tribal language specialist Jason Lewis further clarified that another way to define *hopáki ikhąna* is "knowing or knowledge from long ago."[7] Although the term does not convey a sense of who is telling the stories as *elders' stories* does, it *does* convey a sense of their function: for audiences to learn. Further, it clearly conveys a sense of the past, both in terms of being *about* the past in glossing etic terms such as legends and history, and in being *from* the past, in describing "old stories," passed down over the years from long ago.

The term is clearly in its infancy and may continue to evolve in meaning and usage. With its expansive definitions and inclusion of "old stories" *hopáki ikhąna* offers a useful umbrella term to replace what I have referred to in the past as *elders' stories* or *talk of the elders*. More restrictive usage, however, may suggest it operates more usefully as a synonym for the subcategory of "historical legends" discussed later in this chapter.

In either case, while the distinction between *shokhannǫpa* and *old stories* that describe the past with the gravitas of the elders may not be explicitly articulated in conversation, it is nonetheless understood throughout the community, particularly by men and women in their thirties, forties, and fifties, people old enough to have heard the old stories but who rarely claim the right or accept the responsibility of the elders to perform them. With this distinction, we can understand the seemingly contradictory comments made by Henry Williams about his grandfather and similar comments made by other performers of *shokhannǫpa*. "I am not a storyteller," Hulon Willis says, "but I tell stories." Hulon plays with the double meaning here. He tells stories but not "stories." Hulon accepts the title of comedian but squirms under the label of storyteller. To accept such a title is to claim a knowledge and status in the community that Hulon believes he is too young for and that he is too humble to accept. *Shokhannǫpa* is open to performance by all; "stories," or *hopáki ikhąna*, on the other hand, belong to the elders.

The notion of authority and age implicit in the emic definition of "stories" as well as the new but recognizable *hopáki ikhgna* suggests yet another axis underlying the generic system of Choctaw verbal art: the temporal. The characteristic of being passed down is integrally important to how the Choctaw view these stories. The story rooted in the past is imbued not only with the validation of past wisdom but is by definition traditional, where traditional demands temporal longevity.[8] In fact, storytellers mark these stories in performance with the simple but powerful introductory formula of attribution. As Regina Shoemake notes: "They used to say, 'This is what they said,' when they were sitting around talking." According to Harold Comby, his mother is even more forceful: "It's not my words," she tells her son when recounting the old traditions. "It's the words of the elderly or the old ones before me." Authority is inherent in the claim.[9]

This distinction is so vital, so ingrained, that narratives that people tell about themselves are often not considered "stories" at all, at least not the kind of stories that the Choctaw person thinks of when stories and storytelling are mentioned. Discourse, even nonnarrative discourse, that was passed on by elders is considered part of the genre of "stories" or *hopáki ikhgna* just as situational joking, which does not follow narrative structure, is considered *shokhannǫpa*. All the while, narratives people tell of their own experiences are just that, personal experiences. Clearly the difference between narrative and nonnarrative is not a key axis for Choctaw verbal art. The temporal dimension of being passed down versus having taken place today, however, is.

Again and again, when I asked people about stories they knew, they responded that they simply did not remember any. "Remember" is key. They all refer back to their childhoods, noting the performance situations of storytelling events, but lack of interest or need of sleep at the time has resulted in poor memories today. The notion of stories never conjured up narratives of their own lives. There is one marked exception. Many men and women, particularly those between thirty and fifty years old, recounted personal encounters with supernatural beings in the woods, stories with parallels among the old stories some people do remember hearing as children. A narrative about an encounter with Kashikanchak some time in the past, the specific people involved now long forgotten, was a "story," but a narrative about an encounter with *bohpoli* last month or last year was not. Harold Comby is quick to point out that there is nonetheless continuity here. The *bohpoli* of the past is the *bohpoli* of the present.[10] The phenomenon is stable through time—*bohopoli* is ahistorical. The stories about the supernatural, however, are either legendary or contemporary.[11] The former are more authoritative; the latter more visceral and personal.

The formal structure of the performances of the two kinds of stories differ also. Contemporary narratives may be attributed if they originate from a peer, but generally such stories are personal and have no such introduction. Rather than "They used to say," people begin, "This is true." Both introductions act as a means for validation, but one does it implicitly through attribution to the elders, the other, explicitly by claiming truth directly or further noting that this was something they saw with their own eyes.

More telling, however, is the lack of formal closure. When narrating stories that were passed down through generations, Jeffie Solomon and Odie Anderson, for example, end each of their stories with a formal close: "*Makilla*," translated as "That is all." But it is the rhetorical meaning rather than the literal one that is important here. In recounting more recent stories, this ending is rarely included. There is a sense that passed-down stories have a recognizable form and content, however flexible, that can be marked with a formal closing. More recent stories are not viewed with such coherency. Further, where passed-down stories more often claim authority, recent stories are told as a means to engender further discussion. *Makilla* closes off discussion. But with contemporary stories, the end is left open. Discussion is encouraged, even demanded.

This division of the world into past and long past is reflected in the Choctaw language as well. Two verb endings are used to create the past: *tok* meaning past, and *ttók* meaning long past. Generally, in conversation, *tok* is used for events that happened a month ago or less, *ttók* for a year or more.[12] Anything in between is left up to the preference of the speaker. The temporal split reflected by these verb endings is generally too short a span to be useful in distinguishing contemporary stories from passed-down stories since the difference between these two is generally reckoned in years versus generations rather than months versus years. Nonetheless, the dichotomy in time can be seen as a basic tenet of the Choctaw worldview.

This distinction between passed-down stories and contemporary stories is, then, another important axis operating within the generic system of Choctaw verbal art. Cynthia Clegg makes exactly this distinction when she begins recounting a story to young campers about a man turning into a snake: "My dad told me this when I was a little girl. . . . It was told to him by his grandparents, and their grandparents told him, so it's a story that's been passed down." To be "passed down" is to be imbued with the authority of the past and the authority of the elders. Stories that are passed down are markedly different from those that are not, though to different degrees for different kinds of stories. Being passed down does not mean merely that it is valid by having existed for a long time, but also that it is worthy of being passed down. Again, the importance of the material is stressed.

A clue from the past suggests the validity not only of the genre of *hopáki ikhana* but also of this integral division between past and contemporary.

Carmen Denson remembers that the old stories were often recounted with a formulaic opening:

> They just, elders would tell, and this is the way that they put it, when they tell, they would say, "It was said, and said, and said, and said, and that's why I say it."
> And that's the way that they say it. And I don't know when it was originally, you know, started. You understand what I'm—That's the way, you know. In Choctaw terms, I would say,
> "Makato, makato, makato, achili."
> *Maka* means "it was said"; *to* means "at the time"—
> "It was said at the time, it was said at the time, it was said at the time, now I say it."
> And that's the way it was passed on.
> There was no school; there was no education; there was nothing. Even back in 1950s, '40s, Choctaws were sharecropping on their own. And there was no government intersection, no school education.
> So late at night, then, before, when we get to bed, or when we're in bed, our parents would talk to us then.
> That's where the schooling was kind of, Choctaw school, elders, how it was. To me it was that way.

The stories are not told this way today. Carmen suggests that a few of the oldest of the elders in the more traditional communities such as Conehatta or Bogue Chitto might still narrate this way, but he believes it has otherwise died out, a belief supported by my fieldwork. If the phrase has been lost, however, the division has not.

Shokhannǫpa is not viewed with such awe and respect. These stories may be attributed to an individual, but they are not "passed down" in the way that *hopáki ikhǫna* is. The distinction can be noted in the degree to which storytellers attribute their narratives. Harry Polk, for example, tells *shokhannǫpa* as well as *hopáki ikhǫna* about supernatural beings of the past. In the *shokhannǫpa* story "The Funeral," he introduces the tale without any attribution at all. Nor does he follow up with any at the end. Yet when he tells a story about a supernatural being that used to live in the woods long ago, he frames his discourse by attributing the story to his grandfather, once at the beginning of his narrative and twice at the end. One might presume that the difference in attribution can be ascribed to the fact that one story involves the supernatural, material that might need validation when recounting to a non-Choctaw audience, while the other is a humorous story and, in not being regarded as explicitly true, does not need validation. This is at least partially correct. *Hopáki ikhǫna* need not be believed by the narrator, but the presumption is that they are true. The negotiation of belief by the storyteller is something that emerges in performance, but the generic system, the communal assumptions of the genre, is that *hopáki ikhana* is true, *shokhannopa*, not. Not surprisingly, virtually none of the narrators of *shokhannopa* attributed their stories at all. Those who did attributed the story initially and then not again. Such attribution seems to be more about crediting the past performer for the tale than attributing it to the past. The level of attribution certainly varies according to a number of factors in *hopáki ikhana*, but it is uniformly higher than in *shokhannopa*.

And so, in categorizing Choctaw narratives, two new axes can be added: truth—truth value is important, and the story is true, versus truth value is not important, and/or story is not true—and time—passed down versus contemporary. The generic system of Choctaw storytelling, then, operates primarily according to tone, time, and truth value.

PATTERNS OF PERFORMANCE

While *shokhannopa* and *hopáki ikhana* encompass the range of Choctaw storytelling, Choctaw storytellers distinguish further among their stories, creating smaller subcategories. Sometimes these more specific categories are merely topical and serve to suggest a corpus of common stories without necessarily indicating a unique storytelling structure or aesthetic. This can be seen quite clearly with animal stories, in which people will note that this is a Possum story, Rabbit story, or Turtle story. The number of stories that revolve around these characters make divisions according to dramatic personas possible and logical, although some of these characters are interchangeable as with Rabbit and Turkey in the story of the frequently told race with Turtle.

Sometimes stories coalesce by sheer number. There is a corpus of Rabbit stories because so many stories involve this character. This process can feed upon itself. Recognition of a culturally salient character may engender more and more stories about that animal, and more and more stories confirm the corpus. The characters and their stories' origins, while interesting, need not concern us here. What is important is that the sheer number of stories with a recognizable character, theme, unique time frame, or other unifying characteristic can form a corpus of stories and potentially a subgenre within a storytelling tradition.

Although the cohesion and recognized boundaries of subgenres like the jokes and tall stories of *shokhannopa* are verifiable in other ways and need not be constructed from sheer volume, they nonetheless could be. Categories within the genre of *hopáki ikhana*, however, benefit more directly from this method. Here we find a number of stories that coalesce around types of characters and divisions of time into categories of creation stories, legends, supernatural stories, historical stories, and prophecy.

It would be easy to dismiss these subgenres as recognizable etic categories applied out of habit, carelessness, or lack of fieldwork. However, two pieces of evidence suggest otherwise. First, the dictionary definition for *hopáki ikhana* includes a list of genres that articulate subdivisions: legends, old stories, and history. They are not mutually exclusive, but nor are they synonyms. *Old stories* is the most inclusive, but *legends* is used primarily for stories of creation and of a time before historical time, what folklorists typically call myths. These are distinct from historical stories set in a particular moment in time such as removal. Second, by expanding the view from the individual story to the speech event, one finds confirmation within the community, not merely outside it. Where our previous analysis extended the scope beyond text to context, primarily to incorporate and address introductions to the stories, now we turn to entire events and interviews, tracing the progression the storyteller makes from one story to the next. Understanding the links that allow the narrator to make these moves helps to clarify the categories of Choctaw storytelling even further.[13]

During one of my first interviews in Mississippi, I sat down to talk with Terry Ben, acting superintendent of the Choctaw school system. Our general topic was Choctaw culture, with a focus on things the youth should know but perhaps are not hearing from their elders like they would have in years past. He began with stories he called *legends*, though the term is not used consistently in the community and differs from the academically defined etic term. Terry Ben recounts stories of how the Choctaw were created, how they came to Mississippi, and how they were introduced to corn—again grouping the stories in performance and thus suggesting a natural category. Without a clear native term, I have resorted to the etic term *myth*, the closest approximation for this corpus of stories that are set before historical time and are filled with beings and actions foreign to the world today.

Historical discourse operates much the same way, particularly with "used-to" stories. The term *used-to stories* refers to historical discourse about the cultural practices of the past. These recollections are strung along, one after another, regardless of actual topic; that is, the narrator may move from funeral customs to marriage to cooking without a break in the logic of the performance. Used-to stories generally lack a clear and definite narrative structure but are considered, as noted earlier, to be "stories."[14] This is not unusual. Neither is the fact that used-to stories have counterparts in both temporal sections: passed down and contemporary. Younger speakers recall what life was like for their parents and grandparents; as they get older, they take the role these grandparents did and use their own pasts as source material.[15] We have not included these reminiscences in this collection.

The sheer breadth of such used-to stories demands a book unto itself, one that can address the range of cultural practices past and present and the complexity of community memory. And now, two decades later, Eddie Johnson, Jay Wesley, and I have put together such a book, one that includes used-to stories as well as the first- and secondhand stories people tell friends and family that illuminate the rich cultural history and traditions of the tribe (*Choctaw Traditions*).

The temporal counterpart to historical discourse is prophecy. Discussion of the past often engenders discussion of change in how that past is different from the present. Change through time is the realm of prophecy as well, particularly where change is projected a bit farther, beyond the present and into the future. But prophecy clearly stands as its own category as well. Like historical narratives, which depend on time but explicitly of the past, prophecy depends on time but explicitly of the future. This temporal split quickly separates history from prophecy with regard to narrative genre, even when the content is strikingly similar. The difference becomes even more noticeable when studying formal, stylistic, and affective attributes of the two.

SYNTHESIS: SUPERNATURAL STORIES

Throughout this analysis, supernatural stories have emerged clearly outside the category of *shokhannǫpa*, but their status within the category of *hopáki ikhąna* is less clear. Stories of beings no longer seen in the woods today such as Kashikanchak fit comfortably within the "legends" and "old stories" *hopáki ikhąna* categories. But the more widespread storytelling tradition of recent supernatural encounters are stories told in first or second person, stories that are not old at all. There is no expectation that one must reach the age of elder to share these stories. Rather, stories of the supernatural are regularly shared among all ages, with a range of functions that include sharing tribal knowledge, cautioning people about the dangers of the woods, and scaring each other for entertainment.

Working through the processes for identifying genres, we find no clear native term in Choctaw, but analysis of commentary and context suggests an English one: *hunting stories*. "My dad used to tell me a lot of stories dealing with something called hunting stories," Melford Farve explains.

> I remember there was one story he told me; I can't tell you the whole thing but it had something to do with dogs talking.
> Some Choctaw was walking down the path, and he heard some people coming. He didn't know who they were, but just to be on the safe side, I guess he sort of hid from the path until they passed on. When he saw, it

was only two dogs, but they were actually talking to each other as they were walking down, talking in Choctaw.[16]

Melford follows with a story of a man mistaking his brother for something supernatural, then another about shape-shifting medicine men. Both commentary and performance context make it clear that stories of supernatural encounters exist as a distinct genre in Choctaw storytelling.

Similarly, Terry Ben talks about the *bohpoli*, supernatural little people who train and assist Choctaw doctors with their herbal medicines. He recounts stories of his own encounters with these little people, then moves to stories of encounters by his close friends and family. He then branches out, moving from the *bohpoli* to other supernatural creatures: a manlike creature with a tail, floating balls of lights, and shape-shifters. Terry Ben moves from one supernatural encounter to the next, clearly viewing them as related stories. One story reminds him of another and then another. Memory is a system of categorization. Once that door is open, the entire category is often accessible. That all of these stories are categorized together suggests a generic category; evidence that it extends beyond the individual mind to the larger community is easily noted through comparative analysis where similar performances of such tale-telling is common.[17]

On a less rigorous level of distinction, children also recognize the basic nature of the supernatural tale. At summer camp during storytelling time, the children clamored again and again for "ghost stories." Older members of the community are well aware that ghosts are vastly different from the majority of the supernatural beings recounted in these stories. But while the term itself is too loose for categorization, the corpus described is the same. *Hunting stories* and *ghost stories* both index the same corpus of narrative.

Yet despite the clear connection between the old legends of the supernatural being shared by elders as part of *hopáki ikhana* and the first- and secondhand stories of encounters with supernatural beings more recently, these latter stories do not fit comfortably in the category of *hopáki ikhana*. Old and young alike share these stories. They do not carry the weight and authority of *hopáki ikhana* in the way that older legends do. Yet they dominate the oral tradition. More than another other genre of story, this is the most common by far. Stories of recent supernatural encounters sit slightly outside the simple binary of the Choctaw storytelling system.

Taken all together—native terms, commentary and contextualization, and patterns derived from the performance context—it is possible to chart the generic system of Choctaw storytelling according to key axis points and emic categories. This system (figure 2.1) provides the organizational structure for the stories that follow in this book.

A NOTE ON THE TEXTS

In addition to the generic categorization, the format of the texts that follow also deserves some explanation. The stories in this collection have been drawn from many different sources with many different collectors who had various means and ideas of how to best transcribe and present oral narratives on the page. Before the advent of the tape recorder, tales were either summarized by their collectors or taken down from storytellers who slowed their performances to accommodate the hand of the writer. Collectors followed the procedures prescribed by the times and did the best they could. In light of today's standards, some were more successful than others. I have presented these older texts as written, modifying only punctuation, capitalization, and spelling in an effort to update the texts to the modern eye. This includes keeping the titles for each story, titles almost certainly given by the recorders rather than the narrators. In fact, for virtually all the stories in this collection, the titles have been added by their respective collectors to aid in identification.

More recent texts have benefited greatly from the tape recorder and digital recorder. Beginning with those narratives collected by the staff of the Choctaw High School magazine *Nanih Waiya*, all stories from the 1970s on were collected in this manner. Accordingly, the narratives retain more of the oral quality of the performance. With all of these texts, I have respected the transcriptions (and in some cases, translations) of the material. The choice was an easy one; without access to most of the audiotapes, I could do nothing else.

For the texts I have recorded personally, the range of options was greater, so the decisions were more difficult. For the most part, the texts are exact transcriptions. It is important to recognize that the oral narrative is vastly different from the written ones we are used to reading in books; we omit words when we talk, repeat ourselves, and make reference to our setting. I have attempted to accommodate this shift in medium through punctuation and occasional endnotes only. I have added no words, changed no tenses, nor made any corrections in syntax except, occasionally, in the opening sentence of a story. These narratives occur during conversation, couched in what has been said earlier, moments in larger performances. Often, storytellers begin their storytelling by attributing their stories to a grandmother or grandfather and then refer to that person as "he" or "she" for all subsequent stories. Rather than break up the story with brackets, I have chosen to substitute these initial pronouns with the name of the family member referenced earlier by the storyteller. Further, as a performance by real people in real places, interruptions disrupt the stories: phones ring, visitors drop by, babies cry. I have omitted these interruptions. However, in both of these types of alteration, I have documented the changes in the annotations.

In this new edition, Rae Nell Vaughn and I have also omitted some false starts and filler words such as *you know*. Any omissions of greater significance are explained in the annotations. Ellipses, therefore, indicate pauses and changes in conversational direction, not omitted words.

In doing all this, our hope is that the storyteller will be allowed to communicate with this new reading audience, that the reader will be allowed to understand, and that the scholar will be offered exact translations.

The biggest decision was whether to display the texts in ethnopoetic form with numerous line breaks and indentions to help convey the orality of the performance or to follow more conventional standard paragraph form. Although I firmly believe that storytelling is often more akin to poetry than to prose, and that the oral component of a story is integral to its full appreciation, I ultimately attended to a more basic tenet of presenting texts on the page: clarity. Readers can learn to interpret an array of markers, styles, and formats, but it is hardly a kind invitation into the material. Further, different stories and different storytellers are aided by different textual formats. A prophecy recounted by Billy Amos, for example, is brought to life on the page when its structure of moving back and forth from past to present is displayed through a series of indentions. Another prophecy told by Estelline Tubby, however, more clearly benefits from attention to the various voices she is negotiating. Formatting to distinguish these voices helps make both the prophecy and Estelline Tubby's interpretation of it clearer. However, formatting a story one way highlights some elements, while formatting it another way highlights others. A single format cannot accommodate all of the stories in this collection or even one. One size does not fit all. Further, such formatting requires detailed explanation, something that quickly turns a collection of narratives into a multivolume series of textual analyses. So I have employed the familiar indentions and formatting of prose narrative. It is perhaps not ideal, but I believe it provides clarity in addition to maintaining the open-endedness of performance.

The one addition other than punctuation that I have made is in recording gestures and sounds that impact performance. In cases where gestures are added for words, I have included a description of the gesture in brackets. This includes laughter, which is integral to many of the performances.

A dozen or so of the narratives in this collection were recorded in the Choctaw language. I do not speak Choctaw. Maggie Chitto, a native Choctaw speaker who worked with the Choctaw Bilingual Education Program, transcribed and translated the tapes interlinearly. After her initial work, I sent the interlinear translations to Pam Smith, another native speaker, who works full time translating English and Choctaw. Pam checked both the transcriptions and the translations and helped ensure both were accurate and uniform.[18] Geri and Harry Harm, with whom Pam works, contributed their expertise on some of the more problematic passages. Finally, Roseanna Nickey, head of the Choctaw Language Program, and Jesse Ben, a Language Program teacher, checked the translations one final time for spelling and syntax. The results are translations that are careful and fairly literal. The original Choctaw versions are printed toward the end of the book, primarily for Choctaw readers, though they should prove useful to language scholars as well.

CREATION STORIES AND MYTHS

The Choctaw have often been described as unique in that they have two distinct stories of their origin. According to the migration story, the Choctaw originally lived in the West and migrated to Mississippi by divine providence. In the emergence story, the Choctaw (and often the other native tribes of the Southeast) were created and led out of a mound in Mississippi by divine providence. The first focuses on how the Choctaw came to live in Mississippi, the second, how the Choctaw were created as men.[1] Despite the difference in focus, outside scholars and Choctaws alike have noted the contradiction in the two stories.[2]

Within the tribe today, people generally follow one version or the other, though many know both. The community of Bogue Chitto, for example—one of the communities living closest to the sacred Nanih Waiya Mound—generally follows the emergence story. Other communities are more varied, versions depending more on family than community ties. But the contradiction, while recognized, is not particularly troublesome, perhaps for the same reason that the two contradictory versions of creation described in the Book of Genesis in the Bible are not particularly troublesome for most Christians and Jews. Interpreted symbolically, spiritually, socially, pragmatically, and affectively, the stories are not contradictions at all.[3] By focusing on different aspects of origin, both myths accomplish various goals: they explain cultural and linguistic similarities between the Choctaw and Chickasaw and other southeastern tribes; they express a vital link to the earth; they attribute creation and daily life to divine and prophetic powers; they order social relations between men and women as well as between tribes; they attempt to establish land claims in Mississippi, particularly with White settlers; they create a sense of communal identity; and they create an emotionally charged touchstone to common beliefs, customs, and practices.

This last function has perhaps been the most enduring. These stories cannot be relegated to historical accounts, just as they do not only function to validate land claims. There is a sacred tie between the community and these stories that transcends the mundane. For many, that sacred tie is symbolized by the Nanih Waiya Mound, which can be visited today. While Nanih Waiya is integral to the emergence story, it is an important element of most versions of the migration story as well. In both, it is the spot the Creator chose as a home for the Choctaw. Further, in many versions of the migration myth, Nanih Waiya is described as a burial mound for the bones of the ancestors hauled the many miles from the West in respect of the dead. The mound also figures in a number of other stories as the place where corn was given to the Choctaws and one of the homes of the *bohpoli*. The mound remains a sacred spot in both the mental and physical landscapes of the community today.[4]

The ability of sacred stories to operate on so many levels, in so many ways, for so many people, is one of their most alluring and quixotic characteristics. Such stories are even more flexible when told since individual narrators can stress the points most relevant to them and their audience at any given telling. Perhaps not surprisingly, then, there are a variety of creation stories told among the community. While they can all be reduced to either migration or creation, none fares the better for such reduction. Rather, the sheer breadth of the tales, with overlapping themes and motifs, is testament to the skill of the narrator, the depth of thought involved both in the story and its narration, and the multivocality of the community itself.

Of course, the creation stories of the Choctaw do not end once the earth was created and the Choctaw in it. Balance was sought, and the world changed, in part in accord with God's will, in part as a result of the actions—wise and foolish—of the first beings. Stories chart this transition.

During this time when the earth was new, the natural world's inhabitants were peers. Animals spoke and intermarried with other animals and humans, matching wits against one another. Intelligence and cunning were the most prized attributes, while extravagant heroism was most often rewarded with sorrow. Social customs and moral norms were established, and vital gifts such as corn were given to the people. Eventually, the world settled into a more regular routine. The sun rose and set. Children were born. But regular did not mean safe or understood. Questions of natural occurrence and social interaction remained unresolved. Where does the sun go when it sinks at night? How are people to marry? Or hunt?

These events happened "a long time ago," or at the moment "after God had created the men and the animals." These stories are considered a record of the past and regarded as something like history without dates.

However, there is also the understanding that these past events continue to hold meaning for the world today. Accordingly, the stories reflect the changing world of the Choctaws in historical time. Many of the stories, particularly those of the flood, resonate with similar stories in the Bible, evidence of the Christian missionary influence of the time. Like the stories of creation and migration, these narratives are powerful because of the fact that they are dynamic, not despite it.

THE CHOCTAW CREATION LEGEND

ISAAC PISTONATUBBEE   1901

A very long time ago the first creation of men was in Nanih Waiya. And there they were made. And there they came forth.

The Muscogees first came out of Nanih Waiya, and they then sunned themselves on Nanih Waiya's earthen rampart. And when they got dry, they went to the east. On this side of the Tombigbee, there they rested. And as they were smoking tobacco, they dropped some fire.

The Cherokees next came out of Nanih Waiya. And they sunned themselves on the earthen rampart. And when they got dry, they went and followed the trail of the elder tribe. And at the place where the Muscogees had stopped and rested, and where they had smoked tobacco, there was fire, and the woods were burnt. And the Cherokees could not find the Muscogees' trail, so they got lost and turned aside and went towards the north. And there towards the north they settled and made a people.

And the Chickasaws third came out of Nanih Waiya. And then they sunned themselves on the earthen rampart. And when they got dry, they went and followed the Cherokees' trail. And when they got to where the Cherokees had got lost, they turned aside and went on and followed the Cherokees' trail. And when they got to where the Cherokees had settled and made a people, they settled and made a people close to the Cherokees.

And the Choctaws fourth and last came out of Nanih Waiya. And they then sunned themselves on the earthen rampart, and when they got dry, they did not go anywhere but settled down in this very land, and it is the Choctaws' home.

NANÉ CHAHA

PISATUNTEMA (EMMA)   1910

In very ancient times, before man lived on the earth, the hill was formed, and from the topmost point, a passage led down deep into the bosom of the earth.

Later, when the birds and animals lived, and the surface of the earth was covered with trees and plants of many sorts, and lakes and rivers had been formed, the Choctaw came forth through the passageway in Nané Chaha. And from that point, they scattered in all directions, but ever afterwards, remembered the hill from the summit of which they first beheld the light of the sun.

MEN AND GRASSHOPPERS

PISATUNTEMA (EMMA)   1910

Soon after the earth was made, men and grasshoppers came to the surface through a long passageway that led from a large cavern in the interior of the earth to the summit of a high hill, Nané Chaha. There, deep down in the earth, in the great cavern, man and the grasshoppers had been created by Aba, the Great Spirit, having been formed of the yellow clay.

For a time, the men and the grasshoppers continued to reach the surface together, and as they emerged from the long passageway, they would scatter in all directions, some going north, others south, east, or west.

But at last the mother of the grasshoppers who had remained in the cavern was killed by the men, and as a consequence there were no more grasshoppers to reach the surface. And ever after, those that lived on the earth were known to the Choctaw as *eske ilay*, or "mother dead."

However, men continued to reach the surface of the earth through the long passageway that led to the summit of Nané Chaha, and, as they moved about from place to place, they trampled upon many grasshoppers in the high grass, killing many and hurting others.

The grasshoppers became alarmed as they feared that all would be killed if men became more numerous and continued to come from the cavern in the earth. They spoke to Aba, who heard them and soon after caused the passageway to be closed, and no more men were allowed to reach the surface. But as there were many men remaining in the cavern, he changed them to ants; and ever since that time, the small ants have come forth from holes in the ground.

CREATION OF THE TRIBES

PISATUNTEMA (EMMA)   1909

Many generations ago, Aba, the good spirit above, created many men, all Choctaw, who spoke the language of the Choctaw and understood one another. These came from the bosom of the earth, being formed of yellow clay, and no men had ever lived before them.

One day all came together and, looking upward, wondered what the clouds and the blue expanse above might be. They continued to wonder and talk among themselves and at last determined to endeavor to reach the sky. So they brought many rocks and began building a mound that was to have touched the heavens.

That night, however, the wind blew strong from above, and the rocks fell from the mound. The second morning they again began work on the mound, but as the men slept that night, the rocks were again scattered by the winds. Once more, on the third morning, the builders set to their task. But once more, as the men lay near the mound that night, wrapped in slumber, the winds came with so great force that the rocks were hurled down on them.

The men were not killed, but when daylight came, and they made their way from beneath the rocks and began to speak to one another, all were astounded as well as alarmed—they spoke various languages and could not understand one another.

Some continued thenceforward to speak the original tongue, the language of the Choctaw, and from these sprung the Choctaw tribe. The others, who could not understand this language, began to fight among themselves.

Finally, they separated. The Choctaw remained the original people; the others scattered, some going north, some east, and others west, and formed various tribes.

This explains why there are so many tribes throughout the country at the present time.

ORIGIN OF THE CRAWFISH BAND

PETER PITCHLYNN   1841

Our people have amongst them a band, which is called the "Crawfish Band." They formerly, but at a very remote period, lived underground and used to come up out of the mud. They were a species of crawfish, and they went on their hands and feet and lived in a large cave deep underground where there was no light for several miles. They spoke no language at all, nor could they understand any. The entrance to their cave was through the mud, and they used to run down through that and into their cave. And thus, the Choctaws were for a long time unable to molest them. The Choctaws used to lay and wait for them to come out into the sun where they would try to talk to them and cultivate an acquaintance.

One day, a parcel of them were run upon so suddenly by the Choctaws that they had no time to go through the mud into their cave but were driven into it by another entrance, which they had through the rocks. The Choctaws then tried a long time to smoke them out and at last succeeded. They treated them kindly—taught them the Choctaw language, taught them to walk on two legs, made them cut off their toenails, and pluck the hair from their bodies—after which they adopted them into their nation. And the remainder of them are living underground to this day.

A SHORT STORY OF THE CREATION OF THE FIRST MAN

WAGONER AMOS   1974

A rain-like cloud filled with smoke, two moons in the night. And the spirit of the Lord came upon a man who came and laid the cane on top of the cave. There, people gathered around to see the mountain. They watched and they worshipped the Holy Spirit.

Finally, many moons came and raised the cane, and people shouted and bowed down to the true Spirit. There stood the cane straight up to symbolize the true Spirit and symbolize that the first earth man was born. And so the people sang with joy.

THE CREATION OF THE CHOCTAW

WAGONER AMOS   1975

As in the past and still yet today, people talk of Nanih Waiya. So as not to confuse people, I will translate what I have heard from the old people.

They stated that the events that are occurring now would happen. The creator of man, God, was the one who told them of future happenings. The incidents that have occurred are a prediction of the older generation. It is even talked about in preachings at churches today. The origin of the incidents are all related to the Choctaws.

The Creator, leaving out the woman, created three men: the Choctaw, the White, and the Black. He said that he would return in seventy years. He did return with another God, and they talk.

"It is good that you created man in your own image, and from what I see it is good; but they have not multiplied. So if you wish to, would you be willing to create others?" he said. "It was then that I realized that what you preached and taught was right and I was thankful to you. So it would be in the creation of the three men and others."

Then he said, "Your thinking created men in your own image, now with what I will teach you, you should create others."

"Yes, I feel that I may be able to create. So I feel I am ready to create others. But then we together created them. I grew old. So with that they did not multiply. Staying with them I felt that they should have multiplied. But I see that they haven't. Yes, I do see that. Then we should be able to multiply and grow."

"So you as the creator of man should create the woman."

"Yes, I shall do that. Yes, as many men as I have created, so shall be the women. After I have created the woman, it will then be up to them to continue from thereon."

With that he created the Black and White women and gave them their language as it still is today. He told them that it would be just that and told them, the old men, not to go beyond what had been set.

He then told the Choctaw, "I myself will be your wife."

To this the Choctaw nodded.

"I see that the other two men are somewhat faster than you.

But because I created them as men, I have also given them a wife. But you, being the slower, I myself will be your wife. Together you will follow in learning but will be able to learn faster. I as your wife will also be there to keep you from reaching a high esteem when I am finished telling you what I am to do.

"So that the two of you will be at the same age, I shall sing to you until she reaches that age."

When he finished, he sang, and with that, she aged in stature and age as he said she would.

"Now you two shall be together and pass on to other generations what I have given. If not, they shall come into confrontation with the sun. I have created the day, the moon, the sun, and all. If it is false and bright, many men will follow it. Then will little children not understand. If not spoken to and taught, they will not know what to do. Then and there will the sun begin to die. You will notice the death when there won't be any summers. That is when, as stated, it will begin to die."

So as it was to be, we are now living in what was to happen. For one who did not hear, there are doubts; but we are living now as predicted.

What he said he would do, he did. As clearly seen with the languages and nothing else has been said. As he had laid down the language, it still remains. If we do not believe that, we shall meet something evil. As it is, we are in somewhat of a tangle, and we do not understand all that we do. This he said would lead into losing our summers, and we are leading to that point.

Thinking to myself, sitting in a church, I believe that it is so. For one who heard it can be clearly seen.

Also, in giving the language and the transformation of him to the wife, he said, "I give you a wife, and I'll take my rib and put it in her. I'll also duplicate my heart and give her a likeness of it. So I am truly your wife. I am doing this for the purpose of your unity."

He talked to the man, stating for him to keep what he had given him. "Keep the language!" He told them that in the joining of the two together, "I shall be a part of both of you all the time. So whenever you whip your wife, you will be whipping me. I shall be a part of you always. You may think what of it. Being a part of you I shall always be watching you."

THE MIGRATION LEGEND

PETER FOLSOM   1899

The ancestors of the Choctaws and the Chickasaws lived, in primeval times, in a far western country, under the rule of two brothers named Chahta and Chikasa. In process of time, their population becoming very numerous and their territory overcrowded, they found it difficult to procure subsistence in that land. Their prophets thereupon announced to them that far to the east was a country of fertile soil and with abundance of game where they could live in ease and plenty. The entire population resolved to make a journey eastward in search of that happy land.

In order to more easily procure subsistence on their route, the people marched in several divisions of a day's journey apart. A great prophet marched at their head, bearing a pole, which, every evening on camping, he planted erect in the earth in front of the camp. The next morning, the pole was always seen leaning in the direction they were to travel that day.

After the lapse of several moons, they arrived one day at the mound on Nanih Waiya Creek, where they camped for the night. The prophet erected the sacred pole at the base of the mound. The next morning, the pole was seen standing erect and stationary. This was interpreted as an omen from the Great Spirit that the long-sought-for land was at last found.

It so happened, the very evening the advanced party camped at Nanih Waiya Creek, that a party under Chikasa crossed the creek and camped on the eastern side. That night a great rain fell, and it rained several days. In consequence of this, all the lowlands were inundated, and Nanih Waiya Creek and other tributaries of Pearl River were rendered impassable.

After the subsidence of the waters, messengers were sent across the creek to bid Chikasa's party return, as the oracular pole had proclaimed that the long-sought-for land was found, and the mound was the center of this land. Chikasa's party, however, regardless of the weather, had proceeded on their journey, and the rain having washed all traces of their march off the grass, the messengers were unable to follow them up and so returned to camp.

Meanwhile, the other divisions in the rear arrived at the Nanih Waiya Mound and learned that here was the center of their new home, and their long pilgrimage was at last finished.

Chikasa's party, after their separation from their brethren under Chahta, moved on to the Tombigbee and eventually became a separate nationality.

In this way the Choctaws and the Chickasaws became two distinct though kindred nations.

MIGRATION

JOHN HUNTER THOMPSON   1980

The Choctaws traveled many days following the leader, who went by the stick that he carried. The White man called it a walking stick. When they made camp at night, the chief would place the stick straight into the ground, and whichever direction the stick was pointing to in the morning, that was to be the direction they were to go. He would do this every night when they made camp.

One morning, the stick was standing straight into the ground, and so the chief said that this meant that this was to be the place where they were to live.

Hearing this, the people started building shelter for themselves. The women started making baskets to carry dirt. The dirt was used to make a sacred burial ground, which they called Nanih Waiya.

TRADITION OF THE FLOOD

ISRAEL FOLSOM   C. 1860

A long, continued night came upon the land, which created no small degree of fear and uneasiness among the people. Their fears were increased at seeing the terrible buffaloes and the fleet deer making their appearance, and after them the bears and panthers, wolves and others approaching their habitations. Suspicious at first of their intentions, they thought of placing themselves beyond the reach of the more dangerous animals; but instead of exhibiting any disposition of ferocity, they seemed rather to claim protection at their hands. This presented an opportunity of having a jubilee of feasting, and they therefore indulged themselves to the fullest bent of their propensity and inclinations by an indiscriminate massacre of the animals.

Having thus feasted for some time, they at last saw daylight appearing. But what surprised them much was they saw it coming from the North. They were at a loss what to think of it. They, however, supposed that the sun must have missed his path and was coming up from another direction, which caused the unusual long night; or perhaps he had purposely changed his course, to rise hereafter in the North instead of the East.

While such conjectures were making, some fast runners arrived as messengers coming from the direction of the supposed daylight and announced to them that the light which they saw was not the daylight, but that it was a flood slowly approaching, drowning and destroying everything.

Upon this report the people fled to the mountains and began to construct rafts of sassafras wood, binding them together with vines, believing this expedient would save them from a watery grave. But alas, delusive hope! For the bears were swimming around in countless numbers, being very fond of vine twigs, gnawed them through, thereby setting loose the materials of the raft and bringing the people under dark waters. Their cries, wailing and agony, were unheard and unseen.

But there was one man who prepared and launched a strong peni or boat, into which he placed his family and provisions and thus floated upon the deep waters. For days the Penikbi (boat builder) strained his eyes looking all around for the purpose of discovering the existence of some animal life, and a place at which to anchor his vessel. Nothing met his sight save the cheerless waste of waters.

The hawks, eagles, and other birds of the same class had all, when they found that the tops of the mountains could not render them a lighting place from the flood, flown to the sky and clung on to it with their talons and remained until the flood abated, when they returned to their old haunts and resumed their natural propensities and habits. An indication of the disappearing of the flood thus manifested itself. A crow made its appearance and so much delighted to see the boat that it flew around and around it.

The Penikbi, overjoyed beyond measure, addressed the sable bird, wishing to elicit some information from it as to whereabouts, and whether or not the flood was subsiding any, but it heeded him not, seeming to be determined to consult its own safety before that of anyone else.

But scarcely had the crow winged away from the peni before a dove was described flying towards it and on reaching it the Penikbi with joy perceived a leaf in its bill. It flew several times around but did not alight; after doing so took its course slowly flying toward the West, but seemingly anxious that Penikbi would steer in the direction it flew, which he did faithfully following the course. In this way many a weary mile was traveled before seeing a place to land. At length a mountain became visible, and never did a benighted mariner hail the sight of land as Penikbi did, when its summit became visible. When he had safely landed, the dove flew away to return no more.

THE FLOOD

OLMAN COMBY   1928

One time there came into the Choctaw country a being looking like a man. When he met an Indian, he approached him holding out something resembling a ham, but on the Indian attempting to take it, the being seized and devoured him.

At that same time the people had become disobedient to the law and the authority of the chiefs.

On one occasion a big dance was held. While it was in progress, it began to rain, and it kept on until the water was waist high. It still kept on until, in some places, it was over a person's head. Presently, the dancers observed a light over to the east and they thought the sky was going to clear so they shouted, "Day is coming," but the light was due to a flood of water, which destroyed them all.

The story does not say that anyone survived.

While the waters were upon the earth, the sapsucker (*tcaktcak*), the red head (*tcalantak*), and wood-knocker (*bakbak*) flew to the sky and saved themselves by holding onto it, but the waters came so high that some feathers were cut off of the very ends of their tails.

Because the *tcaktcak* had to ascend to the sky at this time, every September (or at least toward the fall of the year), their young, who are born with black heads, have to go up there to get their heads reddened. At that time of the year, you can hear them late at night high up in the air.

LIGHTNING AND THUNDER

ODIE ANDERSON   1997

There were two children. But because they were orphans, they lived with nobody caring about them. So one said, "You become lightning, and I will become thunder."

Lightning and thunder are orphans, they always said.

THUNDER AND LIGHTNING

HAROLD COMBY   2022

Thunder and lightning. At one point, I guess the flooding was so bad that it hurt or killed many Choctaws. So the Creator wanted to help us and said, "I'll get the Thunder Beings to maybe help the Choctaws out."

So he got two of the Thunderbirds—they're big, enormous birds in the sky—"Can you help us out in some way where the Choctaws will get some kind of warning when a flood is coming or bad weather is coming?"

So the Creator talked to the Thunderbirds, and the female said, "I'll make sound in the sky in the clouds where it will produce big sounds, and it will warn the Choctaws to heed the weather, that bad weather is coming."

And then the male Thunderbird said, "I'll be the one because I'm the male; I will have the stronger power, and I will send lightning to strike a tree or something nearby and warn the Choctaw people that bad weather is coming."

So this is the way our people got thunder and lightning.

FANI LOSA AND THE SUN

RAE NELL VAUGHN   2024

Rae: It's beautiful out here, right? What do you see, Ave?
Avery: The sun.
Rae: The sun? That's right. Do you remember when we had an eclipse? That's when the moon got in front of the sun?
Kids: Yes.
Rae: Yeah? Well, let me tell you a story.
It comes from our brothers and sisters from Oklahoma Choctaw. You know, they are the ones that were forced to leave Mississippi.

Avery: Mississippi?
Rae: Yeah, Mississippi.

So a long, long time ago, there was an eclipse where the moon got in front of the sun. And that's the eclipse. But the Oklahoma Choctaw said, "One day, Fani Losa . . ."

Do you know what *fani losa* is?

Avery: Yeah.
Rae: What is it?
Avery: I don't know.
Rae: It's a black squirrel.

He was getting real hungry and jumped onto the sky, and then did what? Jumped on the sun and started trying to eat the sun. It was biting the sun because he was trying to eat it.

So the Oklahoma Choctaw people started making loud noises with their pots and their parents.

Avery: I'm hungry.
Rae: I know you're hungry. We're going to go get some pizza in just a little bit.

And so the Fani Losa was trying to eat the sun; like you, Ave, he was hungry.

So he jumped in the sky. And he started eating the sun, trying to eat the sun. And since he was Fani Losa, he started covering up the sun. [quietly] It got darker and darker.

And then the Choctaw people said, "We've got to get Fani Losa off the sun. We need the sun because that's what helps grow our crops and makes us feel warm."

Avery: And why was the squirrel . . . ?
Rae: I know, up there in the sky. And so the Choctaw people . . .
Avery: He tried to eat it?
Rae: Uh, huh [*affirmative*]. He tried to eat it.
Avery: Like cheese?
Rae: Uh, huh. [*affirmative*]

And then the Choctaw people grabbed their pots and pans and started making looouuuuud noises with it. They were hitting it, tok tok tok

tok tok tok tok. "Get off there, Fani Losa! Get off there! Get off the sun, Fani Losa!"

Avery: Did he listen?
Rae: He was trying to eat it; he wasn't trying to listen.
   But they did it louder and louder and louder.
   And then Fani Losa got scared. And then he jumped off the sun.
   And then what happened?
   The sun came back and was shining bright.
   And that's the story of Fani Losa and the sun.
   What did you think about that?

Avery: Yeah.
Bellamy: Grammy, what was that?
Rae: That was Fani Losa and the sun. And do you know what?
Avery: What?
Rae: The eclipse is going to come back again in 2045. And if Grammy is still here with you, I'll tell you that story, but if I'm not here, you've got to tell Noel the story because Noel's not here right now; she's sleeping. And so you've got to remember to tell Noel the story when Fani Losa tries to eat the sun again. That'll be 2045.
Avery: But we can't read.
Rae: You don't have to read. You just tell it with your words. Just like I told you.
Aubri: I see the sun!
Rae: I know you see the sun. But when it gets dark, Fani Losa gets on top of it and tries to eat it.
Avery: Fani Losa!
Rae: Fani Losa, get off the sun!
Avery: Fani Losa, get out of here.
Rae: Get out of here! We want the sun! Right, Ave?
Avery: He tries to eat it?
Rae: Right. He tries to eat it. But we need the sun, right?
Avery: Yeah.
Rae: Okay, who's ready for pizza? Raise your hand. Who's ready for pizza? Okay, can we say, "Fani Losa"?
Kids: Fani Losa!
Rae: "Get off the sun!"
Kids: Get off the sun!
Rae: [*laughter*] All right, guys. We'll go get us some pizza.
Kids: Yay!

Rae: Okay. Love you.
Kids: Love you.

DARK SUN

UNKNOWN [BUSHNELL]   1909

Eclipse of the sun, *ashe oklelega* ("sun dark or dirty"). The Choctaw say that since the sun works every day, he becomes dirty and smoked from the great fire within. It is necessary therefore for him to rest and clean himself, after doing which he shines the brighter. During the eclipse, he is removing the accumulated dirt. A similar explanation applies to the dark of the moon, their term being *ninaahukwa oklelega koshsholeje* ("moon dark or dirty, cleaning").

THE ORIGIN OF CORN

TERRY BEN   1996

Supposedly, a long time ago, according to one legend, going back to Nanih Waiya, there were some hunters around Nanih Waiya at nighttime. And they saw or heard somebody crying; I think it was a lady, you know, crying.

The woman was real hungry and wanted food. And so, the hunt was not too well, but they had a little game, and so they shared the meal they had with this woman, at the Nanih Waiya area.

And so the woman was so very thankful, and told the hunters, "One month later, on the night of the full moon, come back."

And so, about a month later, the two men went to the same spot on the full moon night, and there, on Nanih Waiya area, the mound area, the cave mound area, were some strange seeds. They never saw that before.

And of course, the item was corn—corn on the cob or whatever it was. And this was a gift from the lady, who was maybe some kind of a legendary figure who was thankful. And this was a return gift.

And so that's how supposedly the Choctaws acquired corn, via the situation at Nanih Waiya.

CORN-FINDING MYTH

ILAISHTUBBEE   1899

A long time ago it thus happened.

In the very beginning a crow got a single grain of corn from across the great water, brought it to this country and gave it to an orphan child, who was playing in the yard. The child named it *tanchi* (corn). He planted it in the yard.

When the corn was growing up, the child's elders merely had it swept around. But the child, wishing to have his own way, hoed it, hilled it, and laid it by.

When this single grain of corn grew up and matured, it made two ears of corn. And in this way the ancestors of the Choctaws discovered corn.

WILD GEESE AND THE ORIGIN OF CORN

BAXTER YORK   1975

They were supposed to go like wild geese every spring of the year and about September or October. They go back and forth in the spring and fall of the year. The geese are the ones who introduced us the song. They pick up corn way back in Mexico or somewhere. They brought and dropped the seeds. While the land was ripe, the corn would come up and began to grow and make the corn.

They found that the corn was real rich; the raccoon would be on that corn; the squirrel, redbird, jaybirds, crows, and all kinds of birds would be on that corn. Since they are close to nature, I bet you they tasted everything that was good to eat. The Choctaws tried the corn, and it has been the big prey for the human race all this time.

THE GEESE, THE DUCKS, AND WATER

PISATUNTEMA (EMMA)   1910

The geese and ducks were created before there was any water on the surface of the earth. They wanted water so as to be able to swim and dive as was their nature.

But Aba objected and said he would not allow water on the earth as it was dangerous, and he then said to the geese and ducks, "What is the good of water, and why do you want it?"

And together they answered, "We want it to drink on hot days."

Then Aba asked how much water they wanted.

And the ducks replied, "We want a great deal of water. We want swamps and rivers and lakes to be scattered all over the surface of the earth. And also we want grass and moss to grow in the water, and frogs and snakes to live there."

Aba asked the geese and ducks why they wanted frogs and snakes to live in the water.

And they answered that frogs and snakes were their food. And they told Aba how they could dive and swim beneath the water and catch them.

And then Aba told them how he had made the sun, the air, and the earth and asked if that was not enough.

"No," was the reply of all. "We want water."

The alligators then spoke to Aba and likewise asked for water. The alligators told of their desire to live in dark places, deep in the waters of bayous, among the roots of cypress and black gum trees, for there the water was the best.

Aba then spoke to all, saying he would give them all the water they desired but that he had talked with them to hear what they would have to say.

And even now the ducks and geese claim the swamps and marshes.

THE LIFE OF DOGS

OLMAN COMBY   1928

After God had created man and the animals, he fixed a time and a place where he would meet them to determine their several spans of life.

The dog felt happy, intending to ask for a very long life, and he ran to the appointed spot so rapidly that he got there first. Then he told God that he wanted to live a very long time.

"How many years do you want?"

"Ten years," said the dog, for he thought that that was a very long time. So when a dog is ten, he is old.

The rest of the animals did not ask for any particular limit of time. Therefore, God gave them what he thought would be best for them. But to man, he gave two hundred to three hundred years.

God also decreed that the dog should live long according to the master he had. If he had a good master, he would enjoy bread and meat, and in that case, he always wallows; otherwise, he can't wallow.

HOW THE SNAKES ACQUIRED THEIR POISON

PISATUNTEMA (EMMA)   1910

Long ago, a certain vine grew along the edges of bayous, in shallow water. This vine was very poisonous, and often, when the Choctaw would bathe or swim in the bayous, they would come in contact with the vine and often become so badly poisoned that they would die as the result.

Now the vine was very kind and liked the Choctaw and consequently did not want to cause them so much trouble and pain. He would poison the people without being able to make known to them his presence there beneath the water. So he decided to rid himself of the poison.

A few days later, he called together the chiefs of the snakes, bees, wasps, and other similar creatures and told them of his desire to give them his poison, for up to that time no snake, bee, or wasp had the power it now possesses, namely, that of stinging a person. The snakes and bees and wasps, after much talk, agreed to share the poison.

The rattlesnake was the first to speak, and he said: "I shall take the poison, but before I strike or poison a person, I shall warn him by the noise of my tail, *intesha*. Then if he does not heed me, I shall strike."

The water moccasin was the next to speak. "I also am willing to take some of your poison. But I shall never poison a person unless he steps on me."

The small ground rattler was the last of the snakes to speak. "Yes, I will gladly take of your poison, and I will also jump at a person whenever I have a chance." And so it has continued to do ever since.

THE OWL

OLMAN COMBY   1928

One time, a lot of owls agreed to meet at a certain creek to eat crawfish.

After they had assembled at that place, they discovered that one of their number, a female owl, was a stranger. In order to place her properly, they began calling her by various terms of relationship, *sister*, *aunt*, and so on. She did not respond to any of these terms.

And finally, one of them said, "She shall be my wife."

And such she became.

TASHKA AND WALO

UNKNOWN [BUSHNELL]   1909

Tashka and Walo were brothers who lived long ago. Every morning, they saw the sun rise above the horizon, pass high overhead, and late in the day die in the West.

When the boys were about four years old, they conceived the idea of following the Sun and seeing where he died. So the next day, when he was overhead, they started to follow him. But that night, when he died, they were still in their own country where they knew the hills and the rivers. Then they slept, and in the morning, when the Sun was again overhead, they once more set off to follow him.

And thus they continued for many years to wend their way after the Sun in his course through the heavens.

Long, long afterward, when the two boys had become men, they reached a great expanse of water, and the only land they could see was the shore on which they were standing.

Late that day, when Sun died, they saw him sink into the water. Then they also passed over the water and entered Sun's home with him.

All about them they saw women—the stars are women, and the Moon is Sun's wife. Then Moon asked the brothers how they had found their way so far from their home. They told her how for many, many years, ever since they were mere boys, they had followed Sun in his daily journey.

Then Sun told his wife to boil water. Into this he put the boys and rubbed them. This treatment caused them to turn red and their skin to come off.

Sun then asked them whether they knew the way to return to their home, and they said, "No"; so he took them to the edge whence they looked down to the earth, but they could not distinguish their home.

Sun asked why they had followed him as it was not time for them to reach heaven. They replied that their only reason for following him was a desire to see where he died.

Sun then told them that he would send them home, but that for four days after reaching their home, they must not speak a word to any person. If they spoke during the four days, they would die; otherwise, they would then live and prosper.

A large buzzard was then called by Sun, and the two boys were placed on its back. Buzzard then started toward the earth.

The clouds are midway between heaven and earth; above the clouds, wind never blows.

As buzzard flew from heaven to the clouds, the brothers could easily keep their hold; but from the clouds to the earth, the buzzard was blown in all directions. All reached the earth in safety, however, and the boys recognized the trees that stood about their old home.

They rested beneath the trees, and while there, an old man passed by who knew the brothers. He continued down the road, and soon, meeting the boys' mother, told her the boys had come back. She hastened to see them.

When she saw them, she began to talk and made them answer her. Then they told her that, as they had spoken during the first four days after their return, they would surely die. Knowing she had forced them to speak, on hearing this, the mother was greatly worried. Then all went to the mother's home, and the brothers told of all they had seen and how they had followed Sun during many years. After they had told all, they died and went up to heaven to remain forever.

THE HUNTER OF THE SUN

UNKNOWN [COPELAND]   1853

Many, many generations ago, when the Choctaws were assembled on a great national occasion, the inquiry arose as to what became of the sun when it disappeared at the close of the day. None of their great men, chiefs, prophets, or doctors could give any satisfactory answer to the inquiry. The next question was whether it were not possible to ascertain to a good degree of certainty, in regard to the matter, whether by traveling in the direction of the point where the sun disappeared, one could not find the place of its rest? And then, who would voluntarily undertake the task of discovering what became of the sun?

After a long consultation in regard to the matter, a young man, in all the freshness and vigor of early manhood, volunteered for the task. He would leave his people, his friends, and his country, all that the Indian counts dear, and devote his life to the task, that he might gratify his people. Accordingly, he bade them all farewell, charging them to remember him daily and talk of him and his undertaking to their children so that he should be always had in remembrance by the tribe. And assuring them that he would one day return to gratify them in regard to the object of their desires, he departed.

His people remembered him and talked of him, and the object of his journey, and the day of his return. The old men died; the young men became old, and many of them passed away to the grave. Still the young man came not. The people had looked for him, the prophets had spoken of his coming, but he came not. Years rolled away, and even generations passed, but no tidings from the young man, who had gone to find what became of the sun, till finally his name, and the object of his journey, were quite forgotten.

The nation were again assembled. The old men, the young men, the women and children were there. They were suddenly checked in their mirth and rejoicing by the appearance of an old man, a very, very old man. His form was bent, his hair white, his eyes dim, and he leaned upon a staff. The people rose up in reverence for the old man.

He inquired if the young man who went to find the resting place of the sun was forgotten.

The old men remembered the story told them by their fathers.

"Then," said he, "behold the man of whom ye have heard. I am he. Long, long years are gone. I left my friends, my people, and my country. I traveled on, on, and on, till I came to a great water, and standing there on the shore, I saw the sun disappear. I have now returned to you to tell you of my success and to be buried in the land of my fathers. The sun, when it disappears, falls into the water. In the morning it must rise out of it. My mission is ended; my work is done. All, all, farewell."

And the old man laid him down and died.

YALLOFALAIYA

UNKNOWN [HALBERT]   C. 1900

A long time ago there was an Indian with his wife and child that lived in a cabin. One day the woman said to her husband that they ought to go and see a hunter who lived a long ways from their cabin. The man was willing, and they went to the hunter's house. The hunter was not at home. He had gone deer hunting. But his sister, who lived with him, was at home. She gave the people something to eat.

After a while, the man's wife had some bad thoughts. She went to the hunter's sister and said, "I am a poor widow. This man you see is my brother, and the child is my son, his nephew. I have no one to give me help, and my brother may someday bring a wife into his cabin, which would not be good for me. Your brother has no wife. Can I not become his wife?"

The man's sister said, "Yes, my brother has no wife, and I know he would be willing to marry you. Now trust me, and I will fix up everything all right for you. He will come home sometime in the night."

That evening the man's sister spread a pallet for the man and the child and another pallet for the woman and her brother, the hunter. At last, the man and the child went to bed, leaving the two women sitting up.

The little boy said, "Mother, are you not going to come and stay with father?"

The woman knew that she had to keep up fooling the hunter's sister, so she said, "Hush, you little fool. You don't know what you are talking about. That is your uncle, and you know you always call your uncle Father."

The hunter's sister was now badly fooled.

At last, the man and the little boy fell asleep. Then the woman went to the pallet, which the hunter's sister had spread for her. The other woman sat up until her brother came. She then told him about the marriage that she had fixed for him. It was all right with the man.

That night there was born unto the couple a boy child who grew so fast that by sunrise he was up and outdoors making arrows. His mother gave him the name of Yallofalaiya.

After breakfast a strange bird named Yoshobli came near the cabin, fluttering and flying about after the manner of a brooding dove. Yallofalaiya started out in pursuit of the bird. He was decoyed a long ways off. He could not follow back his tracks, and so got lost in a great woods.

Soon after Yallofalaiya had left the cabin, the woman's first husband found out what she had done. So he became very angry and took his little boy and went back home. The hunter, too, now saw that she was a bad woman and had fooled him. So he, too, left the cabin and never came back again. He would not let his sister go with him for he thought that she had helped to fool him. So the two women lived together in the same cabin for several years.

At last, one day, the hunter's sister got very angry and scolded bitterly the other woman—that she was a bad woman, that she had fooled her husband, and her, and her brother, and was the cause of her brother leaving her. She grew more angry. "You are the cause of all my sorrow, and I intend to kill you."

The base woman, at these words, feared for her life, left the cabin, and went out into the woods. She began to weep bitterly.

After a while, she saw an arrow lying on the ground. "Ah," she said, "that must be Yallofalaiya's arrow." Soon after, she saw another arrow. She said, "I know now that these are Yallofalaiya's arrows." Hardly had she said this when she saw Yallofalaiya coming. They knew each other.

Yallofalaiya said, "Mother, why are you crying so?"

"Oh, my son," she replied, "that woman over yonder has threatened to kill me."

He said, "Be quiet, mother, I will kill anybody that wants to kill you. Lead on and show me this woman."

So they came to the cabin of the hunter's sister, but she was not in. She had gone into a winter house not far off. Yallofalaiya then went into the winter house and killed all the people with his arrows. He then came out and said, "Mother, I have killed them all. What shall we do next?"

The woman said, "Yallofalaiya, I have been such a bad woman that I do not wish to live any longer. Let us both die at once. I will die and become a crow."

And Yallofalaiya said, "Then I will die and become a sewing thread."

So the woman died and became a bad old crow.

The crows are the great enemies of the corn fields. They also set a crow to watch and tell them when anyone is coming. And when nobody is coming, they fly down into the field and scratch up and eat the fresh-planted corn. The crow's meanness comes from the base woman, who long ago died and became a crow.

But it was not this way with Yallofalaiya. From the time he had left the cabin until he came back to his mother, he had never seen a woman. So he did a good thing for women. He died, and his body shrank away until nothing was left but his sinews. Women gathered them up and used them for sewing thread, and so sewing first came among the Indians.

NAMELESS CHOCTAW

PETER PITCHLYNN   1870

There once lived in the royal Indian town of Eyasho (Yazoo) the only son of a war chief who was famous for his handsome form and lofty bearing. The old men of the nation looked upon him with pride and said that his courage was rare, and he was destined to be an eminent warrior. He was also an eloquent orator. But with all these qualities he was not allowed a seat in the councils of his nation because he had not yet distinguished himself in war. The fame of having slain an enemy he could not claim, nor had he even been fortunate enough to take a single prisoner. He was greatly beloved, and, as the name of his childhood had been abandoned according to an ancient custom, and he had not yet won a name worthy of his ability, he was known among his kindred as the Nameless Choctaw.

In the town of Eyasho, there also once lived the most beautiful maiden of her tribe. She was the daughter of a hunter and the promised wife of the Nameless Choctaw. They met often at the great dances, but, in accordance with Indian custom, she treated him as a stranger. They loved, and one thought alone entered their minds to cast a shadow. They knew that the laws of their nation were unalterable and that she could not become his wife until he had won a name in war, though he could always place at the door of her lodge an abundance of game and could deck her with the most beautiful wampum and feathers.

It was now midsummer and the evening hour. The lover had met his betrothed upon the summit of a hill covered with pines. From the center of a neighboring plain rose the smoke of a large watchfire, around which were dancing a party of four hundred warriors. They had planned an expedition against the distant Osages, and the present was the fourth and last night of the preparation ceremonies.

Up to that evening, the Nameless Choctaw had been the leader in the dances, and even now he was only temporarily absent, for he had stolen away for a parting interview with his beloved. They separated, and when morning came, the Choctaw warriors were upon the warpath leading to the headwaters of the Arkansas. On that stream, they found a cave, in which, because they were in a prairieland, they secreted themselves. Two men were then selected as spies, one of whom, the Nameless Choctaw, was to reconnoiter in the West, and the other in the East.

Night came, and the Indians in the cave were discovered by an Osage hunter, who had entered to escape the heavy dews. He at once hastened to the nearest camp, told his people what he had seen, and a party of Osage warriors hastened to the cave. At its mouth, they built a fire, and before the dawn of day, the entire Choctaw party had been smothered to death by the cunning of their enemies.

The Choctaw spy who journeyed to the East had witnessed the surprise and unhappy fate of his brother-warriors, and, soon returning to his own country, he called a council and revealed the sad intelligence. As to the fate of the nameless warrior who had journeyed towards the West, he felt certain that he, too, must have been overtaken and slain.

Upon the heart of one this story fell with a heavy weight; and the promised wife of the lost Choctaw began to droop. And before the moon had passed away, she died and was buried on the spot where she had parted with her lover.

But what became of the Nameless Choctaw?

It was not true that he had been overtaken and slain. He was indeed discovered by the Osages, and far over the prairies and across the streams was he closely pursued. For many days and nights did the race continue, but the Choctaw finally made his escape. His course had been very winding, and when he came to a halt, he was astonished to find that the sun rose in the wrong quarter of the heavens. Everything appeared to him wrong and out of order, and he became a forlorn and bewildered man.

At last, he found himself at the foot of a mountain, which was covered with grass, and unlike any he had ever before seen. It so happened, however, at the close of a certain day, that he wandered into a wooded valley, and, having made a rude lodge and killed a swamp rabbit, he lighted a fire and prepared himself for at least one quiet supper and a night of repose. Morning dawned, and he was still in trouble but continued his wanderings.

Many moons passed away; summer came, and he called upon the Great Spirit to make his pathway plain. He hunted the forests for a spotted deer, and having killed it on a day when there was no wind, he offered it as a sacrifice and that night supped upon a portion of the animal's flesh. His fire burnt brightly, and, though lonesome, his heart was at peace.

But now he hears a footstep in an adjoining thicket! A moment more, and a snow-white wolf of immense size is crouching at his feet and licking his torn moccasins.

"How came you in this strange country?" inquired the wolf.

And the poor Indian told the story of his many troubles. The wolf took pity upon him and said that he would conduct him in safety to the country of his kindred; and on the following morning, they departed.

Long, very long was the journey and very crude and dangerous the streams which they had to cross. The wolf helped the Indian to kill game for their mutual support, and by the time that the moon for weeding corn had arrived, the Choctaw had entered his native village again. This was on the anniversary of the day he had parted from his betrothed, and he now found his people mourning for her untimely death.

Time and suffering had so changed the wanderer that his relatives and friends did not recognize him, and he did not make himself known. Often, however, he made them recount the story of her death, and many a wild song, to the astonishment of all, did he sing to the memory of the departed, whom he called by the name of *Imma*, or the idol of warriors.

On a cloudless night he visited her grave, and at a moment when the Great Spirit cast a shadow upon the moon, he fell upon the grave in grief and died.

For three nights afterwards the inhabitants of the Choctaw village were alarmed by the continual howling of a wolf, and when it ceased, the pine forest upon the hill where the lovers were resting in peace took up the mournful sound and has continued it to the present time.

THE HUNTER AND THE ALLIGATOR

UNKNOWN [BUSHNELL]   1909

One winter there were many hunters living in a village, all of whom, with one exception, had killed a great many deer. But one had met with very poor luck, and although he often succeeded in getting close to deer, just ready to draw his bow on them, they always contrived to escape unharmed.

He had been away from his village three days and during that time had seen many deer but had not been able to kill a single one.

On the third day, when the sun was overhead, the hunter saw a huge alligator resting on a dry, sandy spot. This alligator had been without water for many days and was dry and shriveled and so weak that he could scarcely speak. He was able, however, to ask the hunter where water could be had.

The hunter replied, "In that forest, only a short journey hence, is a clear, deep pool of cold water."

"But I cannot travel alone; I am too weak to go so far. Come nearer that we may talk and plan. I cannot harm you; have no fear," said the alligator.

At last, the hunter went nearer and listened to the alligator, who said, "I know you are a hunter, but all the deer escape from you. Now, carry me to the water, and I will then make you a great hunter and tell you how to kill many, many deer."

The hunter hesitated, as he feared the alligator. And then he said, "I will carry you, but not unless I may bind your legs so you cannot scratch and your mouth so you cannot bite me."

The alligator rolled over on his back and held up his legs, saying, "I am helpless. Bind me, and do with me as you will."

Then the hunter bound with a cord the alligator's legs and mouth. Then he lifted the animal to his shoulder and carried him to the water.

When they reached the pool, the hunter loosened the cords, and the alligator plunged into the water. It went down, then returned to the surface three times, then went down again and remained a long time.

At last, he rose again to the surface and spoke to the hunter, saying, "You brought me to the water; now listen, and if you do as I counsel, you will become a great hunter. Take your bow and arrows and go into the woods. You will first meet a small doe, but do not kill it. Next you will meet a large doe, but you must not shoot this one either. Then you will see a small buck, but this likewise must be spared. Lastly, you will encounter a very large, old buck. Go very close to it and kill it, and ever afterward you will be able to kill many deer."

The hunter did as the alligator told him and never again was without venison in his camp.

SUPERNATURAL LEGENDS AND ENCOUNTERS

Tales of the supernatural beings that roam the Mississippi woodlands are common throughout Mississippi's varied cultures and communities, regardless of ethnicity or economic class. Undecipherable creatures are glimpsed in the woods, unexplainable events occur again and again. For the Choctaw, such creatures and events are unusual but not unexpected. Rather than relegate them to superstition, supernatural beings are integrally situated within Choctaw belief systems about power, medicine, and human nature.

There is an internal logic to these accounts of the supernatural. Melford Farve called them hunting stories, suggesting both the context of their telling as well as their content. Until recently, when property rights and "No Trespassing" signs became actively enforced, men in the community headed into the woods in the late fall and winter to hunt for a few days at a time, traveling in groups for efficiency, safety, and companionship. At night, gathered around the fire they had used earlier to cook a rabbit or two from the day's hunt, they entertained and scared one another with stories. In the warmer months, whole families went out into the woods to nearby ponds and lakes to fish for both fun and food. There too, stories were shared, often about the supernatural beings in the woods. Caroline Morris described loading up the family wagon on Friday night and camping all weekend to fish. Her son-in-law, Harley Vaughn, did the same, noting, "That's when they all start telling those scary ghost stories." Caroline joined in the laughter at the recollection. "My grandmother, Sweeny Willis, she used to tell stories. You'd be just listening to what she was saying and all of a sudden, the owl would make a sound, and everybody would squeal!"

Often the characters in their stories were also hunters, many of them also sitting around campfires. Any small solace the listeners could take in the fact that the stories were set long ago, involving men whose names have been forgotten, was lost when another storyteller added his own story of a recent encounter with a similar creature.

Yet many people today say that supernatural beings are slowly disappearing. Logging and population expansion are whittling away the miles of pine, hickory, and black gum that once surrounded the early Mississippians. With the trees vanish the herbs local doctors use for healing, the animals the men hunt, and the supernatural beings that call such places home. Yet while the power and prevalence of the doctors and supernatural beings may be waning, these stories attest that they are not gone.[1]

In fact, recounting supernatural encounters, both personal and those of friends and neighbors, is the most active storytelling tradition in the community today, among young and old alike. Children clamor at summer camp for ghost stories to scare them; adults recount these stories for didactic and personal reasons, partly explained by the social power of having seen one of these supernatural beings. The supernatural are dangerous and only partially understood; they must be treated with respect. Stories of these beings may be told with awe, curious wonder, false bravado, and laughing relief, but they are always told with respect. In doing so, narrators reinforce how such beings must be regarded if encountered.

While the stories serve to instruct young listeners about the dangers in the woods, there is the equally important need of the storytellers themselves to recount their experiences. Encounters with the supernatural are mysterious and often frightening. When something strange is seen in the woods—a ball of light, a small man or men, a creature part animal, part human—there is a need to understand it, discuss it, make sense of it. Interpreting these encounters is made particularly problematic since many of the creatures can appear in various forms that mirror other creatures. A ball of light, for example, could be *bohpoli*, *hashok okwa huiʼga*, a medicine person, a witch, or just lights. This is one reason that medicine men or women, people with esoteric knowledge of the supernatural, are often enlisted to help interpret the encounter.[2]

Virtually everyone has either encountered such a creature or knows someone who has; one need not, therefore, search beyond family and close friends to hear such tales. Yet while most of these stories are personal experience narratives, they nonetheless serve as tribal stories. Each story describes a different, separate encounter, but all are recognized by the Choctaw as part of a communally held belief system.

Some stories are told as legends, some as personal experience narratives. The former are more authoritative, the latter more visceral. The division between legendary and contemporary tales is clearly apparent in the corpus of supernatural stories told throughout the community, but the issue is a bit more complicated. There appears to be an important distinction between whether the supernatural beings are still regularly encountered today. Kashikanchak is not, and there are legends concerning this being, passed-down stories from the past. But for *na losa chito* and *bohpoli*, contemporary encounters are still quite frequent today. Older legends of these beings are simply not necessary since more vibrant contemporary encounters abound.[3]

Yet there are a number of stories told both as legends and in stories of recent encounters. The problem that arises, then, is whether to categorize the stories temporally or thematically. Because the system of supernatural beings is so varied and complex, and because this system is historically continuous, I have chosen to organize by temporal division when possible, but I adhere primarily to thematic continuity, as with the stories "Big, Black, Hairy Monster" and "The Ghost," which are legends but are nestled among contemporary stories that describe similar beings.

THE GIRL AND THE DEVIL

UNKNOWN [BUSHNELL]   1909

A young Choctaw girl was walking alone one day in the outskirts of the village when she suddenly met a young man whom she had never seen before. Soon he spoke to the girl and asked her to accompany him to his home. At first, she refused, but at last he succeeded in persuading her to go with him. They passed through dense woods and over hills and at last entered the yard that surrounded his house. Here various birds and animals were tied to the trees. As they were hungry, food was brought them, and then, and not until then, did the man assume his true character, and the girl saw the Devil before her. Then she became frightened and endeavored to escape, but before she could do so, she was seized and locked in a small cave.

A large frog hopped from a hole in the far corner of the cave and, going to the girl, said, "Do you know what that noise is?"

"No," replied the girl. "What is it?"

The frog told her the Devil and his men were sharpening their knives to kill her.

At this, she became more frightened than before, but the frog quieted her by saying, "Now, if you will listen and do just as I say, you will escape. I will open this door, and thereupon you must run swiftly out and down the wide road. Soon you will reach a road on the left, but do not take it; keep to the broad road. Then you will come to the junction of three roads, and you must take the middle one. Shortly afterward, you will reach a broad bayou where there will be a small boat on the shore. Here you will be safe."

After saying this to the girl, the frog hopped up a beam to the top of the door, which he unlocked. As soon as the door swung open, the girl ran out and followed the roads as she had been directed. Finally, she arrived at the bayou, jumped into the small boat, and, seizing the paddle, pushed out from the shore.

As she neared the middle of the bayou, she heard voices calling her, and looking in the direction of the sound, she saw the Devil standing on the bank just where she had been a few moments before. He called the girl, who was not able to resist him; so she pushed the boat toward the spot where he stood.

"Come nearer," said the Devil, "so that I can step into your boat."

The girl said she could not do so, but she rested one end of her paddle on the side of the boat and the other end on the shore, telling the Devil to walk on the bridge thus made.

He started to do so, but just as he reached the middle, the girl jerked the paddle, and the Devil fell into the water. He sank straight to the bottom of the bayou and never came up.

In time, the Devil's body broke into many small pieces, which became hard, forming the gravel now found on the bottoms of the bayous.

THE EAGLE STORY

ROSALEE STEVE   1998

This is about the eagle story. This is a long, long time ago.

And it used to happen that Indian people used to live in a teepee houses; not a log house or a house like we're living in—they were teepee houses. And the big old eagle used to live in the wood. And they're watching the children, especially crawling baby.

And when the mama and papa's not watching, just a few minutes, the eagle will fly and come get the baby and take him up in the sky. And they will eat the baby while they fly into the sky. And the bones will drop down, back on earth.

And the grandmas and the grandpas and mamas, they will follow the bones, until the eagle fly way up, somewhere, and they can't even follow them no more.

SKATE'NE

UNKNOWN [BUSHNELL]   1909

Late one afternoon, several children were playing near their house when suddenly they saw a woman approaching. She was very old and stooping, and her hair was white. The children were greatly frightened and ran into the house but soon returned to the old woman, who said to them, "Children, do not be afraid of me for nothing will harm you. I am your great-great-great-grandmother, and neither you nor your mother has ever seen me. Now, go to the house, and tell her that I have come."

The children did so. Then they took a deer skin and spread it on the ground for the old woman and carried her food and drink. She then asked the children when their father went to sleep and in which part of the house he lay, and the children told her all.

That night, after all had gone to sleep, the old woman entered the house and cut off the man's head, which she put into a basket she carried for that purpose. Then she covered the man's body with his blanket and quietly left the house.

The next morning, the man's wife was surprised to find him asleep (as she supposed) since it was his custom to go hunting before sunrise. So she spoke to him; and as he did not answer, she pulled off his blanket. When she saw that his head was missing, she became greatly alarmed.

After cutting off the man's head, Skate'ne, the old woman, immediately left the house and started down the road. Soon she met a large bear, who said to her, "What have you covered up in your basket, old woman?"

"You must not see it," said she, "for if you look on it, you will lose your eyes. It is poison and bad."

The bear was contented and went on his way.

Then she met many other animals, and at last came two wildcats. "Stop, old woman, and show us what you have in your basket," called one of the wildcats. "We must see what you carry."

The old woman repeated what she had told the bear and all the others.

"But we must look inside your basket, even if we do lose our eyes," replied one of the wildcats, at the same time seizing the basket and raising the cover. When they saw the man's head, they knew it was the old woman who prowled around during the night, killing men and animals and birds, so they determined to kill her. While one held her, the other went to find a large club.

When he had gone, she said to the wildcat holding her, "Over there is a large club. You would do well to get it and kill me before your companion returns for the one that kills me will always have good luck, and I like you."

So the remaining wildcat went to get the club for he believed what the old woman had told him and hence wanted to kill her. On his return with the club, he could not find the old woman for she was Skate'ne, an owl, and had flown away.

HOKLONOTE'SHE

UNKNOWN [BUSHNELL]   1909

A man away from his village on a hunting trip had killed many deer and bears.

One night, he made a large fire of oak and soon was sleeping soundly. But before long he was aroused by the cry of an owl, and, looking up, he saw a huge owl standing over the fire. Then the hunter thought to himself, "What am I to do?"

Thereupon the owl said to him, "So you wonder what you are to do," and repeated every thought the hunter had.

The owl was really Hoklonote'she, a bad spirit that can read men's thoughts and readily assumes the forms of various birds and animals.

After the owl had stood there some time, repeating whatever thoughts were in the hunter's mind, the latter suddenly jumped up and vigorously stirred the fire, causing the oak logs to send up a myriad of sparks that fell on the feathers of the owl and burned them. So badly frightened was Hoklonote'she that he flew away in haste and never again troubled the hunter.

A STORY OF KASHIKANCHAK

UNKNOWN [HALBERT]   C. 1900

The saying is that a man once went a-hunting and did not come back. So a certain man followed and looked for him. And he came to the hills and valleys, and he went upon the high hills. And towards a hill and valley beyond, he heard a woman pounding. And he went to see. And he got to the hill and went around it and took a search.

Across the valley at the foot of a hill there was a great cave. And inside of the cave, he heard a pounding. And the man said, "What is this?"

He went to it, stooping over, and he saw a very tall woman with long teeth pounding with her elbow. And he said, "Aha, she can never use us up," and so he stealthily went back to where he came from.

And when he got there, everything that he had seen, he told to the people. "Kashikanchak just uses up people," he said to them.

And they thought how they could kill her.

And they chose the men that could run fast that live there. And several men took their guns and went, and the land was level that reached to the cave. And on the ridge, the men with their guns went and sat down overlooking the cave. And the chosen men with their guns went to the cave. And they saw the old woman standing up and pounding with her elbow. And they shot at her and then ran to the ridge.

Kashikanchak came out and said, "Hi, heh, he, yantakkali [*running*], iback [*mixing*], pok, pok, pok." And she pursued the men.

And the men sitting above each one began to shoot. Still, she nearly overtook the men. And the hindmost one shot; and he wounded her in the foot. And Kashikanchak fell down, and the men escaped, so the saying always has been.

And the people returned and went into Kashikanchak's house. And they saw a child there eating a man's leg. And they hacked and killed the child.

And so the saying is finished.

KASHIKANCHAK

JEFFIE SOLOMON   1997

They used to say the Kashikanchak used to exist here. That, I really don't know, but . . .

Two children wanted to go fishing. The two usually enjoyed fishing, so they went to a small pond. While they were walking around, Kashikanchak found them. And then, because he was telling them that at his water hole there's so many fish that if they stand in the water, they would nip their feet, these two children went with him.

So when they did not return—their mother and father were waiting for them—but because the two had not returned, they were thinking they are lost forever since the Kashikanchak had led them away.

He took them to his place and were there, but apparently the old kanchak was there, it is said.

So then she said, "Let me check your head for lice."

And then one of the boys said, "Let me check yours first."

When the boy realized the old Kashikanchak, sitting, had placed a big knife beside her, he said, "Let me check yours first."

And the child was busy with the old Kashikanchak's head when he quietly took the knife and cut her head off, it is said.

Then, because the one that stole them wasn't there, they stayed for a little while. And when he did that to the old Kashikanchak, they put the head in a mortar that was there.

So now, "Let's go." Because they knew when the Kashikanchak saw them, he would follow them, they took off running. They were singing as they were running, thinking, "Don't let him follow us," it is said. And they were singing:

> Let me pick up an acorn
> Let me pick up an acorn
> Give it to
> the skinny
> pig.

He was continually singing, saying, "Roll up land," it used to be said.

Since they took off running, because they were singing as they ran, "It's the children saying that," he said.

And as he looked out and saw it was really them running, going that way.

As the two reached the open shed that was there, as they entered, they slammed the door really hard. And so he did not go in with them.

That is what I used to hear.

That's all.

THE SPECTRE AND THE HUNTER

J. L. MCDONALD AND PETER P. PITCHLYNN   1850

Kowayhoommah, or Red Panther, once started out on a hunting expedition. He had an excellent bow and carried with him some jerked venison. His only companion was a large, white dog, which attended him in all his rambles. This dog was a cherished favorite and shared in all his master's privations and successes. He was the social companion of the hunter by day and his watchful guardian by night.

The hunter had traveled far, and as the evening approached, he encamped upon a spot that bore every indication of an excellent hunting ground. Deer-tracks were seen in abundance, and turkeys were heard clucking in various directions as they retired to their roosting places. Kowayhoommah kindled a fire, and having shared a portion of his provision with his dog, he spread his deerskin and his blanket by the crackling fire and mused on the adventures of the day already past and on the probable success of the ensuing one.

It was a bright starlight night; the air was calm, and a slight frost, which was falling, rendered the fire comfortable and cheering. His dog lay crouched and slumbering at his feet, and from his stifled cries, seemed dreaming of the chase. Everything tended to soothe the feelings of our hunt and to prolong that pleasant train of associations, which the beauty of the night and the anticipations of the morrow were calculated to inspire.

At length, when his musings were assuming that indefinite and dreamy state which precedes a sound slumber, he was startled by a distant cry, which thrilled on his ear and roused him into instant watchfulness. He listened with breathless attention and in a few minutes again heard the cry, keen, long, and piercing.

The dog gave a plaintive and ominous howl. Kowayhoommah felt uneasy. "Can it be a lost hunter?" was the inquiry which suggested itself. Surely not, for a true hunter feels lost nowhere. "What then can it be?"

With these reflections, our hunter stepped forth, gathered more fuel, and again replenished his fire.

Again came a cry, keen, long, and painfully thrilling, as before. The voice was evidently approaching, and again the dog raised a low and mournful howl. Kowayhoommah then felt the blood curdling to his heart, and folding his blanket around him, he seated himself by the fire and fixed his eyes intently in the direction from which he expected the approach of his startling visitor.

In a few moments, he heard the approach of his footsteps. In another minute, a ghastly shape made its appearance and advanced towards the fire. It seemed to be the figure of a hunter, like himself. Its form was tall and gaunt; its features livid and unearthly. A tattered robe was girded round his waist and covered his shoulders, and he bore an unstrung bow and a few broken arrows.

The spectre advanced to the fire and seemed to shiver with cold. He stretched forth one hand then the other to the fire, and as he did so, he fixed his hollow and ghastly eye on Kowayhoommah, and a slight smile lighted up his lived countenance, but not a word did he utter. Kowayhoommah felt his flesh and hair creep, and the blood freezing in his veins, yet with instinctive Indian courtesy, he presented his deerskin as a seat for his grim visitor. The spectre waved his hand and shook his head in refusal. He stepped aside, plucked up a parcel of briers from an adjacent thicket, spread them by the fire, and on his thorny couch he stretched himself and seemed to court repose.

Our hunter was petrified with mingled fear and astonishment. His eyes continued long riveted on the strange and ghastly being stretched before him, and he was only awakened from his trance of horror by the voice of his faithful dog. "Arise," said the dog, suddenly and supernaturally gifted with speech. "Arise, and flee for your life! The spectre now slumbers; should you also slumber, you are lost. Arise and flee while I stay and watch!"

Kowayhoommah arose and stole softly from the fire. Having advanced a few hundred paces, he stopped to listen; all was silent, and with a beating heart he continued his stealthy and rapid flight. Again, he listened, and again with renewed confidence he pursued his rapid course, until he had gained several miles on his route homeward.

Feeling at length a sense of safety, he paused to recover breath, on the brow of a lofty hill. The night was calm and serene, the stars shone with steady lustre, and as Kowayhoommah gazed upwards, he breathed freely and felt every apprehension vanish.

Alas! On the instant, the distant baying of his dog struck on his ear; with a thrill of renewed apprehension, he bent his ear to listen, and the appalling cry of his dog, now more distinctly audible, convinced him that the spectre was in full pursuit. Again, he fled with accelerated speed over hill, over plain, through swamps and thickets, till once more he paused by the side of a deep and rapid river. The heavy baying of his dog told him too truly, that his fearful pursuer was close at hand. One minute, he stood for breath, and he then plunged into the stream. But scarcely had he gained the center, when the spectre appeared on the bank and plunged in after him, closely followed by the panting dog. Kowayhoommah's apprehensions now amounted to agony. He fancied he saw the hollow and glassy eyeballs of his pursuer glaring above the water and that his skeleton hand was already outstretched to grapple with him. With a cry of horror, he was about to give up the struggle for life and sink beneath the waves, when his faithful dog, with a fierce yell, seized upon his master's enemy. After a short but severe struggle, they both sunk; the waters settled over them forever.

He became an altered man. He shunned the dance and the ball play, and his former hilarity gave place to a settled melancholy. In about a year after this strange adventure, he joined a war party against a distant enemy and never returned.

THE HUNTER WHO BECAME A DEER

UNKNOWN [BUSHNELL]   1909

One night a hunter killed a doe and soon afterward fell asleep near the carcass. The next morning, just at sunrise, the hunter was surprised and startled to see the doe raise her head and to hear her speak, asking him to go with her to her home. At first, he was so surprised that he did not know what to reply, so the doe again asked him whether he would go. Then the hunter said that he would go with her, although he had no idea where she would lead him.

So they started, and the doe led the hunter through forests and over high mountains, until at last they reached a large hole under a rock, which they entered. Here the hunter was led before the king of all the deer, an immense buck, with huge antlers and a large black spot on his back. Soon, the hunter became drowsy, and finally he fell asleep.

Now all around the cave were piles of deer's feet, antlers, and skins. While the hunter was asleep, the deer endeavored to fit to his hands and feet deer's feet, which they selected for the purpose. After several unsuccessful attempts the fourth set proved to be just the right size and were fastened firmly on the hunter's hands and feet. Then a skin was found that covered him properly, and finally antlers were fitted to his head. And then the hunter became a deer and walked on four feet after the manner of deer.

Many days passed, and the hunter's mother and all his friends thought he had been killed.

One day, when they were in the forest, they found his bow and arrows hanging on a branch of the tree beneath which he had slept beside the body of the doe. All gathered around the spot and began singing, when suddenly they saw a herd of deer bounding toward them through the forest. The deer then circled about the singers. One large buck approached closer than the others, and the singers, rushing forward, caught it. To the great astonishment of all it spoke, whereupon they recognized the voice of the lost hunter.

Greatly distressed, the hunter's mother begged her companions to remove from her son the deer skin and antlers and feet, but they told her he would certainly die if they should do so. She insisted, however, saying she would rather bury her son than to have him remain a deer.

So her friends began tearing away the skin, which already had grown to the hunter's body. And, as they continued their efforts to remove it, the blood began to flow. Finally, the hunter died. Then his body was taken back to the village and was buried with the ceremony of a great dance.

THE MAN WHO BECAME A SNAKE

CYNTHIA CLEGG   1997

Cynthia: My dad told me when I was a little girl, just like Siah, and just like Hillary, and just like Monique. And it's about a snake. [*kids all scream*]
William: Is this true?
Cynthia: He said it was. It was told to him by his grandparents, and their grandparents told him, so it's a story that's been passed down.

There was this recipe. A long time ago, my dad said there was this recipe. He said that there was a recipe for becoming a snake. There was this recipe where you could get all these ingredients. You get all these and mix it together, and you can become a snake.

And I remember two things that he told me: one was wild cabbage, and another one was wild onions. And there was several other stuff, but I've forgotten because it was a long time ago that he told me. Because when you mix everything together and eat it, you will become a snake.

There was this family, this man and a woman who lived in this house. The man did not believe it could be true. "A man cannot become a snake," he said. He was laughing about it.

After he thought about it, he says to his wife, "Boil the stuff after I get them. Then I will try it."

The wife says, "No, don't do it. It might be true, and you will become a snake."

And this man says, "I am going to do it." He would not listen.

Wild cabbage, wild onion, and whatever all the other stuff—he gathered all the stuff and gave it to her to boil. "And mix it up for me, then I will eat it," he says.

So the wife boiled it and prepared the mix for him.

After she finished, he ate and really got full. He got full. After he got full, he says, "I'll be sitting in the living room."

He started out toward the living room. He sat down on the chair.

The wife washed the dishes and wiped the table. After she finished, she went to the living room and sat beside him. They were talking.

A little later, the man was sitting there talking, but he did not finish. She wondered what was wrong.

His ears were protruding a little and was damp and cold. Then his hands went this way [*she places her hands by her side*] and his legs start going together like this [*she puts her legs straight out in front of her and close together as if becoming one*].

Then, all of a sudden, his body went straight out. He fell. He was sitting; then he fell over. His body was like a snake. The man became a big snake.

William: How big was it?
Cynthia: I don't know. I really can't say, William.
William: Did that really happen too?
Cynthia: Um-hm. He became a snake, they say.

Later, all his hair was gone, like snakeskin. He wasn't human no more. He became a big snake. He was slithering across the room toward the door. He went out the door. His wife was afraid and started to scream. Then . . .

William: Was he mean?
Cynthia: He wasn't mean to his wife.

It's told he went outside, through the door. He slithered across the yard and found a big hole. The snake went down the hole. He thought that was his house.

The wife wondered what she was going to do. She was afraid.

She brought him food every day, whatever it was, because she knew he was her husband. Even though now he's a snake. She knew that was her husband, so she fed him every day.

And he would come out. He ate everything she put out for him.

People in the next village heard about the big snake and were afraid. "What if he eats our children?" they thought. So they went to the wife and asked if she has a big snake in the yard, he asked.

"No," she says. She didn't want to tell the truth.

Finally, she told the truth.

"My husband did not believe, so he told me to boil the ingredients for him. Then he became a snake."

"Well then, you must call him in the morning. When you call and he comes out, we are going to kill him."

His wife cried. Even though he is a snake, he is her husband.

She kept crying.

That next morning, everyone gathered with guns.

She called out to him and said, "Here. Food." Then a big snake crawls out, and the man shot it and killed it. And they buried him.

And that was the end of the snake man.

HORSE MAN

HARRY POLK   1997

My grandfather told me all kind of stories.

Old Choctaw, one time he going hunting, and he meet a big old black bear. And a bear followed him, and he didn't know what to do. He climbed up that little old log like that [*indicates log lying diagonally*]. He climbed up, and the bear had followed him. He's behind, and that tree is about that far ahead [*indicates it is close*]. Go up there, and he didn't know what to do. That bear might kill him; and he was scared. And he sat over there.

He saw just like a horse and a head that's a man's. He got a bow and arrow. He saw him, and he walked over there. And that horse and that kind-of-man is standing over there.

He [the bear] started bad, trying to kill that old Indian. He's [the horse man] standing up, and he gets bow and arrow, and he shot down that bear.

And the old Choctaw said, "Thank you, thank you."

And the kind of horse, that's running, going up there.

And that old Indian was going to skin that bear and get head off and just pulled the skin off. And this fur wrapped on his body; and he wore it home. [*laughter*]

It didn't kill him.

I don't know, he's kind of like horse but head is kind of a man. He got bow and arrow and he killed that bear.

That's what he told me. Used to be an old Indian story, I guess. That's what he told me.

HALF HORSE, HALF HUMAN

JESSICA MILLER   2024

I have not seen that half horse, half human but one of my cousins has seen it and they was telling me about it. It's been a while.

I guess they were going through the swamp area in Bogue Chitto. They said they've seen it before.

When they seen it, they said the car shut down. So the car stopped and shut down and then they couldn't crank it back up.

But that half human, half horse never messed with them. They just seen it and the whole car just shut down. They were freaking out because they were scared! [*laugh*]

KASHEHOTAPALO

AHOJEOBE (EMIL JOHN)   1909

Kashehotapalo is neither man nor beast. His head is small and his face shriveled and evil to look upon; his body is that of a man. His legs and feet are those of a deer, the former being covered with hair, and the latter having cloven hoofs. He lives in low, swampy places, away from the habitations of men. When hunters go near his abiding place, he quietly slips up behind them and calls loudly then turns and runs swiftly away. He never attempts to harm the hunters but delights in frightening them. The sound uttered by Kashehotapalo resembles the cry of a woman, and that is the reason for his name (*kasheho*, "woman"; *tapalo*, "call").

NA LOSA FALAYA

PISATUNTEMA (EMMA)   1910

The *na losa falaya* somewhat resembles man. It is of about the size of a man and walks upright, but its face is shriveled, its eyes are very small, and it has quite long, pointed ears. Its nose is likewise long. It lives in the densest woods, near swamps, away from the habitations of men. In some respects, it resembles Kashehotapalo.

Often when hunters are in the woods, far from their homes, late in the day when the shadows have grown long beneath the pine trees, a *na losa falaya* will come forth. Getting quite near a hunter, it will call in a voice resembling that of a man. And some hunters, when they turn and see the *na losa falaya*, are so affected that they fall to the ground and even become unconscious. And while the hunter is thus prostrated on the ground, it approaches and sticks a small thorn into his hand or foot and by so doing bewitches the hunter and transmits to him the power of doing evil to others. But a person never knows he has been so bewitched by the *na losa falaya* until his actions make it evident.

The *na losa falaya* have many children, which, when quite young, possess a peculiar power. They possess the power of removing their viscera at night, and in this lightened condition, they become rather small, luminous bodies that may often be seen along the borders of marshes.

MANLIKE CREATURE

TERRY BEN   1997

I remember one unique story that my grandfather used to tell over and over in the early days, as far as when he was hunting.

Toward Jackson, the Pearl River gets wider and wider as it goes to the Ross Barnett Reservoir. The swamp, also in that area, is big even now; it's a big swampy area.

And I guess in the past, at some point, they would go hunting there, and they'd be just miles and miles away from the nearest house or cabin. During that time period—talking about maybe in the twenties and thirties, forties—a group of men might, you know at nighttime, after they finished eating, they would sit around and talk about the day's events or talk about women or whatever. And then somebody would tend to the campfire. And maybe around midnight or so, they would retire and go to sleep.

But during that time period, there was a unique creature who supposedly lived way in the swamp during that time period—a manlike creature that had a tail. Everybody knew about it in that time period, and there was a certain name he gave that creature, but I forgot.

Anyway, he would come out of the forest area, the swamp area where the campfire light was, you know, where they were sleeping. Maybe come to the edge of the light and so forth. And he would never do harm to anybody. But everybody knew why that particular creature was there: he was wanting food. And what they did, the last person who maybe fell asleep, was . . . the leftover food for the night, he would leave it off to the side, maybe fifteen, twenty yards away. This creature would come and sit down and just eat. And once it finished eating, it would just go off.

I remember him, again my grandfather, telling me stories like that. He'd seen creatures like that in the old days, time and time again, way in the deep swamp.

OKWA NAHOLLO—WHITE PEOPLE OF THE WATER

HELEEMA (LOUISE CELESTINE)   1909

The *okwa nahollo* dwell in deep pools in rivers and bayous. There is said to be such a place in the Abita River. The pool is clear and cold, and it is easy to see far down into the depths; but the surrounding water of the river is dark and muddy. Many of the *okwa nahollo* live in this pool, which is known to all the Choctaw.

As their name signifies, the *okwa nahollo* resemble White people more than they do Choctaw; their skin is rather light in color, resembling the skin of a trout.

When the Choctaw swim in the Abita near the pool, the *okwa nahollo* attempt to seize them and to draw them down into the pool to their home, where they live and become *okwa nahollo*. After the third day, their skin begins to change and soon resembles the skin of a trout. They learn to live, eat, and swim in the same way as fish.

Whenever the friends of a person who has become one of the *okwa nahollo* gather on the riverbank near the pool and sing, he often rises to the surface and talks with them, sometimes even joining in the singing. But after living in the pool three days, the newly made *okwa nahollo* cannot leave it for any length of time. If they should go out of the water, they would die after the manner of fish for they cannot live in the air.

Heleema, one of the women living at Bayou Lacomb, claims that when a child, some forty years ago, she had an experience with the *okwa nahollo*. She related it with the greatest sincerity.

One summer day, when she was seven or eight years of age, she was swimming in the Abita with many other Choctaw children. She was a short distance away from the others when suddenly she felt the *okwa nahollo* drawing her down. The water seemed to rise about her, and she was struggling and endeavoring to free herself when some of her friends, realizing her danger and the cause of it, went to her assistance and, seizing her by the hair, drew her to the shore.

Never again did the children go swimming near the pool where this incident occurred.

BIG POND

JEFFIE SOLOMON   1997

Well, in front of this house was a big pond.

And at dusk they usually heard a rooster crowing, and they heard a drum beating, it was said.

So then the pond way over there [*she points outside*] was very huge. The White people drained it.

And when the water was almost gone, a big snake that had laid there slithered [*out and away*].

Then it was said there was a big ditch laid out there, they used to talk about.

So when the water was all gone, there lay an *oka nahollo*, they used to say.

THE WATER CHOCTAW

ESBIE GIBSON   1997

Between Union, there is a lady with long hair. There was a creek, and a log lay in the creek beside our house. Whenever somebody is walking, they can see the woman with long hair combing her hair. Then she'll jump in the water. [*laughter*]

How we lived was, when the Water Choctaw took the child, if you follow, you must have a stick to know your direction. If she takes them this way, they can follow the sticks that was laid.

Those women told it, so it must be true.

The log that is in the creek, the limbs are long. If the roots were long, follow it to the water. She'll put them in her house, lay them down.

Then a *hopaii* must go to get them.

They can come steal you from the house.

The Water Choctaw, if they caught him, is not like a real person; he's like a creature.

THE MERMAID

JESSICA MILLER   2024

My parents were at Nanih Waiya Cave at that time. They had some commotion going on, and I guess my dad and my mom had a little argument. My dad was about to leave my mom at the cave, but when my dad seen the mermaid, he turned around, trying to go pick my mom back up because he got scared. And they both got scared at the same time because mom has seen it too.

So when they seen that mermaid . . . the mermaid had half a human body, and the bottom was like a fish tail. So the long hair . . . [she] was sitting on top of the rocks. And that mermaid was sitting there combing her hair.

And then next thing you know, when I was asking my mom a couple days later about it, she was like, "Yeah, we seen it, but it was a human face and that we could see, but it seemed . . . " Well, I guess when they got out of contact with each other, the mermaid jumped in the water.

VOICES ON THE MOUND

JESSICA MILLER   2024

We used to hear stuff on top of the cave mound, getting on nighttime. We hear people playing stickball; we hear people singing. Same thing as the Nanih Waiya Mound, like nighttime when it's real dark. That's when it comes out like singing, hollering, and everything; the spirits be coming up at nighttime.

It's kind of creepy to me because I never experienced that until I got to Nanih Waiya Mound. It was in my teens, and it was like a family get-together, and it was nighttime. When nighttime comes, we was all talking, laughing, joking.

When we got loud, we started hearing people on top of the mound singing and hollering. When we got quiet, their voice was going down; they would quiet a little bit. And then we get started louder, then they get louder too. That's how it was when we was out there.

THE LONG-HAIRED LADY

JESSICA MILLER   2024

I have seen a spirit before with my own eyes. And I got scared because see, okay . . .

One time—I don't know what month it was; I don't know what year it was, but it was really raining hard; it was storming. And me and my friend ran that back way going to Nanih Waiya Mound. And there used to be a tree there, but it's not there anymore. It used to be a big old tree sitting by itself. And there was a lady standing there with the long hair, with the long hair, just standing there. And it's pouring down hard, and I wanted to turn around and see whoever the lady was, trying to maybe use a phone because she had her head down looking at something in her hand. But I never turned around to look.

But then when my friend was like, "Let's go see." I'm like, "What about we see something else?" you know? And then I'm like, "I don't know if I want to turn around." But she's like, "Let's go see." But it was pouring down hard, but I'm like, "Why is that lady standing right there?" Maybe she needs some help, you know? But we never turned around and never went to go see because that lady had long, long hair. Like past the knees.

Yeah, I've seen them before.

PA̱Š FALAYA

CYNTHIA CLEGG   1997

Cynthia: This story is about my *hokni*. Do you know what *hokni* means?
Children: Yes, yes—"grandma."
Cynthia: Grandma is *pokni. Pokni.*
Children: *Pokni.*
Cynthia: My *hokni* had died. *Hokni* is "aunt."

She told me. She passed away years ago. And she told me this story when I was little. See, I'm from Tucker, and my aunt was from Tucker. So then, she said to me, she had been sick and her *ičo̱kašat* was not well. Do you all know what *ičo̱kaš* is?

Children: No.
Cynthia: *Ičo̱kaš* is your heart.

And her heart was not well. And that's what my grandparents died from. They died of a heart attack. So we were scared because she was sick.

So anyway, she lived in this old wood-frame house. And the house was like this [*motions with her hand*]. Door—*okkisa* means "door"—the door stood like this, and the living room was like this. And what was supposed to be the dining room, a table was supposed to stand there, they put her bed there. So that's where she slept. And the door was like this, the wall, and the window was here. [*She motions with her hands to describe the layout of the house.*]

From the dining room you could see whoever came over toward the door.

So anyways what she told me was that one night, *o̱batoh* [it rained].
What is *o̱ba*?

Children: "Rain."
Cynthia: *Hilóhatoh* [It was thundering].

What is *hilóha*?

Children: "Thunder."
Cynthia: *Malattatoh* [It was lightning].

Children: "Lightning."
Cynthia: Lightning. It said, "Boom."

She was asleep. It was almost dawn.

So then she said she woke up. Then she said something went "boom, boom, boom" at the door. And she said she wondered, "What am I hearing?" Then she laid there.

Someone knocked again. It came to the door.

And it rained hard; it was raining so hard that you just couldn't see good outside.

So she said she sat up then stood up. And she said it seemed as if someone arrived.

"Who would be so crazy to come out in this rain?" she thought.

Then she went to the window. And there was a curtain on the window, so she quietly opened, like this [*pantomimes pulling a curtain to the side*], and she looked out.

And at the front door, from the sideways, she said she could see it this way. And she said a tall man was standing there. And he was wearing a black hat, and his hair was long hair.

So when she said "Pąši Falaya," I thought she was talking about my grandma's great-uncle because he died long, long time ago. But he was a medicine man, and his name was Pąš Falaya.

What is *pąš falaya* in Choctaw?

Children: "His hair is long."
Cynthia: "Long hair," yes.

That's who I thought she was talking about. I wondered was it him who came and revealed himself to her.

But she said that when she looked, with the curtain this way [*she pantomimes pulled to the side*], he stood there. And when a tall man with a long, black coat to his knees, was standing there, when she looked at him in this way, his eyes were like this. [*Cynthia rolls her eyes back into her head so only the whites show.*]

Only the whites of his eyes were showing. And it was like this [*repeats gesture; kids all scream*]. Only the whites of his eyes were showing. He didn't have no pupils.

It was said that when she saw that, she was frightened.

But she wondered, "What will I do?"

She said that when she wondered, "Why is he showing himself to me?" she went back to bed, and she was laying there.

She said that the knock stopped, and she just fell asleep.

Then when it was morning, she said she didn't tell anyone about it.

It was several days later, she told me about it.

Her son was certainly sick. So it was he who was possibly going to die, she said. Maybe that is the message he is bringing, she said. But he never passed away.

It was several months later when it was she who passed away. And she passed away; she died.

Child: How?
Cynthia: Her heart; her heart was not good.
Child: Who died?
Cynthia: My aunt.

After she told me that, when she told me only the whites of his eyes were showing, she said, "I was scared, and I could not go to sleep that night."
So when I see movies today, and if it is about ghosts, I get scared when I see it. [*She rolls her eyes back into her head, and the kids scream.*]

Children: Do it again!
Cynthia: One last time. [*She does it again, and the kids scream.*]
Children: Do it again one more time.
Cynthia: It was like this. [*She does it again, and the kids scream.*]

But that's my story, and that's a true story because it was my aunt who told me. That's a true story.

Child: That was true?
Cynthia: It was a true story.

NISHKIN CHAFA—ONE-EYE

REGINA SHOEMAKE   1997

Well, that *nishkin chafa* I was telling you about?

We were playing. It was at my sister's wedding, and we were playing I guess hide-and-seek. And we went toward the back of the house; because the house was sitting this way [*indicates layout of house and road with her hands*], but the road came to the back of the house. But they were having the wedding at the front of the house. So all were running toward there.

We came upon, at the edge of the yard, kind of going toward the woods, there was this real shiny, round thing. It was so shiny, all of us noticed it—not men, but the kids.

So we were asking each other what it was because we didn't know. We started toward it, and then it became big, wide. And so, we all just got scared, screaming, ran back. So I don't know what happened to it.

But find out later, that's what it was. But at that time, I didn't know.

Another time, we were on our way back from the movie. This car we were in, bunch of us teenagers, and when a hill . . . the car wouldn't make it. So, they rolled the car back down the hill; and then they were going to try to bring it up.

In the meantime, we got out, and we got the car up toward the hill, and there was the same thing. And we all stopped. And the guys were wanting to throw things at it, but us girls knew that our parents had told us not to throw things at it because it would multiply, or it would chase us and all that.

But anyway, they went ahead, and they said they were going to. So we were looking at it, and it had gotten big. And then, all of a sudden, it turned into a man and just went like that [*she imitates him grinning*] and walked toward them.

And the boys shouted, "Hey. Hey. I know who you are." And they started calling the person's name but never did look back; it just went on.

That was my experience. I was fine then, but, you know.

And then another time, my kids, and boys, were playing in back of this house.

What they said—I knew what they were talking about because they said they saw this, and they went toward it, and they decided to throw rocks at it. And they did, and it multiplied, and it started chasing them. And they got so scared, they had to get law and order to call an ambulance, and they had to bring them in, to the hospital.

But then when they [the boys] got here, because they [the hospital staff] didn't understand, and they didn't know, they kind of laugh at it. But they had to give them some kind of shot, calm them.

But that happened to them, still—my son and his friends.

HEADLESS MAN

MELFORD FARVE   1997

There was a kind of a little legend there for a while. I don't know the story about it; there just seems to be a figure that shows here and there, over there. You can't really look at him; if you do, people will get sick and die or something like that, if you look directly at him.

My dad told me that story one time.

Him and his sisters had come from the store. At that time, it was still light, but by the time they started getting home, it was getting dark.

And back then there was no security lights and stuff. And it was a dirt road, and it was kind of a hilly road.

At that time, the moon was coming out. It was shining pretty good, so they saw somebody walking up ahead. So they figured it was some old man that usually walks—lives close in, and he is always walking on the road. So they said—they were scared—so they said, "Let's go catch up with him, and we can walk home with him."

So, they said as soon as they start running, and they were about to catch up with him, when the figure was just going on top of the hill on the road, they were about to catch up.

And that's when the moon was the brightest around that area.

He was walking, but they said they saw . . . they didn't see a head. He was just walking.

And they stopped dead in their tracks and went the other way.

THE INHUMAN *NA LOSA CHITO*

JEFFIE SOLOMON   1997

Na losa chito. They used to talk about it.

And this road that lies here—if someone was walking on the road, that someone would meet something inhuman-like. When it was happening like that, they became unable to speak. They were beginning to be like that, it used to be.

So then, they had been looking for a medicine man. That medicine man said he would go catch it. So he prepared and was ready to go, but there was nobody to help him carry his supplies. Although it was said that one man was getting ready, there was no one to help carry the supplies, so they did not go.

That's all.

THE DEMON *NA LOSA CHITO*

HAROLD COMBY   1997

There's a lot of stories. Like this road here. My mother used to live at the edge of this road here, right behind present-day Chahta construction. And she says that we have a demon, I guess. Choctaw has a demon called *na losa chito*, which means "big, black thing." I guess. There was a devil, I guess, according to the Choctaws.

She says that one night, the mules got out, so all the cows got out. And her mom and her sisters came, and the dogs came, and found the mules.

As they were going back, they saw something on the side of the road. And they got closer to it, and that thing was just like a . . . She said it was almost like a black cow with red eyes. And she said it smelled like mud.

But the dogs wouldn't get close to that thing. So they just kept on. The mother recognized what it was and said, "Don't be scared, or you're going to have convulsions, seizures."

So they started walking, and she said one of her sisters started to run because she was scared. And she fell down, and she had a seizure. So they had to carry her too.

As they continued on, that thing just kept on getting bigger and taller and taller. And she says the dogs were even scared of that animal or whatever it was. They couldn't get close to that animal.

Once they got close to the house, toward the light area, that thing just went away.

And she still says that even though we live in the twenty-first century, there's some strange animals in the swamps. Like big snakes or small horses or whatever. And she says that's those medicine men's helpers.

A BIG HOG

GLADYS WILLIS   1996

Even what they call *na losa chito*—it's "a big, black thing" in English. *Na losa chito*, that's "big, black thing." It can turn to a hog or any kind of animal. But they said you don't fool with that because they have some kind of power, that they would spread that power, and it smells bad, and they can kill. When you hear something like that, you just don't go near it.

Used to, in the hot weather, we used to sleep out on the porch, when we was living over there. We used to sleep on the porch.

But one night, I don't know, we all wasn't asleep yet, we was just laying there. And my husband called—Rae's Grandpa [*laughter*]—said he heard something coming. And he said, "Lay very still, and don't say anything."

I was just wondering what it was. And pretty soon, there was something like if you had heard a hog, a big hog, trying to breathe.

And it came closer; and I would have said something. "It's a hog," I would say. [*laughter*] But he jerked me.

I was real still. And it came right by the porch. It came back that way and come past through here. And we could hear when it went up this way, and we could still hear him. And that's where he passed.

He said, "I told y'all not to talk."

And everybody said, "We didn't talk."

And, "Uh-huh. Somebody liked to say something."

That's what it was.

I said, "It's a hog." [*laughter*] Uh-huh.

BIG, BLACK, HAIRY MONSTER

TERRY BEN   1984

Close to a small road leading from Conehatta to Lake was a swamp in the middle where strange things were said to have happened.

One night, a man was riding through the area with his wagon and mules. He was whistling to himself, trying not to think of the stories associated with that place, when he heard a sound coming from the darkness behind him. He turned and saw something that made his heart skip some beats. He saw the big, black, hairy monster called *na losa chito* running after him and catching up easily.

The man coaxed his mules to pick up speed while trying not to show that he was terrified. When he looked behind again, he saw that the monster had reached the wagon and was climbing aboard. Seeing this, the man became so frightened that he jumped from the wagon onto one of his mules. Taking another look back, he saw that the monster was sitting in the same place that he had been sitting a moment ago. The creature was holding the reins, and it appeared that he was trying to take control of the wagon.

The man knew that one of his mules became easily frightened, so he covered the mule's eyes with his hands.

Finally, they were leaving the swamp and entering a populated area, and as they did, the man looked back again, and the creature was gone.

BLACK DOG

THERON "DUKE" DENSON   2021

Now some people swear that *na losa chito* is real. I don't know what their description of *na losa chito* is, but I've often heard that *na losa chito* can change forms. One minute, he can be a dog. One minute, he can be a bird. But that's the thing that *na losa chito* would do.

So this man—and my mother swears it was true, and she was there—after he had gone berserk and they had to chase him, he'd be way over here shouting, hollering. And then men would go there to arrest him. But he'd run away and be way over here somewhere, hollering. Finally, he came running by. They all chased him. They all caught up to him and tied him down. Tied his hands, tied his legs. He went to sleep.

So the next day, he said [what had happened]. He was walking down Highway 16, which is right up here [*points outside his home towards the highway*]. And he saw a black dog that met him on the road. He said he kicked the dog, and all of a sudden, before he knew it, there was a coffin, casket, right in front of him, right in the middle of the road. He stood there and looked at his own body; it was inside of a casket. That's when he went crazy.

So that's when he started running around. He ran for miles. They chased him. They finally caught up to him.

That was the story. It was *na losa chito* changing shape.

CHOCTAW BIGFOOT

THERON "DUKE" DENSON   2021

My story about *na losa chito* is what I witnessed myself back in 1972.

Me and some other boys were camping out back in the early '70s. There was nothing to do. Nothing. There was nothing here. So we had to find something to do. So camping out was a big thing. I had a camp at Beaver Dam. I had these brand new World War II army tents. They were just given out. I took several of them.

We had a camping place on Beaver Dam. We had another camping place at the intersection by the school where the electrical power station is. Beyond there is a trail that goes all the way near to the back of the casino there.

We were out there. We just got there. We had some of the older boys. We had to pitch in a dollar or two dollars, whatever money we had, so we could get beer. So we got our beer. We went into the woods, find a nice clear space. Two loggers had come and cut up all the wood that they needed. And all the ones that they didn't need, they was lying all over the place. Limbs. So we gathered all that up; we built a fire. The fire was yea high [*motions with his hand*]. It was firing up about four feet, I guess. It shined around us. We sat there drinking our beer, talking.

All of a sudden, one boy said, "What's that?"

Everybody got up, stood up and looked. They just all started running. Me and my friend Henry Bucksy Bell, we didn't see anything. At first, I thought they were pulling a trick on us. So we just stood there. All of a sudden, we hear snap of a twig or something. So we look at the direction where the snap came. There was a creature standing there which was eight, nine, ten feet tall. Very, very big and huge. Hairy. You could almost see the hair glistening from the fire.

We looked at it for maybe two or three seconds. We ran down the trail. That creature was right beside us all the way out to the highway.

So that's my story about *na losa chito*. But today, *na losa chito* is what people know as Sasquatch or Bigfoot. In the northwest area of this country, the natives call them Sasquatch. But here in the southern part of the United States, I think especially Choctaws, call them *na losa chito*. So that's what we saw.

I saw that myself, and my mother's seen one. My sister that was here, she's seen them many times. And her daughter has seen them three times.

They all saw it all in my mother's yard. It was during the daytime or nighttime; they were not just one. They were two or a group of them that were living in the woods behind my mother's house, right by the water theme park, that little speck of woods. They were living there for a good week before they moved on.

NA LOSA CHITO'S LAIR

THERON "DUKE" DENSON   2021

There's a graveyard called Isaac's Cemetery.

My cousin was looking for metal. He could trade metal for money. He was looking for metal, and they had made a dumpster out of there.

Anyway, he said he heard a growling noise. It was a deep kind of throaty growling. He said he never heard that before. So he was a little scared. Might have been a bear or something. So he walked to the road and turned around and started recording it with his cell phone.

Sure enough, we saw it. It's about a minute long. A creature just standing there, just standing still, just standing there. Every once in a while, the creature will be turning its head like this [*turns his head slowly side to side*].

The professional Bigfoot hunters came. They slowed the video down. They said, "It's not only that; this one here is a female" because they saw the breasts on it. They said, "This little black spot right there behind the bush is actually a male," because when he was panning back and forth real fast, one time he stood up, and he went back behind the bushes. But it's so fast, you couldn't tell.

So we had that video. I don't know what happened to that one. But I believe that was the best video of Bigfoot ever made. Besides the Roger Patterson one.

So some weeks later, we decided, we'll go look for him. We found a lair, teepee structure. Big, big thing. Big. You could put several people in there. Well, Matt Jackson was just videotaping it with his cell phone. I left early. I said, "Well, I'm going to go to the car because my knee hurts." He said, "I'll be there in a minute." So I got there, and a few minutes later, he showed up.

About midnight that night, he called and said, "Hey, you got to look at this." He brought his laptop. We was looking at the video through the laptop. He said, "Look what it's going to do." You could see the legs moving like this [*moves hands up and down*] under some bushes. But you couldn't see the top of the body. But you could see the leg walking. He went behind the bush in this big old pine tree. This whole thing took about a good five, ten minutes. He said, "Look what he's going to do. He's going to poke his head out behind the tree." So we had to wait several minutes, and finally, he did like this [*imitates poking his head up*]. Went back. He said, "Watch it again." About a minute or two later, he came out and poked his head out behind the pine tree.

He said, "Now watch this." The creature from behind all them bushes and pine tree walked in full view, was just standing there watching. We didn't even see it. He took a video of it. He didn't realize there was this creature standing there watching. We saw it in video. So this is another example of *na losa chito*.

THE BLACK STUMP

NELLIE BILLY   1997

In order to understand this story, it is important to note that Nellie Billy told this story in Choctaw. She plays with the double meaning of na losa chito. *As a single term, it indicates a supernatural being, but the words separately mean simply "big, black thing." Nellie Billy exploits this ambiguity in her story. To attempt to convey this ambiguity, I have capitalized* Big, Black Thing *only toward the end, when she explicitly intends to refer to the supernatural being.*

When I was a little child, maybe about your size, it was dark, but my mom wanted to go see her mom, and we went. We went through the woods.

At night it's real dark in the woods, isn't it?

And when the screech owls were making sounds, and the large owls were making sounds, I was real scared, but I went along. And we walked in the woods; we did not walk on a road.

Then we went through a cow pasture. And there was a big, black thing standing in the cow pasture. And we were frightened even more. And we did not want to go that way because the big, black thing was there, we thought it would be coming.

And we were not going along the road, but we got scared and went to the road. Walking on the road, we went. We went through the woods wanting to get there faster. But since we were afraid, we had to go on the road.

So finally, we made it to my grandma's house.

And that was the first thing we told her because we were scared.

"There was a Big, Black Thing standing there; we were frightened."

But my grandmother laughed at us. "There is a tree that someone had burned, always standing there," she said, and laughed at us.

So it was a burned tree stump that was standing that we were afraid of.

We thought it was a Big, Black Thing [*laughs*]. It was a tree, but we got scared.

When a tree is burnt, it is black, isn't it? Yes. That was what was standing, but we were scared.

It wasn't a ghost, but we thought it was a ghost, but it was a burnt tree standing there.

That's all.

THE CHOCTAW ROBIN GOODFELLOW

UNKNOWN [HALBERT]   1895

The Choctaws in Mississippi say that there is a little man, about two feet high, that dwells in the thick woods and is solitary in his habits. This little sprite or hobgoblin is called by the Choctaws *bohpoli*, or *kowi anukasha*, both names being used indifferently or synonymously. The translation of *bohpoli* is the "thrower." The translation of *kowi anukasha* is "the one who stays in the woods," or, to give a more concise translation, "forest dweller."

Bohpoli is represented as being somewhat sportive and mischievous but not malicious in his nature. The Choctaws say that he often playfully throws sticks and stones at the people. Every mysterious noise heard in the woods, whether by day or night, they ascribe to *bohpoli*. He takes special pleasure, they say, in striking the pine trees.

A young Indian once told me that one night, whilst camped in the woods, he was awakened out of a deep sleep by a loud noise made on a pine tree by *bohpoli*.

Bohpoli, or *kowi anukasha*, is never seen by the common Choctaws. The Choctaw prophets and doctors, however, claim the power of seeing him and of holding communication with him. The Indian doctors say that *bohpoli* assists them in the manufacture of their medicines. Most Choctaws say or think that there is but one *bohpoli*. In the opinion of others, there may be more than one.

THE LITTLE PEOPLE IN NANIH WAIYA CAVE

TERRY BEN   1996

Anytime my grandfather would get together with some of his old friends, they would talk about the Nanih Waiya Cave Mound. And I can remember one thing I'll let you know right off the bat, you know, there's two openings there at the cave mound, I guess the major opening in the front area.

Anytime there's going to be a big old storm coming, lightning, thundering and all that, supposedly maybe at the edge of the woods in front of the mound opening area, if a person would hide, those legendary little people we were talking about, they would live inside the mound supposedly, and they would come out. And I guess the lightning and thundering, rain and all that, really turns them on. So they come out of the mound. And supposedly, you could maybe hear them or see them dance and just having a good time outside. But you had to remain hidden.

And so that's one thing I do remember out of conversations with the older men that my grandfather had a long time ago.

And supposedly, my grandfather used to say, inside the mound was a big old huge snake that held guard over the bones of the dead ancestors. If someone wandered into the cave area, then supposedly they could not get out. These were some of the things older generations of Choctaws told him, and you know, he told me about the cave mound area.

The cave mound area is the sacred mound area.

DOORS IN NANIH WAIYA CAVE

JESSICA MILLER   2024

Inside the cave mound, my uncle went out there. Nobody can't tell him nothing. So he went in there. But when he went in there, he said it was some doors. Their doors was there.

And it had some water in there already because I know. We peeked in, and there's water in there already. But we didn't know there was doors was in there.

So he came and told us that there was some doors in there because he was trying to look for gold because somebody was telling him that it was some gold in there. So he was trying to go look for it. [*laugh*] But he didn't find any, I don't think, because he couldn't open the door because the water was inside.

WATCHER IN THE WOODS

CARMEN DENSON   2000

I don't know if he's joking with me, but one other guy, he's my nephew, he said one time he saw the little people.

You know the Pearl River creek? It runs through Carthage, near Carthage. He was out there fishing. He turned and felt somebody was looking at him. He was standing on a tree that was kind of slanted over the creek, over Pearl River. He wanted a better position, so he climbed up there and was fishing there. And he kind of felt somebody was looking at him. Over the back, he turned around, and one of those guys was standing there. He said he looked peculiar. He turned and looked again, and he was gone.

THROWING ROCKS

TRAVIS WILLIS   2021

My aunt and their family used to live on what is called Gym Road now.

Me and my cousins, we were playing out in the woods one day, and my cousin Barbara, she was running. We were all running around in the woods. And next thing we heard, she screamed out. Something caught her right here [*points to forehead*].

She said it felt like a rock. Never saw where it came from. We looked for that thing for almost two hours, never could find that rock. But she had a big old knot on her forehead.

> Tom: What did y'all do?
> Travis: We got out of the woods. [*laugh*]
> Tom: Did you tell your parents?
> Travis: No, but they saw. We didn't have to tell them nothing. They saw.

> And they knew what it was. So instead of taking her to the traditional [medical] doctor, they took her to this one [Choctaw doctor]. That's what it was [*bohpoli*]. That's what they told them.

THROWING COMPETITION

BRIAN BILLIE   2021

There's a story about the little people.

We were outside, me and Jamie and Jarrett. We were cleaning up the truck, and it was late at night, two o'clock. We just sat up and just talked about movies and laughing about memories.

We were outside, and all of a sudden, you hear something in the woods. Sound like zipping through the woods. And all of a sudden, you hear a big thump. And I hear a big thump, and I was like, "Jamie, you hear that?"

He goes, "Yeah."

I said, "It keeps going, and then it stops, and it hits something, and it stops."

He goes, "That's in the woods, right?"

I said, "Yeah."

Jamie or Jarrett, one of them said, "I was always told that's the little people playing their game."

I said, "What game?"

They said, "They'll be competing to see who can throw the rock..." or the boulder, or the stumps... no, the rock. "They would throw the rock and try to get a hit, knock the stump out, or something."

Ná oklah ittipaknah. Hikma nana zip awah kaniyah mat mash pilah átok. Hikma ish haklokmat ot issa tokosh pilah átok. Ittipaknat ásha kiyọ. Abohli yot ish haklokma washóhash ásha hattak sipokni. ["They're competing, and something like a zip, that one threw it," they said. "And when you hear it [the thump], it [*bopholi*] hits it [the stump], so he throws it [the rock]," they said.]

NO PLAYING AFTER DARK

DAN ISAAC   2021

I think some of the stories that were told was to teach what I call "values," how to treat elders, how to treat the young people. You got to always watch our kids.

There was so many different stories that was told so that children could think about how they're acting, how they're behaving. If you aren't really following what grandma and grandpa said, there are some stories that were scary. So you would be scared.

I remember our grandpa would say not to be out there playing when you are kids. You can't be playing at night because there's things out there. And he would tell us, and we would kind of see proof sometimes because they were telling the truth. What we called the little people. *Bohpoli*. So I remember he used to tell me stories, and I'd be scared.

He said, "Remember that little fire you built out there?"

And I said, "Yeah."

"So, watch that fire."

And I'm like, I'd look out the window, that little fire would flicker a little bit. You could almost see a small being run by or walk by behind it. And it just terrified me. I'm like, "I'm not going to be outside no more."

I still tell that to my kids. As soon as the sun goes down, even if they want to shoot basketball or play outside, "Y'all come on in. You know, grandpa always said kids can't be out there playing if it's dark, it's nighttime. There's things out there." Just to teach them to take care of their kids or that they are sacred, and they need to be watched.

THE FLOATING LIGHT

JAKE YORK   1997

I remember telling somebody this, I don't know if it was you or not, about my dad, used to go out hunting, and about this light that was following him and his friends.

He used to go out hunting, way at night. Or they would set out hooks, and they would check it. He had a White friend that lived nearby, lived on Blackjack Road, too—almost at the end of Blackjack Road where it meets 16. He used to go fishing with my dad a lot. They'd go set out hooks and they'd go check. Well, there was hardly any road leading out to where they set out their hooks; it was just little old trails and stuff. He used to take guns along, the White guy did.

So I guess on one of those nights, they went out to check on their hooks. They were using this old carbide light; they call it carbide lights. They each had one.

They went and checked their hooks out, and they were coming back, and they said—well, back around Beaver Dam area, near the river, I mean the woods is thick. I mean it is dark. The moon's out, and the leaves would cover the trail.

They were walking back, and it was dark, but they said a light, it seemed like, was coming.

They turned around and there was this light among the trees. And they said, "That can't be the moon. It's kind of too low for the moon."

I guess they, through stories you've heard, kind of knew what it was. Well, he kind of knew what it was, but he said, "Let's keep on walking."

And it seemed like that thing, light, kept coming closer to them.

And that White guy said, "I'm going to shoot at it."

He said, "Don't." He said, "You better not." Whatever it was, it would probably go away.

And he said the gun jammed on him. It wouldn't fire. And the carbide light started going out.

Well, anyway, they just started walking. And then the carbide light started faintly coming back on. But that thing kept following them, following them.

Finally, they made it up to a little better clearing than where they were traveling. It seemed like it stopped where they got to that clearing, and it went off.

And they got back almost to that main road, and that guy said, "I wonder what was wrong with this gun?" And he was pulling up, pointing it up in the air, and they said that gun fired.

I guess he asked my dad what it was. And they said the old stories says that, like *bohpoli*, little people, they can shift, change—shift-changer or something like that—where they can maybe turn into light or something. They said that some *bohpoli* have that power; they can do that, or they can change themselves into a light and follow you like that, they said. He had heard stories from his grandmother and father and mother and stuff like that.

But anyway, he said that incident happened to them.

The guy, while they were in the woods, when they saw the light, he tried to fire, but the gun wouldn't fire 'til they got to the clearing. That light went away, and he pulled the trigger and the gun worked fine.

LIGHTS

GUS COMBY   1984

Out by the Neshoba County Fairgrounds, there was a house that had been empty for years. We lived near it.

One night I could not sleep, and my wife said, "Gus, if you can't sleep, why don't you go get us a possum?"

So I got dressed and went out into the woods. I was near that old house where no one had lived for years.

A long, green light showed, then a maroon light, and then an orange light. It was floating along, and it had been in that old house.

KOWI ANUKASHA

AHOJEOBE (EMIL JOHN)   1909

Kowi anukasha is the name of a little spirit—a man, but no larger than a child two or three years of age. His home is in a cave under large rocks, in a rough, broken part of the country.

Now, when a child is two or three or even four years old, it is often sick, and then runs away from its home and goes among the trees. When the little one is well out of sight of home, *kowi anukasha*, who is on the watch, seizes it and leads it away to his dwelling place. In many instances they have to travel a considerable distance through the country.

When *kowi anukasha* and the child enter the spirit's home they are met by three other spirits, all very old, with white hair. Approaching the child, the first offers it a knife; the second a bunch of herbs, all poisonous; the third a bunch of herbs yielding good medicine.

Now, if the child accepts the knife, he is certain to become a bad man, and may even kill his friends. If he takes the bunch of poisonous herbs, he will never be able to cure or otherwise help others; but if he waits and accepts the good herbs, then he is destined to become a great doctor and an important and influential man of his tribe, and to have the confidence of all his people. In this event, *kowi anukasha* and the three old spirits tell him how to make use of the herbs—the secrets of making medicines of the roots and leaves, and of curing and treating various fevers and pains.

The child remains with the spirits three days, after which he returns to his home, but does not tell where he has been or what he has seen and heard. Not until the child has become a man will he make use of the knowledge gained from the spirits, but never will he reveal to others how it was acquired.

The Choctaw say that few children wait to accept the offering of the good herbs from the third spirit, and hence there are comparatively few great doctors and other men of influence among them.

MEDICINE WOMAN

ESTELLINE TUBBY   1976

My mother used to talk about my grandmother and how she became a medicine woman. Her name was Louisa Phillips, and she lived to be a hundred and four years old before she died. When she was a little girl, she used to roam around a lot in the fields and other places that were isolated.

One day a strange thing happened to her. While she was walking in the woods, she heard people laughing. It became louder and louder as she approached it. She got very scared.

Then a strange thing happened. Out of nowhere, a cloud of dust forming a funnel-like shape as if it was a tornado appeared. It hurled around with great speed and went in a thicket of bushes.

The cloud of dust disappeared.

At least that's what my grandmother thought.

She then started toward the bushes where the cloud had vanished. The thorn bushes were making a lot of noises, as if they were alive or something. For some reason or another she happened to look in front of her and there stood an old woman, carrying a pipe, coming her way.

After she saw her coming, she did not stay. She ran home like she never ran before in her life.

When she got home, she was still in a daze and told her mother. Her mother told her that it was a sign informing her that as long as she lived, she would never be hungry or poor.

From then on, my grandmother knew what was to be done. She had to become a medicine woman.

THE LITTLE MAN

TERRY BEN   1996

I was about eleven or twelve, and this was the year I got my first gun. My granddad had certain guns, and he let me have a single-shot .22 bolt action.

I was a big man, all right?

And so he had a couple of hunting dogs. I remember two. He had real excellent hunting dogs, and there were two.

And this was about maybe November, as I remember it. This was on a Saturday afternoon and maybe around maybe five, six o'clock.

Anyway, from the house to the woods, it was about maybe half a mile away. So I took my dogs, Chester-22, and some shells in my pocket, and I went on to the woods. And as I crossed the fence into the woods, there were a lot of just, leaves on the ground and so forth. So when you stepped on the leaves, it just made all kind of sounds, all right? So I tried not to make any sounds. And I was hunting squirrel.

Anyway, my two dogs were going in front of me, just with their noses up in the air, just going all over like that, you know? I was hunting for squirrel. And of course I had my rifle, just taking every couple of steps and standing there listening, and so forth like that.

And all of sudden, I heard some thuds.

And I was going into the neighbor's land anyway. He allowed me to hunt on his land anyway. He had cows and all that, and so he was probably working—maybe a fence broke down; maybe he's putting some posts into the ground or whatever. Maybe he's digging a ditch, whatever. I thought of that.

So I walked a little bit further, toward the sound, you know. I moved a couple of feet.

It was beginning to get a little bit dark. Again, it's in November, and I'd just listen maybe for some talking and so forth like that. And I didn't hear anything like that. The thud, maybe every, maybe thirty seconds, there'd be a big old thud like somebody hitting something into the ground.

And, you know, I'm thankful; even now I've got twenty-twenty vision. You know, way back then, I still had twenty-twenty vision. So I had good hearing, and so forth, and even now. So, you know, I understood that.

The dogs were just running all over, about fifteen, twenty yards. They didn't find anything, no rabbit or squirrels yet. There was no yapping sound yet.

So, I just looked around.

And I saw a big old stump, maybe that high off the ground [*indicates about a foot*], off to the side, you know. I kind of looked real closely—this is maybe about fifty yards away from where I was standing. There was no brush or any other trees—it was sort of a clear path, where I could see real good. And that's where the thud was coming from.

I looked real, real closely, and I saw a little man, facing the other way toward the stump; and he had a little old pick, and he was digging, like that [*imitates overhand motion of using a pickax*]. And every, whatever, you'd hear a thud. Didn't see the face; he was pointed the other way. He was maybe so tall [*gestures about three feet high*], about fifty yards ahead of me.

The dogs were approaching that little man but nothing—no yaps, no signs of getting mad or signs of getting scared, nothing. They were just running all over, just, looking for squirrels, rabbits, whatever.

And I just looked at it, and it just digging away, like that [*repeats pickax motion*]. Definitely, I knew that's where it was coming from.

I looked around, and I looked around, and hey, maybe it was kids looking for something, whatever, this, that, and all that. That's a Saturday night, five or six o'clock at night; it can't be. I don't see no truck, don't see no other dogs around and so forth. You know, "What's this?"

I got my .22 rifle, put the safety off, aimed right at it at first . . .

Then all these stories that my granddad told me that came into me. If you mess around with these little guys, they're going to throw something at you, they're going to hit you, and you're going to get sick, and you're going to die. There's nothing a Choctaw doctor can do about it.

All these stories came back to me. I was not scared at first, but I started getting scared.

And it's getting darker. Dogs still around; not even a sign that they knew what was there. Did I imagine them? No. Still, something was in front of me.

So, what I did was, I backtracked, slowly at first. But with every step, just a big old squashing sound against nothing but leaves and all that. And at that point, it didn't matter anyway; I was panicking. There was the fence there. I quickly jumped over the fence, I think. Got my gun and just ran off towards the house.

When I got to the house, just right at nightfall, I told my grandparents about it.

And, you know, "What you saw was that little man." You know, "What did I tell you? You go into the woods and so forth, and you'll see one of these, maybe."

And what he told me at that point, may be two things. If I had stuck around there, I might have become a Choctaw doctor. Or there might have been maybe some money there, if I'd stuck around, so they told me.

But he told me that, "Since you ran away and so forth, he will never appear to you again. And since you ran away, whatever was there, you'll never find it again, as such."

The next afternoon, Sunday afternoon, after church, I took my granddad, two dogs, of course a rifle again; and I went to the spot, and I showed him where the stump was. You know, I couldn't find where that stump was. The stump was not there. I could not find that stump.

To this day, every now and then, when I go by there, I would still look for that stump, but that stump's not there.

So that's one of those believe-it-or-nots. But I actually experienced that firsthand, as such. There was fear, all right?

And I've got twenty-twenty vision and so forth, and hearing and all that even now. So back then, you know . . .

And I was sane back then. I'm still sane now. [*laughter*]

So I don't know what it was, but I did experience that as such.

PILE OF ROCKS

JUDY BILLIE   1997

You're not supposed to play with that stuff that they have. Like under the pine tree, they used to have these little rocks, you know? Kind of an eggshell, but it's rocks.

But they're so pretty; and we used to gather them.

You could just, you know, when you look at it, the area looks like little kids are playing there. And the way they stack their rocks, and the way they have it in the surrounding area—it's clean, and they have all kind of shapes of rocks. And they be playing with it. And you know, they have it around.

And we used to go over there.

And my grandparents—it's across the road from my grandparents' house. There was a little brook between my house and my grandparents'. It was like one board that you can walk across. I never had learned how to ride a bicycle, so I couldn't balance myself to walk across that board. And I used to get scared, so I used to take the long way—go to the road and go on the other side, across that, to get to my grandparents'.

They used to tell us not to play with those; and if we do, they used to tell us, "If you play with them, they're going to come after you when you're sleeping." And, "They want you to play with them, so they're going to come after you. And we're not going to know."

And I never understood. I used to not believe what they tell me, so I was just laughing at them. "That's not going to happen," you know. "I don't believe that. There's no little kids playing there."

And they used to say, "Then who is playing with those rocks over there?"

And I said, "We are."

But he said, "No." They said, "Well, next time, when you go over there, mess it up and next day, when you go and look at it, and see how it is."

So we did that.

And that night, I woke up; and without knowing, I had blanket over me, and I walked . . . I got out of the house, and nobody knew. I got out of the house and walked on that board and across that little bridge and went to my . . . I guess I was on my way to that place, where we were playing.

And the dogs had to come out, and they were chasing me and barking at me and everything.

So, my grandpa woke up, and he got up; he got out of the house, and he had a shotgun. So, he walked toward the road, and he saw something walking.

And the dogs were just hanging onto the blanket and pulling me and everything.

So he came towards me, and he said that he talked to me, but I didn't do anything; I just stood there. And he opened the blanket, and it was me, under the blanket. And I acted like I was wide awake.

And to me, you know, it was like daylight; I knew what I was doing; I knew where I was going. But when they woke me up, I couldn't remember anything, and it scared me. And every time I turned around, I looked. You know, all these people had different type of shapes, and it was real scary.

And they had to take me to medicine man, and that medicine man told me that I was sleepwalking, what they call sleepwalking. But they told me I was going out there to play with them. Those little people were around me, but I didn't know. And nobody knew.

But that was so weird because it was like daylight to me. And crossing that little piece of wood—I couldn't believe it. Because I couldn't do it the next day. But it was something like real scary, and they thought I was hallucinating. [*laughter*]

So the next day, they went and checked on it. And those little rocks were in different kind of shapes.

So I quit playing over there. [*laughter*]

A WITCH

GUS COMBY   1984

One time a long time ago, I heard that a turkey came into the yard of some people, and the men shot the turkey. But when they looked, the turkey was gone, and just some blood was left.

They couldn't find anything but blood, so they trailed the blood to a spring or a well and found a woman washing herself. There was blood there, and they followed her to her house where she lived with another woman.

Finally, they found her body in the woods, where she had died. She had died of a gunshot wound.

Many hundreds of years ago, Choctaws could turn into animals. They could put a curse on one another. That woman who turned into a turkey was a witch and didn't like the people whose yard she had entered.

CHOCTAW DOCTORS

TERRY BEN   1996

My uncle told me this, that maybe one night, he was walking from the church of Standing Pine to his house at Standing Pine, and this was night.

I guess he wanted to go home early.

Anyway, when he almost got to the house, he heard a pig, coming down the road, parallel road or whatever, making all kind of piglike sounds and all that.

"Hey, the sound's getting louder and louder. Let's see where the pig came from. Maybe it's one of our pigs that got out," and all that.

Anyway, he just stood there; and as the sound came closer, he just stood there. The sound was almost upon him, I guess, maybe in a curved area, or intersection area. When the sound came into focus, it was a man—a man in the community who was known to be a medicine man. It was him making all those piglike sounds. True piglike sounds.

And the mother asked him, "Hey, I thought I heard some pigs coming down."

"You did."

"Oh yeah? Where is it?"

"You're looking at it."

So the real powerful Choctaw doctors can transform themselves into whatever animal—horse, pig, cow, duck, chicken, owl—whatever they wanted to.

SHAPE CHANGER

MELFORD FARVE   1997

We talked about shape changers too, before.

And I remember talking to a friend of mine. And this was in Standing Pine. There was a guy that told him he could do that; he told him, "I can do that kind of thing."

But the other guy didn't believe him. He said, "Really?" So, he didn't believe him.

So, "OK." He told him to turn around. And so the guy turned around.

And say, "OK. Now, look back at me. Now you can turn around."

So he turned back.

And he had told him the guy was standing there, but his head was like the head of a donkey or something like that, that was right there.

And I don't know how true that was, but stuff like that.

But like I said, belief in the medicine, belief in power—it's been here for a long time, so you can't get away from it; it's something that's always going to be there.

THE BASEBALL GAME

MELFORD FARVE   1997

I remember that they used red pepper or something; sometimes considered some kind of magic, not magic, but like it was an effect or something.

I remember my dad telling me a baseball game they played against this Black team. And this team was pretty good, pretty good hitters and everything. But Dad said that their pitcher was pitching against . . . but he was striking these guys out.

They played each other all that summer, and these guys always . . . every one of them was power hitters.

And this particular game, the pitcher was just fanning them left and right.

And finally, their best hitter got up, and, you know, he was joining in: "Throw that ball," and, "I'm going to knock it over there," and all that kind of stuff.

So he threw it, and he didn't hit it.

The next pitch, same thing: he swung and missed.

And finally, he called timeout, and he walked up to the Choctaw pitcher, and he told him, "Turn around."

So he turned around, and he reached into his back pocket and pulled out a little pouch. When he picked the thing out of the pocket, he threw it to the ground, and he more or less stepped on it, just kind of mashed it up; and then he went back to the batter's box and said, "OK. Now throw it."

So the pitcher reared back, threw the same type fast ball he'd been throwing that was striking people out, and the guy just blasted it out of there.

And then after that, every batter that came up started hitting.

So, I really don't know what to base it on, how some of these things work. Sometimes I think it's a mental thing, you know, makes you believe, makes you maybe do a little bit harder than maybe you're accustomed to. Somebody could give you this thing, saying it's going to give you a little bit of help here or something like that. And it might give you that extra . . . you know, if you think it will. But then again, like I said, there's things we don't understand, so it may be one of those situations.

DANCING LIGHTS

MELFORD FARVE   1997

I think I've told you about how witch doctors get their magic, where they have to have the thing to open up their belly and get their intestines or whatever and place it in a can and leave it in the woods. But, I've seen those things flying around, and usually they say that's what it is.

Well, I've never really seen swamp gas, and we don't really have too many real swamps around this area. But I have seen strange lights. Most of the time it's neon colored. It's almost like a neon; by the time you see it, it's streaking across the treetops or something like that. The lasting impression you have in your mind is just almost like a worm type. You see it, and it's gone, and in your mind, "What did I just see?" You remember it was just a neon kind of a streaky thing.

But I've seen that, I don't know, two or three or four times within my lifetime.

One time, I was just looking, happening to look out my door, my house, my mom's house. And it was as tall as the pine tree, and it seemed to be falling. And it just disappeared.

And I said, "What was that?" And I really looked; and I don't know, I really couldn't explain it.

And when my dad was a watchman for that new elementary school, Pearl River Elementary School, when he was out in the front area, sometimes he'd see those same things, go maybe towards Choctaw Greetings, just something dancing along the tree line, you know.

And at the time, there was an old woman that lived there—eccentric woman. They said she's been known to practice some of those things.

So, he just said once he saw the lights dancing, he said, "Well, that's so-and-so doing that."

HASHOK OKWA HUI'GA—DEW DROP (WILL-O'-THE-WISP)

PISATUNTEMA (EMMA)   1910

There is a certain spirit that lives in marshy places—often along the edges of swamps. It is never seen during the day, only at night, and even then, its heart is the only part visible. Its heart appears as a small ball of fire that may be seen moving about, a short distance above the surface of the water.

At night, when a person is passing along a trail or going through the woods and meets the *hashok okwa hui'ga*, he must immediately turn away and not look at it; otherwise, he will certainly become lost and not arrive at his destination that night, but instead, travel in a circle.

THE BLUE LIGHT

MELFORD FARVE   1997

Another thing, I guess I have an active imagination, but also, I love these UFO stories, and Roswell. I like to throw that at my wife. I drive her crazy with that.

One time my father said they were coming back from the store, when he was still pretty young, maybe five, six years old, maybe four. And his sisters and my grandma, and they were walking back to their house. I guess he'd been tired, so he said, "Carry me."

So my grandma picked him up and, you know, put his arms around her and was carrying him.

And he said, all of a sudden, this blue light just hit him, kind of a spotlight surrounding him.

She put my father down and just like, "Where's the light coming from?"

And then all of a sudden, my grandmother started feeling weak. Then she got down on her knees; she had gotten so weak all of a sudden.

And all of a sudden, the light stopped. And the light was gone.

And they were looking at my grandma; and she was still just woozy and just weak, feeling weak.

Then she felt a little better. And then they started up.

But he said they never knew what that light was. It was just a blue light that engulfed them.

DISAPPEARING LIGHTS

GUS COMBY   1984

A lot of things happened to me when I was younger that I can't explain, and I don't know what they were. I know the difference between those things and my imagination. When it is my imagination, I don't believe it. These things were not my imagination.

There was an old, old church at Red Water, where they used to have singing on Sunday nights. An old Choctaw died, and we went to see him. On the way home, while walking past this church, we heard the singing and saw the lights. We went over to the church, and there was not a person there. The lights went out. We went in and touched a light globe, and it was cold.

LINGERING SPIRIT

TRAVIS WILLIS   2021

Pearl River is right there. The river itself winds along that property. And there's a cemetery on top of the hill, on one of the bluffs.

One time, we went there, and we saw the tombstones, old tombstones. Eighteen something. It was written on it, but I can't remember what it was. But it's way back there in the woods by the river. It was about ten, fifteen stones there. Sometimes back then, they didn't put no stone, or they put a rock or something, and that was it. But these bunch had stones. They were high headstones.

It was me and my brother Hulon. We were out there one day. I guess it was the wind; I don't know, but we were out there, and it sure sounded like somebody was talking. So, we sat there. We shoot a look at each other and took off!

Right at the bluff is where it bends like an S shape, back in there. The water was pretty high that day, too. I figured it was the water. I don't know.

After years, coming back and thinking about it, I said, "It's probably the river that was . . . " But it sounded like somebody was talking.

> **Tom Mould:** So was the thinking at the time that it was spirits from the graveyard or . . .

Yeah, that's what it was.

This I experienced myself. The old Hope Church building, before that new one . . . I used to go out there on weekends when I didn't have nothing to do at home. And just go and maybe clean up a while, just go in there to just sit around.

One Saturday, I was there. I was there alone, and I heard people singing. I heard them singing in Choctaw. They was old, old tunes I never heard before. I sat there, and I listened.

And the more I listened, the farther back it went. The voices went further back.

One other time, I was sitting on the porch outside, and they were singing inside. And I'm thinking, "Who's here?" I opened the door. As soon as I touched the handle, the music stopped. But I know I heard music. It wasn't no air conditioner on or nothing.

But it's happened several times, even with this new [church] building.

I was working on cabinets one day. This was late Saturday afternoon. I heard footsteps coming down the hallway as I said to myself, "Whoever is going to show up, is going to show up."

So I was sitting there, and I was just, like I said, working on cabinets. Nobody showed up. That footstep quit just before it got to the sanctuary part, or the fellowship part. It just quit.

And then, another night, I put in a big old stained-glass window. I was doing the finishing touches on it, and I looked up. I looked up, and I saw somebody come into the sanctuary. I saw a body, a figure. I turned, and I looked. There was nobody there.

Things like that happen.

And death is something that is permanent, but sometimes the spirit lingers on, I guess.

THE GHOST

OLMAN COMBY   1928

A certain chief had four wives. Presently, one of them died, but she kept coming back at night. She would seem to be cooking as she had formerly done.

When the chief got up and made a light, he could see nothing, but as soon as he went back to bed, here she came walking in again.

The ghost disturbed him so much that finally he had to move away.

SPIRIT OF THE DEAD

HAROLD COMBY   1997

And another thing is that if you have a spirit in your house, and it seems like it's taking over, and you can't get rid of it any other way, my mom says confront it; speak to it like there's another person in the room. Say, "Hey. This is my house. Get out of my house." And open the door for that spirit.

And I've had people tell me it has worked. I've never seen it done; I'd be scared anyway. But my mom says talk to him, scold him, and tell him to get out of the house. "You no longer live here. It isn't your house anymore."

But recently, this guy told me there's a house in Bogue Homa, relative of his's house, that, they had a spirit. And whatever they did, the spirit wouldn't leave. So finally, the aunt just went out and confronted it.

And he told me that he thought that she was going crazy because she was saying stuff like, "You're dead now." "You don't live here." "Get out. Get out of here."

Open the door, and then after a while—he said that the spirits left.

They didn't have any problems after that.

TWO BROTHERS

MELFORD FARVE   1997

One particular one my father told me was—it was one of his relatives. It was a story about one of his relatives.

And they had sent the son to go get some flour and some other things from the store.

But he was gone for a long time, and they didn't know what had happened to him. It was dark at that time, no streetlights or anything, so you have to go by the moon, the moonlight.

So, the brother went after him.

And they were walking; he was walking down the road, and then they saw somebody coming. He knew it was his brother, but he didn't call out . . . I think he *did* call him by his name.

But the other brother, the one that had gone to the store, was frightened. He said, "I don't know what you are, but you're not going to get me," or something like that. I guess he had been walking down the road real scared.

And even though it was his brother that was standing there, he threw down the sack of flour and whatever else he had in his arms, and just ran off the other way, or something like that.

So, they thought that was pretty funny.

HISTORICAL TALES

Before the advent of a written language, history was shared primarily through oral narrative and was embodied in stories as diverse as sacred myths, legends, and personal reminiscences. Stories of all these kinds exist today and all continue to build the record of the past for the Choctaw. Nonetheless, there are differences among these narratives. Creation stories and myths tell of people who existed long ago. While names may be included, dates are neither known nor meaningful. More recent events, however, are rooted in time and can be discussed as history. Pushmataha is well known by all. Portraits argue for his existence, events assure us of his importance, and dates confine him to specific periods.

While the life of Pushmataha is a favored topic, much of the history that is told in oral narrative is specific to families. As in any culture, elders talk of growing up, of the events that shaped their lives. The narratives are personal because the events were experienced as individuals on an intensely personal level. With time, the stories may lose their rancor and their passion as the people who narrate them remember only the story, not the event. But with removal efforts to Indian Territory in what is now Oklahoma continuing into the twentieth century, subsequent underhanded land deals made in the decades that followed, and acts of discrimination that continue to this day, stories felt personally describe a history shared tribally.

Those histories highlight major points of contact: with neighboring tribes, European colonists, Christian missionaries, the US government, and their primarily White and Black neighbors in a segregated South that continues to try to reckon with this brutal, racist past. Conflict dominates, with injustice pervading virtually every interaction with White people. Despite it all, the resilience of the Choctaw people is inescapable, and their ability to combat and even overcome these acts of discrimination through wit, cleverness, courage, and sheer determination stands as a powerful model for future generations.

THE COMING OF CHRISTIANITY

BOBBY JOE   1999

The year 1440 is when Spaniards came over and had a war against us. Our leader, he's the one teaching the people, our people, things to carry on, religion or heritage or whatever you call it. But after that is when everything was taken over in our country. That's when the Englishmen came, overtook everything.

When they had that war, our leader got killed. His name was Tuskaloosa. He was a traditional leader; people call it a chief. He's the one that got killed. I understood that everything is all vanished. Everything is all gone. You don't have the ceremony anymore. After Tuskaloosa died, there's no one out there showing how to do that anymore.

After that, the Pilgrims came over, and they bring with them the Bible books. They showed them how to live by the Bible. This priest was bringing a Bible book in one hand, and he had a sword in one hand. He tell this Indian people, he said, "If you believe this Bible, we can show you the right way, we can show you to go to Heaven when you die. What you're doing now is the devil's work," because the Indians were wearing their own hair dress and style; it's got the deer horn. And this priest thought these Indian people was devil worshipping. So he tried to show them how to live. "If you don't believe this Bible," he said, "this is what you're going to get." And he dropped the Bible down, and he grabbed that sword, and that sword's got a cross on it. Stuck it through his heart and killed him. And that's when all the rest of the Indian people got scared. So that's when he picked up this Bible, go along with the Bible.

So after that, that's when all our heritage was gone. Because he don't do that no more. Because once he done learned about the Bible, he started going to churches, and they forgot their religion. They left it behind.

HELPING THE NEW IMMIGRANTS

BAXTER YORK   1974

Choctaws had the corn already when they [non-Indians] came here. A lot of them suffered; they were starving. They were going to die out.

But then the Choctaws saved them by knowing how to make vittles out of corn. So they made kind of vittles out of the corn. So they feed some of the non-Indians that just come in and didn't have anything to go on.

Well then, those are the things that they began to feed them where they began to stay alive. And all the time, they thought that since they come in with the Bible in their right hand, why, they thought they were good people. They thought they would treat them right. But it went the other way; didn't happen that way. The Bible didn't work, somehow.

WHITE MEN BRING ALCOHOL

JOHN HUNTER THOMPSON   1979

The Choctaws never really knew what liquor was until the White men brought it over. All they knew about the White man was that they came from the big water and came ashore.

When the White man saw the Choctaws in the forest, they tried to speak to them but had difficulty understanding each other. They returned to their boat and came back with some whiskey and told the people to drink it; but the chief said "No" for he thought it was something that would kill them. So the Whites left for the boat to return later to try again.

When they did return, they saw only a few Choctaws and asked them to come over and try the whiskey. This the Choctaws did. The whiskey tasted sweet to them, so they continued to drink some more.

A little while later, the Choctaws started saying things that made no sense. This caused them to be unable to stand up straight. They would also fall down on the ground.

The White men saw this and went to their boat to get some more whiskey, leaving it on the shore for the other Choctaws to come and get it. The other Choctaws went and got it, and soon everybody was drinking and getting drunk.

That's how the Choctaws started drinking.

FIGHTING THE MUSKOGEES

JOHN HUNTER THOMPSON   1979

There were other Indian tribes near the Choctaws that they didn't know about. They hunted the small game and took it to their people.

The Choctaws found out, got angry, and told the other Indians to hunt somewhere else. This the other Indians did not do, so the Choctaws and Muskogee, which is what they were called, started fighting.

It became a big war. The Muskogees were strong for they used bows and arrows, while the Choctaws used blowguns.

This was told to me by my grandfather and father.

The Muskogee would travel at night to the Choctaw's house. They would knock on the door, and when they opened the door, they would kill them and run.

The Choctaws did the same to them.

When the young Choctaws went hunting in the forest, the Muskogee would hide, and they would catch the Choctaws. And they would gather some black bushes together and put it in between the young Choctaws' legs and push it and pull it out like a saw. This would burn and cut the young Choctaws. They would have to crawl home.

The Choctaw found out and started doing the same to the Muskogee. This was the beginning of a big fight.

The Choctaw started wondering how they could go hunting without being caught by the Muskogees. They needed someplace to hide.

A prophet told them that they should dig a hole and climb into it, when the Muskogees chased them and followed them in, hit them below the knee, and beat them up.

So the Choctaws dug a hole near the stream deep in the hills. They did what the prophet said, and this made the fight even bigger. The Choctaws had help fighting the Muskogees by the Whites.

The Whites helped them by giving them guns. The Muskogees left soon after this to live somewhere else.

This was a hard time for the Choctaws.

CROSSING THE LINE

LOUISE WILSON   1997

There was one incident. It was something that was really stuck in my mind.

And remember, I was about thirteen, fourteen years old. I got out of the home probably when I was sixteen, when I finished high school at seventeen, then I was out of the home. Went to school and things like that. So, I probably was thirteen or fourteen.

One story my grandfather told us was that we were from a different clan. And he told us what it was, but I can't remember that. I wish I did; if I ask my grandmother, she may remember it.

But anyway, he said that everybody was called different clans back then, years ago. And he said that's probably what we have now is different communities. Different communities had different clans.

Since we were from Bogue Chitto area, we were called a name. And he even mentioned something about one clan was called *Fichik Watathbe*, which means . . . I don't know what it means, really. But he was saying one clan was

Fichik Watathbe. And then of course there's one for Pearl River: Biasha, I think is what he called it. Then there was a clan name for Nanih Waiya, and all these other different names is what he was bringing out.

And as he was talking, he said that the leaders from each of these clans, which was probably an elder, the leaders from each of these clans made it known among each other that you stayed within your own clan, and you had a boundary where you lived, OK? You had to get permission before you could go over that boundary in order to do any hunting or anything like that, OK?

Let's say for instance, you want to go hunt rabbit or something like that. You can't go over this boundary for the other clan. That was so, he said, because they wanted to make sure they had plenty to eat within their clan. So, like if you have a lot of rabbits and deer and stuff like that within your boundary, you had plenty to eat there; there was no need for you to go over the other side of the boundary.

So each clan, they had it known that's the way it was supposed to be. It was like a law, I guess, that they had, an unwritten law.

And he said that if one was caught doing that, they were punished by torture. And he said Choctaws were not really known to kill or things like that, but they really could torture somebody in order to teach them a lesson.

He told us of an incident where a young man . . . he knew that he wasn't supposed to go over, but he saw a deer on the other side of this boundary; and he went over there and killed it.

And he said also, you wouldn't think that they had someone to watch around, but they had someone to watch.

And so I guess this particular young man got caught. And so they took him to his leader in that clan, and they talked about it among themselves and said, "OK, what's the discipline that's going to happen to this young man?"

They brought him back to the leader, to this other clan, and said, "Look. Here's this person. We caught him. And we have a rule. Remember, we had agreed that no one was going to go over their boundary to hunt or anything like that."

They brought him back to an elder and their leader, and they said, "We brought him to you; now we're going to punish him."

The elder said, "Yes." Because it was a known law that he was not supposed to do that. "You may take him back and punish him."

So this other clan will take him back, and they punished him by torture. They call it *bissápi*. I can't think of the English word for it right off hand, but you know the blackberries? They have those stickers? And they're kind of like long vines? You see blackberries and they're on these long . . . They'd get those.

And since this man . . . but they had him stand, while they rubbed a bunch of blackberry things between his legs, to torture him. That's what they did. And he was bleeding and everything like that, but that was a way of teaching him a lesson. And once they finished with the torture, they sent him on.

And so other people within that clan saw that "Oh," you know, "this can happen," and, "Yes, he wasn't supposed to do that anyway."

So, you know, that teaches him that he's not supposed to go over the boundaries to hunt. Because we have plenty of food. He said, "There was plenty of food within their area. Why did he go and do that?"

And so he was talking. That was one story that I remember he told us. And I don't know if it was written, but I remember that.

PUSHMATAHA

FRANK HENRY   1997

What little I know about Pushmataha is what I read. What I read was about Pushmataha when he was a young man.

The Choctaws had gone hunting somewhere in the Mississippi River area, Delta country. They were having a big bonfire. And all of a sudden, somebody appeared. A young man. Nobody know where he came from, but he appeared. That was little Pushmataha.

Since he was a young man at that time, they took him hunting. He'd always be the best hunter; he always killed a rabbit or deer or whatever it might be. He always was the one that caught the most.

And finally, they accepted him. And they just called him Pushmataha. He didn't have no last name. Evidently, he had some popularity with the Choctaw people. Eventually, he became a chief.

But Pushmataha was the best of everything. He could wrestle anybody, one-to-one, and he could win. And whatever it is they used, like using rabbit stick to kill a rabbit, he'd beat everybody else. He was just one of those kind. Naturally, he became a chief.

And of course, Pushmataha, the history tells us that he fought with General Jackson in the Battle of New Orleans and expected General Jackson to do him a favor. He wanted to keep twenty million acres right here in Mississippi and keep the Choctaws here.

But he was invited to Washington, DC. And while he was there, they had a big feast. That same night, he got sick. The next day or so, he died.

So I figure, evidently, he was poisoned, food poisoned. Those were not in the history; you don't see it in the history. He just got sick and died; that was it. But he was huge, husky young man. You just don't get sick and die. And all the medical service they have in Washington, DC, should have taken care of him.

But that's what happened. He was there to preserve the culture and preserve the land, Choctaws, and everything else.

When that happened, the second in command took over.

General Jackson at that time was President Jackson. He wanted all the Choctaws to move out of here to Oklahoma—not Oklahoma but New Territory; *now* it's Oklahoma. So they signed treaties, all kinds of treaties. I think the last treaties were twenty million of acres and also that they moved to the new territory.

So Pushmataha lost out. And his family lost out; they lost everything.

DEATH OF PUSHMATAHA

GRADY JOHN   1998

Pushmataha, he was a pretty good chief, very strong chief. And Pushmataha was a well-educated man, too, you know. And when the senators found out he was well educated, they got him to be in the commission, so he went to Washington.

That's where he's dead, in Washington.

So, when he got elected . . . see, a lot of Indians, different tribes, and so, Pushmataha was the man to freedom for all Indians. And he was commissioner; he was a good commissioner because a lot of things Indian need was education, lot of Medicare, lot of these, what you see Indians to have, all tribes.

And so, he lived there in Washington.

But he died with—I can't prove it—but he died with poison, food poison. And so, that's where he's buried: Washington.

PUSHMATAHA'S SUSPICIOUS DEATH

DAN ISAAC   2021

Before the Trail of Tears, Pushmataha, while he was alive, we are told by the elders that he said, "As long as I'm alive, we're not going to Oklahoma or Indian Territory. We're supposed to stay here."

And so the story is, when he went to Washington, they say he got sick, died of croup or whatever. *We* know it that he was poisoned. He was poisoned. That's why they buried him in Washington, DC. And they never brought his body home.

But the elders always say, "Yeah, they killed him because they wanted us to be removed. And he died. After he died, we were removed."

All the other chiefs . . . Not only did he die, but on the way, I think two other chiefs died on the way to Washington. So that's why they had enough strength to get rid of us or remove us.

REMOVAL

GRADY JOHN   1998

1830. President Jackson, he removed a lot of them to Oklahoma. Lot of Choctaw living in Macon coming this way.

You know, Macon, in that area? You know Dancing Rabbit Creek?

They thought that was a peace treaty, signed. But Choctaw signed it to go to Oklahoma. They tricked them.

Choctaw used to be one of the largest tribes in the United States. Anybody ever told you that? We were the largest tribe.

That's when the removal to Oklahoma. All of them didn't make it. Dehydrated. A lot of them just couldn't go. Died. They buried them from Greenwood to Little Rock on to Oklahoma.

If archeologists looked for it, they could kind find the Choctaw burial grounds somewhere—not grounds, but they just covered it up.

They moved from there. Half just made it.

OK, they had the land. All of them had land when you got there. But you know what happened? OK. A lot of Caucasian people made whiskey; went up and drank with them. They got drunk, and they made them sign. And they lost it. Because he didn't know; he was drunk. He signed the paper. And the law say, "Here it is. You done signed it."

HIDING TO AVOID REMOVAL

LOUISE WILLIS   1973

Some wanted to stay here, and they had to hide where the Nanih Waiya Mound is, or the Nanih Waiya Cave. They hid there for so many years until some White man found them there and thought that they needed help because our people were having a hard time of living. And they finally set up a reservation, the government did.

As I recall, the Indians did own land, but taxation came in, and they had to pay tax on their land. And the White men would get the Indians drunk to where they wouldn't pay for their tax. And when they didn't pay for it, they would put it in the trust fund for the government, or the government just took the land away from them.

They said that God wanted them to stay, so they stayed there. But when the White man was going to take all the Choctaws to Oklahoma, some of the people that wanted to stay ran back. It's about two miles back, and you'll find Nanih Waiya. If you walk, about two miles back to the Nanih Waiya Cave.

They ran away, and they hid, and these other Choctaws went on to Oklahoma.

SECOND REMOVAL AND RETURN

FRANK HENRY　　1997

At one time, Choctaws in Mississippi was flourishing with schools and social, economy. At that time for them it was good. But after the removal, people suffered, suffered a lot.

My grandpa was in the last part of the removal in early 1900s. He was moved to New Territory. My grandma didn't want to go. This was her home; she wanted to stay. She cried. She did everything she could. And the soldiers just took her, put her on the train.

My mother was born somewhere in New Territory.

Several years later, they gave them an option: they can go back home, or they can stay. So my grandma came back, and Grandpa stayed. So, they separated themselves. Reason for that was that Grandpa had, all together, probably had about three or four hundred acres of land. They were allotted a hundred and sixty acres. Grandpa had a hundred and sixty, Grandma had a hundred and sixty, my uncle had a hundred and sixty, and my mother had a hundred and sixty.

But like I said, my grandma wanted to move back. So, they all moved back except my grandpa; Grandpa stayed.

And when Mama reached eighteen, married to my daddy, Jim Henry. Of course, my mother was literate. My daddy probably forced her to sell the land. And I don't know how much money she got out of it, I have no idea, but she sold that land, a hundred and sixty acres in New Territory. Whatever happened to that money, I have no idea. I probably wasn't even born then.

But that's the way it was until the government felt the need here in Mississippi. Bought some land, built some schoolhouses, and brought the Indian people out of sharecropping into a community such as this. Had their own forty acres of land, pasture, hay. Plant some corn; plant some peas; plant a garden. They were supposed to be self-sufficient.

And they did. Grandpa had cows and mules and horses and pigs and chickens, all kinds. You couldn't go hungry.

SNEAKING BACK FROM OKLAHOMA

JAKE YORK   1997

My father's great-grandfather was named Solomon York. He's one of those on the removal. Well, his grandfather was, too, but his grandfather came back, Scott York. He went with his dad, Scott York did, with Solomon York. Scott York is my dad's grandfather. And he went with his dad, but he came back. I guess he snuck back, the son did.

So that's where I guess he settled up and got some of the land when they were giving out the head of household; he got some land. And it was in Standing Pine area. So a lot of our relatives from my dad's side are from that community.

When that old guy Solomon—the great-grandfather that stayed in Oklahoma—they said he . . . his wife died, and he married a Caucasian. Well, when he died, I guess he had a big old plantation in Oklahoma where whatever land they gave him down there.

But anyway, when they started breaking it down, he didn't leave no kind of will for who was supposed to get what. But since his land area was so vast, but he had so many children and their children and their children.

They got a check when their estate was sold or whatever assets he had. And [*laughter*] they all got a check for, eventually some got a dollar and twenty-five cents, some got a dollar fifteen, and some got ninety-five cents. I think he got something like a dollar. But my aunt's the one that showed me. She saved hers. It was a ninety-five-cents check.

LAND SWINDLING

JAKE YORK   1997

They got swindled out. See, they didn't understand the written part. Like even if they get groceries, and if you don't pay for it, you'll give up your property or land, but they would put their X there when they get groceries. And that's how they got swindled out of their land.

My dad used to tell me about that all the time, how they got all these lands from the different people, property owners. That's how they were swindled out.

There was lot of different ways they'd swindle them out. Like even liquor. They would get them drunk, and they said, "Put your X over here." They would make it like it was something else; they'd be purchasing a cow or something. It would wind up like it was their land that they were putting up.

GRANDFATHER'S LAND

INEZ HENRY   1986

The land over there was Grandfather's. It was around forty acres. And that is where we lived, long time ago.

And then Grandfather got sick.

So then a White man had already drawn up papers wanting the land, but as long as Grandfather knew what was going on, he would not sign his name.

So when he laid there unconscious, two White men came. As he laid there unconscious, they put a writing pen in his hand and, holding his hand, had signed his name.

When he died, Mama wanted to stay, but the White man got mad. When he got mad at Mama, because Mama wanted to stay, Mama also got mad. When they both got mad at each other, the White man got an end of a hoe and beat her with it, and so Mama moved out.

So then that land was sold to the government.

So then we all moved way across the creek. And so that's where we used to live. And then, moving back, traveling, we arrived near that Bond school. And that's where we used to live.

When the government finished building the houses, they wanted me to go to school. But Mama would not allow it. I did not go to school.

So when I went to school, they wanted us to move there, so we moved to the government house. It was around 1937. So then that's where we all used to live when Mama died.

That's all.

BURNING STICKS

ESTELLINE TUBBY   1997

I'd like to look up what kind of . . . like other Indians have their own kind of religion. But I search for our Choctaw way, but no. Well, I asked one time because, well, I asked my mother about it. I says, "Why don't we have our own way? I'm a Choctaw."

I used to think, "I'm an Indian," so I want to be an Indian doing something.

And she said, "Well, as far as I know, the Baptists said those are sins what we are doing."

And I said, "Well, I thought God made everybody to worship in their own way, in our own tongue."

But she didn't know either.

But she told me this though. This is the way it started, as far as I know.

She said that there was some religion people came here, and they started one time to have school. My mother said that there was some religion that came out here and forced the Choctaws to give up their cultures and everything. And one of them, I think she said, was a Baptist. She just mentioned that name.

And then, well, they'd been playing stickball and so on like that. And they told the men to bring all the stickball sticks. And it said it was a great big pile, and they all burned it. And they burned a lot of things that the Choctaw had.

And then they went on down to Bogue Chitto, I guess, and tried to do that, too, but they said, "No. We will not listen to these people. We'll just keep our things and keep our culture the way it is."

And now today, they are bringing it back from Bogue Chitto to here. That's how it is. Because those older people, older man and people, know about our culture. So that's how we got ours back. That's why we have it today.

ESCAPING SLAVERY

ALICE BELL   1985

Long, long time ago, they had a big war in this country, they said. Big war. It's called Civil War, they call it. And then, there used to be a man that bought Colored people. I don't know what country that was—must be from Africa. Just like you buy mule, horses, like that. They brought him into this country. They had Colored people come into this country that people used to buy when they got big farm. They bought those people, making them work for nothing.

But one day, this slave owner man that owned the slave, one Colored man, I guess he got angry at him. And my daddy was living not very far from there. And then this Colored man got beat up by this slave owner. Beat him up bad, blood just streaming and running off. And then this man went to my daddy—he got three cabin houses; they had three cabin houses—and he want daddy to hide him.

So that's just the way it went. My daddy saved the Colored man's life on the Civil War.

And so, that's what he used to tell us.

SINKING SHIP

PETE DAVIS DYER   1975

I was in the South Pacific. I was on an aircraft carrier called the USS *Lexington*. Boys, I'll tell you what, it was hell that day. And the Japanese got us with a torpedo submarine. And I was down in the hatchery drinking coffee. I had a cup of coffee in my hand. Both hands like that, great big old mug in them. And hell, that damn coffee been setting there about twenty-four hours anyway. See, we never let that coffee pot go empty, so we had all kind of coffee and was almost as thick as syrup. I was standing out there trying to drink it when it was hot. And whenever that torpedo hit that ship, boy, I mean it just rocked the whole thing. And when it did that, I dropped my . . . my coffee went up in the air like that.

Now everybody's hollering, "Every man on the deck! Every man on the deck!"

When we got on top of the deck, heck, half of the deck was sticking up straight like that. Wide open. They told us, "Abandon ship." We did. And I swim six hours. We swim six hours and forty-five minutes.

You know, lot of people say that I was scared to death of the Japanese spraying with a machine gun. But shoot, when I went to seeing them shark fins going around us, that's what I was scared of most. [*small laugh*] It was so funny. I'm telling you, boy, it wasn't so funny. It was time for everybody to realize there's a God up in the heaven. That's the way we felt. Every one of us did.

GERMAN SURRENDER

CARMEN DENSON   2000

My father was drafted into the army when he was about twenty years old. His grandfather told him when he was about four or five years old that he was going into the army. Like I said, he was also a medicine man, and also a prophet.

Twenty years old, and he said he was sitting there drinking coffee, that morning, going into the army, and he remembered back then what his grandfather said. And he went into the army, I don't know how many years, but he said he went to Camp Shelby in Hattiesburg over here. At the time, that was the third-largest base in the United States. From there, he was always proud that he made the PFC [private first class] in six months.

From Camp Shelby, he went to Ft. Bragg. From there, he went to Ft. Jackson. He had artillery training there. He said at that time, the Germans broke through somewhere in Europe and they needed paratroopers. And he signed up for paratroopers. And they sent him to Ft. Benning, Georgia. He had his training in Ft. Benning, Georgia, and at some point in time, he went to Camp Mead in Maryland.

That's where him and a buddy got real drunk. They wanted to see the president. They went to the Capitol and then the MPs escorted them out. [*laughter*]

I think it was at Maryland that his buddy, they had pictures together. This buddy lived in Pennsylvania. On furlough, they went to Pennsylvania; had a good time there he said. They eat; they probably celebrate pretty good in Pennsylvania. From there, he went to camp in New York, Camp Shanks. From there he said he boarded *Queen Mary*, and *Queen Mary* took him to London. He said they had six thousand troops on that. From there, I guess he went through that English Channel. It looked like a big pan, that boat. He said they got to France. From there, from France, he said they didn't stop; they just kept going until they get back to France, and they had a little nap overnight. Then about three, four o'clock in the morning, boarded a plane and jumped behind enemy lines.

When they jumped behind enemy lines that the American infantry were fighting German infantry, and they jumped behind German infantry and started fighting Germans from behind, and Germans surrendered.

They told them that when he was at camp stateside, he said "One jump and you'll come back." They didn't tell him after the *war* they'll come back. [*laugh*]

When he jumped, he joined I think the Twenty-Sixth Yankee Division. He got into reconnaissance. He can tell you that one time, they were up there, and reconnaissance people go before the infantry, and they scout everything where the Germans are, and they radio back. He said first they send artillery, then the infantry come in. But the reconnaissance would go in there and spy and see where the Germans were stationed, and they would radio back how far and where, and they would throw artillery over there.

And he said one time, they were out doing what they were supposed to do. He said in reconnaissance they walk in a V-shape; they don't all bunch together. They go in a V-shape. He said, some of the guys would see it, but he said all of a sudden it was a stack of trees, like fallen trees. He said all of a sudden, he spotted an eye, like your eyes. Like the whites, but they were camouflaged. He screamed. He said, "I think I screamed," because he saw a machine gun right at him. And all that guy had to do was pull the knob like that, and he was gone. But he said he screamed, and everybody fell down. And he said he was there, and he couldn't move. The German guy kind of smiled at him and lifted up a white hanky.

He spoke in German. One of sergeants that was with them could speak in German, so they talked to each other. He had his handkerchief out, and he came out and they got him. Two more was in there. And they also came out. And he said the sergeant told him take them back to where they were camping. He said he couldn't; he said he was scared. And they all went back instead of just him alone, taking the prisoners. He didn't want to be alone taking them back, three prisoners. He was the only one that had a gun, but when he got back and they told him what happened, and the captain there said, he got a glass a water and moved it up and said, "Drink it!" He caught the glass, but he couldn't drink it; he was shaking.

ARMY VOLUNTEER

TERRY BEN   2021

My granddaddy Tom, he was at the age of World War I. World War I was 1917, 1918. The first pandemic—and we are in a pandemic now—and so in 1917, '18, there was a worldwide pandemic. It was called Spanish flu.

And at the same time period, World War I was going on overseas, and America became involved, fighting against Germany and her allies during that time period. My granddaddy, from Standing Pine, Tom senior we're talking about, he volunteered to join the army. He volunteered, and they took him for the United States Army.

And then he trained and all that, and he never went overseas.

But one winter while he was training, it was so bad that he developed pneumonia. So they took care of him and eventually released him. But he never left the United States.

But the war was a short war, as far as America's involvement. It ended in two years. The main thing he always told me was that he was not drafted. He volunteered into the United States Army.

One thing, my granddaddy was a hard worker, but he didn't talk much. He did not talk much. But occasionally, he would tell me something, and he said, "We're going to the courthouse in Carthage, Mississippi, and I want to show you something."

"Oh, yeah?"

And so we went to Carthage, Mississippi. When you go there, there's a large plaque, a little bit bigger than the TV monitor there. Bronze plaque hanging on the wall. It lists all the people from Leake County, Carthage area, who went to World War I who got drafted into World War I. It lists their name in alphabetical order. He went to the B section, and, "Look right here." And his name was there. It had *Thomas Ben*, parentheses *Indian*, off to the side. He was proud of that. He was proud of that. He showed me that. But that's something unique that hardly nobody knows.

PATRIOTS

HAROLD COMBY   1997

My uncle's name is on there [the WWII memorial at the Neshoba County Courthouse]. Wilson Isaac. There's about six or eight [Choctaw].

There's a lot of heroic events. Like my uncle. My mom said he was drafted but failed the physical, so he volunteered and was killed in action.

I know two people; they wanted to take up the military when they were sixteen years old. I think they lied. I heard that they lied and had their uncle sign their names, saying that they were seventeen. Can you imagine going to war at sixteen?

I guess, someone said it's within us.

GO BACK TO EUROPE

BAXTER YORK   1974

I think it happened back in 1929. We were playing ball in Philadelphia, Pennsylvania. It was a night game. And somehow or another, the audience on the right side of the stands began to razz my friend. He was playing center field. I don't know how they got started, but they began to razz him, and he began to talk back to them. He shouldn't have because the audience, you know. But then he went on carrying it out. And I was playing left field, and we both come towards the left-field line, then switch off. He was Jim Thorpe's nephew, and he was a fast runner. He is a good center fielder. But he started razzing this audience, while the audience razzed him, and it just kept on continuing.

You know what he said? "You! Why don't you go back to Europe? You come over here, and you going to ruin everything we got."

That's what he said as he go on.

I still think about that. And it looked like it is going that way all the time. Today, our government is in a heck of a big mess, and our government is using our natural resources in order to buy out the other country. And the other country don't care a thing about us. But they want what we got, so they're pouring in.

So I still think about this guy that made that statement razzing the audience.

POLL TAX

TERRY BEN   2021

In Mississippi, during that time period, not anybody could just vote. You had to pay a poll tax, P-O-L-L tax, in order to vote. My grandfather had to pay twenty dollars every year. He would go up to the courthouse and pay his twenty dollars every year so he could vote in state elections, for governor, in federal elections, for president of the United States. And there was a series of tests during that time period, reading tests or whatever, given to Choctaws, given to Blacks, and if they couldn't pass those tests, even though they had money to pay poll tax, they were not allowed to vote.

So that was one of those things where Granddaddy was unique. I guess he passed those literacy tests or whatever, and then he had money to pay the twenty dollars a year to vote. He did vote in elections for governor, president of the United States, and all that, for senators. So he was one of the few Choctaws.

There were other Choctaws who voted during that time period, but nowadays, we don't have to pay anything. Like tribal election this week: you don't have to pay anything. All you have to do is register to vote. State elections—just go down to the courthouse and register at the right location. You can vote for the governor, for the president of the United States. You don't have to pay anything; just go register, and we can vote. So a lot of things that happened in the past no longer exist, which is good.

SEGREGATION IN THE FIELDS AND AT THE MOVIES

HUBERT WESLEY   1999

All the White peoples would go inside the house to eat their lunch. And after they get through eating, and we had Blacks as well picking cotton with us, and we were not allowed in the house to eat, so we had to eat out in the backyard.

We come up like that.

And then a lot of places back in them days, we weren't allowed to go in places because we were discriminated against just like the Black was.

And I remember well when I got to the point I start going to movies about twelve miles from where we live, which was Macon, Mississippi. The movie cost fifteen cents at that time, and my dad would give me fifty cents a week to ride the pickup truck. Back of the pickup truck was ten cents ride over to Macon to go to the movie. And when we go to the movie back then, we had to go where the Black people go; we Choctaw Indians, we went where the Black people were. In fact, we were told to lot of time, which I didn't mind. Didn't know; I didn't know what was going on anyway.

INJUSTICE AT THE LAUNDROMAT

TERRY BEN   2021

Carthage had a movie house called Fox Theater. I never went there because we didn't have the money to go there. On top of that, Granddaddy, Grandma is not going to take me there, anyway. But for the Choctaws who went, they had to sit up in the balcony to watch the movie.

I have a little story right here that I still remember, going to a laundromat.

Saturday during that time period—going back to growing up on the farm—after you took care of going to the grocery store and taking care of the corn to the mill to be milled into cornmeal, it was time to do the laundry. Grandma would go to the laundromat, certain area in Carthage. But we had to go to the "Colored" side, the back end of the building, for the laundromat.

Most times, there was an attendant there, and if you lost money, they would refund you, and all that.

But that morning, Grandma, for whatever reason, she was mad. So when she went to the back area and put all the clothes inside the washers and all that, she lost money on one machine, and she got mad, and there was no attendant. So Grandma said, "Hey, I'm going to get my stuff. We're going to the front."

And I was there, and Granddaddy was there; Granddaddy just looking at her. I was there. "What's going on?"

So Grandma took up all the clothes, and she went to the front, the White-area-only laundromat portion. So when she got to the front, she didn't look around, nothing. Grandma was mad, and so she just went to the machines and put her clothes that needed to be washed inside the machines. Then here comes this White lady, White attendant, said, "You can't be over here. This is for Whites only. You can't be here. If you all don't leave immediately, I'm going to call the police."

And by that time, Granddaddy came around and heard everything. So Granddaddy said, "Go ahead, call the police."

So sure enough, she called the police. And Grandma just went about her business, and her just tending to them machines; I think she had three machines.

Anyway, real soon, five minutes later, here comes a Carthage police. Came in, White police officer had came in, said, "You all not supposed to be here. You all know that?"

Granddaddy said, "Yeah, but the machines back there are not working right and taking money."

"Well, you're not supposed to be here. If you all don't leave immediately, I'm going to arrest you all."

And Granddaddy said, "Those machines are already paid for. The machines are running. We're going to leave when the machine is done, and whenever it's washed, we're going to leave."

That officer stood there a little bit and said, "All right; I'll let you do that, but you all don't ever come back here again."

As a ten-year-old boy, I still remember that.

And the cops or police officer got in his car and went on.

But that day, Grandma was mad. You didn't want to see Grandma mad. She was mad and got her way that time. But that's part of the civil rights period.

DISCRIMINATION

FRANK BELL JOE   1975

I'd say it was in 1963, I believe it was. This was the time when I first noticed that White people were being prejudiced against Indian people and many Black people down here.

One time I wore long hair, and I went to this drug store, and I got kicked out because I was told that I had filthy hair and that I was an Indian, and they didn't want me in there.

So then I came on to another place called Mary's Coffee Shop. I went to the front door down there. I was met by the manager down there that told me that I was to go out in the back and eat with the Black people down there.

And that's the only time that I started noticing that we were being prejudiced of. That was in 1963, I believe it was.

MURDER OF CIVIL RIGHTS WORKERS

TERRY BEN   2021

Two people I always remember during that time period. The sheriff of Neshoba County, Lawrence Rainey, and Cecil Price were very, very hard on people of color, and they were members of the Ku Klux Klan also at the same time. Whenever Martin Luther King came, they gave him a hard, hard time. When the three civil rights workers were killed . . .

You know where they buried the three bodies at, right? You all know? [*speaking to the YOP students*] You know what I'm talking about? The three civil rights workers who were killed in Neshoba County because of the civil rights? You know where Neshoba County Fairground is? Neshoba County Fairground, right, where they have the fairground? Fairview area?

Anyway, Fairview area, somebody was building an earthen dam, and so when the sheriff of Neshoba County and the members of Klan from Neshoba County and from Meridian, they killed those three civil rights workers close to House, Mississippi. They had to bury those bodies somewhere, and so they came all the way to Fairview community, Fairview, not far from Neshoba Fairground. And they came to a landowner. They killed those three civil rights workers, and they buried the bodies in the earthen dam, and they covered it up, probably close to this height from the ceiling here. They buried the three bodies together in the earthen dam area in there.

So after that, everything became super hard for people of color. Okay? So during that time period, the FBI came in and began asking questions and all that.

MISSISSIPPI BURNING

HAROLD COMBY   1997 / 2021

1997

The swamp area leads from around Bogue Chitto toward that place where they burned that civil rights wagon back in '64. I saw it. My dad took me and my brother out there. It was still smoldering. I remember he said, "Don't you ever forget this. I want you to remember." The station wagon was still burning. All the leaves, I guess the flame had gotten too high, and all the leaves had been burned around it.

2021

Then he took us to this Clayton Lewis Road, I believe, which is next to the reservation. That's where the dam is. And back then it was just red dirt. They was just fixing up the dam, and that's where they placed the bodies and covered it with dirt. But now it's overgrown with trees, so you can't really tell what's there.

When we saw the station wagon, he said, "You guys don't forget this."

Because we have never seen certain things, and maybe the kids that were born like fifteen years ago, they have never seen discrimination. They haven't seen where our kids graduated at eighth grade or tenth grade and couldn't go to public school. They have to go to Meridian or Haskell Junior College to finish their twelfth-grade education. And some of them just stopped there and just only got a tenth-grade education.

BANNED

TERRY BEN   2021

So again, life became harder after that [the 1964 murder of three civil rights workers] with people of color. Let me tell you one story. My granddaddy volunteered for the military, for the army. And so, as a veteran, there's a veterans' group called Veterans of Foreign Wars. In Carthage, Mississippi, there's a building, Veterans of Foreign Wars site. And granddaddy loved to go there. And he knew Whites from Leake County who stopped by in the area who had served in the military. And so, he would love to go there. And there was fellowship. Maybe every six months on a Saturday night, they would go there and just have meetings, talk about military things or veterans' affairs or veterans' benefit checks or whatever. But he would always take something there because everybody ate. Grandma would fix a chicken container for him to take up there, whatever.

This is not far from Standing Pine, where they had this lodge for veterans. He would go there, and he would enjoy himself there. And they had meetings, I think twice a year.

But after the civil rights thing happened in Neshoba County, he was told that he could no longer attend those meetings by some of the leaders at that site. And then, some other person came to him; one of the lawyers who was a veteran, or I don't know, it might've been Ross Barnett. I don't know. Somebody had mentioned, sent word to him, that, "We're going to take a vote on you, whether you can come back and be with that group or not."

And then, later on, somebody came to him, one of the leaders of the veterans' group came to him and said, "We'll take you back. You can come back and join us."

But then after that, he never did go back. He just didn't feel comfortable, so he never did go back. He had something sort of against them.

But he had someone pulling for him.

But previous to that, he enjoyed going to those events with veteran affairs.

I remember that distinctly, still. But this is one of the results of what was going on in the South, and especially after the three civil rights workers were killed in the Neshoba County. Things changed a lot. It became more tense between people of color and the White society in the Neshoba County.

TROUBLING TIMES

LEONARD JIMMIE   2021

I don't know if something needs to be said about racism. And I do because I lived here. I was right kind of in the middle of it. But I'll give you my take on it. It's that I didn't know that was racism. I thought that's just the way people lived. Because I was so young when I came here.

Every year. "Get out of the store."

And I'd be, "Oh, OK, no problem."

"You know that's for White people only."

And I'd be like, "Okay."

"Did you read the sign?"

And I didn't know.

I'll give you another example.

When I was in elementary, in the dormitory, we got the privilege of the school buying us some new clothes for school. So we would go to town. There was this place called Clark's Department Store. And in there, there was a lady . . . they knew we were coming I guess because they'd have extra ladies on the floor. And we'd be walking around looking at clothes. And they'd send out the teachers with us to help us. But there was only so many. So we'd be walking around on our own. And of course being young you're going to walk around, look, point at things, punch things. And those ladies would be hollering at us.

And I remember I would try on some shoes, and this lady would come over, and she said, "They better fit because that's what you're going to buy."

So I remembered the thumb rule. Always make sure your shoes had a thumb [space from the end of the sneaker to the end of your toes]. Anyway. I would always buy bigger shoes than I needed sometimes because I didn't have the time. They would tell us get a pair of shoes and shirts and pants and then move on.

Anyway, go to the shirts, they would have it on this rack, and I'd be looking at the shirts. And then I'd pull one out, and then I'd look at the lady; the lady would be around somewhere, and she'd say, "You better make sure it fits if you try it on because that's what you're going to take with you."

And then some would allow us to try it on to see if it fits. They would take it off the "Brand New" rack and put it in the "Discount" rack after we tried it if we didn't buy it.

But see I was young, and I thought that's just the way people live. I didn't know.

And so my mother was here. She's working in the courthouse, working with the court system. She'd got hired as a secretary or something. And Phillip's wife [Chief Phillip Martin's wife, Bonnie Martin] was working up there, too. Miss Bonnie. They were working together in the same department. They had that infamous civil rights march come through here in Philadelphia.

My mother was working that day, and I remember her telling us about it. And she said Miss Bonnie said that when this happens tomorrow, just get into your office, get under your desk, and stay there 'til it's over. My mother said she sat the whole afternoon under that desk waiting for them to leave. And then she could hear the fighting going on outside the courthouse as the marches went through.

TREATED LIKE A DOG

MARTHA FERGUSON   2021

They didn't put Choctaw inside the police car. They used to use pickup truck that holds dogs, the cage for dogs.

My uncle got arrested then. And we were there. I guess we were heading toward the hospital, and Grandma had to pick up her diabetic medicine. We're heading toward that way. And, "Look, Uncle Charles got arrested. He's in jail. What a dog."

And he was sitting there, and he looked at us. He says, "Don't say anything."

But he always teased. He just a teaser. He don't do anything to nobody; it was fun to see him then. And I said, "Oh." And when he came home, I said, "Look, I think we got a blue jay jailbird." And he used to get mad. He said, "Don't be calling that."

FRAMED FOR MURDER

DOYLE TUBBY   1997

Well, I was talking to my wife the other day that there was a time when my uncle was accused of killing a man. There was an old man living down there: Mr. McCrory. This is a true story. He was eccentric; he didn't believe in banks; he buried his money, hid it away.

I never shared that with my wife until last week. But anyway, the man died. As best as we can figure, he was hit in the head with an ax and died.

The McCrory house was an old shack. What happened was, my uncle was accused of killing the man. Back in Neshoba County, in the fifties, that wasn't acceptable [Mr. McCrory was White].

When they found out he died, they used the bloodhounds. Now he knew the McCrorys pretty well. There was a trail that went between the two houses. So what happened, the sheriff used the bloodhound to trail the footprints back to his house. What my dad always said, when they went up there, they had to find someone who did it. Well, they found the weapon and took it over there. They took that weapon up there and forced him to pick it up. And that was the evidence. He was sent off to prison for a long time.

Now what we've heard is that his [McCrory's] own nephews were bad, and they wanted his money. They say they're the ones who killed him, but my uncle got arrested because they forced him to pick up the ax. There was no evidence at the time, but that's the evidence they were looking for. That was justice back in the fifties.

He spent about twenty years in the pen. I think they considered it manslaughter and not murder. But he always maintained he hadn't done it.

But I remember the offshoot so well. We were living nearby, and the relative of the man that died came over to the house in a drunken stupor and said he was going to kill all of us to avenge that man's death. At the time, my dad said, "Well, if you think you're going to kill us, you've got another thing coming." I remember he told one of his sons to go get his gun, and my mom, even though she was kind of strong about things like that, she told him not to get the gun.

But my daddy was dead set on shooting that man. What he told that man was this: "You threatened my family; I might as well kill you first, right now." He sent his son in for a gun, but my mom stopped him. I remember us going into the house. That man said he was going to bring reinforcement and shoot the house up. So he left. He was lucky.

My mom didn't think he was going to come back and do that, but my dad thought he might because that's what southern justice was. So we got the mattresses and put them up against the door and barricaded them in.

A couple of days later, Sheriff Rainey came over. He was chewing a big old plug of tobacco and spitting it. He told my daddy that, well, I guess that guy told him he threatened him. He said, "I hear you two had a problem."

My dad said, "Look. When a man comes into my house and threatens to kill all my family, I told him what I was going to do, and he's lucky he left."

Mr. Rainey said, "Well, you can't do that, boy."

I remember that. I was standing there listening, and he was still spitting tobacco right and left. He said he ain't going to let anyone shoot him like that; he ain't no dog.

Mr. Rainey said, "Well, I check on it and see if he's threatening you."

But that's related to what happened with my uncle.

But they say the kids did it to steal his money. The White folks said they didn't have any money, but then they had money after he died.

WHITES-ONLY WATER FOUNTAIN

TERRY BEN   2021

My granddaddy, from time to time, he would be served to serve on a jury. He loved doing that because they're going to pay him money, and remember, money was scarce during that time period. Sometimes he volunteered to serve on the jury for lots of time, and they would last for two weeks, three weeks, or whatever, certain cases.

At any rate, at the Leake County Courthouse, when I was growing up, in the basement area, you had restrooms for Whites only; you had restrooms for Colored only. Up there inside the courthouse, outside, you had water fountain for White only; you had water fountain for Coloreds only.

So those times I would go with my granddaddy to go there. Of course, I was not allowed to go inside the courtroom, and so what I did before I go is go to the side of the house and get a little stick that looked like a little gun, whatever, and I would take it with me, put inside the back of the truck, would take it with me. In my mind, I'm going to play all day. Then when Granddaddy gets out at lunch, I'm going to eat something good: ice cream and maybe a little chips and can of drink or whatever. That was my motivation to go with him. I was around maybe ten, twelve years old during that time period.

Granddaddy, first time he took me, he said, "You see that? See the restrooms, 'Colored only'? That's where you go if you need to go. You don't go to the White. You see the water fountain? If we get thirsty, you don't go to the White water fountain. You go to the Colored water fountain. If you don't follow my direction, they're going to put you in jail." And he said that, and he went to the courthouse inside.

So I would take my little gun and just play, pretend, just around the courthouse. I would behave, and then I would play, whatever.

But one day I got thirsty, and so what am I going to do? In my mind, what's so good about this water here as opposed to that water? And so nothing planned, but I looked around and looked around and looked around and looked around, and there was nobody around in the whole court square of Carthage. There was no car coming, nobody coming down the hallway of the courthouse, and so I quickly ran up to the White-only water fountain, and I drank from it. I looked around, looked around, nobody around, and so I got my little toy wooden pistol type, whatever, and went on.

I never told Granddaddy. If I told Granddaddy, I would never go again, and I knew what's coming right here on the leg, right there [*points to upper thighs*]: switches coming right here. Never told Granddaddy, but that's my experience, and I didn't do it again, but that's one of those things during that time period.

SHORTCHANGED

HAROLD COMBY   2021

My mom used to say, "Learn the White man's way so that they won't cheat you."

I guess the old truth about the Treaty of Dancing Rabbit Creek, it was told in families. So they said, "Watch out."

She had several stories.

I guess there was one time where this Choctaw man went uptown and got some stuff and got some change back. But he looked at it and said—he couldn't write his name—but he looked at the money and said, "Hey guy, you shortchanged me." And although they got into an argument, he was right, and he got whatever was coming to him, the change back.

OVERCHARGED

FRANK BELL JOE   1975

One time my wife bought something, and she knew. She was a good mathematician I guess in her background, so she was looking at this person who was adding this. She had a blouse or something that she bought one time, and this saleslady added up the prices on that, and I guess she overcharged her about, at least two dollars and something. She was looking at her doing that, and in her mind, she figured out the numbers and all that. And it turned out that she was to pay eight dollars and something, and she was supposed to wind up eleven dollars and something. She caught her doing that, and the only thing she did was that she complained to the manager. The manager wouldn't do anything, so she threw the shirt on the floor. She walked out.

I remember that one time. I believe that was in the Parks Department Store. So I imagine it's been that way for us in the other stores, like if you buy things on credit. I guess it's typical, mostly; I guess other than people that you can trust.

SOME BAD, SOME GOOD

TERRY BEN   2021

At Standing Pine, there was an old man; he had a bald head, short man. He liked to wear overalls. Anyway, he ran the store, and anytime a Choctaw from Standing Pine would go up there and buy meat, maybe smoked sausage or salt meat or whatever, he would cut it up, and if somebody wanted two pounds or whatever, he would cut maybe a pound and a half. When he put it on a scale, he would put his hand on a scale and make it two pounds, and he would sell it. The Choctaw, we were paying for two pounds of meat, but actually it was only a pound and a half because he was holding the scales like that, pushing them down with his hand.

Just little things like that was going on during that time period.

But generally, the people who kind of knew each other—Whites, Blacks, Choctaws—they generally got along. They generally got along and did little things to maybe help each other out.

It was a little unusual, but my grandparents had a neighbor, White man, during that time period, eating at our house. At a certain other time, a Black man for a different reason came to the house, and he ate inside the house, and that was unusual, but it happened. We went to a White man's house to help him kill a hog, and we would eat inside their house, you know? Little things like that was going on between neighbors. So it wasn't all just like that.

NO TRUST AND NO CHOCTAW

HAYWARD BELL   2021

I know that the BIA [Bureau of Indian Affairs] schoolteachers were trying to teach us to speak English. In order to do that, they used to spank us if we get caught speaking Choctaw in the classroom. That kind of put a fear in a lot of the kids, which I thought was not good.

Another thing that they did is when they'd send me to another teacher's classroom to give a message. They'd write it down, give it to me, but then he'd send another student with me to go over there. I could say, "You tell me what you want us to tell him. I can tell him myself, but then you want to write it down, and you send another person with me. What am I supposed to do?"

If you made a teacher mad, you get whipping for asking questions like those.

SERVED IN THE BACK IN HIGH SCHOOL

TERRY BEN   2021

Standing Pine and Red Water, one time a year in the spring, would have athletic competitions: who had the fastest runners, long jump, high jump, things like that. Standing Pine would compete against Red Water.

So on one occasion, as we were passing through Carthage, there was a drive-in called the Mug 'n' Cone, and they had hamburgers and ice cream and all that. We told our teacher, principal, that if we did well, can we get an ice cream on the way back? He said, "Yeah, if you all do well, we'll stop there, and I'll ask."

So we did well.

On the way back, at the Mug 'n' Cone, the bus wheeled into the Mug 'n' Cone drive-in. The principal got out. He was the bus driver, too, I think, that day. He got out and went inside, and he said, "Yeah, they said they could serve us." They could serve us, but we had to be served on the back end.

So we got off the bus and went to the back end and stood in line and got our ice cream cone, vanilla ice cream cone, and went back to the bus.

But that's just one example of during that time period, how it was in Carthage, Mississippi. But we got our ice cream cone; we were happy.

We beat Red Water that day also. It was better after the competition.

EAT IN THE BACK

EDDIE GIBSON   2021

I've had a couple of experiences that I've eaten in the back of restaurants here in town. During the summer, I was lucky enough to work something similar to YOP [Youth Opportunity Program]. But back then, we did a lot of outside work cutting grass and trimming bushes and stuff like that. And I'd work at BIA office [Bureau of Indian Affairs], and we were going out. I was with a group of guys and men, and we'd go eat lunch.

And I really didn't understand all of that.

And so we drove up to the restaurant, and one of the older guys says—and I was going to the front—he said, "Hey, no. We're going to the back."

I said, "Why?"

And he said, "That's the way it is. Because you walk in there, they're going to tell you to go to the back."

So we winded up in the back. And we ate there, among the dirty dishes, dishwashers, and it wasn't really that clean.

And there was another place . . . I could name these people and these places. They're not there, anyway. But I won't name them, to protect the innocent . . . I mean guilty. The guilty. Protect the guilty.

We went to the back, too, at another place. And I was with these people, and working in the summer, and these older guys, they've been there before. Then they knew what to do, so I just followed them.

A SIMPLE HELLO

BRIAN BILLIE   2021

I learned how to speak English because they had an ESL program that taught English as a Second Language. A lady worked with us, watching movies and learning how to speak, shake hands, greet, say hello, and look for a response.

But it's not as simple as the teachers wanted it to be. There was a time there where the non-Indians and the Indians didn't really coexist. Or some have their own belief of what they come from.

After one session, they told us when we're in town, we'll meet people to use our English. I remember the first non-Indian I told, "Hello, good morning." It was an older lady that looked at me and goes, "Hmm." [*snorts*] And she walked away to her husband. And her husband, they talked. I thought they were being receptive, so I went to the gentleman, and I said, "How are you doing?" And

I stuck my hand out. And the older gentleman said the same thing, "Hmm." [*snorts*] And walked away.

I couldn't wait to get back to class because I had a bone to pick with the teacher. It didn't work like the movie did.

She asked everybody, "Did you all get to use your words?"

I said, "Yeah." I kept waving my hand.

She goes, "What?"

I was like, "That movie though is not true. It lies."

She kind of pulled me to the side and said, "What happened?" I told her. She goes, "Oh, wait." She put everybody busy to look at the movie and books and pulled me outside and asked me what happened. And I told her.

Man, she said she was so sorry. She was so sorry that some people still hold on to that old . . . to their ways.

BELIEVE IT WHEN YOU SEE IT

EDDIE GIBSON   2021

To prove a point, in high school, I think it was a drama club class, or something that I was in, and we were telling this lady, this teacher, that we get kicked out of barbershops and stuff like that. And she didn't believe us. So I said, "Okay. Go to this barbershop, and I'm going to go in." And I said, "But if he decides to cut my hair, now I don't have no money, now." I said, "You might have to bail me out."

And so I walked in, and the guy met me at the door and said, "We don't cut Choctaw's hair." Said, "You're going to have to go somewhere else."

And the teacher had her window down, so she heard it. And so she believed it.

And I did that just to prove a point. I wasn't about to get a haircut.

SEGREGATION THEN AND NOW

DAN ISAAC   2021

I remember the Neshoba County Fair. I remember one year, I was small, but I remember that we went to it, and they were very, very disrespectful, and we were actually scared. I remember.

And even in town, I remember being younger in Philadelphia. I think it was called Dot's Cafe back then. They used to make all the Choctaws sit in the back rooms. In fact, you couldn't even go through the front door; you had to go . . . We tried to go through the front door; they said, "Hey, you're supposed to go to the back door." And we're like, "Wow."

I didn't know nothing about it. I'm little, so the whole time they're like, "Oh, don't worry about it. Don't say nothing."

And I'm like, "Why?"

I never understood because we're not taught. Because I'm going to tell you, racism is taught. They say, "Don't talk to so-and-so." You can even see grown people holding their babies and teaching them. And I'm like, "Wow, it *is* taught." It's not just they know it from being born. They are taught. "Don't talk to so-and-so."

A little kid would come up and play with any other kid, but then they'll see the grown-up pull them away and say, "They're not your friend" or whatever.

But yeah, it was very prevalent here in Philadelphia growing up. We couldn't go to certain areas.

Or let's say we was at the park, Northside, even Northside Park. If we were there, and then some other people came, Mom and Dad would say, "Get in; let's go home."

And we're like, "We just got here."

"No, there's some people here, and they're looking at us like we shouldn't be here."

And they would say it: "You shouldn't be here. This is not your park."

Even today they would say stuff like, "You all have your own."

That's why I know a lot of the stuff that are made today, here, is so that we have our own. Young people may look at it like, "It's great we have our own." But us older people, we know it's because they want us to be what I call "out of sight, out of mind."

HOUSING DISCRIMINATION

HAYWARD BELL   2021

Craig's mom and I got married, and we were looking for a house, and of course we went uptown to Philadelphia. One of the real estate guys, he was a redneck, prejudiced guy. I knew that, but my wife didn't know that. She said, "Let's go and talk to him."

I said, "Okay."

Went over there. All the houses he showed me was run-down shack. And every time I see it, I say, "No, keep walking." I got tired of it. I told my wife then, I said, "Let's just go. Na hapiyápila chį kiyoh alih." ["He's not going to help us"].

She said, "How come he don't want to give us a good house?"

"Well . . . You had to be certain Choctaw. Robert Ben, Phillip Martin, if you're that type then you can get this bigger house or expensive house. It's not the money to me. It's not the money, but you just you think your shit don't stink. And I don't like White folks like that."

I don't like to use that word. [*laughter*]

I mean that's what I said. I told him right in his face, and he left. He went and told some people. He said, "That guy don't like White folks."

And every time announces election, some of my opponents want to compete with me, they go and tell him [the real estate agent] that I was running, and he goes around, "Hey, don't vote for him because he's a crazy Choctaw," and all this stuff. [*laugh*]

But I mean, I'm sorry I used them words, but I want to stand on what I think is right. And if he thinks that this guy is better than me, then he can jump in the lake as far as I'm concerned. You know?

And I guess his dad never taught him.

PROPHECY

Prophecy is a natural extension of history. Historical narratives tell a story of the past; prophecy tells a story about the future. If history is a story of the past, told in the present, intended for the future,[1] then prophecy is a story of the future, told in the past, and intended for the present. All of these prophecies depend upon attribution to the past; the establishment of authority and belief demand it. And their utility is bound less to the future than to the present, when life decisions can be usefully made. After all, one of the primary and most compelling functions of prophecy is to interpret the world. Events are measured and filtered through prophecies, as people examine their current path. The process is ultimately evaluative. It is through the recounting of prophecy that people can construct a moral history that extends both forward and backward.

This moral endeavor is easily seen in the content of Choctaw prophecy. One group of prophecies addresses the human endeavor through war, removal, loss of identity, and the deterioration of society, where money becomes more important than people, and traditional values are subsumed by modernity. The other group of prophecies addresses the natural world, with prophecies of the loss of land, farming, and forests, and a general deterioration of nature, with the ultimate destruction of all—the end of the world.

The seeming exceptions to these deteriorating states of affairs are the prophecies of new technology, virtually all of which have been fulfilled. Here, storytellers awe audiences with stories of predictions of cars, telephones, paved roads, electricity, running water, airplanes, TV, and VCRs. Many of these prophecies are told like riddles: beasts with two eyes roaring across the land turn out to be cars, spiderwebs that cover the land, electric wires.[2] Yet these prophecies are not so dissimilar to those that carry intensely moral and often dire warnings. In fact, when told in the context of other prophecies, many of these seemingly innocuous prophecies are viewed as signs of darker things to come. Paved roads seem wonderful in contrast to their muddy predecessors until other prophecies are told where paved roads are the crucial development that allows foreign armies to invade Choctaw land.

Yet for all the doom and destruction, there is hope. By applying these stories of the future to the present, people can prepare for the worst, work to mitigate the negative consequences, and in some cases, avoid them altogether. Determining what is inevitable and what can be avoided is not easy, but considering what is at stake, the endeavor is worth it.[3]

CHANGING LANDSCAPE AND INTERMARRIAGE

JOHN HUNTER THOMPSON   1979

The older men of the tribe would sit around the campfire and talk about things that they saw happening among their people.

They said that one day the trees will be few, and the people will grow and feed it to the cows. I found out this to be true. Today there are many fields of grass.

Another thing they would talk about was a couple getting married.

Back then, a couple could get married, live together, and have children. As the years passed by, the people started feasting over weddings. Today, they buy a marriage license.

The old men said that the Choctaws will become a chicken and be spotted. I would ask how, and they would say, "You will see." I know what they meant now. When a Choctaw marries a White or a Black person, the children become spotted.

Back then also, people had no way of getting married to a different race; they also had no idea of a separation until later in the years. The children only were spotted when their parents were of a different race.

INVENTION OF THE AIRPLANE

MARK PATRICK   2021

My grandmother told me, years ago, when I was a child, she said, "There's some things that our elderly people told us that it seems like it was so far-fetched, it felt unbelievable. We would say, 'No.' It's almost like, 'I think it's going to rain; my knee hurts a little bit.' It's almost like that. We'd laugh at it when we were young. 'We don't think it's real.'"

My grandmother, she said, "'One day,' he said, 'people are going to be able to travel across the sky. Get from one point to another, in no time.'"

And they said people would just laugh, and laugh, and laugh. And they would say, "No."

He said, "No, I'm telling you. I know. This is what was told to me, by my parents, and then it was told by their parents, on and on."

So before you know it, the airplane was invented.

They told that story before the airplane was ever invented.

PLANES, ROADS, AND CULTURE

GRADY JOHN 1998

You know, my grandpa predicted lot of things I didn't believe but that's happened.

He said, "You see that bird?"—one time I was a small kid—"We going to see, like that, going to be flying over you."

"And *hinakta sa losa*?" He said, "That's blacktop. It's going to be all over. People be driving the car; he's going to see car; people be driving. You're going to hear the wagon; you're going to put it away. These things going to change."

One day, he picked one time: "The tractor. You ain't going to find any more like that horse."

I didn't believe him. "Ah, quit telling me that, Grandpa," you know?

I thought I knew it all at ten years old. I didn't know a thing. I'd rather listen to my granddad now.

But, you know, he predict something.

He said, "All these schools; there are going to be bunch of new schools. You know what? They're going to study about you. You better keep your blowguns; you better keep your things. You can be sure then. That's how it's going to be—education."

And it's true.

I used to sit there and think, "Grandpa, what do you know?"

And he'd say, "Grady, you're going to find out. It'll be too late then."

"Don't be ashamed to wear your shirt." He said, "Choctaw shirt—wear that when you go to the Choctaw Fair. You're a Choctaw. Be proud of what you are."

That's what he used to say.

INTERMARRIAGE, ROADS, AND CHANGING SEASONS

HAROLD COMBY   1997

There are stories where the elderly used to say that there's going to be a time when you won't be able to recognize the Choctaw.

And my mama says we're up to that point because we're integrating with Whites and Blacks and other races.

She said there was a lot of people that prophesized events. Like, she said, she has heard from her mother that her mother, her grandmother, used to tell her that they were going to have roads that were black, like asphalt. And they were going to have things that flew without being an animal. And the winter and the summer was going to switch.

And she thinks that the time is now because, you know, at night, it's cool. And she says the days were going to get shorter.

And, you know, when you think about it, it seems like the year goes on and on and on, quickly.

CHANGING WORLD

BOBBY JOE   1997

Talk about this future. Sounds like it's going to be just kind of like be continuing what I was talking about. What my father always tell me, even my grandpa, and all that, and they was saying, like I said, we don't know when the year 2000 going to be here. And I never thought about that year, you know?

They said, like all these factories was going to go out. He said that's when you're going to know that something's going to come to the future. There's lot of things going to happen once you see it. And my father said even though you're living after I die, after so many years after, you're going to learn some more, what we've been telling you, they said. He said in years come, if you realized everything, they're watching it, they said it's going to be step by step. Now you're going to know something. Then you be thinking, "Well, this time, it's time's coming." That's what you going to be think, that's what he said.

And he told me, said, "Even though you'll want to plant a little garden somewhere in the back of your house, somewhere, keep watching it." Said, "The things you planted, it's not hardly going to grow anymore. You ain't hardly going to make corn anymore. You ain't hardly going to get rain anymore and put that water in that plant." And, "Someday, you're going to learn some more. If you plant it, it maybe won't, nothing won't come up anymore." He say, "Then you be know when the time is getting close." Said, "That's the future's going to coming." He said, "That's how we know what's going to happen."

He said, "Even you see something in the sky, you ain't never see it before. But yet, you're going to see lot of stuff in the sky. It's going to be flying all over.

"You may have something better than the TV we got now," he said. "They going to tell you lot, every day." Say, "You're going to like, knowing everybody around your area, the people you know, telling you something every day. It's going to be just like that. You're going to be know everything what's going on in the world."

What he was talking about was this satellite and TV, tells you all kind of news and whatever little pieces that happen somewhere, just like earthquake is happening in California, and within five minutes, you'll be listening to that TV, and it tells you. That's what he was talking about.

And talking about a lot of things, flying around in the sky; he was talking about airplanes.

"Even," he said, "even we going to have spiderweb all over the country." Said spiderweb's going to cover us. I didn't know spiderwebs, what he was going to be talking about. I thought he was talking about everywhere you go, spiderwebs everywhere, you know.

You know what the spiderweb was? [*Tom shakes his head no.*]

This electricity wire. That's what he was talking about. [*long pause*]

And they said you're going to know something little bit more, and you're going to learn some in the future.

Yeah, "That's the way you're going to know the end of the world is coming soon," he said, "if you live to see it. If you don't, your kids going to see it. And it's coming."

Even though, you know, foods we eat is poison. Like we was talking about earlier, you know.

And things, some things you see it in the wooded area, it's not going to grow anymore. So these wild apples or plums and stuff, they don't grow anymore.

Everything what they says, taking it step by step. And I know it; I know why my father used to tell me about it. That's what it happened now today.

ELECTRICITY, PLUMBING, AND SOCIAL DANCING

BILLY AMOS   1999

But at that time, some of the things in the future was going to come up. That's how they sit down and explained it. And some of the things that I saw today and in the past has come true. And most of them, I haven't seen yet. But once in a while, they come up. So it's true.

Back then, what I was talking about was the sharecropping that I was talking about.

Same time was, we didn't have no electricity back then. Then we have to go and use a toilet outside. Or we have to tote water from the spring or wells. And that's how did we used to cooking. Or maybe we didn't have no electricity on the stove. We had a fire on the stove. And we have to build a fire to make it cook. Everyday. I don't care if it's hot, you still have to cook, unless you cook outside. Most of the time, some of them was cooking outside, like we do today, cook outside. And that's how they lived.

"But," she says, "someday, you'll be sitting inside a house, and they'll just put on the water and the water come in, in the house." And then electricity. "You just flip the button, and the lights coming on."

We had a lamp to clean back then. Because I remember going to school, had to clean that lamp to get study. Clean it out every night. Lamp tops, you know, lamp globe in other words. Kerosene lamp.

And I can't believe that, when she said that. "How can that be? Just put the water on the inside the house, and it come on. And you got your hot water and cold water."

Well, we have to take a bath, we have to tote water from the spring or wells and then pour it in the washtub, washpot, and build a fire to heat it up, warm water to take a bath with. That's how did we go.

But like they said was, someday that you could flip the faucet, then you're ready to take a shower. And in a few minutes, you'd be finished taking a shower.

And I can't believe that, how that could be.

And then, I used to go out to TV, I mean movie. They had set up the tent; once a week that movie comes out. And then—I used to be crazy about it—so I have to go up there at nighttime, in the evening. Then I come back, and I'm kind of scared coming down the road, but I go up there every week. And they had movies come out, chapter-continued movie. What happens, it goes off, then next week it continues. And I want to watch the whole chapter, I have to go up there.

She says, "Someday—you'll be running around, go up there walking, go see the White people's movie—but someday you going to be sitting in your own house and going to watch them. You don't have to go out; you just flip that button and you'd be watching the White people's movies, pictures, in other words."

And I can't believe what she was saying.

But after all that time, there was . . . the first to come up was TV, black and white. And that's the way it was.

And beyond that, they got this VCR tape. What kind of movie you want, you just go to the store and rent it and clicked it on, and then you can watch the movies, what you want to see.

But like I said, I don't know where they got the ideas, but in the future times that they look ahead of times, and those things was come up.

"And the social dances is going to fade away," she said, "someday." These are dancing on the weekend, Saturday night; they dance all night long in the ball field. But they think it's going to be disappeared if they don't watch it. So is the house dancing.

And today, that's where we at now, if we don't watch it. So many things has changed. Only time we have our social dances is go out at some schools and performing, or Choctaw Indian Fair. Stickball game; you see that. But that's the only time. The rest of them, when the fair is over, they done forgot about it. Then the next year time, will be month of time, and here they're trying practicing dancing or stickball.

But at least we still got culture, a little. Some other state, I don't think they have their culture.

CARS, ROADS, AND CHANGING VALUES

ODIE MAE ANDERSON   1997

Well, it was my father and Bike Williamson, the two together, I heard sitting around talking as a child.

But they said, "Even the little road that is laid out here, that road will be laid out wide. It will be paved," they said as they sat.

"How do they know?" I sat wondering.

But then, and something with two eyes would be running on it, I heard him say.

And then—never even imagined there would be houses here—there will be rows of brick houses.

When I heard him say, "And then it will be all paved, other places; it will be paved going side by side," that he had said, I can see.

I think it is the interstate he was talking about. I am thinking, it probably was, as I now think.

And when the brick houses are all built, when the daycare is built, they will just drop the little children off and will continually go. "Money will mean more than the children," he used to say.

That, I see, is true.

And even though he kept saying, "I am the chief," however, when he said the Choctaws vote "Yes," "No," when they vote and defeat it, the Choctaws will not have a place to live. And then they will not have a place for their bundles.

And when they don't have a home, it will be full of White people, even where it was thought the Choctaws used to live.

Then when they go carrying the bundles, they will go to bury the buffalo feces.

They will go eat little frogs.

I used to hear it said.

That has not come about yet.

That's all.

GENDER ROLES, ROADS, AND HOUSING

EVALINE DAVIS   2021

I've been told by my grandpa, this has been years ago, years and years back, that my grandpa used to tell these kind of stories that someday—and I didn't know he knew this far because it was way back in the years, and he was pretty old when he was telling that, and he said—"One day, some day from here," he said, "everything is going to be changed up."

He said, "Women are going to be the workers, and the men are going to be staying home babysitting."

But that's what I heard from my grandpa.

And it's true.

He used to talk about the roads because back then it was a paved road. But he said, "You never know where these houses . . ."

From the time that we was living, the house used to be far back yonder and over there, and they weren't really close. "But one day that's going to change. It's not going to be like this anymore." He said in Choctaw that "even the houses were going to be so close, and there's going to be houses here and there, and it'd be just short distance that they're going to be sitting around."

And it's that way today.

And the road. You never seen that road anywhere because back in that time there wasn't much of a road. And then he said, "The roads are going to be changed. It's going to be going different ways. And it's going to be blacktop."

And it is true today because you never seen that road before, and then there's a lot of roads. And I guess he was talking about this interstate.

But I never knew. But I'm up to see it today. And I'm living in the house, even the brick house that he used to talk about. I'm in one of the houses at the time that I was told that there's going to be houses like that.

So also, he said that the houses was going to be sitting around the short distance, sitting together. I guess he meant that motel or all these houses that are newly built and everything like that. I guess he was talking about that. I thought about it today; that's what he meant.

But there's another thing I remember. He said, "There's a lot of Choctaws over here. But y'all going to be losing your language because everybody's going to start speaking English."

But I never raised my kids like that. I heard my grandpa. So I didn't want my language to pass away. So, I taught; I raised my kids with Choctaw. It's good that they know how to speak English because not everywhere you go there's going to be a Choctaw there.

So it's not that you know how to speak English, but today these young people are losing it because everybody speaks English. Even my grandkids today. None of them speak Choctaw. And I got two at the house that really don't speak Choctaw. They don't understand a word of Choctaw, what I'm talking about. I said, "If you can easily learn how to speak English, you can learn your language."

A FEARFUL FUTURE

LORENA ALEX   2021

I remember when we were little . . . Oh, at night, Mama used to scare us, too. She would tell us some stories, but it would be scary, and we had a hard time going to sleep.

But one time she told us about . . . But we always wondered how did she know this stuff? Who tells her this stuff? But you never questioned Mama. You never talked back at all. In those days, you didn't. And if you did . . . [*laughter*]

Anyway, she said, "And as time goes on, at your times or your kids' time, there will be kids having babies."

And it has gotten to that.

"And there will be time for . . . " I'd never seen an airplane, and she talked about how . . . she said the Choctaw word, but I can't remember. She said there were going to be some airplanes and trains.

And also, there will be some disease where a lot of people, a lot of Choctaws, are going to die.

And this is what we see. And in a way it's scary because since last year up to now, a lot of friends of mine, a lot of relatives of mine, have passed on. And it's still sad for me.

Anyway, she used to bring all that stuff back, and it makes me wonder.

A GREAT ILLNESS

LOUISE WILSON   1997

I remember the old house I grew up in is still there in Bogue Chitto.

And we were sitting out in the back.

Grandpa had built a shed for his truck. And the shed is still standing there as a matter of fact.

But one time we were sitting out there close to the shed, and I guess it was in the nice summer afternoon, and we were through with our tasks. Like I said, we were sitting around there talking, and he was telling us one time that he said, more or less, telling us to listen to him. He said that y'all don't listen to me, but these things are . . . times are going to change.

And he said there's going to be an illness. He said that his grandfather told him that there's going to be a great illness that a lot of people is going to have. That back in the history, there was an illness back then which killed a lot of the Choctaw people.

And see, I didn't know about the history of this. And to this day, I still, you know, know a little bit. I need to read more about our history.

But he said back in his grandfather's time, there was an illness where it killed a lot of the Choctaw people. And that they were told that an illness is going to come here that's going to kill a lot more Choctaw people in the future.

He said it will be an illness not only for Choctaws but for all the people. People are going to be greatly touched by it. And he said that we don't know what it is, and he said, "I couldn't tell you what it is, but that's what my grandfather said," he said.

And he said now, in his time, he sees a lot of TB that gets people. And he said he sees a lot of this sugar diabetes that gets a lot of people. And he said, "I don't know if that's what he was talking about," he said, "but it could be other illnesses that he was mentioning that he knew of that we just . . . that I just didn't see," is what he was saying. And he was telling us about that.

And today when I look back, I was wanting to know. He said that everybody was going to be touched by it. Well, you know, now that AIDS is here, I wonder if that had anything to do with what he's talking about now.

It hasn't killed a lot of our Native American people, but it's killed a lot of other people, too. But we have been touched by it, even within our own tribe here. You know, we've been touched by it. And a lot of other tribes up North and elsewhere have really been touched by AIDS.

So I don't know if that's something that was a prophecy, like you say, that he was talking about. But in my grandpa's time, like he said, there was that diabetes, you know. And there's the other—what did I say?—the TB, that was there. And I think there was another that almost wiped the whole people out. Smallpox. It may be in the history book, that it almost wiped the people out back then.

PROPHECIES OF DISEASE

HAROLD COMBY   2021

It's kind of strange that the pandemic that made us MBCI [Mississippi Band of Choctaw Indians] back in 1918, 1920, almost a hundred years later, another pandemic came by. And knock on wood, it seem like we're going to survive this one, too. But even back then, they say we had a lot of deaths.

But you know, that was prophesied.

SNATCHED FROM ABOVE

MARK PATRICK   2021

From what I heard, this is more of a prophecy.

This is something that has not happened yet. But according to the Choctaw beliefs is going to happen. They said, "One day, toward the end of the world," he said, "Mother is going to be outside with her kids." And he said, "This big bird is going to come out of nowhere and is going to swoop down and capture one of the kids." He said, "That mother will be crying and screaming and pleading, and running around in circles. That bird will circle around, and," he said, "then there will be bones, where he's picking that child apart in the air. And bones will be falling to the ground, from the dead child."

I was really scared, the way she would explain it to me. Said, "This is what my parents and grandparents told me," is what she told me. She said, "That day is coming."

THE THIRD REMOVAL

ESTELLINE TUBBY   1996

One thing was that our great-grandmother said that one day we will have a third removal, here. And she told us that; she said why it will be third removal is when Indians have good homes, electricity, and all of these. And then one night . . . well, but I believe that it might be an ending of a world or ending of time. I kind of believe it must be that because she said this will not be the removal by Washington or government or whatever. It will be removal by some person in a long robes, will be coming at night and tell us that if we stay there, we will suffer in days to come. So we need to be gathering up somewhere in North. And this will not be the Oklahoma or, or something like that.

And the children, well, he'll be . . . they'll be talking to your children because they know more about the English, and they understand. And the children, well, the older person would ask them, said, "What are they saying to you?"

Said that, "Well, if we stay here, we're going to suffer." And, "They want us to go tonight, right now."

But they say, "Oh, we were born out here. We will not go. We will stay and suffer."

But the older boy will say, "Well, if it's going to be suffering, I don't want to suffer so I'm going."

And all we have to do is pick out a few clothes, and that's all we need. And everybody will say, "Well, if you go, we'll go."

And from house to house everybody will go. But few will be left, just few will be left, after all night.

After whenever, I don't know who is the person that will be here. And they will be moving overnight, just overnight. And then someone will tell the agency that the Choctaws have moved. And they'll send a word to Washington. And that's when the Washington people find out. And a few of the representatives will come down and look at the houses. But they have been hearing, seeing and hearing about the Choctaws making progress and this and that. But all in one night, they will be gone. Again.

Third removal, to the North, where the buffalo used to roam. That's what they say. And I, I hope I don't live to see it. [*laughter*] It'd be a lot of work getting up there, I guess. [*laughter*]

My great-grandmother was the one that used to sit down and tell. They didn't have . . . nobody wrote anything at that time. They just sit down and talk to their grandchildren what's going to happen in the future.

That's what they used to do. And that's why they told that story to . . .

And my mom heard about it, so she repeat it over again.

[Estelline returned to the topic about thirty minutes later.]

I was talking about that removal. Well, I was writing about it. One day I thought I'd write about it, and no one was here, and I went wri—ting about it.

And I was thinking, well, I guess we'll be hungry when we go. And there's nothing else . . . if we take our clothes, we're still going to suffer, look like.

And I keep thinking about it.

And then there was a voice talking to me and said, "You read Moses and my people in the wilderness, how they survived."

And so I went to the Bible and read the Scripture a-ll the way down to it, and it said that—the people that Moses took to that wilderness, these people—said, "Well you come, you bring us here out to suffer and die. And you said we were God's people. But you didn't tell us we going to suffer this much. We are rea-lly getting hungry."

And then, Moses said, "Well, tomorrow you will be fed."

But they couldn't believe it. They got on to Moses about it. They didn't have anything to do. I guess in the wilderness you just go there and stay.

So finally in the morning, it rained. And it was the manna that came down and fed these people.

And that came into my mind while I was thinking about it. And the thing that came into my mind at that time was the spiritual walk. It was not just the removal like the other ones.

And maybe that's why the Lord is telling me what they going to do. Maybe it was a spiritual walk, and we'll be leaving.

So that's the third removal. That's the good story that I got it from my mother that my grandmother told. She died when she was hundred and four. So she told my mother some of the things. So she remembered and told me about it.

WAR

LINDA WILLIS   2000

And then my grandfather would tell us that there's going to be a great big war coming to the United States, where, he would tell us, there would be more houses in the future where you can see everybody, neighbors to neighbors, just like we're living right now. And he would say there would be no place for us to hide, so we're going to end up being killed.

"Not unless," they said, "if you're truly Choctaw, you would have Choctaw shirt or Choctaw dress hanging up in your porch. That way they'll know that you're Indian living in that house. And they'll pass by you."

LAND GETTING OLD

LOUISE WILSON   1999

My grandfather said, "You see young people get white hair, now," he said.

And I said, "Yeah."

And he said, "Well, it's because the earth is getting older. This earth is not..." I can't think of the word. "It's getting old now, and so it's about to break loose," is what he was saying.

I don't know what he meant by that, whether it was going to blow up or whether or not...

And you know, as I got older, I see these predictions that Jeane Dixon—is it Jeane Dixon? Yes—that Jeane Dixon said about California going under the water and things like that. Well, that's exactly what he was saying back then. He didn't say California, though, but he said this land that we're living on is going to go back under water eventually, he said.

He said, "Might not be in the Bible," he said, "but I know that's what's going to happen." And he said, "If people don't take care of the land like it is, we're not going to have that much food," and all of that. And he said, "That part might be in the Bible, but..."

I was thinking, "No, that's plenty of food. You know, right there in the garden we got plenty of food, as long as you got a garden." But now, yeah, you see, in Ethiopia and all these other places, it's so dry that they don't have no food and things like that.

And even here in America there's a lot of families that don't have much food because they're living on the street or homeless or things like that. So now I see what he was talking about. But maybe he meant that if we don't continue to till the land and keep our garden growing, that we won't have no food.

But then you see where a lot of farmers have to, they lose their land because they couldn't come up with the payments every year. When they farm, they lose money more than make money. And what are the farmers going to do? We're not going to have any more farmers; maybe that's what he was talking about. Eventually, all that's going to be gone. I don't know.

But he did talk a lot about [that]. Grandma too. And she would say, "You..."

When my son was born, the one that was hearing impaired, the one I was telling you about, it wasn't until he was four or five years old, and he had white hair, started to have white hair in his hair.

And I asked Grandma about that.

And she said that's one of the signs that this land is getting old. So you'll find that there's a lot of other young people who have white hair that this land is getting old.

And she says, "Don't pick it. Because if you pick it, you're going to have a lot more in there." So I never picked it. But you can find . . . I've seen it even, some young kids, would have a lot of white hair. And she said back then, a lot of young people are not supposed to have white hair and things like that. But they'd be young, and they'd have white hair.

EXTINCTION

PISATUNTEMA (EMMA)   1910

Many generations hence the country will become crowded with people. Then there will be tribes that do not now exist. They will so increase in numbers that the land will scarcely sustain them. And they will become wicked and cruel and so fight among themselves, until at last Aba will cause the earth to be again covered with water. Thus, mankind will be overwhelmed, and all life will become extinct.

Time will pass, and the waters will subside; the rivers will flow between their banks as before. Forests of pine with grass and flowers will again cover the spots of land thus left dry by the receding waters. Later man and birds and beasts will again live.

SNAKE RETURNS

BRADLEY ALEX   2021

My father, up to teenage years, Nanih Waiya, he lived there. Him and his friends and relatives, they used to play over there.

There's a prophecy.

When the time comes, before the last day, he said, there's a big snake there that is going to come out, revealing that the time is coming. It's a huge snake. It's in that cave. There's a tunnel or somewhere underneath that goes into the water alongside that.

But he said they used to say that it's there. It's going to come out, eventually reveal itself when the time comes.

END OF THE WORLD

LINDA WILLIS   2000

My grandfather Cameron Wesley used to tell us that if his children didn't see it, that we would see it, or our children would be the last to see the world being destroyed; that's what he used to say.

And he would tell us what to do. He would tell us that it's going to be the people destroying the world. It's not going to be God destroying the world, he said; it's going to be people destroying the world.

Because, I guess, when I remember those, and when they're making these nuclear bombs and everything, and I would think back to what he was saying. I said that's why he used to tell us that these things were going to happen, that people were going to destroy each other. Destroy the world.

And I kind of believed that because it's happening all over the world. People are destroying one another, killing one another, and I think we're going to face that.

BIG FIRE

HAROLD COMBY   2021

On the end of the world, my mom used to say that it's going to be a big fire. You know flood didn't kill mankind, so it's going to be fire.

And the thing is, there is so much problem with nuclear weapons. Everybody wants it. So once that starts flying . . .

JOKES AND TALL STORIES

People tell jokes and tall stories for a laugh, and they are rarely disappointed. Gathered under carports, in living rooms, at lunch tables, and in office corridors, men and women joke with one another, trading stories back and forth to the delight of both the small group that watches outside the fray and the storytellers themselves. Many of the stories depend on specific knowledge of those present and can be described as good old-fashioned ribbing. Stories are exaggerated to the point of outrageousness. They are the *shokhannopa*—literally "hog talk" but more accurately translated as "hogwash"—that friends and family engage in regularly. Most of these stories are embarrassing—that is often the good-natured goal—and are appropriate only in the small groups in which they are told.

However, other stories and jokes employ legendary funny men such as Ashman and Jim Dixon rather than audience members for their humor. These are the stories told throughout the community, stories that are understood if not always known outside small, familiar circles. The same can be said of those stories told with self-effacing humor in which narrators place themselves as the scapegoats. Such stories parallel the experiences of others, making them appropriate and resonant to the larger community. "*Shokhannopa*. That's pig tales," explains Doyle Tubby. "Sometimes it's called a fib. But they would tell it in a way that that fib is so real. They tell it in such a way where you'll be part of that story. Sometimes it's embarrassing for you, but it's just a whole lot of fun because friends, family know how to laugh among each other."

The focus of many of these stories is human foible. In laughing at missteps, misjudgments, and naivete, storytellers and audiences acknowledge a shared concept of how we ought to act. There is also the recognition that not conforming to these ideals is natural and naturally funny. Foolish behavior reaps negative, but humorous, consequences.

Each story has its own multiple interpretations, its own particular issues and dilemmas. Yet as Carmen Denson says, there is a broader level upon which such stories operate: "The moral of the story is, well, that happens in life, too. You got to be careful. You tell them to your kids, and they go out in life, and into society, and they'll be more aware. You don't teach them anything, they won't know what to do; they'll be walking into like a jungle." Morals in stories, metaphors for living—the parallel to biblical parables is not an arbitrary one. The majority of the community is Christian, and such values often underlie these raucous tales.

The narratives in this section strike a balance between their functions as entertainment and instruction. While some stories suggest moral imperatives, others comment on social behavior and cultural traditions. Customs of mourning the dead and courting a wife are reflected and remembered in these tales. Some people continue to practice such customs, while others have adopted Christian rituals for such rites of passage. Either way, these customs remain a part of the common heritage for all Choctaw.

While negotiations of proper behavior and cultural customs involve complex relationships within the community, the Choctaw are also engaged in interaction outside the community. And while some tribal members might wish that such interaction was not necessary, their expanding role in Mississippi economics has made isolation impossible. More frequent contact on decidedly more friendly terms than in years past has not made interaction with non-Native people completely comfortable. Yet the Choctaw storyteller understands that tense, ambiguous, and particularly sensitive topics can be dealt with effectively with humor. Further, such topics make great fodder for humorous stories. So do stories of encounters with new technology, such as automobiles, air conditioning, and running water. While these stories can comment on relationships with non-Native people, they also suggest a humorous look at modernity. Change is not always easy, and it can be frightening, but in these stories, it is always funny.

THE CAR

LILLIE GIBSON   1997

They used to call it campgrounds. It was sort of like this Neshoba County Fair they got on now. They'd have little houses built out there, for some of them. We stayed out there for a week, every year.

Our house wasn't too far from the camp where we were camping, but we had cows, and we had hogs and mules. Our daddy couldn't go out there to feed them, so me and my mom walk out there and feed them. My sisters would go with us, and we'd go feed them every evening.

And one day, there was a car coming down the road. I never had seen a car before, and I was scared. [*laugh*]

And well, whoever he was, he stopped, and he said, "I'll give y'all a ride."

But I wasn't going to get in there because I didn't know what it was. [*laughter*]
And so, Mama wasn't that scared, I guess. She said, "Yeah, he'll give us a lift."
"Well," I said, "I don't know, but I'm not going to get in there."
And so Mama told him, "No. We'll just walk."
And so we walked on over there and fed all the animals, and then we came back. And there's another car going the way we were going. Well, they wanted us to ride in their car.
I wouldn't get in that car.
Mama said, "Well, I don't think it'll hurt us."
And I said, "It might hurt us, though. We don't know." [*laughter*]
And so we walked back to the camp.
I'm still scared. I never got over it. [*laughter*]

RUNNING WATER

LILLIE GIBSON   1997

Mama got married. Well, our daddy died, and when she married a man, she married one from Conehatta, and so he already had a house. And so we had to move up here.

And we didn't have no way to draw water; we didn't have no running water.

So one day, a nurse, a home health nurse, came to my house, after we moved here, now.

After I got married and we moved over here, when we moved over here, I got married.

And so, she came around and asked, do we have running water.

And I told her, "Yes ma'am. We've got running water . . . if we run and go get it." [*laughter*]

WHATYOUSAY

GLADYS WILLIS   1996

They used to call him Ashman. This is a Choctaw man. I think this was a Choctaw because when he met a White man, this Choctaw asked him, "What's your name?" I mean, in English it's "What's your name"—"Katah chihohchifo," akmano.

"What you say?"

"Where are you from?" really. The Choctaw asked the White man, "Where are you from?" but in Choctaw. He said, "Katima ish minti," akmano.

The White man said, "What you say?" akmano [he said].

The Choctaw said, "Whatyousay minti mjyah," atok miya ["He said he came from Whatyousay," so he said]. [*laughter*]

He thought he came from Whatyousay. [*laughter*]

That's the way it was.

TIME TO KILL HOGS

GLADYS WILLIS   1996

Ashman was walking down the road, and a White man came by with a car and gave him a ride. He got in there; the car had the air conditioner . . . He had the air conditioner on, so it was pretty cold in there [compared to the heat] probably from walking.

So, he said if this weather keeps up, it will be a good hog killing time tomorrow. [*laughter*]

Which in those days, they didn't have refrigerator or freezer. So, first cold spell comes, they usually kill a hog for the winter. They salt it down or hang it up in smokehouse and smoke the ham, meat. And that's the way they used to keep their food a long time ago.

THE HORSE'S EGG

OLMAN COMBY   1928

An Irishman once met a man plowing and asked what he was doing that for.

The man answered that he was going to raise cotton and also corn with which to feed his horse and colt.

"How do you hatch a colt?" said the Irishman. "Does a horse lay eggs?"

"Yes, indeed," said the man.

"What kind of eggs does he lay?"

Then the man pointed to a pile of pumpkins and said that they were horse eggs and that if one of these were laid on the gallery in the sun, it would hatch.

"How much will you take for an egg?" said the Irishman. "Ten dollars."

So the Irishman handed over the ten dollars and started off with a "horse egg."

After he had traveled for about a mile, however, he came to a fence. He climbed to the top of this with his burden, but just then the rail slipped, and he dropped it, and it burst open.

There was a rabbit close to the spot where this happened, and he started up and ran off as fast as he could.

The Irishman, however, thought that it came out of the pumpkin, and he ran after it, crying, "Whoa! Whoa!" until the rabbit was out of sight.

The Irishman walked on after it and presently came to another man plowing. "Did you see my colt come by?" he said.

"No."

"My colt came right this way. I followed him but could not catch him."

Just then, another rabbit sprung up and ran through the woods, and the Irishman started after it and has not been seen since.

THE FUNERAL

HARRY POLK   1997

This one story, then, is about Choctaw people planting corn at a place called "the bottom," the area by the edge of the creek they usually planted corn. That's the way it was.

The name of this Choctaw was Ashman.

So, as Ashman was going along, the corn which he planted he was fixing to plow.

It was like now; he hooked up the mule and was plowing.

It was said that it was so very hot. And it being this hot . . . because beyond there, below where the bank is high, way down below was a creek running. He kept looking over at it. But he got so very hot that he took the mule to the edge and tied it and took off his clothes and, only with his undershorts on, ran toward it, it was said.

When he reached the bank, he went down like this [*imitates drowning*], and he went like this, it was said.

But like the alligator there today, like that, it was an alligator that . . . the man was moving this way when the alligator looked at him. It opened this way [*imitates jaws opening wide*], it was said.

And he just went in this way [*motions falling into opening*], the alligator swallowed him, it was said.

So he was in the alligator's stomach, but he himself thought he was taken out quickly. [*laughs*]

But it happened that the alligator let him out a year later. [*laughs*]

That's where he was standing on sand, because he was let out; he laid there 'til he got dried. He went, and when he arrived and saw the corn he had plowed before, the corn was hanging all dried up, it was said.

Then as he went, when he arrived at his home, his family . . . Choctaws long ago, when someone died, they would have what was called a "cry" for that person. When it was like that, to represent his bones, sticks were connected, and they usually placed them in the middle of the room.

So that's what they were doing when he arrived, it was said. [*laughs*]

They were having a cry with the bone when he appeared. Because it had been a year.

THE WHITE CAT

CARMEN DENSON 1996

One story I learned: this is a lesson for boys, and it's a lesson for young women, too. It's kind of funny, you know.

They say that sometimes it happens in life that an older woman will be interested in a younger man.

So one time, this guy was visiting his girlfriend. Her mother was interested in this guy. So, it was about sundown, so it was kind of dark inside. So she acted like a young one, you know?

There was a vase on the side of the wall, sort of like a book stand there. She was older, so her eyes were not that good, but she pretended they were good. She thought it was a cat, a white cat sitting there.

She said, "Oh, this white cat thinks he can hide from me, that I can't see good."

So she slaps that vase down onto the ground, and it breaks up. [*laughter*]

The moral of the story is that happens in life, too. So you've got to be careful.

You tell them to your kids, and they'll go out into life, into society, and they'll be more aware. If you don't teach them anything, they won't know what to do; they will be walking into like a jungle.

THE MAN AND THE TURKEY

HENRY WILLIAMS   1997

Grandpa was not that old, so he didn't tell us about any stories. He tells us about jokes, you know.

Before, people got married without knowing each other. Parent usually used to make arrangement for these two—couple to get married—especially mamas. Mamas used to talk to the other mama. This guy don't know that he's going to marry this lady. Parent be talking, you know.

Grandpa told me one time that this guy . . . I mean, if they're going to marry, they used to look for a good hunter and good stickball player. Those are persons they used to pick.

And this guy was a lousy ballplayer and lousy hunter, so nobody picked him. But he likes this girl in that family.

So he finally killed one turkey.

So he went by one morning, carrying that turkey. He goes around and brings that turkey where he kills it at.

Each morning, he had a shotgun. And each morning, he fired that shotgun, carried that same turkey by the house. And the family looked at him, "Oh, this guy finally become a good hunter." "Look at him, carrying turkey."

Next morning, he carried that turkey and goes around and drop it over there.

Third morning, he fired that shotgun again. He carried that same turkey. So they decided to talk to him.

But they found out he had that same turkey all week! [*laughter*]

So this guy got locked out because they found out he had the same turkey. [*laughter*]

They had flies all over that turkey. [*laughter*]

I thought that was funny. I don't know how they do it, but families used to find their boys a woman. I guess that was the traditional role of the parent. If this was the same today, I'd die. [*laughter*] They'd probably take their time finding me a woman. [*laughter*]

TALKING FROGS

BRIAN BILLIE   2021

I worked with a guy named Robert Christopher Tubby. They call him Bullos. We're eating lunch, and he sat there, and he goes, "You ever heard about the frog?"

I was like, "Frog?"

He goes, "Yeah." He said, "Yeah." Frog mat abohlih binílihmat, "Ribbit, ribbit," chimáchih? "Ish hakloyo alih." [The frog that is sitting in the woods, "Ribbit, ribbit," he says to you? "Have you heard it?" he says.]

I looked; I laughed at him. "No, I want to hear it. Tell me."

He said, "One time, Chahta pat hakloh bannah tokósh [This Choctaw wanted to hear it]. He went fishing and a frog at ólah kaniyahahma yakot folótat pisa tokako [made a sound; he turned around like this to look at it].

Hm. Then he prayed, "Chihówa hina okma shokatti pat nanokachika hakloh sannah áttok. Hikma hina okma issa haklokma, haklotoh im íkkanalánah nanokachika áttok. [God, if possible, I want to hear what this frog is saying. And if possible, if you allow it, I will understand it.]

Then all of a sudden, he said he heard, "Mitih! Mitihka!" [It's coming! It's coming!]

"Katomma? Katomma?" [Where? Where?]

As he's saying that, I could hear the frogs, in my memory, how it's in the woods. It makes it a sound like "ribbit, ribbit," and it goes "rrrraann rrraann." He explained it to me, and I was like, "Yeah, I hear that way." He goes, "Well the frog is saying," and he goes,

"Mitihka! Mitihka!" [It's coming! It's coming!]

"Katomma? Katomma?" [Where? Where?]

He goes, "Yak ayah! Yak ayah!" [He's here! He's here!]

One far away goes, "Nataho? Nataho?" [What? What?]

Another goes, "Siti, sit, siti mitika!" [Snake, snake, snake is coming!]

He sat there, and he laughed. He said, "That's a story I heard from an old person about the frog and what they're saying to each other," because he said, "There are snakes, and they eat frogs. They'll be going around, and the frogs are telling each other where the snakes are."

A PRAYING BEAR

BRIAN BILLIE   2021

Then later on, Bullos said, "You ever heard about the bear that was a praying bear?"

Wow. He just come up with stories.

He said a bear, the guy was hunting bear, and he didn't see this bear come up behind him and knock his gun down. The bear reared up real tall.

Hattak mat [That man], he turned around and he prayed on his knees, and said, "Oh Lord, let this be a God-fearing bear," ahnish makatok [he said, hoping for that].

Chihowa i yimmish, Chihówa ahnit nana anokhaklo atokiya ahni tokakobear [Believing in God, hoping God would have mercy on me, but the bear], all of a sudden, bear mat akka iyacha ibbak yakomichicha [bear went down and did his hands this way [*indicates praying*]. "Thank you, Lord, for the food I'm about to receive. Thank you, áchih ho. Hattak ma apatok miya makah [he said. It is said that he ate that man]. [*laughter*]

He laughed about it. [*laughter*]

THE DOG WHO SPOKE CHOCTAW

JAKE YORK   1997

When I was seven, my mother . . .

Delta City, it was called. My uncle lived there, and we used to go there. We went to pick cotton. I was the water fetcher.

When the elders went to pick cotton, my uncle used to say he raised a puppy. Bounty was the dog's name.

My uncle could not speak English, not very much, so he didn't speak much English. He spoke Choctaw to this dog. This dog had a good mind.

Mail carrier, White people call it; he brings the mail.

When they threw the newspaper outside—"Holisso hót amálah ákma" [Go bring me the paper], calling to the dog, then the dog used to bring it. When it brought it in its mouth, he'd say, "Yakókih" [Thank you], and acknowledged it by shaking its hands, even though it's a dog.

Then, "If you want to eat, you'll have to walk here to eat the food," telling the dog in Choctaw. "Even though you stand on all fours, you must walk here on two to get the food," he said. And it used to stand up and walk there. And then he gave it biscuit, chicken bone, or something.

Then, "Binílih" [Sit], he commands, and it would sit.

"Ittólah" [Lie down], he commands, and it would lie down.

"Nosih" [Sleep], he commands, and it would close its eyes.

That dog was never spoken to in full English, which is how it learned Choctaw. Uncle never spoke to it in English, but "Ittólat tonólih" [Lie down and roll], he'd say, and the dog would lie and roll.

"Illjpah" [We eat], you'd say to make it walk on its hind legs and make it walk there to eat.

"A holisso hoyot alah" [Fetch the paper]. As commanded, it would bring it in its mouth.

That is what I want to tell you. If a dog can learn Choctaw, then you all can learn, too.

English was never spoken to that dog. My uncle only spoke to it in Choctaw.

So those of you who do not know Choctaw, you all know. Listen when they talk to you. When Choctaw is spoken, you can learn if you listen. This dog understood my uncle when spoken to only in Choctaw.

That is the way it was said, and I wanted to tell you. If a dog can learn, you can, too, okay?

That is all.

THE TRIP TO ARKANSAS

JAKE YORK   1997

My dad had a friend that he used to talk about, and his name was Jim Dixon. And I guess Jim had a knack for telling tall stories.

So, a friend of mine was visiting with me, and my dad was out in the yard; he likes to work on fishing lines—putting bobbers on, putting hooks on, testing his line.

So, he was telling us about this Jim Dixon.

He said Jim was going to Arkansas one day. But since he had no vehicles, no horses, he was going to go on foot. So, he took off for Arkansas on foot—had his little old knapsack, and he was going to Arkansas.

And back then, the trail was kind of winding. It was just like homemade trails that people had just walked on, where it was just like a little narrow road.

Since he was walking, it took a long time. He figured he was going to take a long time. So that night, when it got dark, he would go into the woods. But in order for him not to get bugs on him or snakes, he would climb up a tree and find a big old limb and lay on the limb where bugs won't get in his ears or snakes wouldn't bite him. So he would climb a tree and lay on top of a limb, and then the next morning he would get down and start walking again.

He came up to the Mississippi River; and it was evening time when he came up to the Mississippi River. He decided to sleep before he crossed the river, or he'll wait 'til daylight to cross the river the next day. He laid on a big log, and pretty soon, he fell asleep.

But the log he was laying on started to move. He thought it was the current from the river making the log move. And he kept moving 'til he crossed the river. And he got off, and it turned out the log was an alligator. [*laughter*]

He still had quite a ways to go even though he crossed. I guess he was into Louisiana. See, he still had quite a ways to go.

So, on one of those evenings, he stopped off and got on a limb to rest.

He fell off while he was asleep.

And it just so happens a big old buck was eating the acorns underneath the tree that he was laying on top of.

And he landed on the back of the deer, and the deer took off.

And that's how he had made most of his way to Arkansas. [*laughter*]

TALL STORIES

JAKE YORK   1997

And it just so happens that not too long after that, maybe a year later, same friend and I, my dad—we were all going to the store because, you see, he smokes cigarettes a lot and wanted a pack of cigarettes. So we were riding to the store.

There was an old Indian guy walking down the road. So, we stopped, gave him a ride, and he got in the car with us. He shook hands with my dad.

And, see, elderly Indians don't introduce their friends to their kids. I don't know, for some reason, I don't know if it's convention or not.

Well, anyway, this guy got in. They shook hands and asked how each was doing.

And we sat there. And I was driving, and my friend was in the back; that's where the guy was sitting, with him.

Yeah, he started telling he was living in the Delta now—Mississippi Delta area, where they had cotton plantations. He said he's under some White guy that he works for, helping out with the plantation.

And he start telling my dad that one day, a guy drove up, and he said he was out of money; he was real hungry.

So he said—at that time he had a bunch of dry goods and eggs and meat—well, he said he cooked a big ol' breakfast for that guy that came to his house and was real hungry.

So he said after the guy got through eating, he said he'd be on his way. But since he didn't have no money for gas and stuff, he said he gave the car to him for providing food for him.

Well, we got to the store. He got off, thanked my dad and all that, and he went on. My dad got his cigarette. We was coming back towards the house, and my friend says—because he's heard stories about this Jim Dixon guy—he said, "Who is that guy anyway? Man, he tells stories like I heard about Jim Dixon, these tall stories he tells."

And he said, "Fellas. Y'all just got through hearing Jim Dixon himself." [*laughter*]

THE LUCKY SHOT

OLMAN COMBY   1928

One time, a number of men were out hunting. One of their number remained at home for a considerable time while the others went after game. But at length, he went out by himself and made a bow and some arrows.

Traveling on a short distance, he saw a fox squirrel sitting on the limb of a tree and aimed an arrow at it. His arrow passed through its heart and going on, pierced a hawk which happened to be flying past. Then it fell back into the grass; but at the point where it struck, there lay a deer. The arrow wounded this deer mortally in the head, and in its death struggles, it kicked out and killed two terrapin.

And so, when the man went to get the squirrel, he also found the hawk; and when he went to recover his arrow, he found the deer and the terrapins.

Then the man went back to camp and related what had happened, and on account of his lucky shot the chief gave him his daughter in marriage.

HELP FROM ABOVE

HARRY POLK   1997

This is not an old story. I heard this in Nashville.

The kids were about your size. His mom was home.

It was almost dark, and the little boy was sitting watching TV, just before dusk. There was nothing good to watch. The boy went outside to play but there was nothing to play with.

He looked in the closet; there was a mop. He took the mop out and made a horse. He went around the house by himself.

He put the mop by the side of the house, went back to watch TV.

He forgot about it and started to play with a train.

The boy stood by the door at night; then he got frightened.

His mom said, "I need the mop. Where is it?"

The boy says, "It's over here."

It wasn't there.

He started looking for it. He couldn't find it. He thought, "Did I take it way over there?"

He ran to the door, but he couldn't go outside. He went back.

His mom asked, "Where's the mop?"

"I think I took it way over there. I can't go get it," he says.

"Why?"

He says, "I'm afraid. If I go way over there, something might happen," he says.

She felt he was going to cry, so she held him and said, "You should not be afraid. God is out there, so you shouldn't be afraid. He is watching over you," she said.

He says, "Is God really out there?"

The boy ran to the door but could not go out. "I'm still afraid."

He yelled, "God, if you're out there, bring in the mop!" [*laughter*]

ANIMAL STORIES

In these stories, animals match wits against animals—Turkey versus Terrapin, Bear versus Rabbit, Hummingbird versus Crane. Egos clash; bravado is mocked. The physically strong are inevitably defeated by the smaller, wilier animals. Cleverness is rewarded, pride punished. The winners in these contests often enjoy a laugh as their reward; the losers fare far worse, losing not merely their dignity but often their food, the fur on their tails, or even their lives. Death is common and not particularly tragic, for the animal will surely return the next time these tales are told.

If laughter is the reward for the winners in the story, it is the motivation for the storytellers. These stories, like jokes and tall stories, are also called *shokhannopa*. The audience invariably laughs—at the foolishness of some animals, the cleverness and wit of others. Yet there is also the recognition that the animals' foibles are human foibles, too. Although actual human beings rarely appear in these tales, our foolishness, greed, and gullibility certainly do. For as much as we may laugh at the animals, raising ourselves above them, separating ourselves from them, the storytellers remind us that they only look so foolish because they are acting like us.

And so the storyteller teaches. Most often, these lessons are implicit in the story. However, in more recent stories, morals are stated clearly at the end: "And so someone who is just fooling will almost precipitate a fight."

More often than morals, these tales end with explanations of why an animal looks the way it does. "That is why the possum has no hair on his tail," or "That is why rabbit's skin is loose." Often, these physical alterations serve as very visible, very real reminders of the consequences of unchecked desire and foolish attempts at imitation.

Such endings are not confined to a single story. An explanation of why the bear has no tail is provided in three vastly different stories. Nor do versions of the same story uniformly include such explanations and morals. Versions of the race between the turkey and the terrapin end variously. One ends, "The moral of the tale is that the proud and scornful are often outwitted by those they look upon with contempt and disdain." Another, "This was to teach the Indians that 'slow and sure wins the race' and that steadiness beats showy irregularity." Others explain, "That's why the turkey has a lot of tendons in its leg," or "That is why terrapins never get fat," or most often, "That is why the terrapin has seams in his shell." Often, these endings are formulaic additions, masking much deeper meanings elsewhere in the narratives.

The storyteller is an artist; the elements of a story are like pigments on a palette. Endings, plot devices, characters, even full episodes of a story can be recombined at the storyteller's will. The story will be faithful to some extent to versions the storyteller has heard before, but the storyteller seems to work as much from a wellspring of these elements as from particular, remembered narratives. Since animal tales do not purport to be legend or history, such dynamism of form is conventional, not merely inevitable.

In fact, these stories are so malleable that they, more than any other type of story, seem most easily adopted and adapted into other cultures. Many of the tales that follow will be familiar to the reader from popular media such as children's books and television cartoons, as well as from oral traditions of people throughout the South—American Indian, Anglo-American, and African American. Such tales inspired Joel Chandler Harris to write his stories of Uncle Remus. Questions of the origin of these tales are hotly debated and have never been resolved.[1] Likely, stories of this kind were known to Native America, as they were in Europe and Africa. As people mingled, stories were shared. Today, animal tales remain both popular and traditional among the Choctaw.

THE BALL GAME

SIMPSON TUBBY   1929

Once the bat wanted to play a game of ball with the squirrels. The game was to run around and up a tree as a squirrel does.

At first they told him that he did not look like a squirrel, that he had indeed a head like one but no tail, and besides he had wings like a bird.

But the bat replied that he was once in a game and his opponents pulled his tail off.

So, after he had teased them for some time, they agreed to let him play.

The play continued for a time without any trouble arising, but by and by, the bat thought that he was beaten, so he flew away with the ball.

Then the squirrels said, "You see that. I told you that he was a grand rascal," and afterward they said they would never let a squirrel of that kind play with them again.

RACE BETWEEN THE HUMMINGBIRD AND THE CRANE

UNKNOWN [HALBERT]   C. 1900

A very long time ago the hummingbird was a large bird.

He was one day sitting on a tree near a pond. The crane came there to catch fish. The hummingbird looked at him a while and said, "You are a very lazy bird, and you cannot fly fast. As for me, I can beat all the birds in flying."

The crane, spoken to in this manner, became very angry and said, "I will bet that I can beat you flying to the end of the world and back."

The hummingbird took up the bet.

The bargain was that the one that won the bet should do what he pleased to the other.

They both now began to fly. The hummingbird was like an arrow shot from a bow, and he soon left the crane far behind.

They were to fly to a place in the North which was the end of the world.

They flew all that day. Night came on, and the hummingbird went to sleep in a cedar tree. But the day and the night was all the same to the crane, and by daybreak, he got near the cedar tree in which the hummingbird was sleeping. The hummingbird waked up and again flew far ahead of the crane.

The two birds in this way flew several days. The hummingbird flew only in the daytime, and the crane flew both in the day and in the nighttime.

On the morning of the sixth day, a little after sunrise, the crane got to the end of the world. Here he waited for the hummingbird. But it was nearly midday before he came. Both now ate their dinners, rested, and slept.

The next morning, they started back. They flew back in the same way. The hummingbird flew only in the daytime and the crane flew both day and night.

And the crane got back to the pond before the hummingbird, and so won the bet.

The crane now took the hummingbird, and with a sharp flint, he cut him down into a very small bird not much larger than a butterfly.

It was in this way that the hummingbird became the smallest bird, as the saying is.

THE HUMMINGBIRD

UNKNOWN [HALBERT]   C. 1900

Another myth about the hummingbird says that a very long time ago, he was a large bird and had sense like a man, so that in all things, except speech, he was the equal of man.

But in the course of time, he became very evil-minded and took great pleasure in destroying the people's crops. So, for this, a prophet killed him with poison.

But he was permitted to arise from the dead, and he became a very small bird but did not anymore have the sense of man.

THE DOVE STORY

JEFFIE SOLOMON   1997

When a dove who had children went and arrived from killing a turtle, they ate the turtle.

And when the children were eating, the mother did not eat. But then the mother asked for the liver, but they did not give her any.

Then, "Do you all want water?" she said.

When they who wanted water said yes, she who went to the well, arriving at the well—it so happened that she died with her head in the water.

When they saw that, they cried the sound that the dove makes, which they kept making, the crying sound, they were crying.

That is how the sound came to be, it is said.

HOW THE *BISKANTAK* GOT WATER FOR THE BIRDS

UNKNOWN [HALBERT]   C. 1900

In ancient days, everything was frozen hard. There was no way to get water to drink. Though the hard-billed birds pecked the hard ice, they could not dig through it.

The little birds then hired the *biskantak*. And the *biskantak* went and stood on the frozen lake, and he sang, "I am male, bis, bis, bis, kant, kant, kant, tak, tak, tak," and so saying he broke through the ice. And so he was named *biskantak*, as the saying always has been.

WHY THE BUZZARD HAS MORE OFFSPRING THAN THE OWL

UNKNOWN [HALBERT]   C. 1900

A very long time ago, the buzzard and the owl had a quarrel as to which should have the most offspring. They agreed to settle it with a fight. The owl chose the fighting ground in the fork of two creeks. He then sat on a cherry tree. The limbs of a big dead oak hung over the cherry tree. The buzzard came and flew against the dead limbs. They fell upon the owl and knocked him to the ground. So the owl was whipped.

And from that day, there are more buzzards than owls.

And this is why in flying, the buzzard is more apt than all other birds to knock down dead limbs from off the trees.

WHY THE GUINEA HEN IS SPECKLED

OLMAN COMBY   1928

A man had a cow, which he left in the pasture while he went off hunting.

During his absence, the cow had a calf, and a wolf came up and wanted to get it. The wolf walked round and round the cow, but the cow kept facing him.

An old guinea hen, seeing what was going on, came there and began walking back and forth between the cow and the wolf until such a dust arose that the wolf could not see the cow, and the latter ran her horn through him and killed him.

At that time, the guinea hen was dark blue in color, but the cow was so grateful to it that she sprinkled it with milk, making it speckled as it is today.

BOATMAKER

OLMAN COMBY   1928

A man named Boatmaker lived on a certain river, and there was a woman living near who wished her two daughters to marry him; so she gave them directions as to where he was to be found and started them off.

By and by they came to a crane walking along by the river. Crane said, "Where are you sweet girls going?"

They replied, "Mother says we are to marry Boatmaker."

"I am he," said Crane.

Now their mother had told them that when they came to Boatmaker, they were to ask him to fill his mouth with water and blow it out; and if the water came out red, they would know that it was Boatmaker with whom they had to deal. They therefore asked Crane to do this, and when he blew the water out, it was reddish from the crawfish legs, which came out with it.

One of the girls believed that he was Boatmaker and married him, but the other refused to accept him and walked on down the river.

Presently, she came to Boatmaker himself standing by a boat. She put him to the test also, and when he blew the water out, it came forth red like a rainbow. So she married him.

By and by, the other sister came where they were, and she also wanted to marry Boatmaker.

"Have you slept with Crane?" Boatmaker asked.

"No."

"Well, then, try to duck under water three times, and if you can, it will prove that you are telling the truth."

She could not do this, and Boatmaker sent her back to Crane; but her sister accomplished it easily.

One morning, Boatmaker's wife arose, combed and parted her hair, and went out where Boatmaker stood. Boatmaker seized a stick and struck her suddenly on the middle of her head so cleverly that he divided her into two women. He did this because his wife's mother had sent him two wives, and he thus got two wives back.

The next time he met Crane, the latter wanted to know how this was done, and Boatmaker explained what he must do, but when he struck his own wife, he killed her. When he was in the act of striking her, he became frightened and jumped back, and that is why Crane is now humpbacked.

THE HUNTERS AND THE BEARS

UNKNOWN [HALBERT]   C. 1900

The saying is that a long time ago, the bear had a long tail, and his body had a strong odor. So the hunters often found the bears by the wind blowing their scent to them. And the bears were all getting killed by the hunters.

So one of the bears went to the wind and complained that the wind carried their scent to the hunters, who were killing them so fast that soon there would be no bears.

The wind agreed to take away the scent from the bears if they would consent to lose their tails.

The bears agreed to this, so the wind cut off their tails.

So from that time, the bears have no scent, and the hunters do not find them so easily.

RABBIT AND THE BEARS

GUS COMBY   1990

Rabbit lived at the edge of the swamp, on the bank of a creek, and a big old pine tree was there.

He run around in the swamp and got lost. He got away up in the swamp—don't know where to go.

And he heard a noise and went over there; and there was a bear, having a meeting. And they was talking about who was the meanest and the smartest one.

One bear, a young bear, said, "I'm the smartest and the meanest."

And the Rabbit was sitting there. He wanted to go home. So Rabbit told the Chief there, "Naw, uh-uh. Man is the smartest one."

And at that time, before that happened, the bear used to have long tails. Now they don't have but about that long [*shows with hands*].

And so, that mean bear wanted to see the man who was meaner and smarter than he is. So Chief told Rabbit to lead him down where the man is.

Rabbit told him, said, "I live on a creek bank next to the biggest pine tree. I live under it."

So Bear know where it was. So he took him down there, come out of the swamp—open place, walking down there.

And here come a boy. Bear said, "Ooooh. Is that a man?"

He said, "No. He will be someday."

After a while, here come the old man with a walking stick. He was humped over. Bear said, "Is that a man?"

He said, "He used to be. He used to be, but now he's about gone."

After a while, here come a young man with a shotgun, a double-barreled shotgun. Rabbit said, "Here comes a man. Go meet him. I'll see you later." He didn't care because he got home. He knowed where he was at.

And Bear went down there. And this man look at that bear, and he said, "Them bears live in the swamp. What the hell he doing down in the open here?" He said, "If he gets close enough, I'm going to shoot him."

He had buckshot in one barrel and birdshot in the other one. So he got close enough to shoot him in the face with birdshot.

The Bear, he was walking on his hind foot. He got down and started running with his four foot.

Then the hunter let him have it with the buckshot and cut his tail off.

He got back, though, and the Chief said, "How is it?"

And he said, "He sure is. That man is smarter than me and all of us put together because he's got thunder and clouds," he said.

"I lost my tail."

HOW THE BEAR LOST HIS TAIL

OLMAN COMBY   1928

A bear once met a fox with a fish in his mouth and said, "How did you get the fish?"

The fox directed him to a certain big lake, which was frozen over because it was winter, and told him to cut a hole in the ice, stick his tail down into the water, and when he felt a fish bite it, jerk suddenly and pull the fish out.

The bear did as he had been directed, but he did not feel a bite for a long time.

Meanwhile, however, ice began to form about his tail, and presently, when he became restless, he pulled against it and thought that a fish was biting. Consequently, he jerked suddenly, but his tail was so firmly frozen in that it came off.

And that is why bears do not now have them.

HOW THE RABBIT GOT A SHORT TAIL

INEZ HENRY   1986

A rabbit wanted to catch a fish, it was said.

And there was a frozen pond.

The rabbit broke the frozen ice, and he hung his tail in the water and sat, it was said. And then something came and nibbled. He thought it was a fish, but it was an alligator who had bitten his tail off.

That's why the rabbit has a short tail.

HOW THE BULLFROG LOST HIS HORNS

UNKNOWN [HALBERT]   C. 1900

The saying is that a very long time ago, the bullfrog had horns, and the deer had no horns.

One day, the deer came to a lake to drink. The bullfrog was at the lake. The deer began to say things to please him. He said, "My friend, you have fine horns. They make you look well. How do you think they would look on me? Let me try them on, and then you tell me how they look on me."

The bullfrog lent the deer his horns. The deer put them on his head. He then ran off a little ways and then came back. He said to the bullfrog, "My friend, how do the horns look on me?"

The bullfrog said, "They look well on you."

The deer then said, "Now look at me again while I run up yonder and back, and see if they don't make me look better than you ever saw me look before."

"Go ahead," said the bullfrog.

The deer trotted off a little ways. Then he ran away very fast to the woods.

The bullfrog waited a long time for the deer to come back. He then began to bellow for the deer to come back. But the deer never came back again.

And so the bullfrog lost his horns. He has never forgotten them. And now whenever he thinks of them, he bellows dolefully for a long time. Then people say, "The bullfrog is bellowing for his horns."

But the horns do not do the deer good all the time, for he has to lose them every year. This is because he acted so mean in stealing them from the bullfrog.

HOW THE ALLIGATOR GOT HIS BACK

GUS COMBY   1990

You know the small wild animals? The biggest ones, to my understanding, was monkey and fox. Rest of them was smaller—rabbit, squirrel.

And they lived down in the swamp.

And there was just one place where they could drink water. There was a big lake there. And at that time, the alligator used to have a hide like a fish—smooth back. And he used to sleep on that side.

But every time the little ones got to be a pretty good size, they disappeared. And the animals had a meeting. They said, "What happened to our children? They disappear all the time." They talked about it. "We don't know."

But you know, that Alligator would sleep by the bank. Looked just like an old, dead tree. The little animals would play there; and with one swing, he'd get about four, five of them.

Monkey caught up with him because Monkey was up on a tree playing. And he told the Rabbit about it. He said, "I know what's been getting our little ones."

He said, "What's that?"

Said, "That thing in that lake."

And they had a meeting and said, "We got to do something about that. We've got to make him move or something."

But they was scared of him. They couldn't do nothing because he was too big, you know? So they talked about it and couldn't do anything about it.

But he was lying there sleeping one day, and they seen smoke way out there. And Rabbit told them, he said, "Y'all gather anything you can burn and put it on top of the Alligator. I'm going after fire."

Rabbit left, and when he come back, they had everything they could pile. Even Mouse was there. And they set that fire, that thing on fire, and it burned. That Alligator burned.

And now, you see, his back is all wrinkled up because they scorched him.

They say people wasn't like that. Mouse didn't do much, but they didn't say nothing.

They said, "We got him." And they say that people ought to live like that, but they couldn't do it. Ain't that right?

So, Alligator moved out.

RABBIT AND TURTLE RACE

GUS COMBY   1990

Rabbit and Turtle, they had a race.

Rabbit was bragging about it because he run fast. And Turtle, you know, he was slow. So Rabbit was bragging about how fast he could run, and the Turtle he say he don't care. He said he'd get there. And Rabbit said he'd like to race him.

So they set the date, one time. And they were going to have a race at a certain creek about two miles down, way up in the woods. That was going to be the finishing line.

So Turtle, he told his cousins.

All turtles, you know, look just alike. You know, the terrapin? All just alike, so they helped one another.

And Rabbit was by himself. He didn't get his buddies.

And so, going up the hill, they had a turtle laying there. Next hill, another turtle. All the way to the creek.

And Rabbit was so fast, you know, he didn't pay attention to that.

And they start off running. Rabbit looked back, as he was hopping over the hill, and a turtle was going down the hill. Running fast, got to the bottom of the hill, turtle be going up the hill. He thought that he couldn't catch him.

When he got to the creek, one of them was there. He said, "Ha. I been here a pretty good while."

So he fooled him.

RACE BETWEEN THE TURKEY AND THE TERRAPIN

UNKNOWN [HALBERT]   C. 1900

The saying is that one day, long time ago, the Turkey was bragging before the birds and beasts how fast he could run. The Terrapin told him that he could beat him running. The two then made a bet. If the Turkey should beat the Terrapin running, he was to take off the Terrapin's shell. But if the Terrapin was the fastest runner, he was to put white oak splints in the Turkey's legs.

A day was set for the race, and the Terrapin prepared the running ground. The Terrapin covered his side of the track, from one end to the other, with a thick bed of leaves. He then hid on his side of the track, a little distance apart, many terrapins under the leaves. Every terrapin held a white feather in his mouth.

The day came for the running. The Turkey and the Terrapin were there. The Terrapin held a white feather in his mouth. The two began to run.

Just as they began to run, the Terrapin ran under the leaves. The leaves made a rustling. The first terrapin in front of him heard the rustling, and he quickly jumped from under the leaves and began to run with the white feather in his mouth. The Turkey saw him and his feather and was fooled. He thought it was the first Terrapin.

The second terrapin now ran under the leaves, and the third terrapin heard him. He jumped from under the leaves with his feather, started to run, and then went under the leaves.

The fourth terrapin with his feather heard the rustling and jumped up from under the leaves and started to run.

And so one after the other, all the other terrapins with their feathers did the same thing.

The Turkey ran very fast, but all the time he saw in front of him a terrapin with a white feather in his mouth. He thought it was all the same terrapin.

The Terrapin now won the race. There were many terrapins at the other end of the running ground. When the Turkey got there, he stared to run away into the woods, but these terrapins caught him. They threw him down and held him fast. They then put white oak splints in his legs, and from that day to this, the turkey has them in his legs.

TURTLE AND TURKEY

PISATUNTEMA (EMMA)   1910

Turkey met Turtle on the road one day and said to him, "Why are you so hard, without any fat?"

"I was born that way," replied Turtle.

"But you cannot run fast," said Turkey.

"Oh, yes I can; just watch me."

And with that, Turtle walked along the road.

"Well, even if you walk, you are not able to run."

And then Turtle raised his head and went, as fast as he was able, down the path.

But Turkey, by walking only slowly, could easily overtake him and so passed him. That being so easily accomplished, Turkey laughed at Turtle and said to him: "You are too slow; let me have your shell; I will put it on and run with the other turtles and easily beat them in a race."

Turkey then took Turtle's shell and, getting in it, assumed the appearance of a turtle. Soon meeting four other turtles, all decided to race, and, of course, Turkey was victorious.

WHY TERRAPINS NEVER GET FAT

OLMAN COMBY   1928

One time Turkey met Terrapin crawling along and asked him how long it would take him to reach a certain place, making fun of him because he was so slow.

Terrapin kept straight on, saying, "I will get there all right."

After Turkey had teased him for some time, he stopped and said, "If you give me time to rest, I will beat you running."

So they agreed upon a date and parted.

Then Terrapin got other terrapins and placed them upon the tops of three hills over which the course lay and one at the goal.

When the time came for the race to start, Terrapin placed himself at the starting point, and the word was given. Of course, Turkey at once left Terrapin behind, but when he neared the first hill, he saw what he supposed was the same one just crawling out of sight over the top. He redoubled his speed, but when he had reached the place, the terrapin had concealed himself, and presently the Turkey saw another terrapin going over the top of the next hill. The same thing happened at the third, and another terrapin was lying at the finish, which he supposed was his antagonist, and he believed that he had been beaten.

Turkey was now angry with Terrapin for having bested him and told him that the next time he encountered him he was going to cut off his head with an ax.

One day, when Turkey was carrying a sword, he met Terrapin and ran upon him to carry out his threat. Terrapin withdrew his head into the shell so that it could not be cut off, but Turkey slashed at his back until he was nearly dead.

Presently, great numbers of ants came that way, and Terrapin said to them, "I would give all the fat I have to have my shell completely sewed together." So the ants sewed him together and received his fat in exchange.

That is why terrapins never get fat.

TURTLE, TURKEY, AND THE ANTS

PISATUNTEMA (EMMA)   1910

Turtle was asleep in some high grass when along came Turkey, who stepped upon him, crushing his shell but not killing him.

Turtle became angry and asked Turkey if he was not able to see him in the grass.

"No," replied Turkey. "You are so low; you should learn to walk as I do and hold your head up, that you might be seen."

But Turtle said he was not able to do so.

And then Turtle told Turkey to call the ants to come and repair him.

Soon the ants arrived with many strands of colored thread. First, they gnawed away the flesh and fat and so cleaned the broken bones. Then, with their colored threads, they sewed together the fragments of bones, thus making a hard bone covering on the outside of Turtle.

The colored threads used by the ants may still be seen as colored streaks on the outside of Turtle's shell.

WHY THERE ARE SEAMS IN THE TERRAPIN'S SHELL

UNKNOWN [HALBERT]   C. 1900

A long time ago the terrapin had much fat under his shell.

A man wanted this fat to eat, so he lifted the terrapin up and threw him hard on the ground, so his shell was broken. The man then took out the fat.

The terrapin was much hurt and groaned much.

The ants saw him and were sorry for him. So they took some thread and sewed his broken shell together.

This is why the terrapin has seams in his shell and has no fat in his body, so the saying is.

WHY THE TURTLE'S SHELL IS SEWED UP

INEZ HENRY   1988

It is said, a turtle was laying on the path.

And it is said a woman who is going along sees the turtle.

The woman, seeing as she goes on by—the turtle said to the woman a bad word, it is said. The woman is angry, and she doesn't like it; and she comes back to where the turtle is lying and comes and stomps, stomps on the turtle, and breaks the shell in pieces, it is said.

Because the turtle shell broke up in pieces, the ants came to sew him back together.

That's how it came to be, why the turtle's shell looks sewed up.

HOW THE TERRAPIN LOST THE ABILITY TO CLIMB TREES

UNKNOWN [HALBERT]   C. 1900

The saying is that in ancient days there was a lizard, and there was a terrapin. The lizard was a tree climber, as is the saying. The terrapin was also a tree climber.

The lizard sharpened a switch, and as the terrapin was climbing up a tree, the lizard went up with him and jabbed the terrapin behind with the sharp switch.

And the terrapin started to say "*pahihko*" but said "*yahohio*" and fell down to the ground.

And it was thence forth so fixed that the terrapin could not climb a tree.

And so the terrapin is no tree climber, so the saying is.

POSSUM'S TAIL

THERON "DUKE" DENSON   2021

These stories by the Choctaw with the animals in general, these stories are intended to teach the Choctaw people what is good and bad, ethical and moral. When you hear the story, it's always some animal doing something right, some animal doing something wrong. So they want to teach the younger folks about benevolence and morality, ethics, and all the other qualities that a human being should have.

For instance, I remember a story, how the raccoon got his tail so beautiful.

The story is the Possum had a shaggy tail as well, but he was always jealous of the Raccoon because the Raccoon had a very beautiful tail. Said he wanted a tail just like that.

So one day, he asked the Raccoon, "How in the world did you get a tail like that? I sure would like to have a tail like that."

Well, the Raccoon didn't want any other animal to have a tail like his, so he told him a big lie. He said, "What I did is I gathered some wood, and I made a fire. I tied up my tail with tree bark so it wouldn't burn there. Then I laid my tail on the fire."

So then the Possum decided, "I'm going to do what he had done." So he built a fire, tied his tail separated apart, just like the Raccoon's—there's a space between each color. So he wanted to do it that way. So he built the fire; he tied wood bark around his tail.

Who would tie wood bark around his tail and put it in the fire? [*laughter*] But the Possum, he didn't think. He just wanted so badly to have that tail of the Raccoon.

So he stuck his tail into the fire. And the tail caught on fire. It burned up all the hair.

So ever since then, all the possums have a tail that is hairless.

That's the story I've heard. You see what the basis for that story is. Don't do anything foolish.

POSSUM AND COON

GRADY JOHN   1998

You know, here's another legend.

Possum and Coon, they were swimming in the creek. And after a while, they'd be rubbing each other, washing; they were just like us—they take a bath too, you know.

After a while, the guy got up, and boy, they shake their body; they're wet. So he's shaking, dry them up quicker.

After a while, they say they were a little cool, so they decide they'll build a fire. Sit around, gossip a little bit. Said, Coon had a beautiful tail. Possum just had white hair. Possum said he didn't like it. He asked, "How come you got pretty tail? Striped. And I don't."

Here he was. Coon was about to tell a tale.

He said, "I slapped that thing in the fire and cooked it 'til it just come out pretty."

He was just telling a tale.

They was sitting around there a long time. Coon just got really tired, so he went home. Before he got halfway home, he said, "You know, I was telling a tale. I hope he don't burn his tail." He turned around and came back. He said he took off.

He was too late. Possum had done burned his tail.

Boy, when he got down there, he got mad and chased him. They chased, they were up and down, up and down.

And Possum tried to catch the Coon, but Coon got smart and got in the hole, and the way its top—the hole was in the top, and Coon took off or whatever.

Possum was still in that hole; he got stuck. So finally, he gave up, and what he done, he fall down. So he looked and looked and looked, and he said, "Boy," he said, "my tail is all skinned up."

So he found a tree, a fork in the tree. He said his tail was nearly come off. He put it in the fork in the tree. He thought he was going to put it back, his skin. He slide it back, twice. When he slide it back, next time he pulled hard, and that's when that skin all came off.

That made Possum mad. He was started looking at Coon. He was trying to whip up all the coon he see. [*laughter*]

That was some of the things my grandpa used to tell a lot. I wished I had wrote it. I wish I had kept a tape because I lost quite a bit of it.

THE PANTHER AND THE OPOSSUM

UNKNOWN [HALBERT]   C. 1900

A long time ago, as the panther was traveling through the woods, he came across a lean, starving opossum. The panther said to him, "My friend, you look like you are almost dead."

The opossum replied, "Yes, I cannot live long for I have not had anything to eat in a long time."

The panther was sorry for the opossum. He said to him, "My friend, I can fix it so that you can get plenty to eat. You know I am the deer's enemy. They hate me and would be glad to know that I was dead. Then they would not be afraid of my jumping down upon them from the limb of a tree when they are passing underneath.

"Now I will make out I am dead. Then do you bury me and then go and tell the deer to come and have a big dance around my grave."

Straightaway, the panther stretched himself out on the ground and feigned death. The opossum dug a grave and put him in it. He then laid a soft, rotten log along on the panther's body. He then filled the grave with earth but left a small hole for the panther to breathe through. The opossum now went to look up the deer.

In a little while, he met a deer. He told him of the death of the panther and to go and tell all the deer. All must come and have a big dance around the panther's grave.

The opossum now went back and sat near the grave.

First, a big buck took a sharp stick and stuck it down into the grave. The stick went into the rotten wood. The buck thought the rotten wood was the panther's body. He told all the deer that the panther was really dead. The deer then began to dance around the grave. When they were dancing, kept singing, "Toshbi pullasi, toshbi pullasi" [He is nearly rotten; he is nearly rotten]. The deer were very glad and danced a long time.

At last, the opossum said, "He will catch you soon."

Just as he said this, the panther jumped out of the grave and caught and killed the big buck. The other deer ran away.

The panther gave the dead buck to the opossum.

The opossum now had plenty to eat. He ate a long time.

At last, he became frightened. He was afraid the deer would come and kill him because he had been so tricky with them. Some blackbirds were feeding on the leaves not very far off. They flew up and made a noise like thunder. The opossum was now in great fear. He put the deer's backbone in a basket, fastened the basket to his body, and started away on a trail.

At last, he came to a creek, where there was a foot log. He climbed a bending tree that overlooked the foot log. He then took the backbone out of the basket and began to eat it.

After a while, a wolf came along. He got on the foot log and began to cross the creek. When he was nearly across, he looked down in the water and saw the shadow of the backbone in the water. He thought to himself, "There is something mighty good to eat." So he jumped down into the water. He dived to the bottom but found nothing but mud and leaves. He was badly bothered and went back to the bank that he had left.

Just then, the opossum overhead said to him, "Open your mouth, and I will throw into it something good to eat."

The wolf heard the voice but did not know where it came from. He ran out on the foot log, and again he saw the shadow of the backbone on the water. He jumped down again. Again he got only mud and leaves. He went to the shore again, ran around the tree, and looked everywhere.

At last, he lay down. He howled and threw up his head. Then he saw the opossum up in the tree.

The opossum again said to him, "Open your mouth, and I will throw into it something good to eat."

The wolf did so, and the opossum threw the backbone into his mouth. The wolf tried to swallow it, but it stuck in his throat and choked him to death.

The opossum came down from the tree. He took a sharp flint and went and cut off the wolf's head and put it in his basket. He then crossed the creek on the foot log.

He was traveling slowly along in the trail when he met a gang of wolves. The leader of the wolves spoke to him and asked him where he was going. The opossum said, "I am going over to yonder hill. My grandmother is a potter. She told me to go over there and get some clay to make a bowl." The wolves were satisfied and passed on. The opossum too passed on.

After a little while, he met a lame wolf who asked him many questions. At last, he peeped into the basket and saw the wolf's head. He howled a signal for the wolves to return. They did so. The lame wolf then told them of the wolf's head in the opossum's basket. The wolves looked at it. They told the opossum that he must die.

The wolf leader said to him, "We will let you choose the quickest way to die, for die you must."

The opossum said, "Over on the other side of the hill, you will find a lightwood knot. You can kill me quicker with that than with anything else."

The wolves left the lame wolf with the opossum, and all started off to get the lightwood knot.

When they were all out of sight, the opossum said to the lame wolf, "Over on the other side of that log yonder is another lightwood knot. Go and get it and kill me before the others get back, and you will become a big *mingo* [chief] among them."

The lame wolf hobbled off after the knot.

Meanwhile, the opossum sneaked off.

After going a little ways, he picked up a rattlebox and a sharp thorn and then burrowed down into a sinkhole.

Soon, all the wolves together with the lame wolf came to the sinkhole. The lame wolf had told the other wolves on their return about the opossum's trick, and they soon tracked him up to the sinkhole.

The wolves began to grabble down after him. The opossum now shook his rattlebox. Then one of the wolves said, "We must be mistaken. This must be a rattlesnake hole."

Another wolf said, "May be so, but no matter what he may be, drench him with your water." The wolf obeyed, and the brine, running down into the hole, struck the opossum on the throat.

Then another wolf ran his paw down into the hole. The opossum stuck the thorn in it. The wolf jerked back his paw, and all now believed it was a rattlesnake in the hole and not the opossum. So the wolves went away and left the opossum in the hole.

This shows how cunning the opossum is; how he can fool animals that are bigger and stronger than he is. And it shows, too, how the opossum got the yellow spot on his throat when the brine struck him.

HOW THE POSSUM TRICKED THE WOLVES

HAZEL THOMAS   1980s

It was said that one day an opossum was walking home. Then a pack of wolves saw him.

The wolves were all growling because they wanted to kill the opossum and eat him. The opossum knew that the wolves were trying to kill him. So he told them, "Rabbit sticks, blowguns, and all cannot kill me, but only pine needles can. Over beyond the second hill, I had placed some pine needles. If you all can go and get it, you all can kill me."

The wolf leader told one of the wolves, "You stay and watch over the opossum." So one of the wolves stayed and watched him.

The opossum lied to one of the wolves and said, "If you go and get pine needles that are close by, you can be the first one to kill me," he told him.

The opossum lied to the wolf, but the wolf believed him and left. The opossum said to himself, "Not one day will they ever be smart like me," and started laughing.

The end.

POSSUM AND THE FOX

HARRY POLK   1997

My grandfather used to tell all kind of story. When he build a fire, he said he's going to tell a story—just sitting around, tell a story. All kind of story. He tell me about animal story, too. And the Possum and the Fox. [*laughter*]

Possum was over there and, you know that 'simmon tree? It got kind of yellows? But that time, it's good. When it's rotten it's yellow.

That Possum he climbed up, and he picked all he want, and then go home. And Fox met him; he said, "What you got down there?"

And Possum said, he just showed him like that [*opens and lifts his hands*].

And Fox said—tried to eat one of them—he said, "It's good. Where'd you get it?"

"Back there."

"How you get it? It's too high. How you get it?"

Possum, he climbed up, he said. He tell him lie, you know. "I just went over there and running, just—I hit my head on that tree, and the 'simmon fall off, and I pick it up."

Fox did believe it, going, "OK. I'm going to try it."

Possum was standing up there watching Fox going up there. Said to go up there and run, fast as he can, and just hit that tree.

He hit it on head, and he fall over unconscious.

Possum, he laughed. [*laughter*]

He tell a lie. That's why he wanted to do.

He tell me all kind of stories, used to be.

POSSUM AND THE WOODPECKER

EDDIE JOHNSON   2021

This one deals with a hungry possum and a gullible woodpecker. The story goes like this.

This Possum one day was walking through the woods, foraging for food, but he found nothing to eat, and he's really starving. His stomach was making hunger pain noise, and he kept on saying, "Oh, I'm so hungry. I wish I could find something to eat." And as he was foraging around, going forward further into the woods, in the distance, he heard a woodpecker pecking on old dead trees, and he's really working away. The woodpecker's working hard on that tree. And the Possum is still not really listening, but he kept on going, and he ends up at that tree where the woodpecker is.

So he looks up, and then he gets the idea, "Hey, there's my meal." [*laughter*] So he looks at that tree, and there's a hole at the bottom. He looks into it, and it goes way up to the top where the woodpecker is. And he said, "Maybe I can get me some meal right here." So he goes up that tree, and what he does is he acts like he's stuck. He got up as close as he could get to the woodpecker, and he starts hollering out saying, "Help, I'm stuck. I can't get out."

So the woodpecker, being a kindhearted animal, decides to go help that Possum and says, "Where are you?"

And he said, "I'm stuck. Help me. Get me out. I can't get out. I thought this hole was a little bit bigger, but it's not."

The woodpecker says, "Wait. I'll poke a hole in this tree where you're at."

And he starts pecking away, and he said, "Naw, just wait." He starts pecking away, and then he pokes a whole through the tree, and he sees the head of the Possum, and he [the Possum] says, "It's not big enough."

And the Possum waits. He starts pecking and [the Possum] saying, "Make it a little bit bigger."

And so the woodpecker works away and makes that hole bigger, and then [the Possum] says, "Now, stick your head in here and see if it is bigger so I can get out. We'll see how big it is."

The woodpecker decides to go see how big that hole is, and when he does, the Possum takes a good chomp on him.

That was his meal of the day. [*laughter*]

WHY THE RABBIT'S SKIN IS LOOSE

OLMAN COMBY   1928

Wildcat was suffering from some sort of itch; so he lay down on the ground and let Rabbit scratch his skin. He turned over several times until he had been thoroughly scratched.

After a time, Rabbit wanted Wildcat to scratch his skin; so he lay down in his turn. When Wildcat began, he passed his paw down over Rabbit's skin with his claws withdrawn, saying, "I have lived a long time, and my claws are worn out."

At that, Rabbit begged him to scratch harder.

And, protruding his claws, he made a sudden grab at Rabbit's skin and pulled it entirely off.

That is why Rabbit's skin is loose.

BEAR AND RABBIT

GUS COMBY   1990

Rabbit met the Bear, and he went home with Bear. He got to Bear's house. Bear started cooking peas. He said he was going to cook some peas. Said he's going to put some meat in it.

Look around [*indicates Rabbit looking around, wondering where the meat is*].

So after a while, Bear said, "Grrrowrrr." Cut his side [*mimics cutting with a knife*], put it in the peas, and they ate it.

So when Rabbit was going home, he invited Bear to come visit him. So Bear did. Got over there, and he was going to cook peas. But he didn't know his side was pretty thin. So, Rabbit grabbed his side and stuck a knife through his ribs and died.

HOW THE RABBIT FOOLED THE TURKEYS

UNKNOWN [HALBERT]   C. 1900

One day, a long time ago, the Rabbit was thinking how he might fool and catch the turkeys. As he looked towards the bottom of a high ridge, there was a flock of turkeys there.

And the Rabbit got into a bag and was rolling towards the bottom, so they say.

And when the flock of turkeys came forward to see, and as the Rabbit in the bag was rolling towards them, the turkeys only said, "Tak, tak, tak, tak, tak, tak," so they say.

And the Rabbit said, "It is mighty good. Do you all get in and roll."

But only one got in the bag; and as they were rolling, he said, "It is mighty good."

And the Rabbit said, "If two of you were to get in the bag and roll, it would be much better," so they say.

And two got in the bag; and as they were rolling, they said, "It is mighty good."

And the Rabbit said to the turkeys, "Do you all get into the bag, and I will roll you to the bottom. That will be a great deal better."

And when the whole flock of turkeys had got into the bag, the Rabbit tied it up, took it up, and carried it to his home, so they say.

And he shut them up in his house and made a blind rabbit the watcher.

And the blind one said, "What is this that is here?" And so thinking, he went and opened the door, and the flock of turkeys that were therein flew out and far away, as the saying always has been.

RABBIT AND FOX FARM TOGETHER

UNKNOWN [HALBERT]   C. 1900

In ancient days, the Rabbit one summer made a bargain with the Fox to farm together.

They raised a crop of beans together.

And the Rabbit said, "I will take the vines, and you take the roots." And the Fox got the bean roots, and the Rabbit got the bean vines.

And when their potatoes got ripe, the Rabbit said, "The other time I took the vines, but now I take the roots."

So the fox got the potato vines, and the rabbit got the potatoes.

The Rabbit so cheated the Fox very much, so the saying is.

RABBIT RIDES WOLF

GUS COMBY   1990

One time Rabbit and Wolf, male wolf, been courting a female wolf.

So Rabbit been talking to the other animals, said, "Wolf is my horse."

So the girl heard it and told him about it. That made Wolf mad. So he went looking for Rabbit. He finally found the Rabbit and he told him, he said, "You been telling lies on me."

He said, "What?"

He said, "You been telling that girl I was your horse."

"Naw, she just made that up, told you that."

Said, "Let's go down and see what she says. Let's go."

Rabbit says, "Oh, my leg is hurting so bad I can't walk."

Wolf said, "I'll tell you. Get on my back. We'll ride close to the edge of the yard." He said, "You'll get off, and we'll walk."

So, "All right."

Rabbit got on Wolf. When they got to the edge of the yard, he pinched Wolf right on the side, and the Wolf run in the house. And the Rabbit riding on him said, "See? I been telling you about the Wolf being my horse."

RABBIT GAINS A WIFE

OLMAN COMBY   1928

Rabbit was calling at the house of a woman who had two daughters. He was full of fun; but after a while, the mother became tired of his antics and said, "You had better go away, you long-eared Rabbit."

Rabbit replied, "Do you know why my ears are so long and stand up so straight?"

"No."

"Do you want me to tell you?"

"Yes," she said.

"It is because I have been in so many battles and have had to camp out for a long period and have smoked so many pipes."

"And what makes the sides of your jaws look yellow?"

"Tobacco smoke. You see that I am a brave man. Will you not, therefore, let me have one of your daughters?"

The woman agreed to this, and she gave the other one to Fox.

The two families lived near each other for a long time.

Then, however, Rabbit became rich and filled his house with beautiful furniture, and he had plenty of good food.

When Fox's wife saw that her sister had lots of good things, she said to her, "How much property you have."

She went to her own husband and said, "Rabbit's wife has lots of stuff. Why haven't you?"

Fox became angry at this and told her not to visit Rabbit's house again; but sometime later, she went there and told her sister that she would also like to marry Rabbit if it could be arranged.

"The only way to do that," said the other, "is for you to come right down here and stay with us."

And so she began going there, concealing the fact from her husband as well as she could. She now had all she could eat.

By and by, however, Fox discovered what was going on and said to her, "If you are going to stay at Rabbit's house so much, you need not come back at all."

This was exactly what she wanted, and she went down there and became Rabbit's wife.

This happened because Rabbit was smart.

HOW RABBIT MADE THE ANIMALS ANGRY

OLMAN COMBY   1928

One time, Rabbit heard someone felling a tree. Feeling very good, he ran frisking along until he met Fox. "There is a big racket back there," he said, "and it must be caused by a multitude of people."

Fox was frightened at this and started off on the run.

Presently, he met Wolf and told him as he ran past that he heard a lot of folks were coming.

At that, Wolf also started off and presently came up with Possum. "Lots of folks are coming," he said, and Possum also began running. Possum then met Coon, whom he set in motion in the same way.

Coon met Bear with like result, and Bear met Panther.

Finally, Panther came to Terrapin's house, and the rest of the animals soon joined him.

But when Terrapin got the news from Panther, he wanted to know who had told him.

"Bear told me," said Panther.

Bear, on being asked, said that he had learned of the matter from Coon.

Coon referred him to Possum, Possum to Wolf, and Wolf to Fox. Fox in turn referred him to Rabbit.

"Where is Rabbit?" asked Terrapin.

But Rabbit was not among them. So they sent to Rabbit and asked him about it. Rabbit said, "I did not tell them to run. I was feeling good and said that I heard a big racket."

But all of the other animals had become so thoroughly stirred up that they were ready to fight.

And so someone who is just fooling will almost precipitate a fight.

RABBIT AND THE GARDEN

OLMAN COMBY   1928

A man named Uncle Remus owned a garden. One time, Rabbit went to this garden and ate a lot of his beans. This happened a number of times, and Uncle Remus wanted to catch the thief but at first was unable. Finally, he went around the entire garden and stopped up the holes in the fence so that Rabbit could only get out by the gate. Then he went away, leaving the gate open.

Late that evening, Rabbit came along and, finding no entrance except by the gate, went in that way.

Uncle Remus had gone away, leaving his girl on guard with orders to close the gate as soon as Rabbit had entered and keep him there until he came home. The girl did as she had been told.

And, after Rabbit had eaten all of the beans and peas he wanted, he could not find a way to get out. So he went to the gate behind which the girl was standing and asked her to open it. She refused. Then Rabbit showed his teeth and said, "See my teeth. If you don't let me out, I will bite you."

The girl became frightened and let him go.

Presently, Uncle Remus came back, learned what had happened, and said to his daughter, "Why did you let him go?"

"I got scared and had to," she answered.

"Well, next time he goes in there, shut him in and keep him there until I come."

Next evening, very late, Rabbit went into the garden again, and the girl shut the gate upon him. Again, Rabbit ate all of the beans he wanted. Afterward, he came to the gate, shook it as hard as he could, and asked to be let out.

"I am not going to let you out," said the girl.

"Let me out," said Rabbit, showing his ears. "See my long horns? If you don't let me out, I will hook you."

The girl again became frightened and opened the gate for him.

When her father came home, he discovered what had occurred and said, "Why did you let him out?"

"Because I got scared."

"Well, what did he say?"

"He said he was going to hook me with his horns."

"The Rabbit has no horns," said her father. "The next time you get him shut up, keep him there 'til I come."

Next morning, the old man opened the gate.

Late in the evening, Rabbit hopped back into the garden, and the girl shut the gate upon him. He ate all he wished, came to the gate, and asked to be let out. But this time his threats were of no avail. She kept him shut in until Uncle Remus returned.

The latter then went into the garden and chased Rabbit round and round until he caught him. He seized Rabbit by the ears, and though Rabbit begged for his life, he was about to cut his head off.

But just then, his wife made a racket at the house and called to him to come there quickly. So he shoved Rabbit into a sack and hung him up on a limb while he went to see what was the matter. After that, it was too dark to cut Rabbit's head off, so he put it off until morning.

Late at night Possum came crawling along under the place where Rabbit was hung.

Rabbit heard him and said, "Climb up that limb, untie this sack, and get inside, and you will hear the most lovely music."

Possum did so.

Rabbit tied him in, climbed down from the tree, and swaggered away, smoking and chewing tobacco as he went.

Next morning, Uncle Remus came back to kill Rabbit, looked into the sack, and saw Possum lying there. He told his wife about this, and she said, "You had better let him go. He will get fat, and later on you can eat him."

So Rabbit and Possum both escaped.

This is what happens when a woman begins to interfere with things.

THE CAT TRICKS THE MOUSE

ENGLISH AS A SECOND LANGUAGE STAFF   1986

Long ago, there was a cat. The cat was chasing the mouse.

The mouse ran into its hole, and before long, it heard something barking outside.

The barking kept on for a long time.

Then the mouse thought, "A dog has chased the cat away," and came out of his hole. The cat was waiting for him outside and caught him.

The cat said, "You have to be bilingual to eat these days!"

MOUSE, ROOSTER, AND CAT

CHOCTAW COMMUNITY NEWS   1987

"Today you get to go outside for the first time," said Little Mouse's mother. "But be very careful. There are some animals who are friendly to others. But there are some who are not friendly. Those will hurt you."

Little Mouse promised to be careful and went out.

He saw many different animals. Some were very pretty, and he took care to remember them so that he could tell his mother what he had seen. When he returned home, he told his mother about what he had seen.

"Mama," he said, "I saw lots of pretty things while I was out. I saw one animal sleeping in the sun. His hair was shiny and yellow, and his tail was long. I also saw an animal that was no good. His hair was red and black. He made loud ugly noises and shook his wings."

His mother said, "I don't know for sure what animals you saw, but it sounds like the red-and-black one you saw was a rooster. You don't have to be afraid of that one, but the pretty yellow one was probably a cat. You must be very careful of the cat. It likes to catch little mice and eat them."

MORAL: Just because you see someone who looks like he's good, that doesn't mean he will be good.

STORIES IN CHOCTAW

THE CHOCTAW CREATION LEGEND

ISAAC PISTONATUBBEE   1901

Hopahki fihna kash hattak at atoba ammona kat Nanih Waiya yo̱ atobat akochchat tok oki. Mashkoki yosh tikba Nanih Waiya akochchah mat, Nanih Waiya yakni banayya yo̱ ilayo̱hofkah mat, shilat tahah mat, hashi akochchaka ilhkolit tok oki. Atok osh, Itombi Ikbi ola ho̱afohah mat, hakchoma shonkah mat, lowak bohlit tok oki.

    Mih man, Chilakki yosh atoklant Nanih Waiya akochchat tok oki. Mih mat, yakni banayya ya̱ ilayo̱hofkah mat, shiulat tahah i̱mat, akni at atiyat tok a̱ iyakkayat ilhkolit tok oki. Mashkoki at afohat hakchoma ashonka cha iyat tok o̱ lowak at ittonlat tok o̱, kowi at lowat tok o̱, Chilakki at Mashkoki at atiyat tok a̱ ikithanoh mat, yoshoba cha, filammi cha, falammi imma akon ilhkolit tok osh, falammi imma ako̱ ont ayoklachit tok oki.

    Mih man, Chiksha yosh atoachchinat Nanih Waiya akochat tok oki. Mih mat, yakni banayya ya̱ ilayo̱hofkah mat, shilat tahah mat, Chilakki at atiyat tok a̱ iyakkayat ilhkolit tok osh, Chilakki at ayoshobat tok a̱ onah mat, filammin mat, Chilakki at atiyat tok akinli ho̱ iyakkayat ilhkolit to oki. Atok osh, Chiksha at Chilakki at ont ayoklachit tok a̱ onah mat, Chilakki bilinka ayoklachit tok oki.

    Mih man, Chahta yosh ont ayoshtah man Nanih Waiya yaman isht ayyopi akochchat tok oki. Mih mat, yakni banayya yan ilayonhofkah mat, shilat tahah mat, kanimma ikayoh osh yakni ilappakinlih on abinohlit tok osh, Chahta at ayyashah oki.

LIGHTNING AND THUNDER

ODIE ANDERSON   1997

Híhma alla toklot a̱šwat oklahtók hitokako̱ ałtakla yátoko̱ kanát i̱ holíto̱pa kiyoho̱ ašwa yattók. Hitóš "Çišnáto malahta iš tobakma̱ anáto hilóha tobáläna," áčíttok o̱.

Hilóha, malahta mat alla ałtakla yátoko̱ oklah makáchih bíkattók.

CORN-FINDING MYTH

ILAISHTUBBEE   1899

Nittak hopaki hash yakohmi tok.

Ámmona fihna ka̱ fala hosh oka chitto mishtánnáp o̱ tanchi niki acháfa ka̱ aiishit yakni ilapa isht ála mát álla álhtakla hosh wanuta awashowát anta ka̱ ima ma álla át tanchi hochifo tok. Mihmat wanuta ya̱ ahokchi tok oka.

Atuk o̱ tanchi yash ot chahát ia ma, álla i̱ shakli hash ot pih apa̱sh pullichi tok. Mihma álla yash osh yakmichi hinla ahmi kát allelit lukfi isht ahopochi tok.

Atuk o̱ tanchi niki acháfa kash osh waya mát tanchi ampi tuklo ho̱ isht toba tok.

Yámmak atok pulla ho̱ Chahta in tikba tanchi ya̱ ithana tok.

A STORY OF KASHIKANCHAK

UNKNOWN [HALBERT]   C. 1900

Hattak át on attát ia tok mát falamát iklo bika hatok mia. Yohmi haták o̱hattak acháfa kát iakaiyát hoyo tok osh nánih okfa aiina ahaya tok osh nánih hiohli abaia hosh a̱ya tok. Mihma okfa in tonnáp pilla ha̱ ohoyo hoponsi ka̱ pit haklo tok.

Mihmát pisát ia tok osh nánih ont apakfopát pit hoyo ma okfa in tánnáp a̱ yakni chuluk chitto kát nánih akishtula hikia tok. Mihma yámma anukaka yako̱o̱ hoponsi ka̱ pit a haklo mát hattak ak osh, "Nanto hohcho?"

Achi mát ia tok osh ont wakkali ma ohoy sipokni chaha fihna hosh i̱sha̱kani akinli ho̱ pisa tok.

Mihmát, "Okoko ilap akosh pi tahli hatoshke," achi mát luma hosh falamát aminti tok át ia tok.

Yohmi tok ash onamát nana ilappa putta okla ha̱ ont im anoli tok.

Mihmat Kashikanchak yash hattak a pi tahlishke, okla ha̱ im achi tok. Yohmi mát kanimikchit ába hinla kát anukfillit pisa tok. Mihmát hattak balili pálhki achukma hosh anta chatuk a̱ atokoli tok. Mihmát hattak kanohmi hosh tanampo ishi ban hosh ia tok. Atuk osh yakni aiitilaui achukma hosh yakni chuluk a̱ ona hatuk o̱ yamma hattak át abali chi̱ ka̱ apisa tok. Mihma báchcha ittilaui ka̱ hattak áhleha át tanampo ishi bano hosh binohlit ia ka̱t yakni chuluk a̱ ont tikili tok. Mihma hattak álhtoka tok át tanampo ishi cha ia tok osh yakni chuluk a̱ ona tok. Mihma yámmak atok okát ohoyo sipokni yash osh i̱sha̱kani ishit hoponsi hosh hikia na ont pis tok. Mihmát ontokafi cha báchcha pit baleli tok.

Kashiknachak ash osh kocha mát, "Hi, he, hi, yantakkali, ibak, pok, pok, pok," achi tok. Mihmát hattak ash hliohli tok.

Mihma abaia binohli ash osh acháfaiyokát ha̱ssát isht ia tok. Yohmi kia hattak ash sakkit ishi pulla̱si tok. Mihma ont ishtaiyopi kash osh hüsa tok.

Micha iyi fihna náhli na Kashikanchak ash osh akkia na hattak ash osh hlakofi tok, achi chatuk oki. Micha falamát ilhkoli tok osh Kashikanchak in chukka okla onchukowa tok. Atuk o̱ álla yosh hattak holhki ápa hosh asha na okla pisa mát okla chanli hosh álla yash ábi tok oke.

KASHIKANCHAK

JEFFIE SOLOMON   1997

Kašika̱čikat ma̱yah bíkattók miyaho̱ oklah makáha̱yakak mano̱ ikkánalih a̱łih kiyo kiya—

Alla yat nani hót ittiyáčih bannahtók. Nani hoyokat imačokmáš a̱ha̱šwatokla bíka tokósh, bók oši ittiyačitóš bók oši o̱t hihi̱lina̱ Kašika̱čakat ahóčittók.

Hihmat imáyóčih ya̱ nanít lawakat o̱t oka hikíyakma̱ iyyi ya̱ kobliho̱makát išti̱ miya hátoko̱ alla toklo pat awa̱t ittiyáčittók.

Makáttóš ikittálačohma̱ iški, i̱ki, to hoho̱yo kako̱ ittaláčih kiyo hátoko̱ pi kaniyat ammómikat a̱łi áhnit a̱šwa tokako̱, kašika̱čak at pihlíčit kaniya tok ókat pihlíčit ónača o̱t a̱tta tok ako̱, Kašika̱čakat at a̱tta tok áči̱nih tok mi̱yah.

Makátokósh, "Issap akči̱hoyo akmat," átok miya.

Hihma̱, "Ti̱ba ákčihoyona," átok miya.

Hihma̱ alla makášoš bašpo čito yo̱ Kašika̱čakat mat hót bolih cha binilihọikkanahmat, "A̱naš, ti̱kba akči̱hóyo háyo̱," ácha alla mak átokat Kašika̱čakat noškobo ištatta tok ókáš bašpoma̱ lo̱mat pit áyišihmat ikko̱la ča̱t tablih tok miyah.

Hihma̱ ho̱kopa fihnatok kato kaniyatóš ikšo hatoko̱ a̱šwatóš Kašika̱čakat mičihma̱ kiti hat hiki̱yatoko̱ noškoboma̱ o̱t fokki tok miyah.

Hihmat, "Átokkiya kiliya," áhnihma̱.

Kašikačakat mat písakmat iyákayyáčįkạ ikkạna hátokósh tiłáyattok miya.
Makátokóš tákolit oklakat "Piyákayyannáh," ahnísh takọhli hókásh talohọwáš tokọhlitók miyah. Hihmat talówahkat:

Nusisita, ákmọna (Nu-si-sii-taaaaa, ákmọna)
Nusisita, ákmọna (Nu-si-siiii-taaaa, ákmọna)
Šokka   (Šo-kka)
čọnnah (čọ-nnah)
ímača   (iiii-ma-ča)

"Yakni bonọta," áhạyaš talówa tok miyah čátok.
Hikat tiłáyatókat takọhlikat talóhọwat takọhli hatokọ, "Álla yášoš mákaški," átokmiya.
Hiča pit písahmat tiłáya hósh íttakọhli kat ạłih mạ, čokkóšit wakammat hikịyatokọ, yàmmạ ittalačikat ạtáłokat okissa išit kámak at kạči hátokọikiba čokkówottók miyahọ hạkloli bíkattók.
Makilla.

THE MAN WHO BECAME A SNAKE

CYNTHIA CLEGG   1997

Cynthia: Story pan ạ dad ash ạmanolihtok when I was alla tik ossi siya ma, just like Siah, and just like Hillary and just like Monique.

And it's about a snake. [*kids all scream*]

William: Is this true?
Cynthia: He said it was. It was told to him by his grandparents and their grandparents told him, so it's a story that's been passed down.

Hopaki ohkas ạ dad at makachimat. There was this recipe.

He said that there was a recipe for becoming a snake. There was this recipe where you could get all these ingredients hicha ma ish ishi cha itti bạnit ish tahlihma sinti tohba na miyatok.

And I remember two things that he told me: one was wild cabbage, and another one was wild onions. And there was several other stuff, but

I've forgotten because it was a long time ago that he told me. Because ya ma ittibannit ish tahlicha inipah ma sinti tobanna miyatok.

Hitoko̱ there was this family, hichi hatak pa hicha hoyo pa chiki ma choka pa mayatok, hatak mat ikyimotok "Na hatak at sinti. Tohba hikiyyo kiyo," achi cha yoppash atah tok miyatok.

Hina, anukfilit tahlih ma akmaksitoh tikchi imakatokmiyatok. "Hobit tahli akmat ont ahyowaht tahli likma. Hikma michit akpisa achi tokmiya."

Hina, tikchit, "Kiyyo ish michi na. Axi atok bhinikma sinti ish tohbana achi tok miyatok."

Hina, hatak pakosh michitachi. Hakla hakiyyo tok miya, hina, wild cabbage, wild onion, and whatever all the other stuff ish a̱natokma ont ayowa tahli tok miyatok, hina immatok miyatok "honit tahlih ikma, ittibanit ish tahlikma issa tahlalikma. Impalachi achitok miya."

Hina tikchit askat honit tahlicha itti ba̱it tahli tok miyatok. Hima tahlali toy hima impat shatablih. He got full. Hima kayattahama ma kayatahama makhit sakaya hokat, "Ont binilli la chi living room aboha iya," living room imma iyatok miyatok. Ihma chair ont a̱sha tok miya.

Ihma tikchit áskcho áchifat tahlicha nanta table pit kasočit tahlima, living room ont apa̱tah tok miya itima̱ opolish chi̱yatoko̱.

Chibanahama, hatakmat anopolish bi̱nillitokosh anoplit ont iktaho̱ tok miya tok kiyo̱. Hima katimmi anoti a̱nilima haksobis at iski̱tini yakot kochat ka̱niya tokosh, kapasat niyatok.

Hima yohmima bi̱nillitokosh ibbakat yakot iyatok miyatok hima, and his legs start going together like this. [*She puts her legs straight out in front of her and close together as if becoming one.*]

Hima, all of a sudden, i̱bodyat yakkot straight out ittolahtok

miya bi̱nillitokash ont ittolahhokma. Hima, i̱bodyat snake tohbat iya tok miya. Hikash sinti čito. Hatak átoko.

William: How big was it?
Cynthia: I don't know. I really can't say, William.
William: Did that really happen too?
Cynthia: Um-hm. Sinti tobah tok miya.

    Hima áchibah nahama pạshit iksho [pi], you know, like snake skin ohm. He wasn't human no more. Hima sinti čito tobah me shalali hosh. Okissa iyatok miyatok okissa maont kocha ma. ˆ Tikchit nokshopa cha chalạka tokmiyatok. Hima . . .

William: Was he mean?
Cynthia: He wasn't mean to his wife.

    Hima, kocha tokmiya kịyo okissa ma. Takạlima nanta áwanata ma ạya tok osh nata cholak čitot takạli miyatok, a hole. Ihma sinti mat pit chokowah tok miya. ˆ choka immayatokkịyo.

    Hima tokchihat katimilachi anicha pi nokshopa katimi tok miya ha everyday ạ illipah im ist tiya tokmiya nata ạ hatak atuk anih atoko. Even though now he's a snake. Ạ hatak atok anihcha illapah ont ịtahlalih.

    Hikkma ạt kochacha ạt impah sinti akkini okkako nanna họ italalihhokma.

    Itokosh people in the next village hokma nanakat okla á haklo tok miya tok. Sinti čito ạtah kạ okla nukshopa tok hapimalla apah naokla anihka. Hima nata sinti čito nata chị wạ nạtahọ tikchi ma ont ị maká.

    "Kiyyo" achi. Ị holabih bạna ịholabihi kiyyo.

    Pulạk immạnolitok miya ạlikạno ạhatakat.

    "Ikyihmocha hobih achi na. Hobit tahlilima sinti tobah tok."

    "Hina nata akmakhitoh ish impayachiki onakma."

    "Ish ịpayakma kochakma okla illibachi."

    Ima tikchi mat yaytok miyatok. Sinti akịni ihokash ịhatak akịni tok osh ịyaya.

Atoko, that next morning, ma okla nata itahobat taha tok tinapo okla ishshicha.

Impa̱yatok mi̱ti illipat a̱sha mi̱ti. Himma sinti čito itkocha tok miya tok. Hitak axihat hiyomaya tokosh ho̱sat okla abit tok. Himma okla hopihtok.

And that was the end of the snake man.

THE BIG POND

JEFFIE SOLOMON   1997

Akma̱ čokka itikba ilappak átokma̱ okhata čito yóš tala̱yyattók.
  Híhma okiyat tahákma̱ aka̱kát ola ka̱ oklah ha̱kloh, ano̱ti alhípa čito kiya olat kanihi̱ya ka̱ okla ha̱kloh bíkattók miyah.
  Makátoko̱ okhata o̱mat [pit biłłih] čitóš tala̱ya toka̱ náhollot olah yanalličittók.
  Híhma̱ oka mat tahah fokálihma̱ sinti čito yóš itto̱la tokóš pit šalallih toko̱—ano̱ti kolokbi čito hóš bácha̱ya miya ho̱, oklah ištáno̱poho̱li bikattók.
  Makáto̱ oka mat táhahma̱, oka náholloši óš itto̱la tokmiya, oklah maka bíkattók.

PA̱Í FALAYA

CYNTHIA CLEGG   1997

Cynthia: This story is about my hokni. "Hokni" hat nána haš kanaho̱?
Alla: A̱ha̱, a̱ha̱ "grandma."
Cynthia: Grandma is "pokni." Pokni.
Alla: Pokni.
Cynthia: A̱hokni illittoh. Hokni is "aunt." A̱m ano̱lihtók. She told me.

  She passed away years ago. And she told me this story when I was little. See, I'm from Tucker, and my aunt was from Tucker. Hitoko̱ a̱makáči kat, náta, abíkáš attahtók and ičo̱kašat ikkachokmotók. "Ičo̱kaš" hat nána haš kanaho̱?

Alla: Ha̱ a̱.
Cynthia: "Ico̱kaš" is your heart.

Hicha i̱co̱kašat ikkačokmottók. And that's what my grandparents died from. Heart attack a̱ išt illittók. Hitoko̱ abíkat attah ná hapi nokšópaš oklah ilášattók kiyo̱.

Hitoko̱, anyway she lived in this old wood-frame house. Hika̱ čokká at yakohmittók. [ibbak išit mihčit ano̱lih] Door—"okkisa" door yakkót hikki̱yattók—hikma̱ living room at yakohmih. Hikma̱ dining room ánato, table at hiki̱yana̱ tokakósh i̱bed mako̱ oklah hilíčittók [ibbak išit mihčit ano̱lih]. Hitoko̱ má ittót nosi attók.

So anyways, what she told me was that one night, o̱batoh.

Qbát nata?

Alla: "Rain."
Cynthia: Hilóhattók. "Hilóhát" nata?
Alla: "Thunder."
Cynthia: Malattatoh.
Alla: "Lightning."
Cynthia: Lightning. "Boom" áchihtoh.

Nosiš ito̱lattók. Onnat iyásh a̱yatok.

Hitokásh okča tokmiyattók kiyo̱. Hihma̱ okčama̱ nátah, nánát "Boom, boom, boom" áttok miyah tók ki̱yo̱ okissa ma̱. Hihma̱ "Náta hakloli," ahnitokmiyattók kiyo̱. Hihma̱ ito̱la tokosh, hima̱kma̱ knockatok kanát. Okissa alatok.

Hihma̱ o̱bakat nánohmih, o̱bakat nanomikat, nátah, pí ačokmat iš pi̱sáhíkiyotok kočama̱.

Hitoko̱ tániča pit bini̱littók miyattók ki̱yo̱, hihma̱ wakáyattók.

Hihma̱ kanáš alah ahwa kaníya, "Kataš tasi̱bokat, o̱bakat yakohmika̱ alána toko̱," ahnitokmiyattók ki̱yo̱.

Hihma̱ windowma̱ iyattók. Hihma̱ curtainat taka̱littók óka̱, hitoko̱ lómmat yakót [ibbak išit tiwwih ilá hobbih] o̱t towih tokmiya tokkiyo̱ hihma̱ pit pisatoh.

Hihma̱ front door ma̱, sideways yakót pit pi̱sa tokmiyattók kiyo̱. Hihma̱, hatak čáhat hiki̱yattók miyattók ki̱yo̱. Hihma̱ šapo losa šapólih hikma̱ ippa̱shít faláya.

Hitoko̱ "pa̱ši faláya" ahma̱, ánákíto, I thought she was talking about my grandma's great uncle because he died long, long time ago. Hikáš, he was a medicine man and his name was Pa̱š Falaya.

"Pa̱š faláyat" nátah in English?

Alla: "His hair is long."
Cynthia: "Long hair," a̱ha̱.

Mako̱ išt ano̱polih amahwattók kiyo̱h. Mako̱š o̱t i̱hayaka toko̱ ahnilittók.

Hikaš, she said that yakót curtain yakót [*ibbak išit tiwwih ilá hobbih*] pi pisahma̱ hiki̱ya tokmiyattók Hihma̱ coat losa faláya, i̱knees ona, hatak čáha áš hiki̱yama̱ yakót pit pisahma̱ iniškinát yakomi tokmiyattók [*Cynthia at niškin tobhi illah hayákachih*].

Niškin tohbi ilaš haya̱kah. Hihma̱ it was like this [*hima̱kma mihčina allyat oklah čala̱kah*].

Only the whites of his eyes were showing. He didn't have no pupils.

Ma̱ pisahma̱ nokšópattok miyattók.

"Hikáš katihmiláhih" ahnima̱.

She said that "Kátina yakot a̱t a̱hayáka," ahnima̱ fala̱t i̱ bed o̱t ittóla ča itto̱lama̱.

Knock kat issattók miyattók hihma pí nosittók miyattók.

Hihma onnát tahahma̱ náta, kanah iki̱makáčottók miyattók.

It was several days later a̱makáchittók.

Hitoko̱i̱ son at abíkáš attah mał̱ittók. Hitoko̱ maš o̱t tahači̱ha áčittók. Mako̱ annót a̱yahah achittók. Hitoko̱, but he never passed away.

It was several months later ilápaš o̱t tahattók. And she passed away, illittók.

Alla: Katíča?
Cynthia: ˆ heart, i̱čo̱kaš at ikačokmóttók.
Alla: Who died?
Cynthia: A̱hokni.

And after she told me that, when she told me, "ˆniškin tóhbi illáš hayáka," áčihma̱ sánókšópahtók, hiča nósiláhíkiyohtók that night ma̱.

Hitokóš movies himáka̱ pisálikma̱ šilop yómit a̱yaka̱ pisálikmat sanókšópah [*Hima̱llma niškin tobhi illah hayákáčina̱ allayat oklah čala̱kah*].

Alla: Do it again!
Cynthia: One last time [*Hima̱llma niškin tobhi illah hayákáčina̱ allayat oklah čala̱kah*].
Alla: Do it again one more time.
Cynthia: Yakomittók [*Hima̱llma niškin tobhi illah hayákáčina̱ allayat oklah čala̱kah*].

Hikáš that's my story and that's a true story, because a̱hokni aš amánólittók my aunt told me. That's a true story.

Alla: That was true?
Cynthia: It was a true story.

THE INHUMAN *NA LOSA CHITO*

JEFFIE SOLOMON   1997

Na losa chito. Náta ho̱ oklah išt ano̱po̱ho̱li bíkattók.

Hihmat hinát pa̱ pit bača̱ya mako̱, kanáš a̱yakmat kanah makátokmat nánah kiya afámah, yohmi hósh ášakma̱, pí ikano̱pólo tobah. Okla yómmit ištiyahóš áša bikattók.

Makátoko̱ alikči oklah hoyot áyyáša tók ako̱, alikčimat iyat yokácha hi̱na míya ná iyači̱hoš imałtáha tók ako̱ ná ibbáyišá hi̱nakat ikšóttók. Áčaffa katoh imałtahah mihi̱ya hókako̱ ibbáyišánakat ikšona okla ikiłkolo háto̱ oklah ikyokáčottók.

Makilla.

THE BLACK STUMP

NELLIE BILLY 1997

Alla ossi siya móma, hačišnohmilittók kanimmah, hihmą okłilíkat tahah ihhokakǫ ąmámát įmáma pisat iyah banna ná ililkólittók kiyǫ. Hayáka pit okla íłipólihttók.

Okiya okmą hayaka okmat ókłilikahka?

Hikmą ofǫla ałiha yǫkat makat kaníyakmą, opah ałíhat makat kaniyakmą, sá nokshópa kásh ąyalittók. Ihmat hayáka oklah ilittanowattók, hina ilittanowattók kiyyoh.

Hihmą wak áyasha pit oklah íłopolihtók kiyǫh. Hihmą ná lósa čitót hikįyattók wak áyáshamą. Ihma įshalit hapi nokshópattók. Hihmat mimmanǫ iłkoli ikhapinnottók, ná losa číto mat hikįyahmą mįtánah hapimahwattok.

Hiča hina kililkolottok ásh hapi nokshópača hina ililkólihtók kiyǫ. Hiną yǫ okla ilittanówa hósh ililkólihtók. Hayáka pit oklah íłopollikmat čikkósi ona hapinnah tók kiyǫ. Itokkásh hapi nokšópa mato kaníkkiya hina íliłkólihtók. Hitokósh nánit áyyašat sappokni į chokka oklah ilónattók kiyǫ.

Hihmą tįkba makǫ ǫt oklah ilimanǫlihtok, hapi nokšópa hókat. "Ná losa čítót mą hikįyatok; hápi nokšópatok."

Hitokakǫ sappokni mat hapį yoppahtók. "Hihmat, iti kanásh hokmitokǫ yammą hikįyákahlįh," ácha hapį yoppahtók.

Ihtokkǫ iti lowa yósh hikįyakakǫ hapi nokšópahtók áčįnihtok.

Ná losa číto hapimahwattók [*yoppah*]. Iti ókakǫ oklilįnokšópatok áčįnitok.

Itít lowakma nánakmat losat kanįyahka? Ąhą. Yohmi ósh hikįyakakǫ hapi nokšópahtok. Ná šilop kiyokak shilop hapimahwatoką, iti lowa ósh hikįyakakǫ.

Makilla.

CARS, ROADS, AND CHANGING VALUES

ODIE ANDERSON 1997

Akma ąki akoš Bike Williamson ittatoklóš čįt anǫpolihǫ hąklolihttók siyalla yó.

Hikakǫ makáčih kat "Hína, osi yóš pą bačąya makoš, hínát áwatahóš bačąyáčį. Tali yósh patałpáčį," áčit oklah čįyąh mą.

"Nátit ikkąnaho?" ahnit ąšalittók.

Hitokakǫ anǫti hikmą nánát niškin toklóš áyiłípáčįh áką hąklolittók.

Hikmą anǫti čokkát pa tallayátok ahnih kiyyo mákǫ lokfi nona čokka yóš ittapakkačit talóha tahačįh áčihǫ hąklolimą, "Anǫti hikmą tali patałpo bąnokmą naksika yą talipałpo yóš ittapátáš iyačį," attóką pįsali.

Interstate mák makáha ahnilih. Hittóka ahnit himakak anokfillilih.

Híkmat lokfi nona čokka tobat táhakmą alla čipįta áyášat tobakmą alla čipįta yą pí ǫt bohliča iłkohǫláčįh. Iskalli ásh imíšahláčįh alla yą, áhąyattó.

Yammanǫ ąliką pįsalih.

Hikkat "Anákóš Chief siyá" ahąyattók mákoš, hitok makǫ čahtat "yes," "no," ači vóta ná okla vótat imayyačikmą, čahtat áyáša ikimikšo kačį ačihhǫhąklolih bíkattók.

Makokmat ná bonǫta kiya áyášat ikimikšokmat čokkát ikimikšokmą náhollo yóš alóta taháčį čahtat á mąyatok áhnih mákǫ.

Hikmą ná bonǫta šáli ča iłkólikmat yanaš į yałki hoppit iłkóláčįh. Yalǫboši ápat iłkóláčįh áką hąklolih bíkattók.

Manǫ ikǫnokįša.

Makilla.

THE FUNERAL

HARRY POLK   1997

Story ačaffah pat ąnoti, čahtát tąči hokčih, hikmat bottom áhǫ bók oka ałi yakómi mą oklah tąči hokčíkattók. Yohmi attók.

Çahtah pat hohčifo kato Ašman hohčifo attók.

Makátokóš Ašman mat ąya mat tąči mą hokčih tós ábašličačįsh ąttah.

Himmak ohmi mą mule takalitčitahlih cha bášliš ąyattók.

Lašpa kat ná ohmi tokmiya. Hikką lašpa kat yakohmih ką, miša akka mąbank at čáhah mą akka pílla hǫ bók at ąyah hatokǫ, yamma pit pihįst ąya ámonah tok. Hitokakósh į lašpahkat į palámit tahah mat mule ałi ǫt hilíčiča, takči ča, ilí fokka pít šowít tahliča short illahóš pít takąlihtók miyah.

Bank mą onahmat yakohmihmat [*nokłamalli hobáčih*] pít akkiyat yakot iyah tókmiyah.

Hitokakǫ, himáką mą ątta mohmi alligator, makohmi hačǫčoba yóš hattak at pą pit takallika hačǫčoba mat ít pisahmat yakot [*itakha čitót towwi hobáčih*] pit įtohwih tok miya.

Ihmat pí yakot ǫt čokkohwa, alligator hat nanablittókmįyah.

Hiną alligator ittakobba foką ná, ílap akįna katoh pi chikkosih kohchi imahwah tók mįyah. [*yoppah*]

Hitokakǫ alligator matoh áfammi ačaffahǫ kohčitok á čįnittók. [*yoppah*]

Makǫ kohčat sand ǫt ikkíya ča, kohči tokǫ mitǫt šilat tahahmat, iya tós ǫnah mat, tąchi ábashli cháshǫ ǫt pisahmą tąčít šilat kániya yósh takomąya tok miyah.

Ihma iya mat įčokka onah mą į family ałíhat, čahta hopáki to kana hat illi tokmá makǫ áyakšo áčįh hós ąša hóką mohmi mą iti yǫ į bone hobáčit ittačakliča abóha iklanna boliča mąya bíkattók.

Yohmi hátokǫ mičih cha mąya hǫ ǫt hayaka tok mįya. [*yoppah*]

Foni áyakshočih hoš mạya họ ọt hayákattók miyah.
Áfammi ácaffah ona akịni átokọ.

THE DOG WHO SPOKE CHOCTAW

JAKE YORK   1997

Qntoklo afammi siyah mạ sashki yat . . .

Delta City, áhọ amọshit ạtta họ ililhkólih bíkah tók. Ponóla amot okla ililhkólih bíkah tók. Anáto okassa hoyo siyah tók.

Pọnola okla amokmạ, assanóchi alhíhát, amóshi mat ofi osi yạ assanóchi attók miya tósh makah tók. "Bounty" hohchifo attók ofít.

Amóshi yat náhollo anọpolí híkiyoh hátok ósh, fíhnah kiyoh, náhollo anọpolih ạlhi kiyoh tók. Chahta yọ ofi pạ imanọpolikạ. Ofi pat imánokfila ạshat kaníya attók.

Mail carrier, okla náhollo tók; holisso isht imọnakmạ.

Newspaper kocha pit okla ịpilakmạ—"Holisso hót amálah ákmạ," ofi ịhowakạ, ofi mat ọt hoyot alah bíkah tók. Qt kapáli cha isht imálah, ikmạ, "Yakókih," áchi cha ayokpachikmạ ibbak ịshákah, ofi yókakọ.

Hikma, "àpah chinnak mat nówat ishlak másh illipa ishpá chịh," Chahta imanọpolih ósh ofi mạ ịmakáchikmạ. Oshata ọhikíya ihókásh ish nówat ishlakmạ illịpa ish íshánah," ákmạ ofi mat wakáyat hikíya cha nówásh iyah híkah tók. Hikma imah biscuit, kaka foni okmah nánah.

Hicha, "Binílih," ákmạ binílih.

"Ittólah," ákmạ ofi mat ittólah.

"Nosih," ákmạ nishkin akammih.

Ofi mat náhollo mọmah imanọpolih kiyo kakọ Chahta ikkanah tók. Náhollo imanọpoli attók kiyoh amóshi mat, ikakkọ ofi pat, "Ittólat tonólih," ákmakopi mạ ittót tonólicha.

"Illịpah," ish áchih makósh ị hind leg ikkíyah ósh nówat ọna cha ọt ịpah.

"A holisso hoyot alah." Ákmạ ọt kapáli cha isht imálah.

Makọ chimanólih sannah. Ofít Chahta imannọpa ikkaná hịnakmạ, hikmạhachishnak mash hashikkaná hịnah.

Náhollo imanọpoli attók kiyoh ofi mạ. Chahta illa imanọpolih amóshi mat.

Mak átokọ hash kaníkat Chahta chikikkạno hash mạyah pat hash ikkạnah. Ho hạkloh, hachim anọpolikmạ. Chahta annọpa okla anọpolikmạ ish haklokmat ish ikkaná hịnah. Ofi pạ amóshít imanọpoli kạ imikkạnat kaníya attók Chahta annọpa illahọ imanọpoli kạ.

Makánoh tók hachim álih sannah, ofit Chahta annvpa ikkaná hịnah okmạhachishnák másh hịnah, okay?

Makillah akịnih.

HELP FROM ABOVE

HARRY POLK   1997

Anot patoh hopakino kiyyo akịni chata. Nashville ont atat hoklilitok.

   Chimanolilachi. Alla ash bịnomaya pakomih fokalli toká. Hikma, iskit ạtah.

   Hokyạhitaha hima allat TV pisash bịnillitokash hokyáhił tahama. Nana achokma achomak iksho tahama.

   Allamat kocha iya cha washoha bọnatok nana ist washohanakat ik shotok.

   Closet ont tohwihma mopat hikkịyatok. Hima mop ont ishshi cha, issoba ọ bịnilli. Illahobit chuka ma apakfobat ạtah tok.

   Itokkakosh mop ma chuka ałima bohlicha falammat TV ont a bịnillitokosh.

   Makatokosh immi naksicha, pịni ont ish cha aboha ọna tokọ, okłilikat taha átokọ.

   Allamat door ont hikkiya mat noshopa tokmia.

   Ịmommat ị makachi mat, "Mop sạnahoki atok mịa. Katak hikịya họ?"

   Allamat pa, "Hikkiya," achi tokakọ.

   Iksho tok mia.

   Ikshoma hoyotok akọ, iksho moma ma. Allamat anukfilimat, "Mapilla bolili tok cha ánit anukfilit hikịya?"

   Balit door ọna nokash nạit iya hikiyyo tok. Falamat ona ma.

   Iskimat ị pạ akola moma, "Mop atoh?" achi tok.

   "Mapilla bohlih li toka chini. Nạ it hoyt allalihi kiyyo," á tok mịa.

   Hitokako, "Katina" atok ahkọ.

   "Sa nokshopa. Mapila ona likma nanakatoh kạnimma na" achi cha.

   Ya yachi ikkanacha shoht bịnillicha imạnopolih "Na chi nukshopa hikkiyo." Chihowat ma ạtah hatokọ, na chi nukshopa hikiyyo. "Chi ya pisạchi kiyọ," im achi tok.

   Ạłi á ma "Chihowat ma ạtah họ?" achi tok mịa ihma ạ atok mịa.

   Ihma alla makash osh bahlit pa iya tok mịa door ont takali tok mịa nanit iyah hikiyyo. "Sa nukshop moma."

   "God mishạtahak mat mop isht amalah" achi tok mịa. [*yoppah*]

THE DOVE STORY

JEFFIE SOLOMON   1997

Pačišóbat allat imaya tokóš loksi abit alah ma, loksi ma oklah apahtók.
 Hihmat allá šóš impáš áyyáša ma iškít ikipohtók.
 Hitokáš salakkáno sapita hila áhníš maka tokkako oklah ikipítottók.
 Hihma "Oka oklah hachinnaho?" ahma.
 Oka bannáš oklah makah ma, áyóchi iya tokóš áyóchi ot oka ayakchošót illittók achiniho.
 Oklah pisahmat yáya kat. Pachišóba ola máš nánokahaya yammakóš makahayahtók oklah yaya toš máko.
 Ola toba tok miyah.

HOW THE *BISKANTAK* GOT WATER FOR THE BIRDS

UNKNOWN [HALBERT]   C. 1900

Nittak chashpo ka momát kalampi tok. Mihma kaniohmit oka ya ai ishit he a iksho ma hoshi ibishakni kállo putta kát okti kalampi yá chanli kia kola he keyu kitok.
 Mihma hoshi osi át biskantak ash o tohno tok. Atuk o biskantak ash osh okháta kalampi ont ohikia cha taloa mát, "Nakni sia hokáno, bis, bis, bis, kant, kant, kant, tak, tak, tak," achit okti kalampi ya koli tok osh, biskantak hohchifo tok, achi chatuk mia hoke.

HOW THE POSSUM TRICKED THE WOLVES

HAZEL THOMAS   1980S

Himmona ka Shokkata yat i chokka iyah ósh ayah tók miyah. Hitok akoNashóba alhíha yat oklah pisah tók.
 Nashóba alhíha yat Shokkata abit apah banna kat oklah kilehat kaníyah tók. Shokkata yat Nashóba alhíha yat abih bannaka ikhánah tók. Hihátok ósh i makamat, "Iti isht nipa, oski lhopa, yómikat sabá híkiyoh." "Tiyak hishi akillá hinah," imáchih tók.
 "Ommá ma, nanih isht atoklá ma tiyak hishi asháchi li toka hoyot hash áyalak mato oklah hash sabá hinah," imáchih tók.

Nashóba pihlíchi makásh ósh, Nashóba isikópa achaffah ma̱ i̱ makah mat, "A̱ttat apísa̱chih chishnáto" imáchih tók. Hina Nashóba achaffa kato shokkata abínịlih tók.

Shokkata yat Nashóba i makah mat "ola̱si pakini ho̱ tiyak hishi hót ishlak mat tikba issabánah kiyo̱," áchit i̱ holábih tók.

Shokkata yat Nashóba i̱ holábi kako̱ Nashóba mat i̱yimmi chá iyah tók. Hina Shokkata yat "Nittak himmah kiya ná i̱ ponna kat oklah salawwíchi áchi̱h kiyoh," ácha i̱ yokpah tók.

Toff.

THE CAT TRICKS THE MOUSE

ESL STAFF   1986

Hopákichásh katosat a̱ttatok. Katosmat pi̱ti lhohlih bíkatok.

Pi̱yat i̱cokka ano̱ko pit chokwatok, iktopa̱kohma na̱nahó, kato wóhanah hohlotok.

Wóhanah hopakitok.

Hihma̱, "Ofimat katosma̱ lhohlit kani pit caffichih," imahwa̱chah pa̱tiyatsit i̱cokka ít hochchatok. Hito̱kah, katosat kochchamo̱ i̱hiki̱yatokachi̱lichah hoklitok.

Hihma̱ katosat óchih, "Himak hikityakano bilingual chiyakmós ishi̱páchih!"

MOUSE, ROOSTER, AND CAT

CHOCTAW COMMUNITY NEWS   1987

Pi̱ti osit nittakat imóna imabóha ákochchat kocha ammóna pisáchi̱ka̱.

Ishkiyat áchihmat, "Kocha attat ish nowánaka̱ nittakat chimo̱nah. Hihókásh ish ahahnikmakáchi̱h. Nánalpowa kani̱kat kana i̱kanah, hikak la̱wakato kiyoh. Kani̱kat chittopálih bannána."

Pi̱ti osiyat ahahnáchi̱hósh makácha kochchat kaniyah.

Nánat la̱wakat i̱lat kani̱ya pisah hicha kani̱kat hóchokmah. Hihókásh ahahni nánalhpowa pisahokmato.

I̱chokka ónacha ishki ímano̱li bannakat imahchibah.

"Máma," áchih. "Nánat hóchokmah pisálih. Nánalhpowa achókmat osísh itto̱lana pisálitok to̱mi inniho. Hishiyat halasbit kaniya hicha hishimat lakna hasi̱bis faláya."

"Nánalhpowa ikachokmo máko̱ pi̱salitok.

Hishimat losa hicha homma ittibalhlho. Olakat hakshobáchi hicha sannihchi wináchitok."

Ishki ásho áchihmat, "Nanakat pisa kano yohmih ahwah makos nana lawakat ali kiyoh.

Nánalhpowa hishi losa hicha homma mato aka̱k nakni. Yammato chittopálá híkiyo."

"Hishi lakna mato katos kiyo̱. Yammato nánalhpowa ikachokmo̱ kiyo̱ katosat pi̱ti chopo̱ta apakat ímachokma̱ kiyoh."

MORAL: Nanakat pisakano yohmih ahwah makos nana lawakat ali kiyoh.

ANNOTATIONS TO THE STORIES

CREATION STORIES AND MYTHS

The Choctaw Creation Legend—Recorded from Isaac Pistonatubbee by H. S. Halbert. 1901:269–70. See "Stories in Choctaw" for the story as it was originally told in Choctaw. Halbert adds: "Pistonatubbee stated that in his boyhood he had often heard the legend, just as he gave it, from some of the old Choctaw mingoes [chiefs]. While perhaps not apparent in the text, Pistonatubbee stated that the creation of the different tribes all occurred in the same day" (268). The motif of losing the trail by accidental fire also occurs in Olman Comby's version. Drying on the side of the mound is also a common motif in many of the versions of this tale; Halbert notes that "Old Hopahkitubbe (Hopakitobi), who died several years ago in Neshoba County, was wont to say that after coming forth from the mound, the freshly-made Choctaws were very wet and moist, and that the Great Spirit stacked them along on the rampart, as on a clothes line, so that the sun could dry them" (1899:229–30). Other versions: Swanton 1928b:1 (published in Stewart 1931:5–6) told by Olman Comby; interview with Terry Ben, May 30, 1996; interview with Estelline Tubby, August 5, 1997.

Compare this story to the humorous versions currently in circulation among the community that explain the creation of "White, Black, and Red" people according to how long they were "cooked" (for example, the story by Harley Vaughn in the introduction of this book). Other humorous versions: interview with Melford Farve, July 10, 1990; interview with Frank Henry, July 23, 1997.

Nané Chaha—Recorded from Pisatuntema by David I. Bushnell Jr. 1910:526. Bushnell introduces this story with the following: "Nané chaha (nané, 'hill'; chaha, 'high') is the sacred spot in the mountainous country to the northward, always regarded with awe and reverence by the Choctaw" (526).

Nané Chaha most probably refers to Nanih Waiya, which stood to the north of the Louisiana Band of Choctaw. Bushnell records a series of narratives as chapters of a single myth cycle, beginning with this narrative and following with "Men and Grasshoppers," "Creation of the Tribes," "The Returning Water" (not reprinted in this collection but compare to "Tradition of the Flood" and "The Flood"), and "Extinction."

Men and Grasshoppers—Recorded from Pisatuntema by David I. Bushnell Jr. 1910:520. John Swanton reprinted this story in his book *Choctaw Social and Ceremonial Life* and noted that "eske ilay" was "a play upon 'chishaiyi,' the word for 'grasshopper'; 'chiske ilay' would be 'your mother is dead'" (1931:37 ff.). The theme of creation of the Choctaw from other creatures below the earth is paralleled in Peter Pitchlynn's story of the "Origin of the Crawfish Band" in this collection. Compare also to the Reverend Alfred Wright's summary of Choctaw creation (1828:181).

Creation of the Tribes—Recorded from Pisatuntema by David I. Bushnell Jr. 1909:30. Titled by Bushnell as "Creation Myth." Bushnell footnotes the story with: "Version related by Pisatuntema (Emma) at Bayou Lacomb, April 15, 1909" (30 ff.). Bushnell published the story again a year later with minor changes in syntax (1910:527–28).

Origin of the Crawfish Band—Recorded from Peter Pitchlynn by George Catlin. 1841:128. Compare the connection between man and animal in this story to that in "Men and Grasshoppers" in this collection. The Choctaw had many different clans or *iksas* that divided up the tribe. Such division is mentioned in much of the early ethnographic material and is referenced in the story "Crossing the Line" told by Louise Wilson in this collection. Division by clan can be equated loosely with the division by community that exists today. Citing Horatio B. Cushman, John Swanton argues that the "Shak-chuk'-la (or in full Shakchi humma okla, 'red crawfish people') undoubtedly represented the formerly independent tribe of that name incorporated among the Choctaw" (1931:80). Bushnell noted that the Choctaw at Bayou Lacomb had a group called Shatje Ogla or Crayfish People but that only one man remained (1909:16).

A Short Story of the Creation of the First Man—Recorded from Wagoner Amos by the staff of *Nanih Waiya*. 1975:53. Translated by Oneva Thompson, "a Choctaw woman from the Bogue Chitto community" (53). I have followed the original translation housed in the Neshoba County Library since the published version contains a few typos. Compare the cane in this story to the pole in "The Migration Legend."

The Creation of the Choctaw—Recorded from Wagoner Amos by the staff of *Nanih Waiya*. 1975:21–24. The story is also printed in Choctaw as it was originally told by Wagoner Amos (1975:25–28).

The Migration Legend—Told by Peter Folsom and published by Henry S. Halbert. 1894:215–16. Halbert adds:

> This tradition was related to the writer ten years ago by Mr. James Welch, of Neshoba County, he receiving it from the Rev. Peter Folsom, a Choctaw from the nation west, who was employed in 1882 by the Baptists of Mississippi to labor as a missionary among the Choctaw people in Mississippi. Mr. Folsom stated that soon after finishing his education in Kentucky one day in 1833 he visited the Nanih Waiyah mound with his father, and while at the mound his father related to him the above migration legend of his people. (216)

Despite Folsom's later move to Oklahoma, at the time the legend was told, neither he nor his father had been to Oklahoma. Rather, both lived in Mississippi until Peter went to school in Kentucky. Accordingly, the narrative should be viewed as belonging to the Mississippi Band (though it is also told in Oklahoma). How the story was passed from Peter Folsom to James Welch and then to Henry Halbert, whether orally or in writing, is unclear. Halbert does publish this story again five years later with some minor alterations, this time asserting that it came "direct from the lips of the Rev. Peter Folsom," and does not mention James Welch at all (Halbert 1899:228). Today, this version has become relatively standardized by the tribe, serving as the base for summaries used in tribal pamphlets and brochures. Compare it to the story the Choctaw Indian Princess reads during the fair (as recorded in the introduction).

Other versions: Bacon 1973:2–3 told by "a tribal elder"; interview with Terry Ben, May 30, 1996; Claiborne 1964 [1880]:483–84; Cushman 1899:18–21, attributed to missionaries who collected the story from Choctaws in 1820; Cushman 1899:298–300, told by Israel Folsom; Gregory and Strickland 1972, unattributed; Lincecum 1861:13; Wright 1828:214, attributed to an aged interpreter familiar with the traditions of the Choctaw. Compare also to John Hunter Thompson's version in this collection.

Migration—Recorded from John Hunter Thompson by Cynthia Thompson. 1980:26–27. The belief that the Nanih Waiya Mound is a sacred burial ground is included in many accounts, including other legends and myths that mention Nanih Waiya. (See notes to "The Migration Legend.")

Tradition of the Flood—Written down by Israel Folsom and published by H. B. Cushman. 1899:303–5. Cushman pulled this information from an unpublished manuscript written by Israel Folsom just before removal (Cushman 1899:315). At the end of this written narrative, Folsom adds: "Though this diluvial story is in some respects absurd, still, the intelligible portions of it coincide with those evidences which are embalmed in the convictions and understanding of the Christian world, in the authenticity of the inspired Word. It is strange that the Choctaws should have been in possession of those particulars long before the white man spread before them the pages of life" (Cushman 1899:305).

Other versions: Bushnell 1910:528–29, told by Pisatuntema; Cushman 1899:222–24, and 225–27, both unattributed; Lanman 1850:220–22, 1856:429–31, and 1870:494, told by Peter Pitchlynn (with slight variations between versions); Swanton 1929:35, told by Simpson Tubby. Cushman's first version (pp. 222–24) is virtually identical to Lanman's version published forty-nine years earlier in 1850 that he eventually attributes to Peter Pitchlynn in 1870. Oddly, Cushman attributes the story to the Choctaws as related by them to the missionaries in 1818 (1899:224). One wonders whether both Lanman and Cushman received their narratives from the written records of missionaries, which may then trace back to Pitchlynn. Lanman did engage in personal correspondence with Pitchlynn, and Cushman also notes he knew Pitchlynn personally, but exactly where, when, and how these narratives were recorded remains a mystery.

The Flood—Recorded from Olman Comby by John R. Swanton. 1928b:2. Compare to "Tradition of the Flood" in this collection. The "sapsucker" is translated in other texts as *biskinik*, as in Cushman's second version of the flood story, which parallels, though is more elaborate than, the one presented here by Olman Comby. Although Adair mentions only "a small uncommon bird" (1775:26) and Romans "a species of motacilla" (1775:84), Henry Halbert suggests both are referring to the tomtit (also translated as *biskinik*). Both Adair and Romans note that this bird is a bad omen during war. Halbert confirmed this bird as the tomtit (*biskinik*) based on his own observations among the Choctaw during the end of the nineteenth century, further noting that in times of peace, the bird signals that a friend is coming (c. 1900:9–11). It is unclear what Comby is referring to when he describes the being at the beginning of the story, though its actions seem to resemble those of Kashikanchak (see "Kashikanchak" in this collection). It is possible that he is referring to the coming of Whites.

Lightning and Thunder—Unpublished. Tape-recorded from Odie Anderson on August 12, 1997, by Tom Mould, Glenda Williamson, and Meriva Williamson. See "Stories in Choctaw" for the story as it was originally told in Choctaw. David Bushnell Jr. records that "thunder and lightning are to the Choctaw two great birds—Thunder (Heloha), the female; Lightning (Mala'tha), the male. When they hear a great noise in the clouds, Heloha is laying an egg, 'Just like a bird,' in the cloud, which is her nest. When a tree is shattered, the result is said to have been caused by Mala'tha, the male, he being the stronger; but when a tree is only slightly damaged, the effect is attributed to Heloha, the weaker" (1909:18). Other versions:

Harrel 1995 (a children's book). After reviewing the Choctaw-language transcripts, Roseanna Nickey noted that she remembered hearing a longer version of this story but could not remember how it went. The following story by Harold Comby offers such a version.

Thunder and Lightning—Video recorded from Harold Comby by Josh Foreman on February 24, 2022.

Fani Losa and the Sun—Unpublished. Digitally recorded from Rae Nell Vaughn on April 28, 2024, by Rae Nell Vaughn. As the Choctaw Nation of Oklahoma prepared for a total eclipse on April 8, 2024, many of their members shared a story of a black squirrel who ate the sun, including on Facebook, where Rae saw it for the first time. Soon after, she told the story to her grandchildren. Neither of us had heard it from Mississippi Choctaw, but John Swanton quotes two versions of the story, one from Cushman, the other from Israel Folsom (Swanton 1931:210–11). He includes a third explanation for both solar and lunar eclipses (included here). After Rae told me this, we agreed it would be great if she could tell the kids the story again and record it this time. So, after a day of playing on a slip and slide in the backyard, Rae gathered five of her six grandchildren (the youngest, Noel, only four months old, was napping) to tell the story. Avery, the oldest (age seven), asked the most questions. The others—Addison (five), Bellamy (three), Aubri (three), and Emerson (two)—chimed in from time to time.

Dark Sun—Recorded by David I. Bushnell Jr., 1909:18.

The Origin of Corn—Unpublished. Tape-recorded from Terry Ben, June 3, 1996, by Tom Mould. I asked Terry where he learned this story, and he said he thought it was "from the books." Charles Lanman first printed an unattributed version of the story under the title "The Strange Woman" (1850:249–50 and 1856:463–64), and then attributed it to Peter Pitchlynn under the title "The Unknown Woman" (1870:495). Cushman seems to borrow this tale from Lanman when he publishes it himself in 1899 (214–16).

Corn-Finding Myth—Recorded from Ilaishtubbee by Henry S. Halbert. 1899:231. Halbert notes that "the version here given is a translation by the writer of a version which was written down for him in the Choctaw language by Ilaishtubbee (Ilaishtobi), a Six Towns Indian" (230–31). Both the English and Choctaw version of this legend are recorded in Halbert's manuscript. See "Stories in Choctaw" for the Choctaw version. Halbert also records another similar version of the legend in both languages in which the mother of the child who finds the corn is the one to plant and care for it (c. 1900:17). In his manuscript, Halbert notes that "the great water" refers to the Gulf of Mexico (c. 1900:18). Current scientific theories agree that corn seems to have been introduced to North America from South America or Central America. Other versions: Bushnell 1910:529, unattributed; Gregory and Strickland 1972, unattributed;

Barney Wesley 1982. Barney began his story as the origin of hominy, one of the staples of traditional Choctaw food.

Wild Geese and the Origin of Corn—Recorded from Baxter York by *Nanih Waiya* staff members Hulon Willis, Bradley Alex, Jimmy Ben, Ricky Billy, and Johnny Osceola. 1975:16. The song Baxter York is referring to is the song that accompanies the corn dance. During our conversation on July 8, 1997, Harry Polk related some of the things his grandfather told him:

> He used to tell me about old Choctaws. They used to live on the Mississippi. When the wintertime comes, wild geese go south. When it's springtime, wild geese come back here. Choctaws used to be the same way. In the winter, they went down south and got all kinds of fruit, pecans, and bananas and bring it back here. Then in the summer they grew pumpkins and corn and all this stuff. When it's winter, Choctaws all go south. My grandpa told me about it. That's what he said. Choctaw used to be like wild geese. That's what he told me, all kinds of stories.

The Geese, the Ducks, and Water—Recorded from Pisatuntema by David I. Bushnell Jr. 1910:534–35. All of the myths recorded in Bushnell's 1910 article are apparently from Pisatuntema, though others may have added parts during the storytelling (526). In the creation myths, Bushnell glosses Aba as "the Great Spirit," and "the good spirit above," credited with the creation of man.

The Life of Dogs—Recorded from Olman Comby by John R. Swanton. 1928:19 (also published by Stewart 1931:12). Swanton added at the end of the narrative: "How man's life happens to fall so much below the limits allowed was not explained."

How the Snakes Acquired Their Poison—Recorded from Pisatuntema by David I. Bushnell Jr. 1910:532. All of the myths recorded here in Bushnell's 1910 article are apparently from Pisatuntema, though others may have added parts during the storytelling (526). The difference in geography between the Choctaw in Louisiana and those in Mississippi is reflected in this story in which bayous replace swamps. It is worth noting that this story might also be categorized as an animal story since the main characters are animals, and this story shares the common explanatory ending of how something looks the way it does today. The difference is that where animal stories often tack on this etiological explanation, this story focuses on it. This focus on the act of creation places it more firmly here, among creation stories and myths. The same might be said of a number of the other stories in this section.

The Owl—Recorded from Olman Comby by John R. Swanton. 1928b:18 (also published by Stewart 1931:6).

Tashka and Walo—Recorded by David Bushnell Jr. 1909:35. Other versions: see "The Hunter of the Sun." There is some ambiguity about how the characters in the story are meant to be presented. "Sun" begins as "The Sun" but is clearly intended as a distinct character. It is less clear with "Buzzard," who is portrayed both as "a buzzard" and as "Buzzard." The same ambiguity occurs in "The Tradition of the Flood" with the boat builder (see this collection).

The Hunter of the Sun—Recorded by Rev. C. C. Copeland. 1853:170–71. Copeland adds: "Such is the tradition, and, whether true or false, the expressions for the rising and the setting of the sun, in use among the Choctaws at this day, are in accordance with it: *Hushi ut okatula. Hushi*, the sun; *oka*, water; *itula*, to fall. The sun falls in the water." Scholars have argued over the prominence of the sun in Choctaw cosmology, many arguing that sun worship was a prominent feature (see Halbert's manuscript that draws from Wright 1828:179–80; Swanton 1928a and 1931:195–96). Other versions: Lanman 1870:495–96, told by Peter Pitchlynn.

Yallofalaiya—Recorded by Henry S. Halbert. c. 1900:28–36. Titled by Halbert as "Origin of Sewing." I have changed the title since such endings—like the origin of sewing—are generally formulaic rather than indicative of the focus of the story. "Yoshobli" is defined in Byington's dictionary as "one who misleads; a deceiver." The name may also refer to *yoshoba*, the Choctaw word for dove, translated literally as "lost pigeon" (Swanton 1938:37).

Nameless Choctaw—Recorded from Peter Pitchlynn by Charles Lanman. 1870:496–97. A derivative version was published by Cushman 1899:217–22.

The Hunter and the Alligator—Recorded by David Bushnell Jr. 1909:30. Other versions: Whitman 1875 as told by Father Adrien Rouquette, who had heard it from the Choctaw in Bayou Lacomb, where he worked as a missionary (D'Antoni 1986:103). This version, as compared to Bushnell's recorded at least thirty years later, expresses a very different relationship between hunter and alligator. In Bushnell's, the alligator, while weak, still seems powerful, and he dominates the plot of the story. In Whitman's, the alligator does as the hunter tells him, even being told to splash around. Further, the hunter dismisses the alligator as powerless and is surprised to find that he is lucky in the hunt. And finally, in Whitman's version, there is no interdiction not to kill any of the first deer he comes across, and he kills everything in sight.

SUPERNATURAL LEGENDS AND ENCOUNTERS

The Girl and the Devil—Recorded by David Bushnell Jr. 1909:33–34.

The Eagle Story—Unpublished. Tape-recorded from Rosalee Steve on February 21, 1998, by Tom Mould. Other versions: interview with Esbie Gibson, July 25, 1997, Linda Williams, June 5, 1997 (not tape-recorded). Before she told the story, Linda said that her grandmother told her that if she and her siblings sneaked out at night to play, "a big bird would swoop down and get us. I assumed she meant an eagle." See also "Snatched from Above," by Mark Patrick, in the Prophecy section. The story may be based in a historical incident reported by Henry Halbert:

> At the time of the treaty of Dancing Rabbit, in 1830, Anumpulitubbee was the chief of Hankha aiola. His cabin stood upon a ridge, about a quarter of a mile east of the pond. A sad and singular event occurred in the life of this chief. Early one summer morning, some years prior to the treaty of 1830, an infant child of Anumpulitubbee was crawling in the yard, on the north side of the cabin, when all at once a large eagle swooped down upon him and bore him away in his talons. The mother heard the child scream, and ran to his rescue, but it was too late. The eagle soon bore the child far away out of sight, and nothing was ever seen or heard of him afterwards. This incident produced a great impression upon the Hankha aiola people. But according to their customs, in due season, they held their funeral obsequies over the lost child. (1902a:422)

Skate'ne—Recorded by David Bushnell Jr. 1909:30–31. Compare the similarity in motifs of escape with "The Panther and the Opossum" in this collection. Also, see "Hoklonote'she" and "The Black Stump" for instances where owls are tied to witchcraft and the supernatural. This connection is a commonly held belief among tribal members.

Hoklonote'she—Recorded by David Bushnell Jr. 1909:33.

A Story of Kashikanchak—Recorded by Henry S. Halbert. c. 1900:71–75. Original Choctaw language version: pp. 67–70 (see "Stories in Choctaw" for this version). In Byington's dictionary, one of the terms for witch is given as *chuka ishi kanchak* (chuka = dwelling, *ishi* = someone who seizes, *kanchak* = corncrib). *Kash* or *kashi* by itself can signal past tense or mean a bird that eats pokeberries or blackgum berries. However, as part of a larger term, its meaning is far more diverse. The song that Kashikanchak sings is not exactly translatable but could mean something like "Hi heh he, running, mixing, pok pok pok." Rosalee Steve's daughter Norma Hickman told a similar story about a cannibalistic babysitter in an unrecorded conversation in 1999. Mark Patrick remembered his mother telling him scary stories of Kashikanchak carrying her sack through the woods, knocking on trees (Tom Mould interview, July 7, 2021).

Kashikanchak—Unpublished. Tape-recorded from Jeffie Solomon on August 12, 1997, by Tom Mould, Glenda Williamson, and Meriva Williamson. See "Stories in Choctaw" for the story as it was originally told in Choctaw. The chant in the story posed problems for translation, just as it did for Henry Halbert (see previous story). In talking with Jeffie about some of the songs she sang as a child, she says she didn't remember what they meant but only remembered the words and tune that went together. Commenting specifically on the song in this story, she believed the children sang it to comfort themselves and that any song would suffice. Odie Anderson, her friend, concurred. For the English translation, I have rearranged the chant into a structure more similar to English. In Choctaw, the verb follows the noun being modified. The actual order would be: "Let me pick up an acorn, / Let me pick up an acorn, / pig / skinny / give it to." In this story, there are a number of these creatures, though the elderly female in the cave seems to be the leader. All of the other creatures are referred to as male.

The Spectre and the Hunter—Written by J. L. McDonald and published by Charles Lanman. 1850:264–66 and 1856:478–80 (also published by Ada Stewart 1931:64). Lanman introduces the tale, noting,

> The following legend was originally translated into English by an educated Choctaw, named J. L. McDonald, and subsequently embodied in a private letter to another Choctaw, named Peter P. Pitchlynn. The former of these very worthy Indian gentlemen has long been dead, and it is therefore with very great pleasure that I avail myself of the opportunity, kindly afforded me by the latter gentleman, of associating the legendary relic with my own. I have ventured, by the permission and advice of Mr. Pitchlynn, to alter an occasional expression in the text, but have not trespassed upon the spirit of the story.

Other versions: interview with Harry Polk on July 1, 1997.

The Hunter Who Became a Deer—Recorded by David Bushnell Jr. 1909:30. The singing described is part of the traditional way of mourning called "a cry" that is remembered but infrequently performed within the community today.

The Man Who Became a Snake—Unpublished. Tape-recorded from Cynthia Clegg on July 27, 1997, by Tom Mould and Liasha Alex during an afternoon storytelling session at the Choctaw Language Immersion Camp. Siah, Hillary (Hillary Meagan Vaughn, mentioned in the introduction), Monique, and William are four of the twenty or so eight- to ten-year-olds listening to the story. See "Stories in Choctaw" for the story as it was originally told in Choctaw.

Horse Man—Unpublished. Tape-recorded from Harry Polk, July 8, 1997, by Tom Mould and Curtis "Buck" Willis. This story was told as one story among many in a longer conversation. Harry Polk identifies the man who told him the stories as his grandfather. I have substituted "My grandfather" in the first line; Harry originally began with "He." During an interview with Terry Ben on June 10, 2021, YOP student Meka Willis mentioned hearing stories about such beings from her mother.

Half Horse, Half Human—Unpublished. Digitally recorded from Jessica Miller on April 11, 2024, by Tom Mould and Eddie Johnson.

Kashehotapalo—Recorded from Ahojeobe by David I. Bushnell Jr. 1909:31. This is a summary description of a supernatural being rather than a specific narrative. In Byington's dictionary, *kasheho* is female gendered, meaning aged or old. At the end of his description of this creature, Bushnell adds: "This myth was told by Ahojeobe at Bayou Lacomb in March, 1909, and he assured the writer that only a few days before, one of the boys, while hunting in a swamp not far from the bayou, had been frightened by Kashehotapalo, whom he saw distinctly, and that he immediately ran home and related his experience." Compare to the discussions in the introduction and endnote 3 in this chapter. Other versions: Conklin 1975:34–35, told by Bob Henry; Hirschfelder and Singer 1992:36, written by James Henry as heard from his grandfather Bob Henry. Compare to Terry Ben's story "Manlike Creature" in this collection. In 2021, Terry described "a certain creature, a humanoid creature that had a tail. And that creature would come into near the camp for the purpose of just eating. And of course, the hunters knew about it." The hunters treated the creature with respect, leaving the leftover food fifty to a hundred feet away for it to eat.

Na Losa Falaya—Recorded from Pisatuntema by David I. Bushnell Jr. 1910:532. This is a summary description of a supernatural being rather than a specific narrative. I have standardized *losa* for *lusa* as it appears in Bushnell. All of the myths recorded here in Bushnell's 1910 article are apparently from Pisatuntema, though others may have added parts during the storytelling (526). Bushnell suggests similarity between *na losa falaya* and *hashok okwa hui'ga* (later in this collection). The ability to remove the viscera and fly at night as small balls of light is often attributed to *hopaii* (bad doctors), as well as *bohpoli*: see "The Floating Light," "Choctaw Doctors," and "Dancing Lights" in this collection.

Manlike Creature—Unpublished. Tape-recorded from Terry Ben, May 30, 1996, by Tom Mould and Rae Nell Vaughn. For clarity, I substituted "my grandfather" for "he" in the opening line. After telling this story, Terry said he wished he could remember the name of this creature. He said many of the other old men back then told similar stories over and over to one another. He believes his grandfather told him such stories partly to teach him to be careful in the woods. Compare this story to "Kashehotapalo" in this collection.

Okwa Nahollo—Recorded from Heleema by David I. Bushnell Jr. 1909. I have standardized *nahollo* for *naholo* as it appears in Bushnell. The Abita River runs through St. Tammany Parish, Louisiana. *Okwa* means "water"; *nahollo* is the term for White people. *Okwa* (or *oka*) *naholla* has been translated more recently as "mermaid" or "merman."

Big Pond—Unpublished. Tape-recorded from Jeffie Solomon on August 12, 1997, by Tom Mould, Glenda Williamson, and Meriva Williamson. See "Stories in Choctaw" for the story as it was originally told in Choctaw. This spot would be between Union and Conehatta, according to where the story is being told. Compare this story to "*Okwa Nahollo.*" Other versions: interview with Esbie Gibson, July 25, 1997, Lakylee Martin, July 1, 2021, during an interview with Eddie Gibson: "I was told that there was mermaids and a snake, a big snake, underneath the pond. And they had drained it, but they never found anything. And they have like a secret tunnel, too, in there. But my mom had told me that once the end of the world is coming, that the big snake will start to come out, and the mermaids will, too" (compare to "The Water Choctaw").

The Water Choctaw—Unpublished. Tape-recorded from Esbie Gibson on July 25, 1997, by Tom Mould, Glenda Williamson, Meriva Williamson, and Lionel Dan. Esbie Gibson told the story in Choctaw. A *hopaii* is a Choctaw medicine man. The gender of the Water Choctaw seems to shift in this story. Likely, Esbie Gibson uses both since Water Choctaw could be male or female. The specific one she refers to in the beginning is the female, though others can be male. Compare to "*Okwa Nahollo.*" Other accounts: written version by Norma Hickman, January 30, 1996; interview with Terry Ben, June 10, 2021, noting, "They've seen a mermaid-type creature at the water area at the edge of the cave mound. Somebody told me that years ago now."

The Mermaid—Unpublished. Digitally recorded from Jessica Miller on April 11, 2024, by Tom Mould and Eddie Johnson. Jessica said that she never heard a Choctaw term for this being her parents saw in the water; they just used the English term "mermaid." She said others had seen it too, but they described the mermaid as having a different colored tail such as purple.

Voices on the Mound—Unpublished. Digitally recorded from Jessica Miller on April 11, 2024, by Tom Mould and Eddie Johnson.

The Long-Haired Lady—Unpublished. Digitally recorded from Jessica Miller on April 11, 2024, by Tom Mould and Eddie Johnson. Eddie added: "There are sightings of an old woman often seen around the mound," confirming that Jessica and her friend were not the only ones to see this "woman."

Paš Falaya—Unpublished. Tape-recorded from Cynthia Clegg on July 27, 1997, by Tom Mould and Liasha Alex during an afternoon session at the Choctaw Language Immersion Camp. See "Stories in Choctaw" for Choctaw language version. The Choctaws' neighbors used to call them *pashi falaya* or "long hairs" (Howard and Levine 1990:3; interview with Harold Comby, June 4, 1997).

Nishkin Chafa—Unpublished. Tape-recorded from Regina Shoemake, June 3, 1997, by Tom Mould and Curtis "Buck" Willis. Regina begins the story by referring to a point earlier in our discussion when she mentioned *nishkin chafa* as one of a number of supernatural beings. When Regina says, "So all were running toward there" about the wedding in progress, she is referring to the practice of having the groom and his family chase and catch the fleeing bride. The idea is that if he cannot catch her, he cannot marry her. I asked Regina if the people at the hospital were Choctaw, and she said no, that's why they didn't understand. Regina recounts three different encounters, not all of which may be referring to the same thing. The second encounter, for example, seems to be referencing a medicine man, as the children yell that they recognize the person from the community. Regina was not sure whether or not *nishkin chafa* are supposed to be medicine men. Other accounts: Melford Farve shared two stories of encountering *nishkin chafa* late at night in the woods (December 14, 2018; not recorded).

Headless Man—Unpublished. Tape-recorded from Melford Farve on July 10, 1997, by Tom Mould.

The Inhuman *Na Losa Chito*—Unpublished. Tape-recorded from Jeffie Solomon on August 12, 1997, by Tom Mould, Glenda Williamson, and Meriva Williamson. See "Stories in Choctaw" for the story as it was originally told in Choctaw. Israel Folsom described *na losa chito* in 1828: "They also believed in the existence of a devil, whom they designated Na-lusa-chi-to, a great black being, or soul eater, who found full occupation in terrifying and doing all manner of harm to people. He accords well with the one described in the Scriptures; 'who goeth about like a roaring lion seeking whom he may devour'" (Cushman 1899:301, citing Folsom's unpublished manuscript). Sightings of *na losa chito* remain prevalent today. In addition to the stories included in this book, dozens more stories have been shared by community members young and old, with many located in the Conehatta community.

The Demon *Na Losa Chito*—Unpublished. Tape-recorded from Harold Comby, June 4, 1997, by Tom Mould and Liasha Alex. Harold is referring to his mother here, so I substituted "My mother" for "She" in the first line of the story. Harold shared this story with me again on December 12, 2018, during a casual, unrecorded, conversation, noting again the importance of not running or you'll fall down and have seizures. He also said that when he worked for the Choctaw Police, they sometimes got calls from people who saw strange things in the woods, including one woman who said she had seen *na losa chito*. "I'm Indian, but I was trained to track in the armed forces," he explained. "I looked at the disturbed leaves and hoofprints, and it looked like a large deer to me." He told her this, but she wasn't satisfied with the explanation. So Harold told her to stay in the house, keep her outside lights on, and be watchful and careful. On Febtuary 24, 2022, Josh Foreman videorecorded Harold's version of the story, which is almost verbatim to this one.

A Big Hog—Unpublished. Tape-recorded from Gladys Willis on May 23, 1996, by Tom Mould and Rae Nell Vaughn, Gladys Willis's granddaughter, the "Rae" she refers to in the story. Other versions: interview with Rae Nell Vaughn, March 14, 1996, interview with Linda Williams, June 15, 2021; Keyes and Carleton 1990 told by Gus Comby. Comby tells two stories; in the second, he describes *na losa chito* as a white cloud.

Big, Black, Hairy Monster—Roy Ketcher. 1985:98. Terry Ben added that this event was supposed to have taken place around 1920. The lack of quotation marks around this story suggests it is not a verbatim transcript from Ketcher's interview with Terry Ben in November 1984. See the notes for "Big Pond" for other supernatural encounters that take place near water in Conehatta.

Black Dog—Unpublished. Digitally recorded from Theron "Duke" Denson on June 17, 2021, by Tom Mould. Duke told this story over the phone to me a few days earlier when I was not recording. In that version, he recounts the story in a linear fashion, beginning with what happened to the man when he saw the black dog and casket and ending with being chased down and tied up to control him. Here, he tells the story from his mother's perspective as an eyewitness, first seeing the strange behavior of the man, and only finding out the following day when he calmed down what he had seen that made him "go crazy."

Choctaw Bigfoot—Unpublished. Digitally recorded from Theron "Duke" Denson on June 17, 2021, by Tom Mould. Other accounts of people using the term Bigfoot: Henderson Williams, July 25, 1997, Donald Cotton, June 27, 2021; Lorena Alex, June 10, 2021. There seems to be some discrepancy between the *na losa chito* that can shape-shift that Duke and others describe in some of the previous stories, and *na losa chito* as Bigfoot, a cryptid typically described without any supernatural abilities.

Na Losa Chito's Lair—Unpublished. Digitally recorded from Theron "Duke" Denson on June 17, 2021, by Tom Mould. Roger Patterson was one of two men who recorded video of a tall creature walking in the distance among the rocks and trees; it is the most well-known and frequently viewed Bigfoot footage in the world. The professional Bigfoot hunter Duke describes is Tom Biscardi, whose visit to Pearl River in April 2012 was covered by the local media including the *Neshoba Democrat* and Meridian's ABC News 11.

The Black Stump—Unpublished. Tape-recorded from Nellie Billy on June 30, 1997, by Tom Mould and Liasha Alex during afternoon storytelling at the Choctaw Language Immersion Camp. See "Stories in Choctaw" for the story as it was originally told in Choctaw. The story depends on the linguistic play between describing the stump as a big, black thing and the name of a well-known creature discussed earlier in the chapter, *na losa chito*, which is literally translated as "big, black thing." Also, when Nellie Billy refers to owls, she uses the term *opaho*, which probably specifies either the owls used by medicine men as helpers or the owl form adopted by such men. These doctors would be considered witches, whose intent was to do harm.

The Choctaw Robin Goodfellow—Recorded by Henry S. Halbert. 1895:57. Compare to "*Kowi Anukasha*" in this collection. Other versions: Blanchard 1981:147–48, told by "a Choctaw male of college age," and 1981:148, unattributed; Gregory and Strickland 1972; interview with Rae Nell Vaughn on March 14, 1996.

The Little People in Nanih Waiya Cave—Unpublished. Digitally recorded from Terry Ben on June 3, 1996, by Tom Mould. Compare to the "Snake Returns" story in the "Prophecy" section. Terry shared the story of the little people coming out to dance during rainstorms again in 2021.

Doors in Nanih Waiya Cave—Unpublished. Digitally recorded from Jessica Miller on April 11, 2024, by Tom Mould and Eddie Johnson.

Watcher in the Woods—Unpublished. Digitally recorded from Carmen Denson on January 12, 2000, by Tom Mould.

Throwing Rocks—Unpublished. Digitally recorded from Travis Willis on June 14, 2021, by Tom Mould.

Throwing Competition—Unpublished. Digitally recorded from Brian Billie on June 30, 2021, by Lakylee Martin, Tom Mould, Makaylin Alex, Taylor Ben, Lexi Flint, and Jaeden Wesley.

No Playing after Dark—Unpublished. Digitally recorded from Dan Isaac on June 23, 2021, by Tom Mould, Makaylin Alex, Taylor Ben, Lexi Flint, and Lakylee Martin. See also story titled "Don't Play after Dark," by Martha Ferguson in *Choctaw Traditions*.

The Floating Light—Unpublished. Tape-recorded from Jake York on July 29, 1997, by Tom Mould. "16" is Highway 16, a well-traveled road that runs through Pearl River, where this story takes place. Compare to "Lights" in this collection.

Lights—Recorded from Gus Comby by Roy Ketcher. 1985:102. Ketcher interviewed Gus Comby at Pearl River on November 26, 1984, and added that "Gus believes that what he saw . . . was the *bohpoli*, not like he is known to look, but in a different form" (102).

Kowi Anukasha—Recorded from Ahojeobe by David I. Bushnell Jr. 1909:30–31. This is a summary description of a supernatural being rather than a specific narrative. Bushnell's original spelling is "Kwanoka'sha." See "The Choctaw Robin Goodfellow" for translation of this name according to Henry Halbert. Bushnell adds: "This legend, as related to the writer by Ahojeobe (Emil John), is given by the Choctaw as explaining why some men do good and help others, while many are ignorant and harm those whom they should assist. The existence of a 'spirit' such as *kwanoka'sha* [*kowi anukasha*] was evidently believed firmly by all, as it is by the few now living at Bayou Lacomb" (30). Other versions: Gregory and Strickland 1972; interview with Esbie Gibson on July 25, 1997.

Medicine Woman—Recorded from Estelline Tubby by Vernon Tubby. 1976:15–16. Other versions: Blanchard 1981:147 told by "one young woman who had previously aspired to be a doctor"; another version by Estelline Tubby recorded by Tom Mould on May 31, 1996. It is not clear from the narrative whether the old woman in the story is meant to be one of the *bohpoli*. The role of teaching medicine is the same, but nowhere else have I found the *bohpoli* described as female.

The Little Man—Unpublished. Tape-recorded from Terry Ben on May 30, 1996, by Tom Mould and Rae Nell Vaughn. It is perhaps worth noting that in popular American culture, animals, particularly dogs, are often the first to sense the supernatural. In this story, the dogs never sense the little man.

Pile of Rocks—Unpublished. Tape-recorded from Judy Billie on June 3, 1997, by Tom Mould and Curtis "Buck" Willis. From our conversation, it is clear that Judy Billie is talking about *bohpoli*.

A Witch—Recorded from Gus Comby by Roy Ketcher. 1985:101–2. Ketcher interviewed Gus Comby at Pearl River on November 26, 1984. Witches and bad Choctaw doctors are synonymous. Compare to the stories that immediately follow.

Choctaw Doctors—Unpublished. Tape-recorded from Terry Ben on May 30, 1996, by Tom Mould and Rae Nell Vaughn. Terry Ben added that a medicine man can do the things that the animal he turns into can do. Doctors might do it to get around faster or scare someone or show off their power. "Stories like that can go on and on and on," he says. Similar stories are told throughout the community, often naming people specifically. Such naming, however, could be considered dangerous.

Shape Changer—Unpublished. Tape-recorded from Melford Farve on July 14, 1997, by Tom Mould. Terry Ben tells a version of the same event (1997), as does Mack Jimmie (2021), who attributed the story to Gus Comby, who describes witnessing the event. This story seems to be circulated widely throughout the community and is therefore somewhat unusual. Most of the stories about the supernatural are similar in nature but describe unique events. This story seems to have become a legend. See also "The Baseball Game" as another possible example of such widespread circulation.

The Baseball Game—Unpublished. Tape-recorded from Melford Farve on July 14 and 16, 1997, by Tom Mould. Melford's duties as tribal councilman interrupted his story just after "and pulled out a little pouch." Two days later, when we met again, I played the last few lines of the story to him, and he picked up the narrative without hesitation. There are a number of stories that connect witchcraft with sports—baseball and stickball in particular. Kendall Blanchard discusses the relationship between the two in his book *The Mississippi Choctaws at Play*. In it, Blanchard includes an unattributed story about a ball game in the 1950s that is strikingly similar to Melford Farve's version, suggesting the two stories describe the same game. Further, Melford mentioned to me that some of his father's stories were in Blanchard's book.

Dancing Lights—Unpublished. Tape-recorded from Melford Farve on July 16, 1997, by Tom Mould. The notion that a witch must take out its intestines to fly is repeated throughout the community.

Hashok Okwa Hui'ga—Recorded from Pisatuntema by David I. Bushnell Jr. 1910:532. This is a summary description of a supernatural being rather than a specific narrative. All of the myths recorded here in Bushnell's 1910 article are apparently from Pisatuntema, though others may have added parts during the storytelling (526). Bushnell adds that the "name is derived from the three words: *hashok*, grass; *okwa*, water; *hui'ga*, drop." He also suggests that this tale as well as the one titled "*Na Losa Falaya*" in this collection refer to *ignis fatuus* (532–33), also known as will-o'-the-wisps—flickering phosphorescent lights seen at night in marshy areas.

The Blue Light—Unpublished. Tape-recorded from Melford Farve on July 10, 1997, by Tom Mould. Roswell is the name of a New Mexico town where, in 1947, there were claims of alien sightings. The name is now inexorably linked to the incident.

Disappearing Lights—Recorded from Gus Comby by Roy Ketcher. 1985: 101–2. Ketcher interviewed Gus Comby at Pearl River on November 26, 1984.

Lingering Spirit—Unpublished. Digitally recorded from Travis Willis on June 14, 2021, by Tom Mould.

The Ghost—Recorded from Olman Comby by John R. Swanton. 1928b:18 (also published by Stewart: 1931:3).

Spirit of the Dead—Unpublished. Tape-recorded from Harold Comby on June 4, 1997, by Tom Mould and Liasha Alex.

Two Brothers—Unpublished. Tape-recorded from Melford Farve on July 14, 1997, by Tom Mould. Melford Farve is referring to his father, so I have substituted "my father" for "he" in the first lines of the story. Melford follows this story with one about shape-shifters (see "Shape Changer"), suggesting that this is what the boy in the story thought he had seen. Compare to "The Black Stump," another humorous tale about an encounter with what is mistakenly believed to be the supernatural.

HISTORICAL STORIES

The Coming of Christianity—Unpublished. Tape-recorded from Bobby Joe on July 30, 1999, by Tom Mould. Bobby heard this story from Cameron Wesley, a man he admired for trying to maintain Choctaw traditions. Bobby explained that, ironically, it has been White people who have questioned why so many Choctaws are Christian today.

It's a lot of people told me, "If you're Choctaw, you knew who created your people." This guy was a White guy. "God created us too. We're all human. You got to know something about your religion way before our people came over here to this part of the country. I'm pretty sure your people was doing something, believing your own way in your religion. Why don't you go around and ask these old people and pick it up from here and there and use it?" He said, "You know you're not a White because you're an Indian. God created you like that. And God wants you to be like that. He said, "Why you go to church?"

Helping the New Immigrants—Recorded from Baxter York by the *Nanih Waiya* magazine staff, June 21, 1974.

White Men Bring Alcohol—Recorded from John Hunter Thompson by Cynthia Thompson. 1979:25–26. Other accounts: interview with Baxter York, "Baxter York Again" 1975.

Fighting the Muskogees—Recorded from John Hunter Thompson, by Cynthia Thompson. 1979:29–30.

Crossing the Line—Unpublished. Tape-recorded from Louise Wilson on June 10, 1997, by Tom Mould and Danielle Dan. At the beginning of the second paragraph, Louise Wilson actually says "he," referring to her earlier identification of the storyteller as her grandfather, John Hunter Thompson, who describes similar warfare against the Muskogees (see "Fighting the Muskogees"). From the early 1700s until 1750, English and French settlers pressured the Choctaws (as well as neighboring tribes) to ally themselves with them. The Choctaw did but not uniformly, creating factions within the tribe that frequently engaged in civil war (Howard and Levine 1990:3). Biasha (or Bihiupiashah, according to Baxter York) was a local term for the community of Choctaw living in and just north of today's Pearl River community. It is unclear what community Fichik Watathbe refers to, although *fichik* means star. *Bissápi* are blackberry briers, as Louise Wilson describes.

Death of Pushmataha—Unpublished. Tape-recorded from Grady John on February 22, 1998, by Tom Mould. Many of the versions told throughout the community suggest Pushmataha was poisoned; others say he was stabbed. History books attribute his death to pneumonia. During a conversation with Grady a year later, he explained that Pushamataha was one of the greatest leaders the tribe had ever known, adding that he was poisoned in Washington, DC, because he was so smart. "People were nervous. They thought he might be President of the United States" (interview with Tom Mould, July 17, 1999).

Pushmataha's Suspicious Death—Unpublished. Digitally recorded on June 23, 2021, from Dan Isaac by Tom Mould, Makaylin Alex, Taylor Ben, Lexi Flint, and Lakylee Martin. The story that Pushmataha was murdered is well known throughout the community. Many agree with Dan Isaac and Grady John that the murder was to facilitate removal. After sharing her version of Pushmataha's death, an elder concluded, "So I think they had to murder him, and the fact was to get the Mississippi lands, which was Choctaw lands. So their belief—the *nahollos* believe, the White men believed—at the time was, 'Okay, if we kill him off, there's that way for Chahtas here not to say much. That's our way of ... We got to get those lands'" (2021).

Removal—Unpublished. Tape-recorded from Grady John on February 22, 1998, by Tom Mould. Compare to "Land Swindling," by Jake York. Apparently, this kind of deceit occurred in Oklahoma as well as in Mississippi.

Hiding to Avoid Removal—Recorded from Louise Willis on December 4, 1973, by John K. Mahon. It is unclear exactly where Louise meant when she described two miles between where people were when they decided to hide. It might have been from where she was at the time of the interview, a place where families were living and had gathered, or the distance between the Nanih Waiya Mound and the Nanih Waiya Cave. In either case, it is not the distance from the site where the Treaty of Dancing Rabbit Creek was and the cave, which is ten and a half miles as the crow flies. Other accounts: interviews with Lela Solomon, February 1982, and Nettie Tubby, March 1982.

Second Removal and Return—Unpublished. Tape-recorded from Frank Henry on July 23, 1997, by Tom Mould. This story immediately followed his story "Pushmataha," making it clear that the leader's death allowed the US government to remove the Choctaw to the West, despite the fact that the tribe was flourishing and life was good. Frank estimates that his grandmother and other family members returned to Mississippi around 1910. This would have been after the second removal efforts that occurred at the turn of the century. In the audio, it is unclear whether he describes his mother as literate or illiterate. I have erred on the side of education, but the context of the story suggests that "illiterate" may be more accurate.

Sneaking Back from Oklahoma—Unpublished. Tape-recorded from Jake York on July 29, 1997, by Tom Mould. Harold Comby also notes that he had heard of many people returning to Mississippi soon after arriving in Oklahoma.

Land Swindling—Unpublished. Tape-recorded from Jake York on July 29, 1997, by Tom Mould. Grady John also spoke about such swindling that occurred in Mississippi (as well as in Oklahoma—see "Removal" in this collection).

Grandfather's Land—Unpublished. Tape-recorded from Inez Henry on February 20, 1986, by Geri Harm.

Burning Sticks—Unpublished. Tape-recorded from Estelline Tubby on August 5, 1997, by Tom Mould. The community of Bogue Chitto is generally recognized as one of the most traditional of all the communities.

Escaping Slavery—Recorded from Alice Bell in 1985 by Susan Weill, Julia Williams, and Bob Ferguson (Weill et al. 1985).

Sinking Ship—Recorded from Pete Davis Dyer by John Lee Chickaway and Baron Gardner, staff of the *Nanih Waiya* magazine on November 4, 1975. It is unclear which ship Pete was on. He mentions later they lost three hundred of the four hundred soldiers when the ship went down on December 11, 1943. The list of US ships sunk during WWII does not include one on that date. Throughout Pete's story, he seems to act out some of the actions, marking some of these gestures with the words *like that*. Twice, Pete refers to the enemy as *Japs*, a term that would have been common during the war but is recognized fairly universally as offensive today. I have replaced it with *the Japanese*.

German Surrender—Unpublished. Tape-recorded from Carmen Denson on January 12, 2000, by Tom Mould. I asked Carmen why he thought the Germans surrendered. "Germans told them that hungry men can't fight." The details Carmen includes here align with the 1973 interview of his father, Charlie Denson, with Sam Proctor, including the bases where he trained, the *Queen Mary* that took him to Europe, and the reconnaissance unit he served in. That interview does not, however, include the story Carmen shared here.

Army Volunteer—Unpublished. Digitally recorded from Terry Ben on June 10, 2021, by Tom Mould, Taylor Ben, Lakylee Martin, Thomas Saunders, and Meka Willis. Terry added that he had many uncles who were drafted during World War II.

> I would say they didn't really enjoy going away from the reservation previously, but once they got into it, they felt proud to be part of the army representing the United States. I would say that was a big deal going into the military, getting drafted. Once they got in, they did all right. And often times, even nowadays, whenever my uncles get together, they talk about wartime—Okinawa, the closing days of when they were in Germany around Hitler's defeat, they would talk about times like that.

Patriots—Unpublished. Tape-recorded from Harold Comby on June 4, 1997, by Tom Mould and Liasha Alex.

Go Back to Europe—Recorded from Baxter York by the *Nanih Waiya* magazine staff, June 21, 1974. Baxter played semiprofessional baseball for a few years for the Oklahoma Indians on a traveling team. Because Philadelphia, Mississippi, is so close to the Choctaw community, he makes a point of clarifying that this story took place in Pennsylvania. Unfortunately, racial slurs cast during sporting events has hardly disappeared; Leonard Jimmie referenced accusations that Mississippi State fans cast racial slurs at their opponents during the 2021 College World Series (interview with Tom Mould, July 11, 2021).

Poll Tax—Unpublished. Digitally recorded from Terry Ben on June 10, 2021, by Tom Mould, Taylor Ben, Lakylee Martin, Thomas Saunders, and Meka Willis.

Segregation in the Fields and at the Movies—Recorded from Hubert Wesley on December 18, 1992, and archived by the Center for Oral History and Cultural Heritage at the University of Southern Mississippi.

Injustice at the Laundromat—Unpublished. Digitally recorded from Terry Ben on June 10, 2021, by Tom Mould, Taylor Ben, Lakylee Martin, Thomas Saunders, and Meka Willis.

Discrimination—Recorded from Frank Bell Joe on April 16, 1975, by Lonus D. Hucks. Frank notes that most people went to Meridian to shop since Philadelphia was so prejudiced. Sarah Jane Sampson McMillan says she never bothered going to a restaurant in Philadelphia again after being told she had to eat in the back (December 2, 1973).

Murder of Civil Rights Workers—Unpublished. Digitally recorded from Terry Ben on June 10, 2021, by Tom Mould, Taylor Ben, Lakylee Martin, Thomas Saunders, and Meka Willis. Terry added that Sheriff Lawrence Rainey and Deputy Sheriff Cecil Price were tough on Choctaws and Blacks alike. "If you're out beyond, say ten o'clock, somewhere, they would stop you and throw in jail for no reason, simply because you were out. That was the rumor during that time period. So my granddaddy, if he had any business done in Philadelphia, before dark, he would always say, 'Let's go home.' He would never stick around Philadelphia during that time period." He also explained to the YOP students that the murder of the three civil rights workers James Chaney, Michael Schwerner, and Andrew Goodman was retold in the film *Mississippi Burning*, noting that some tribal members were cast as extras. He said the film took some liberties with the facts, but he recommended the students watch it for a more complete understanding of the event and the times.

Mississippi Burning—Unpublished. Recorded from Harold Comby on June 4, 1997, by Tom Mould and Liasha Alex, and on June 1, 2021, by Tom Mould, Lexi Flint, Jaeden Willis, Taylor Ben, and Eddie Johnson. Harold is referring to the infamous murders of three civil rights workers: James Chaney, Andrew Goodman, and Michael Schwerner. Harold explained that the KKK burned the car, but the police were involved in it too (some of the police were members of the KKK). When I asked about the story that a Choctaw man had a house across the road from where the three civil rights workers were buried, he noted that the man had since passed away, but the old frame house he lived in was still there. He told the story again in 2021, adding the part about visiting the earthen dam where the bodies were buried (that part is added here). In addition to the FBI who came to investigate the murders, more than four hundred members of the US Navy were deployed to search for the civil rights workers. Melford Farve remembers being a kid when this happened. Military personnel were regularly in the streets to keep the calm. Some handed out fruit or other snacks to the children to engender trust, but his mom told him not to accept them (interview, n.d.)

Banned—Unpublished. Digitally recorded from Terry Ben on June 10, 2021, by Tom Mould, Taylor Ben, Lakylee Martin, Thomas Saunders, and Meka Willis. Ross Barnett was born in Standing Pine in 1898 and is remembered by some Choctaw as a relatively fair and respected neighbor. However, his deeply segregationist policies as governor of Mississippi and aggressive stance against civil rights has shaped his historical legacy, so it is not surprising that Terry imagines that it might have been Barnett who orchestrated a vote to determine whether his grandfather would be allowed to continue to attend the local Veterans of Foreign Wars (VFW) lodge.

Troubling Times—Unpublished. Digitally recorded from Leonard Jimmie on July 11, 2021, by Tom Mould.

Treated like a Dog—Unpublished. Digitally recorded from Martha Ferguson on June 14, 2021, by Tom Mould and Jaeden Wesley.

Framed for Murder—Unpublished. Tape-recorded from Doyle Tubby on July 2, 1997, by Tom Mould. The *Clarion Ledger* newspaper covered the murder with a number of newspaper stories, including two front-page stories: "Neshoba County Man Found Beaten to Death" (May 5, 1961) and "Indian Admits Killing Farmer" (May 13, 1961) that claimed "McKinely Tubby" confessed to the murder, misspelling the defendant's name, which was McKinley Tubby, an army veteran.

Whites-Only Water Fountain—Unpublished. Digitally recorded from Terry Ben on June 10, 2021, by Tom Mould, Taylor Ben, Lakylee Martin, Thomas Saunders, and Meka Willis. Harold Comby noted, "We didn't go into the White restaurant or even the bathroom. It said "White" and "Colored." I used to go to both, but the White people would look at me, but they didn't say nothing" (June 1, 2021). The water fountains and bathrooms in the courthouse also stick out in Travis Willis's memory as symbols of the discrimination they faced long after Jim Crow laws were supposed to have been abolished (June 14, 2021).

Shortchanged—Unpublished. Digitally recorded from Harold Comby on June 1, 2021, by Tom Mould, Lexi Flint, Jaeden Willis, Taylor Ben, and Eddie Johnson.

Overcharged—Recorded from Frank Bell Joe on April 16, 1975, by Lonus D. Hucks.

Some Bad, Some Good—Unpublished. Digitally recorded from Terry Ben on June 10, 2021, by Tom Mould, Taylor Ben, Lakylee Martin, Thomas Saunders, and Meka Willis. Clay Gibson concurs, saying that in the past, neighbors typically got along; "When we were younger coming up, the Whites and the Indians were neighbors, and you could always depend on each other for survival. Because of the way our society is today, it seems like we are distant rather than being closer now" (Weill et al. 1985).

No Trust and No Choctaw—Unpublished. Digitally recorded from Hayward Bell on June 30, 2021, by Tom Mould, Taylor Ben, and Lakylee Martin. In a conversation on June 6, 2023, Hayward added, "I was a kid, but I was disturbed this situation. Teachers didn't have confidence in the students that they taught."

Served in the Back in High School—Unpublished. Digitally recorded from Terry Ben on June 10, 2021, by Tom Mould, Taylor Ben, Lakylee Martin, Thomas Saunders, and Meka Willis. After this story, Terry Ben also tells of buying a burger, fries, and a drink at the local drive-in after he graduated high school and also being served from the back of the restaurant.

Eat in the Back—Unpublished. Digitally recorded from Eddie Gibson on July 1, 2021, by Jaeden Wesley, Tom Mould, Taylor Ben, Lexi Flint, Lakylee Martin.

A Simple Hello—Unpublished, Digitially recorded from Brian Billie on June 30, 2021, from Lakylee Martin, Tom Mould, Makaylin Alex, Taylor Ben, Lexi Flint, and Jaeden Wesley.

Believe It When You See It—Unpublished. Digitally recorded from Eddie Gibson on July 1, 2021, by Jaeden Wesley, Tom Mould, Taylor Ben, Lexi Flint, Lakylee Martin.

Segregation Then and Now—Unpublished. Digitally recorded on June 23, 2021, from Dan Isaac by Tom Mould, Makaylin Alex, Taylor Ben, Lexi Flint, and Lakylee Martin.

Housing Discrimination—Unpublished. Digitally recorded from Hayward Bell on June 30, 2021, by Tom Mould, Taylor Ben, and Lakylee Martin. Hayward explained in a conversation on June 6, 2023, that it was understood that Choctaw didn't go into Philadelphia for a house because of discriminatory real estate practices.

PROPHECY

Changing Landscape and Intermarriage—Recorded from John Hunter Thompson by Cynthia Thompson. 1979:30. Other accounts: interview with Linda Willis, January 7, 2000 (see Mould 2003:182).

Invention of the Airplane—Unpublished. Digitally recorded from Mark Patrick on July 7, 2021, by Tom Mould.

Planes, Roads, and Culture—Unpublished. Tape-recorded from Grady John on February 22, 1998, by Tom Mould. 2003:158. I have omitted a brief exchange where I asked Grady John how long ago he heard a prophecy between talking about the prophecy of the tractor and that about people studying the Choctaw in schools. Parallel prophecies about the coming of paved roads and airplanes are common throughout the community. Other accounts: interview with Sally Allen, Regina Shoemake, and Judy Billie, June 3, 1997. Compare to "Intermarriage, Roads, and Changing Seasons."

Intermarriage, Roads, and Changing Seasons—Unpublished. Tape-recorded from Harold Comby on June 4, 1997, by Tom Mould and Liasha Alex. Other accounts: interview with Sally Allen, June 3, 1997; interview with Charlie Denson, March 12, 1996, and May 25, 1996; interview with Viola Johnson, 1974; interview with Linda Williams, June 15, 2021; interview with Louise Wilson, June 10, 1997.

Changing World—Tape-recorded from Bobby Joe, January 6, 2000, by Tom Mould. 2003:72–74. See Mould 2003:72–74 for a discussion of this passage. Bobby paused between "some time in the future," and "Yeah, that's the way." So I could flip the audiotape over to continue recording. Other versions: Casey Bigpond June 24, 2021: "There's going to be a spiderweb crossing the whole country . . . power lines."

Electricity, Plumbing, and Social Dancing—Tape-recorded from Billy Amos, August 1, 1999, by Tom Mould. 2003:44–47, 69. I have omitted my question to Billy after his first commentary about the prophecies coming true when I asked him about a prophecy he had told me about electricity. This question prompts the prophecy that follows. When Billy talks about cooking outdoors and he adds, "like we do today," he is referring to my visit earlier that afternoon when he and two friends were cooking outside under his backyard arbor.

Cars, Roads, and Changing Values—Unpublished. Tape-recorded from Odie Mae Anderson on August 12, 1997, by Tom Mould, Glenda Williamson, and Meriva Williamson. See "Stories in Choctaw" for the story as it was originally told in Choctaw. The thing with two eyes that will be running along the road refers to a car. Bundles can be understood as belongings. In older times, bundles would have been how such personal effects were carried and described. Other accounts: interview with Viola Johnson, 1974; Annie Tubby, recorded by John G. Wallace, 1977; interview with Estelline Tubby, July 22, 1999 (Mould 2003).

Gender Roles, Roads, Housing, and Language—Digitally recorded from Evaline Davis on June 3, 2021, by Tom Mould, Makaylin Alex, Taylor Ben, and Lexi Flint.

A Fearful Future—Unpublished. Digitally recorded from Lorena Alex on June 10, 2021, by Tom Mould, Taylor Ben, Lakylee Martin, and Jaeden Wesley. The deaths she is referring to are those from the COVID-19 pandemic.

A Great Illness—Tape-recorded from Louise Wilson on June 10, 1997, by Tom Mould and Danielle Dan. 2003: 150–51. In 1918, an influenza epidemic devastated the Choctaw community. Due to crowded living conditions and poor housing, the Choctaws fared far worse than their neighbors. John Peterson records a local nurse at the time who witnessed the decimation: "They were dying like flies, often without any medical attention" (1971:110). From the census records and birth rates, Peterson surmised that nearly 20 percent of the Choctaw population died during the epidemic (111). Just as Louise Wilson wonders if the prophecy may predict more than future epidemic—not just smallpox or TB, but perhaps also AIDS—others more recently have wondered if these prophecies also predicted COVID-19. Harold Comby reflected: "It's kind of strange that the pandemic that made us MBCI back in 1918, 1920, almost a hundred years later, another pandemic came by, and knock on wood it seem like we're going to survive this one, too. But even back then, they say we had a lot of deaths. But you know, that was prophesied. Don't you have it in your book?" (he is referencing the first edition of this book) (June 1, 2021).

Prophecies of Disease—Unpublished. Digitally recorded from Harold Comby on June 1, 2021, by Tom Mould, Lexi Flint, Jaeden Willis, Taylor Ben, and Eddie Johnson. After saying this was prophesied, Harold asked, "Don't you have it in your book?" (referring to the first edition of *Choctaw Tales*). I responded yes, noting that John Hunter Thompson and his granddaughter Louise Wilson after him talked about a disease that would return and kill tribal members (see previous story). He responded, "And my mom used to tell us, too." Historically, Harold seems to be referring to the hearings held in 1917 in Union, Mississippi, to assess the needs of the Choctaw, resulting in improvements to healthcare, housing, and schools. Formal reorganization and formation of the Mississippi Band of Choctaw Indians progressed with the signing of the Indian Reorganization Act in 1934, followed by the signing of the Choctaw Constitution in 1945.

Snatched from Above—Unpublished. Digitally recorded from Mark Patrick on July 7, 2021, by Tom Mould. Compare to "The Eagle Story" by Rosalee Steve. Although she says this happened a long time ago, she uses the future tense for much of the story, suggesting that she, too, may have heard this as a prophecy rather than a legend. After telling this story, Mark recounted reading a book that described fossils found along the Mississippi River of a large bird with a wingspan of twenty-six feet that they called a Thunderbird.

> For years, I've always seen the medallions. The Native Americans, Choctaws wear it all the time. I said, "What is that?" They said, "It's a Thunderbird." . . . The thought in my mind went right back to my grandmother's story. I was saying, "I wonder if this bird is going to make a comeback." And I said, "If it's extinct or it is no longer here, I wonder if it somehow is going to come back and attack, like the old legend says. But then I started asking around because my curiosity kind of got the best of me. So I said, "Why do you wear that?" Everybody would say, "I don't know." They said it just looks cool. So I said, "A Thunderbird. Do you know what a Thunderbird is?

He said, "The reason they called them a Thunderbird ... I've heard two sides of the story. The book says because the flapping of their wings sounded like thunder, as they took off. And then another one says that it was more illusional, something about the weather. When it's foul weather, and it's thundering and lightning or whatever, these birds seems to appear." Compare to "Lightning and Thunder" by Odie Anderson and "Thunder and Lightning" by Harold Comby.

The Third Removal—Tape-recorded from Estelline Tubby on May 31, 1996, by Tom Mould. 2003:93–95. A van pulled up during her account, interrupting her briefly between "Few will be left, just few will be left, after all night" and "After whenever, I don't know who the person is . . . " I have omitted my questions at the end of the narrative; I learned later to wait longer for Estelline to finish. Estelline Tubby recounted this prophecy twice more during interviews on August 5, 1997, and July 22, 1999. Other accounts: interviews with Sally Allen, June 3, 1997; Charlie Denson, March 12, 1996; and Regina Shoemake, January 10, 2000. In Charlie Denson's account, the third removal will be instigated by the Chinese, who will kill anyone who cannot speak the Choctaw language.

War—Tape-recorded from Linda Willis on January 7, 2000, by Tom Mould. 2003:184–85. This narrative comes after she has been talking about the things her grandfather told her. I have changed "he" to "my grandfather" in the opening line. Other accounts: interview with Sally Allen and Regina Shoemake, January 10, 2000. Compare to Estelline Tubby's "The Third Removal" and the additional accounts listed there, particularly Charlie Denson's (all of which can be found in Mould 2003).

Land Getting Old—Tape-recorded from Louise Wilson, July 29, 1999, by Tom Mould. 2003:76–77. This narrative comes after she has been talking about the things her grandfather told her. I have changed "He" to "My grandfather" in the opening line. Other accounts: interview with Bobby Joe, January 6, 2000 (Mould 2003:73–74); Regina Shoemake, January 10, 2000 (Mould 2003:76–77).

Extinction—Recorded from Pisatuntema by David I. Bushnell Jr. 1910:529–30. This prophecy is the fifth and final "chapter" of the myth cycle Bushnell recorded (see "Nané Chaha").

Snake Returns—Unpublished. Digitally recorded from Bradley Alex on June 30, 2021 by Makaylin Alex and Tom Mould, with Taylor Ben. See the annotations for "Big Pond" that also describes a prophecy of a snake emerging from water when the world is about to end, as well as Terry Ben's story of "The Little People in Nanih Waiya Cave" where a large snake lives. Jessica Miller also heard there was a big snake living in Nanih Waiya Cave back where the doors that her uncle saw (see "Doors in Nanih Waiya Cave").

End of the World—Tape-recorded from Linda Willis on January 7, 2000, by Tom Mould. 2003:186. Other accounts: interview with Harold Comby

(Mould 2003):60, 220; interview with Bobby Joe (Mould 2003):127–30, 220; interview with Grady John (Mould 2003):220; interview with John Hunter Thompson (Thompson 1979). The cause is varied in the numerous accounts of the end of the world. Most frequently, however, people point either to natural disaster or war.

Big Fire—Unpublished. Digitally recorded from Harold Comby on June 1, 2021, by Tom Mould, Lexi Flint, Jaeden Willis, Taylor Ben, and Eddie Johnson.

JOKES AND TALL STORIES

The Car—Unpublished. Tape-recorded from Lillie Gibson, August 5, 1997, by Tom Mould, Glenda Williamson, and Meriva Williamson. The week-long get-together that Lillie Gibson refers to commonly involved stickball games, feasting, dancing, and general celebration. It took place toward the end of the summer and can be equated with today's annual Choctaw Indian Fair. The Neshoba County Fair that she refers to is a parallel celebration that was traditionally celebrated by the White community in the county and also involved moving to a campground (with houses) to live for a week.

Running Water—Unpublished. Tape-recorded from Lillie Gibson, August 5, 1997, by Tom Mould, Glenda Williamson, and Meriva Williamson.

Whatyousay—Unpublished. Tape-recorded from Gladys Willis, May 23, 1996, by Tom Mould and Rae Nell Vaughn. Ashman was a well-known character in the community's stories. Harry Polk told a story about Ashman's encounter with a bullfrog (unrecorded); Eddie Johnson told a version of the "Time to Kill Hogs" story, also with Ashman as the main character (June 11, 2021). Neither Harry Polk nor Gladys Willis was clear as to the exact identity of Ashman, though Harry Polk believed he had died while Harry was still alive. Gladys Willis's son Travis Willis, however, remembers him well: "They called him Ashman. He used to live down the road from us. He was a grumpy old man. You couldn't even walk on that side of the road without having him mad. He used to stand at the side of the road and throw rocks at us. If we were going to go down . . . like we walked to the house or something, we would have to walk on this side of the road. We could never walk on this side." Travis said his family name was Bale, and, "They never had a vehicle. If they wanted to go town, they walked, or somebody would pick them up on the side of the road" (June 14, 2021). This detail makes the following story about him all the more fitting. Other versions: interview with Grady John, February 22, 1998.

Time to Kill Hogs—Unpublished. Tape-recorded from Gladys Willis, August 6, 1997, by Tom Mould. When she says, "So it was pretty cold in there.

Probably from walking," she is referring to the air feeling cold because Ashman had been walking in the sun and was so hot. Other versions: Eddie Johnson, June 11, 2021, who ended his story by summing up, "So that's a little cultural 'new-meets-old' kind of thing," and Mark Patrick, July 2, 2021, who said he heard the story from a White coworker.

The Horse's Egg—Recorded from Olman Comby by John R. Swanton. 1928b:21 (also Stewart 1931:15). In a note, Stewart adds: "Told to Swanton August 26, 1928." This is a popular story throughout the Southeast and is addressed by Joel Chandler Harris, who had heard many versions from African American storytellers (1955: xxv–xxvi). He suggests the rabbit stands for the slave; the Irishman, the slave master. While such an interpretation suggests possible parallels to the Choctaw, particularly considering the period of removal when many Choctaw hid in the swamps to avoid the move, the more obvious parallel is between the farmer and the Choctaw as he is the one who dupes the Irishman in this story. This story has been cataloged by Antti Aarne and Stith Thompson as Tale-Type 1319: Pumpkin Sold as Ass's Egg. It is found throughout the United States but not, apparently, in Europe or Africa, suggesting the story is American in origin.

The Funeral—Unpublished. Tape-recorded from Harry Polk on July 1, 1997, by Tom Mould and Liasha Alex during an afternoon storytelling session at the Choctaw Language Immersion Camp. See "Stories in Choctaw" for the story as it was originally told in Choctaw. The cry Harry Polk refers to is a traditional mourning practice. Harry is referring to the alligator seen near the camp that day when he says, "like the alligator there today."

The White Cat—Unpublished. Tape-recorded from Carmen Denson, May 25, 1996, by Tom Mould. Carmen Denson told this story in the presence of his father, Charlie Denson.

The Man and the Turkey—Unpublished. Tape-recorded from Henry Williams, June 24, 1997, by Tom Mould. Other versions: interview with Grady John, February 22, 1997; Blanchard 1981:8.

Talking Frogs—Unpublished. Digitally recorded from Brian Billie on June 30, 2021, by Lakylee Martin, Tom Mould, Makaylin Alex, Taylor Ben, Lexi Flint, and Jaeden Wesley. The word *yakomichicha* was unclear.

A Praying Bear—Unpublished. Digitally recorded from Brian Billie on June 30, 2021, by Lakylee Martin, Tom Mould, Makaylin Alex, Taylor Ben, Lexi Flint, and Jaeden Wesley.

The Dog Who Spoke Choctaw—Unpublished. Tape-recorded from Jake York on June 30, 1997, by Tom Mould and Liasha Alex during an afternoon storytelling session at the Choctaw Language Immersion Camp. See "Stories in Choctaw" for Choctaw language version. Compare to stories such as "The Dog Who Spoke Choctaw," where bilingualism is a valuable asset.

The Trip to Arkansas—Unpublished. Tape-recorded from Jake York on July 29, 1997, by Tom Mould. Other versions: Harold Comby, June 1, 2021, and February 24, 2022.

Tall Stories—Unpublished. Tape-recorded from Jake York on July 29, 1997, by Tom Mould. Jake York and others in the community point out that Jim Dixon was a real person.

The Lucky Shot—Recorded from Olman Comby by John R. Swanton 1928b:20. Swanton adds that Olman Comby said, "This story was obtained from a Choctaw in Oklahoma, but one who had lived in Mississippi until 1903." This story has been cataloged by Antti Aarne and Stith Thompson as Tale-Type 1890: Accidental Discharge of a Gun. A few versions of this tale type have been recorded in Europe, but the majority come from the United States.

Help from Above—Unpublished. Tape-recorded from Harry Polk on July 1, 1997, by Tom Mould and Liasha Alex during an afternoon storytelling session at the Choctaw Language Immersion Camp. See "Stories in Choctaw" for the story as it was originally told in Choctaw.

ANIMAL STORIES

The Ball Game—Recorded from Simpson Tubby by John R. Swanton. 1929a:35.

Race between the Hummingbird and the Crane—Recorded by Henry S. Halbert. c. 1900:38–41 (see also pp. 23–26 for a virtually identical translation). Halbert notes: "The myth of the race between the crane and the hummingbird, differing in several features from the Choctaw version, is to be found among the Creeks and the Cherokees (see Mooney 1892:290, 291, 456)."

The Hummingbird—Recorded by Henry S. Halbert. c. 1900:26–27.

The Dove Story—Unpublished. Tape-recorded from Jeffie Solomon on August 12, 1998, by Tom Mould, Glenda Williamson, and Meriva Williamson. See "Stories in Choctaw" for the story as it was originally told in Choctaw. In one of the versions of the Great Flood that H. B. Cushman records, the cooing of the doves is explained as a cry for salt that was taken away from them by the Great Spirit because their grandmother once forgot to use the salt as proscribed (1899:226).

How the *Biskantak* Got Water for the Birds—Recorded by Henry S. Halbert. c. 1900:77 (see also p. 45 for a slightly different translation). See "Stories in Choctaw" for the story as it was originally told in Choctaw. Halbert translates *biskantak* as "tomtit." I have retained the original name *biskantak* in the story since the sounds the bird makes explains its naming. I have also retranslated one word in Halbert's version. He translated *nakni* as "a man," so the *biskantak*'s song begins, "I am a man." However, *nakni* is translated in Byington's dictionary (edited, ironically, by Halbert and Swanton) as "the male sex of all creatures, where the distinction of sex is known; a man; a brave" (268). As an adjective, it means courageous and brave, manly. The *biskantak* is declaring his power in being male, not as a man, which suggests an anthropomorphic interpretation that may not be intended.

Why the Buzzard Has More Offspring than the Owl—Recorded by Henry S. Halbert, c. 1900:41–42.

Why the Guinea Hen Is Speckled—Recorded from Olman Comby by John R. Swanton, 1928b:22.

Boatmaker—Recorded from Olman Comby by John R. Swanton 1928b:3. Swanton adds: "Boatmaker is the American green heron, called in Choctaw Okataktak ("discolored water"), and the mother of the two girls is a bird called Wishakchi homa ("red top")." In a parenthetical note in the story, Halbert notes that the crane is known as *hushi tcaha*, tall bird.

The Hunters and the Bears—Henry S. Halbert. c. 1900:22 (see also Halbert manuscript p. 37 for a slightly different translation). Originally titled "How the Bear Lost His Tail."

Rabbit and the Bears—Unpublished. Tape-recorded from Gus Comby on December 16, 1990, by Greg Keyes and Ken Carleton. An audio version recorded in Choctaw around 1985 can be found online on the Choctaw Legacy website: https://choctawculturallegacy.com/audio-resources/. Translation by Eddie Johnson.

How the Bear Lost His Tail—Recorded from Olman Comby by John R. Swanton. 1928b:12. This story has been cataloged by Antti Aarne and Stith Thompson as Tale-Type 2: The Tale Fisher. Aarne and Thompson further suggest that this story is European in origin.

How the Rabbit Got a Short Tail—Unpublished. Tape-recorded from Inez Henry on October 28, 1988, by Geri Harm. This story, like the one before it, has been cataloged by Antti Aarne and Stith Thompson as Tale-Type 2: The Tail Fisher, a story that can be found in Europe, Asia, Africa, and North America. This story's ending, however, more closely parallels motif K1021: Deception into self-injury in which a bear is persuaded to fish with his tail through a hole in the ice.

How the Bullfrog Lost His Horns—Recorded by Henry S. Halbert. c. 1900:49–51.

How the Alligator Got His Back—Unpublished. Tape-recorded from Gus Comby on December 16, 1990, by Greg Keyes and Ken Carleton.

Rabbit and Turtle Race—Unpublished. Tape-recorded from Gus Comby, December 16, 1990, by Greg Keyes and Ken Carleton. Other versions: interview with Gladys Willis, May 23, 1996. See also "Race between Turkey and the Terrapin." This story has been cataloged by Antti Aarne and Stith Thompson as

Tale-Type 1074: Race Won by Deception: relative helpers. This story has been recorded throughout Europe, America, and West Africa. Note that I have included a number of the versions of this story in order to provide the reader with at least one example of how different versions of the same general tale can be told.

Race between the Turkey and the Terrapin—Henry S. Halbert. c. 1900:37–40 (numbered out of sequence). Compare to the version by Simpson Tubby, who ends his story: "This was to teach the Indians that 'slow and sure wins the race,' and that steadiness beats showy irregularity" (Swanton 1929a:4; also Stewart 1931:11). The version Randy Jimmie and Leonard Jimmie recorded in *Nanih Waiya*, 1974, 3:10–11, ends with "The moral of this tale is that the proud and scornful are often outwitted by those they look upon with contempt and disdain." The version published in a pamphlet by the tribe ends with "That's why the turkey has a lot of tendons in its leg." Other versions: interview with Harry Polk, July 8, 1997.

Turtle and Turkey—Recorded by Pisatuntema by David Bushnell Jr. 1910:533.

Why Terrapins Never Get Fat—Recorded from Olman Comby by John R. Swanton. 1928b:17 (also published in Stewart 1931:11). The end of this story in which ants sew the terrapin's shell back together is a motif that has been identified in European and African folktales as well under motif A2312.1.1 (and B511.+ by Kenneth Clarke for a similar West African story). The specific use of ants as helpers may be connected to motif K256.+, also from West Africa.

Turtle, Turkey, and the Ants—Recorded from Pisatuntema by David Bushnell Jr. 1910:534.

Why There Are Seams in the Terrapin's Shell—Recorded by Henry S. Halbert. c. 1900:42.

Why the Turtle's Shell Is Sewed Up—Unpublished. Tape-recorded from Inez Henry on October 28, 1988, by Geri Harm.

How the Terrapin Lost the Ability to Climb Trees—Recorded by Henry S. Halbert. c. 1900:66. See "Stories in Choctaw" for Choctaw language version. Originally titled "How the Terrapin Lost the Facility of Climbing a Tree." It is unclear what *pahihko* and *yahohio* refer to.

Possum's Tail—Unpublished. Digitally recorded from Duke Denson on June 15, 2021, by Tom Mould. Other versions: This story is one of the most frequently told animal tales among the Choctaw and is popular throughout the southeastern tribes. Other versions: Bushnell 1910:534; Halbert c. 1900; interview with Gus Comby, December 16, 1990; interview with Harold Comby, June 4, 1997; Leonard 1974:6–7, unattributed; Swanton 1928b:12 (also published by Stewart 1931:13) told by Olman Comby; tribe pamphlet, unattributed; interview with Henry Williams on June 24, 1997 (printed here in full in the chapter "The Genres of Choctaw Storytelling"). Compare also to the following story by Grady John in which Coon does not appear to be trying to trick Possum.

Possum and Coon—Unpublished. Tape-recorded from Grady John on February 22, 1998, by Tom Mould. Compare to "Possum's Tail" by Duke Denson.

The Panther and the Opossum—Recorded by Henry S. Halbert. c. 1900:52–62. *Mingo* is the Choctaw word for "chief." Three episodes can be identified in this story: (1) the rouse played by the possum and the panther (or bear); (2) the killing of the wolf by throwing a bone into its mouth; and (3) the clever escape by the possum when confronted with a whole pack of wolves. (The final episode is similar to the escape Skate'ne makes in the story "Skate'ne" in this collection.) The version recorded by Swanton from Olman Comby (1928b:13–15) also includes all three episodes in the same order; however, the version recorded by Jimmie and Jimmie (1974:9–10) include only episodes 2 and 3. The version told by Tom Tubby (*Nanih Waiya*: 1973) includes all three episodes but in exactly the opposite order of the version printed here.

How the Possum Tricked the Wolves—The story was originally published in the 1980s but updated and revised with the new orthography by the Choctaw Language Program in August 2007 from "Šokkatayat našoba ałíha haksičittók" (Thomas n.d.). The story is described as an "Original Choctaw Oral Tale as told by Hazel Thomas," suggesting both that Hazel Thomas created this story herself and that it was originally shared orally. This is in keeping with the open-ended nature of *shokhannǫpa*, where storytellers continue to add to the corpus of stories by creating new ones. Hazel has done this by incorporating motifs that also appear in other stories in this collection such as "The Panther and the Opossum" as well as motifs that appear throughout southeastern narrative traditions such as the Br'er Rabbit story the "Tar Baby." See "Stories in Choctaw" for Choctaw-language version.

Possum and the Fox—Unpublished. Tape-recorded from Harry Polk on July 8, 1997, by Tom Mould and Curtis "Buck" Willis. For clarity, I have substituted "My grandfather" for "He" in the first line of the story. "'Simmon" is an abbreviated version of "persimmon." Most versions pit the possum against a deer, although one describes a wolf. Other versions: Bushnell 1909:32; Halbert c. 1900:74–75; interview with Inez Henry on October 28, 1988, by Geri Harm; Tuggle 1973:171.

Possum and the Woodpecker—Unpublished. Digitally recorded from Eddie Johnson on June 14, 2021, by Tom Mould. After telling the story, Eddie added his interpretation: "The story has two sides. It has a meaning of don't be gullible. Don't believe everybody that wants help, really needs help, or something will happen to you. The other side of the story is that if you're really hungry, you'll find a way to get what you want." A few years later, Eddie explained that it was common for elders to end their stories with an interpretation since storytelling always offered a chance to teach.

Why the Rabbit's Skin Is Loose—Recorded from Olman Comby by John R. Swanton. 1928b:16.

Bear and Rabbit—Unpublished. Tape-recorded from Gus Comby on December 16, 1990, by Greg Keyes and Ken Carleton. Vegetables are frequently seasoned with meat in Choctaw, as well as general southern cooking. Other versions: interview with Hulon Willis on May 27, 1996 (printed here in full in the introduction); Swanton 1928:16 (also Stewart 1931:16) told by Olman Comby; tribal pamphlets. Kenneth Clarke has found numerous versions of this story in West Africa. Clarke has followed Stith Thompson's motif index, identifying this story as motif J2425: The Bungling Host.

How the Rabbit Fooled the Turkeys—Recorded by Henry S. Halbert. c. 1900:46–48. See "Stories in Choctaw" for the story as originally told in Choctaw.

Rabbit and Fox Farm Together—Recorded by Henry S. Halbert. c. 1900:47–48. Original Choctaw-language version: pp. 46–47. Halbert adds, "With the white race, the fox for ages has been accepted as the emblem of cunning. But with the American Indians, the fox has no such a reputation, and the rabbit is the great trickster. With the Choctaws, he shares this reputation with the opossum." Ernest Baughman has found numerous versions of this story throughout North America, identifying the story as Aarne-Thompson tale-type 1030: Crop Division.

Rabbit Rides Wolf—Unpublished. Tape-recorded from Gus Comby on December 16, 1990, by Greg Keyes and Ken Carleton. In versions of this story told by Simpson J. Tubby and Olman Comby, this narrative acts as one episode in a series that describes the tricks Rabbit plays against Fox (Swanton 1928b:5 and 1929a:30 [also published by Stewart 1931:17–20]). Compare this structure to "The Panther and the Opossum" and "How the Possum Tricked the Wolves" in this collection. Kenneth Clarke has found numerous versions of this story in West Africa. Clarke has followed Stith Thompson's motif index, identifying this story as K1241: "Trickster rides dupe horseback. Usually by feigning sickness, he induces dupe to carry him and then boasts that dupe always acts as his horse."

Rabbit Gains a Wife—Recorded from Olman Comby by John R. Swanton. 1928b:8 (also published by Stewart 1931:23).

How Rabbit Made the Animals Angry—Recorded from Olman Comby by John R. Swanton. 1928b:9.

Rabbit and the Garden—Recorded from Olman Comby by John R. Swanton. 1928b:10–11 (also published by Stewart 1931:24–26). In Joel Chandler Harris's Uncle Remus books, Uncle Remus is the storyteller—a device Harris uses to give the stories a performance context. The Uncle Remus named in this version told by Olman Comby corresponds to the character of the old man in Harris's collection.

The Cat Tricks the Mouse—English as a Second Language Staff. Published in the *Choctaw Community News* 11(6): 14, August, 21, 1986. Compare to stories such as "The Dog Who Spoke Choctaw," where bilingualism is heralded as a powerful skill. See "Stories in Choctaw" for Choctaw-language version.

Mouse, Rooster, and Cat—Published in *Choctaw Community News*, Choctaw Fair Edition, 17(5): July 6, 1987, 10. See "Stories in Choctaw" for Choctaw-language version.

NOTES

PREFACE TO THE SECOND EDITION

1. For scholarly works, see for example Akers 2013 and Haag 2016. Fiction author Mary Anna Evans also used stories directly from the book for her novel *Effigies* (2006).

INTRODUCTION

1. The designation of Cameron Wesley as a chief requires some explanation. His son Hubert said that sometime in the 1930s, a group of families were unhappy with the current tribal organization and split off from the tribe, settled around Mashulaville, and elected Cameron Wesley as their leader or "little chief" and his wife as "queen" (interview with Hubert Wesley December 18, 1992). In a follow-up interview on May 22, 1993, Hubert explained that *little chief* would have been *mingo osi* in the Choctaw language, but he could not remember what term they used for "queen." The chief was in charge of the men; the queen in charge of the women. His stepmother, Eunice Wallace, was queen until she stepped down and Sarah Cotton became the last queen. There have been no big or little chiefs or queens since the current Choctaw Constitution was ratified in 1945. Cameron Wesley, Eunice Wallace, and Sarah Cotton are all buried in the graveyard at the spot of the signing of the Treaty of Dancing Rabbit Creek. For a discussion of the tribal political system in the 1930s, see Osburn 2017.

2. The quote from Du Pratz can be found on pages 216–17 (1758). Friedrich Max Müller and the solar mythologists, who have since been generally discounted, argued that myth often works according to just such metaphors and that, through a breakdown in language, the metaphor is adopted as a myth rather than its original inspiration. For Müller, that original inspiration was nature; here it appears to be historical event.

3. There is great debate about the interpretation of myth, which these stories of origin must be considered. Claude Lévi-Strauss argued that even with the prosody, artistry, rhythm, and flow disrupted, even in the worst translations, the meaning of the myth remains intact (1973:210). Scholars in the field of ethnopoetics such as Dell Hymes (1981) and Dennis Tedlock (1983) argue that much of the meaning of a myth depends upon careful translation,

attention to breath pauses, and introductory phrases. Ethnographic analyses that position myth within their broader social, historical, ritualistic, and interpersonal performance contexts continue to offer inductive approaches that are more emic than etic, focusing on myth as a culturally constructed form more than a universal genre, although general theories of the relationship between myth and religion, science, and daily life continue to be developed (see for example Schrempp and Hansen 2002 and Thompson and Schrempp 2020).

4. George Catlin's quote can be found in his book *Letters and Notes on the Manners, Customs, and Condition of the North American Indians*, vol. 2 (1975:1).

5. The quote from Charles Lanman about his alterations of the text can be found on page 187 of his book *Records of a Tourist* (1850). The collection of *Zuni Folk Tales* by Frank Cushing (1931 [1901]) is perhaps the best-known example of an author attempting to translate the poetic aesthetic of one culture into that of another via transitory styles jarringly out of date to today's reader. When Lanman published the bulk of these legends in 1850 and again in 1856, he only attributed two of the five Choctaw stories: one to Pitchlynn, the other to J. L. McDonald, who recorded the legend in a letter to Pitchlynn, who then passed it on to Lanman. When he republished the legends in 1870 in an article about Peter Pitchlynn, Lanman dropped McDonald's story, added one titled "The Hunter of the Sun," and credited them all to Pitchlynn.

6. H. B. Cushman declares his sentimental connection to the Choctaw frequently throughout his book *History of the Choctaw, Chickasaw and Natchez Indians*. The two quotes here can be found on pages 214 and 215, respectively.

7. Henry Halbert made his derogatory claim about the Choctaws living in Bogue Chitto in his biannual report as state superintendent (1895b:536). Halbert published the migration legend told by Jack Henry in his article "Nanih Waiya, the Sacred Mound of the Choctaw" (1899:228). The corn-finding myth attributed to Ilaishtubbee can also be found in this article (1899:230–31). Henry Halbert's manuscript is a compilation of his own observations coupled with those of recent scholars and observers. Although Halbert criticizes the origin myth Alfred Wright collects, he nonetheless pulls extensive material about sun worship from him in his manuscript. Halbert provided J. F. H. Claiborne with a substantial amount of information regarding the Choctaw for his book *Mississippi, as a Province, Territory, and State* and in turn uses much of Claiborne's in his own, though much of this must be inferred from paraphrasing since Halbert only rarely cited his sources. In his article "Story of the Treaty of Dancing Rabbit," Halbert identifies three of his main informants, all members of the Neshoba County community rather than Choctaw, and all presumably White (1902a:373).

8. Jesse O. McKee and Jon A. Schlenker argue this chronology in their book *The Choctaws: Cultural Evolution of a Native American Tribe* (1980:132).

9. Alfred Wright 1828:178–79.

10. Horatio Cushman 1899:148. Adam Hodgson was apparently the first to note this formal instruction as told to him by a Choctaw man in 1820 (1823:278–79). John Swanton raises some questions of the authenticity of this Indian's statement, arguing that other documents show that very few of the Choctaw at that time were able to swim (1931:125). Many of the descriptions that follow Hodgson's seem derivative. Wright reports it like hearsay, and both Wright and Hodgson were missionaries. Henry Halbert paraphrases Wright as he does often in his manuscript. Cushman suggests formal instruction but with young adults during council meetings rather than younger children (147–48). In other places in his book, Cushman has borrowed liberally without citation, but his description here is unique in its detail.

11. The text read by the Choctaw Indian Princess each year was originally written by Nell Rogers as a play to be performed at the 1973 Choctaw Indian Fair. In between narration, characters acted out various scenes of the community's history.

THE STORYTELLERS

1. The majority of the photos were taken by Tom Mould at the time of each interview. The photos of Billy Amos, Grady John, Rosalee Steve, and Estelline Tubby were taken by Allyson Whyte in 1997. The photos of Gus Comby, John Hunter Thompson, and Gladys Willis were taken by Sue Weill in 1984. The rest are credited in alphabetical order (a question mark indicates the exact date or photographer is unknown with credit being attributed to the fieldworker): Ahojeobe (Emil John): photo by David Bushnell Jr.?, 1909; Wagoner Amos: photo by Jimmy Moore, n.d.); Olman Comby: photo by Frances Densmore?, 1933; Israel Folsom: photo by Antonio Zeno Shindler, 1868; Peter Folsom: photo by Antonio Zeno Shindler, 1869; Heleema (Louise Celestine): photo by David Bushnell Jr.?, n.d. (likely 1909); Inez Henry: photo by Julie Kelsey, 1990? (courtesy of Pam Smith); Pisatuntema (Emma): photo by David Bushnell Jr.?, 1909; Peter P. Pitchlynn: photo by Antonio Zeno Shindler, 1868.; Harry Polk: photo by Roseanna Nickey, 1997; Simpson Tubby: photographer unknown, n.d.; Hulon Willis: photo by Rae Nell Vaughn; Baxter York, Tribal Archives. Special thanks to the Smithsonian Institute for permitting the publication of the photos of Ahojeobe, Olman Comby, Israel Folsom, Peter Folsom, Heleema, Pisatuntema, and Peter P. Pitchlynn, and to the Department of Chahta Immi for the use of photos of Wagoner Amos, Odie Mae Anderson, Nellie Billy, Gus Comby, Esbie Gibson, Harry Polk, John Hunter Thompson, Gladys Willis, and Baxter York.

2. For mention of Peter Folsom, see Kidwell 1986:83 and Roberts 1986:95.

3. Henry Halbert records this note and narrative twice, first in 1894 on pages 215–16 and again in 1899 on page 228. The story is reprinted here titled "The Migration Legend."

4. Halbert records this note and narrative in 1899 on page 231.

THE GENRES OF CHOCTAW STORYTELLING

1. Brief portions of this section have been printed previously in *Choctaw Prophecy: A Legacy of the Future*, published by the University of Alabama Press (Mould 2003).

2. This dual nature of *shokhannǫpa* is mentioned by many in the community. See in particular interviews with Doyle Tubby (1997) and Katie Mae Johnson (1997), copies of which I have deposited in the Tribal Archives.

3. The creation of new animal tales has been particularly common within the Tribal Language Program. In addition to the examples here, the Bilingual Education for Choctaws of Mississippi (BECOM) program that operated in the 1980s created a number of booklets in the Choctaw language of stories drawn from previously published sources, both non-Choctaw and non-Indian, but also included some created by staff members, such as the "How the Possum Tricked the Wolves," in this collection. For other recently created stories in this collection, see "The Cat Tricks the Mouse" and "Mouse, Rooster, and Cat."

4. This definition comes from Gerald Thomas's entry on tall tales in *American Folklore: An Encyclopedia* (1996:700).

5. Harold Comby shared this observation during an interview on June 1, 2021.

6. This comment was recorded by Barre Toelken during his extensive fieldwork with the Yellowman family (1981:80).

7. Personal correspondences July 3 and 7, 2023. Jason said that Jesse Ben originally created the term in the early 2000s, work Jesse often undertook for the language program, though typically for new inventions rather than long-standing ones: "I make words, but then I say, well, somebody has to do it, we don't have [words for] anything technical or anything like microchips, spaceship [or computer]" (interview April 8, 2009, in Gantt 2013:125).

8. While scholars have developed useful definitions for the concept of tradition (see particularly Handler and Linnekin 1984), the vernacular use employed in speech by most, including the Choctaw, is one of a tangible passing down of the knowledge and customs of the past. There is not only a sense of long ago but also a sense of ethnic identity involved in the term.

9. Louise Wilson for example remembers that her grandfather, John Hunter Thompson, always distinguished between the stories that had been passed down and those he made up himself (2000).

10. Kashikanchak, *bohpoli*, and *na losa chito* are all supernatural beings and are defined and discussed in the chapter "Supernatural Legends and Encounters."

11. The division between legendary and contemporary tales is clearly apparent in the corpus of supernatural stories told throughout the community, but the issue is a bit more complicated. From my initial analysis of these tales, there appears to be an important distinction between whether the supernatural beings are still regularly encountered today. Kashikanchak is not, and there are legends concerning this being, passed-down stories from the past. But for *na losa chito* and *bohpoli*, contemporary encounters are still quite frequent today. Virtually every adult either has had such an encounter or has a close family member or friend who has. In some ways, communal and passed-down legends simply do not seem necessary since more vibrant contemporary encounters abound.

12. The spelling and orthography for modern Choctaw has changed since the first edition of this book, published in 2004, At that time, *tuk* rather than *tok* was used for the recent past, and *tok* rather than *ttók* was used for the distant past. While we have revised this section accordingly, we have not retranslated the stories in this book since spelling and orthographies change over time, and these were correct when they were initially shared and translated. Thanks to Tribal Language Program specialists Jesse Ben for helping me understand the initial usage of *tuk* and *tok* and Jason Lewis for helping me understand the new dictionary that now uses *tok* and *ttók* today.

13. John McDowell has usefully employed this approach of attending to the sequence of the performance to understand cognitive systems in riddling (1976) and Henry Glassie to understand how history often operates typologically rather than chronologically (1999:17).

14. This category of story was brought vividly to my attention when I showed a copy of my master's thesis "Choctaw Folk Tales" to Meriva Williamson, who had helped me collect many of the narratives from the Conehatta community. After glancing through it, she asked where Lillie Gibson's stories about the fair were. Lillie Gibson had talked generally about the fair and what they used to do there, but did not include any specific, bounded narratives, so I had overlooked them. This omission has been rectified with the publication of *Choctaw Traditions*, which takes as its focus the stories people tell about participating in their various cultural traditions, including clearly bounded narratives, generalized experience narratives, and used-to stories.

15. Used-to stories appear to be common throughout the world, though their classification and peculiar forms and functions vary. Only preliminary remarks can be made here. See *Choctaw Traditions* for an extended discussion and inclusion of these types of stories.

16. Melford Farve told these stories on July 14, 1997.

17. The performances of supernatural encounters by Harold Comby (1997), Melford Farve (1996), Berdie John (1996), and Rae Nell Vaughn (1996) are particularly noteworthy in this respect.

18. It should be noted that there were two orthographies in use during the initial publication of this book and a newer modern orthography that has been developed since. The second and third orthographies attempt to more accurately reflect pronunciation with diacritics and in some cases, new characters. However, many of the older tales in this book, particularly those recorded by Henry Halbert, used the old orthography. All three are still in use today. For example, one may see the community of "Bogue Chitto," "Bok Čito," or "Bók Chito." It seemed reasonable, therefore, to adhere to whichever orthography was used by the translator. In Halbert's case, it is the old; in Maggie Chitto and Pam Smith's translations in the 1990s, the second; and in Pam Smith's translations in the 2020s, the third.

CREATION STORIES AND MYTHS

1. The origin myths of the Choctaw focus on explaining the creation of man and of tribal divisions and rarely that of the world. Alfred Wright records,

> The Choctaws state that, at a remote period, the earth was a vast plain, destitute of hills, and a mere quagmire. The word, which they use to express this primitive state, is applied to clotted blood, jelly, etc., which will serve to explain what their ideas were. The earth in this chaotic state, some of them suppose, was produced by the immediate power of the Creator; but others, indeed the majority with whom I have conversed relative to this subject, have no knowledge how the earth was produced in this state; nor do they appear ever to have extended their thoughts so far as to make a single inquiry with respect to it. (1828:181)

In no version of the origin myths extant today is there any reference to this creation, and except for Wright's notation here, virtually no reference to the land before the Choctaw inhabited it. There are local legends as to the creation of a certain river or mound (see "Big Pond" in this collection, for example), but not of the world as a whole.

2. Of course, this has not kept outside scholars from attempting to explain the occurrence of the two narratives historically. The first explanation was provided by the first person to record the myth in writing, Antoine-Simon Le Page du Pratz: "According to the tradition of the natives this nation passed so rapidly from one land to another and arrived so suddenly in the country which it occupies that, when I asked them from whence the Chatkas came, to express the suddenness of their appearance they replied that they had come out from under the earth" (1758:216–17). In this brief summary, Du Pratz records evidence of both myths, suggesting a metaphoric connection between the two. It is possible that Du Pratz has recorded not the Choctaws' explanation of their origin but rather his own

rationalization, stemming from an inability to fathom creation out of a mound. However, if he is reflecting the Choctaws' view, then from this metaphor evolved a complete narrative in which not only the Choctaw but the other tribes of the Southeast emerged out of the mound known as Nanih Waiya, eventually resulting in an entirely separate creation myth. An interpreter known to missionary Alfred Wright suggested a similar interpretation but attributed the development of an emergence myth as a guilt reaction for the violent takeover by the Choctaw of the eastern lands. Gideon Lincecum records a lengthy version of the origin of the Choctaw in which the storyteller adamantly declares that the Choctaws lived at Nanih Waiya but did not come from out of it, saying, "Ever since the white people came amongst us they [the Choctaw] . . . have lost the truth" (1861:13). However, Patricia Galloway makes a convincing argument that Lincecum's history is primarily a fabrication, pointing to inconsistencies in his narrative and the fact that all of the information was available to him through other published sources (1995:332–33).

Galloway provides an explanation of her own for the two narratives, tracing them to two different communities: one the group of Choctaw that migrated from the West, the other from scattered people living in the East who eventually became incorporated into the Choctaw upon their arrival (1995). Here, the two stories developed independently. Adherence to one or the other would depend primarily on familial ethnic history.

Recognizing the occurrence of similar emergence myths in the Southeast is important. If other eastern groups were using emergence from the land as validation of land rights, then for the Choctaw to adopt similar means for the right to live and hunt and plant alongside the Mississippi River seems perfectly natural. If this is the case, then it is particularly interesting to note how the Choctaw use the myth during removal in the 1830s. Once again, land rights were challenged. The Choctaw who wanted to stay in Mississippi argued, according to J. F. H. Claiborne, that they would not leave this land as long as Nanih Waiya remained. In one version of the migration legend recorded at the time by Claiborne, the Choctaws are told by an emissary of the Great Spirit: "I give you these hunting grounds as your homes. When you leave them you die" (1964 [1880]:483–84). The tie to the land as authenticated by the emergence myth was far stronger in accounts of emergence than migration, which could actually work against them by suggesting their rightful home was to the west and not their present location.

3. In fact, Harold Comby made the same analogy in 2021:

Sometimes in the native world, there is no why. There is no answer. Sometimes it's just because it's been passed on from generation to generation. It's because of the things like legends. Legends are stories that may be true, may be not. And sometimes when we tell our legends, non-Indian thinks that it's crazy. Like Nanih Waiya. "How could people come out of the ground?" But one time they asked me that, and then I told them, "Well, how can God take ribs off the man and make a woman? Isn't that the same thing?"

4. There are two mounds called Nanih Waiya: the state park mound and the cave mound. The state park mound is of obvious human construction consistent with the mounds of the Middle Woodland Period (AD 0–300). The cave mound, which lies about a mile away and has also been incorporated as a park, is held to be the sacred mound described in the myths. The entrances to the caves in the mound have been closed since the 1960s, but those who have

SUPERNATURAL LEGENDS AND ENCOUNTERS

1. As early as 1909, David I. Bushnell Jr. recorded people saying that doctors have always been few since the process of becoming a doctor is one that few complete (see "*Kowi Anukasha*" among others in this collection that address this process).

2. In cultures where the belief in the supernatural is more heavily contested, these personal experience narratives of the supernatural (often called memorates) usually accompany a more general legend. In these cases, the primary function of the narrative is to validate the legend. However, in the narratives told among the Choctaw, the memorates themselves are the legend; there is no core story. This can be seen in the context of the performance of the narratives. With no core legend to precede the story, the memorate is told first. It is usually followed by the explanation or naming (often done by an elder or a Choctaw doctor) that identifies the supernatural being encountered. Such identification acts to validate the encounter, rather than vice versa. However, in cases where the narrator is speaking with someone outside the community, or with small children who do not yet know about the supernatural beings, the narrative may work to validate the belief.

3. Both Henry Halbert and John Swanton provide descriptions of these supernatural beings in summary rather than legend narratives. David Bushnell Jr. does the same but footnotes these summaries with encounters told by the storyteller. It would appear that there is no one legend that could have been recorded since such stories were always told as personal experience narratives. Halbert, Swanton, and Bushnell seem to have extrapolated from such narratives to provide a summary of the creatures. Therefore, it seems that while stories were told, it was and is the core belief and general understanding of the supernatural that is adopted and reincorporated by new storytellers. Such is the case today, where the stories exist in a multitude of personal narratives rather than one tale describing one encounter. These stories stand in contrast to the hunting stories that also involve the supernatural but are told as legends—nonpersonal, single events. Hoklonte'she, Kashikanchak, and skeleton ghosts are not encountered today. Perhaps such encounters were common in the past but from lack of sighting have been reduced to single instances. Such a process has been suggested by scholars who view the memorate—personal experience narratives of the supernatural—as pre-legends. If the supernatural continue to disappear as many of these storytellers suggest, there may come a point where these voluminous personal experience narratives, too, are reduced to a few, communally held legends.

PROPHECY

1. I am paraphrasing Henry Glassie, who has written eloquently on the topic of history and its practical functions for people (1999:6).

2. For a discussion of the generic parallels between prophetic narratives and riddles, with particular attention to Choctaw prophecy, see Mould 2002.

3. For a more complete study of prophetic narratives of the Choctaw, see Mould 2003.

ANIMAL STORIES

1. The question of the origin of Uncle Remus tales is not restricted to debate between African Americans and American Indians but has been carried throughout North America and Africa to Europe, South America, and even India (Baer 1980:9; Harris 1955:xxii). Alan Dundes succinctly narrows the possibilities for the origin of African American tales: either "(1) The tale came from Africa. (2) The tale came from Europe. (3) The tale came from American Indian tradition. (4) The tale arose in the New World as a result of the Afro-American experience there" (1976:183). There is, of course, a fifth: that the tales arose in the New World as a result of the Anglo-American experience there, such as seems to be the case with many of the tall tales popular throughout the United States. Further, stories can emerge at the intersections of contact among these groups, as stories bleed and blur in the processes of cultural sharing, offering a joint origin shared among multiple groups.

A parallel question is who influenced whom here in the Americas? Did stories flow from Native Americans to African Americans (and Anglo-Americans), or vice versa? J. W. Powell, head of the Bureau of American Ethnology at the turn of the century, believed the African American tales were "borrowings" from the North American Indians (Baer 1980). Joel Chandler Harris not surprisingly points to Africa (Harris 1955:xxv). All of those who have collected such tales or attempted their analysis, Powell and Harris included, agree that the answer is a complex one. However, there have been advances made toward answering this question. Tale-type and motif indices already exist for much of Europe and North America (excluding American Indian cultures, regrettably), and similar indices of African folklore are slowly being amassed. Finding (or not finding) analogs in other countries or continents can help form hypotheses of the origins of some of these stories.

At some level, however, the question of origins would seem to be moot. There is no doubt that these groups interacted; outside of contact as neighbors, some Choctaws owned slaves. Borrowing of stories would likely have happened from both ends, in both directions. Each group would then tailor the tales to their views, lives, and worldview, creating tales that belong specifically to their own culture. In a few cases, the direction of borrowing seems obvious, as in Simpson Tubby's story where he refers to Uncle Remus by name, or in Gus Comby's story in which he includes the nonindigenous monkey as a main character. Yet while analogs can be found, most of the stories indicate only that they are Choctaw stories now, regardless of origin. The stories of rabbit outwitting fox that has analogs with Uncle Remus tales, therefore, belong in collections of the Choctaw as well as the African American.

SOURCES CITED

Aarne, Antti, and Stith Thompson. 1961. *The Types of the Folktale: A Classification and Bibliography*. FF Communications no. 3. Helsinki: Academia Scientiarum Fennica.

Adair, James. 1965 [1775]. *The History of the American Indians*. New York: Johnson Reprint Corporation.

Bacon, Willard Keith. 1973. "Legends of Nanih Waiya." *Nanih Waiya* 1 (1):2–3.

Baer, Florence E. 1980. *Sources and Analogues of the Uncle Remus Tales*. FF Communications no. 228. Helsinki: Academia Scientiarum Fennica.

Baird, David W. 1972. *Peter Pitchlynn: Chief of the Choctaws*. Norman: University of Oklahoma Press.

Bartram, William. 1791. *Travels through North and South Carolina, Georgia, East and West Florida*. Philadelphia: James and Johnson.

Baughman, Ernest W. 1966. *Type and Motif-Index of the Folktales of England and North America*. The Hague, Netherlands: Mouton.

Blanchard, Kendall. 1981. *The Mississippi Choctaws at Play: The Serious Side of Leisure*. Urbana: University of Illinois Press.

Bushnell, David I., Jr. 1909. *The Choctaw of Bayou Lacomb, St. Tammany Parish, Louisiana*. Bulletin 48, Bureau of American Ethnology. Washington, DC: Smithsonian Institution.

Bushnell, David I., Jr. 1910. "Myths of the Louisiana Choctaw." *American Anthropologist* 12:526 35.

Byington, Cyrus. 1915. *A Dictionary of the Choctaw Language*, edited by John R. Swanton and Henry S. Halbert. Bulletin 46, Bureau of American Ethnology. Washington, DC: Smithsonian Institution.

"The Cat Tricks the Mouse." 1986. *Choctaw Community News* 11 (6):14, August 21.

Catlin, George. 1965 [1841]. *Letters and Notes on the Manners, Customs, and Condition of the North American Indians*. Vol. 2. Minneapolis: Ross & Haines.

Chickaway, John Lee, and Baron Gardner. 1975. "Pete Davis Dyer," in *Nanih Waiya*, November 4.

Claiborne, J. F. H. 1964 [1880]. *Mississippi as a Province, Territory and State*. Baton Rouge: Louisiana State University Press.

Clark, Kenneth W. 1958. "A Motif-Index of the Folktales of Culture Area V, West Africa." PhD dissertation. Indiana University.

Conklin, Paul. 1975. *Choctaw Boy*. New York: Dodd, Mead.

Copeland, C. C. 1953. "A Choctaw Tradition." *Transactions of the American Ethnological Society* 3:169–71.

Cushing, Frank. 1931 [1901]. *Zuni Folk Tales*. New York: Alfred A. Knopf.
Cushman, Horatio B. 1962 [1899]. *History of the Choctaw, Chickasaw, and Natchez Indians*. Oklahoma: Redlands Press of Stillwater.
D'Antoni, Blaise C. 1986. *Chahta-Ima and St. Tammany's Parish*. St. Tammany, LA: St. Tammany Historical Society.
du Pratz, Antoine S. Le Page. 1975 [1774]. *The History of Louisiana*, edited by Joseph G. Tregle Jr. Baton Rouge: Louisiana State University Press.
Dundes, Alan. 1976. "African and Afro-American Tales." *Research in African Literatures* 7:181–99.
Galloway, Patricia. 1995. *Choctaw Genesis: 1500–1700*. Lincoln: University of Nebraska Press.
Gregory, Jack, and Rennard Strickland. 1972. *Choctaw Spirit Tales: Tribal Folklore, Legend and Myth*. Muskogee, OK: Indian Heritage Association.
Haag, Marcia. 2016. *A Listening Wind: Native Literature from the Southeast*. Lincoln: University of Nebraska Press.
Halbert, Henry S. 1894. "A Choctaw Migration Legend." *American Antiquarian and Oriental Journal* 16:215–16.
Halbert, Henry S. 1895a. "The Choctaw Robin Goodfellow." *American Antiquarian and Oriental Journal* 17:157.
Halbert, Henry S. 1895b. "The Indians in Mississippi and Their Schools." In *Biennial Report of the State Superintendent of Public Education to the Legislature of Mississippi, for Scholastic Years 1893–94 and 1894–95*, pp. 534–45. Jackson, MS: Clarion-Ledger Printing Establishment.
Halbert, Henry S. 1899. "Nanih Waiya, the Sacred Mound of the Choctaw." *Publications of the Mississippi Historical Society*, pp. 223–34.
Halbert, Henry S. 1900(?). "Choctaw Folklore." In *History of the Choctaw Indians East of the Mississippi River*. Housed in the Alabama Dept. of Archives and History, Montgomery.
Halbert, Henry S. 1901. "The Choctaw Creation Legend." *Publications of the Mississippi Historical Society* 4:267–70.
Halbert, Henry S. 1902a "Bernard Romans' Maps of 1772." *Publications of the Mississippi Historical Society* 6:413–49.
Halbert, Henry S. 1902b. "Story of the Treaty of Dancing Rabbit." *Publications of the Mississippi Historical Society* 6:373–402.
Harrell, Beatrice Orcutt. 1995. *How Thunder and Lightning Came to Be*. Illustrated by Susan L. Roth. New York: Dial Books for Young Readers.
Harris, Joel Chandler. 1955. *The Complete Tales of Uncle Remus*. Boston: Houghton Mifflin.
Henry, James. 1992. "My Grandfather." In *Rising Voices: Writings of Young Native Americans*, edited by Arlene B. Hirschfelder and Beverly R. Singer, p. 36. New York: Charles Scribner's Sons.
Hickman, Norma. 1996. Unpublished stories shown to author.
Hirschfelder, Arlene B., and Beverly R. Singer, eds. 1992. *Rising Voices: Writings of Young Native Americans*. New York: Charles Scribner's Sons.
Hodgson, Adam. 1823. *Remarks during a Journey through North America*. New York: J. Seymour.
Holy Bible. 1972. New York: Thomas Nelson.
Howard, James H., and Victoria Lindsay Levine. 1990. *Choctaw Music and Dance*. Norman: University of Oklahoma Press.

Hymes, Dell. 1981. *"In Vain I Tried to Tell You": Essays in Native American Ethnpoetics.* Philadelphia: University of Pennsylvania Press.

Jimmie, Randy, and Leonard Jimmie. 1974. "Choctaw Tales and Legends." *Nanih Waiya* 1(3):6–11.

Ketcher, Roy. 1985. "Choctaw Perceptions: Legends and Superstitions." In *A Choctaw Anthology III*, edited by John Anderson and Nina C. Zachery, pp. 96–112. Philadelphia, MS: Choctaw Heritage Press.

Kidwell, Clara Sue. 1986. "Choctaw Land and Identity, 1830–1919." In *After Removal: The Choctaws in Mississippi*, edited by Samuel J. Wells and Roseanna Tubby, pp. 64–93. Jackson: University Press of Mississippi.

Lanman, Charles. 1850. *Hawhonoo or Records of a Tourist.* Philadelphia, PA: Lippincott, Grambo.

Lanman, Charles. 1856. *Adventures in the Wilds of the United States and British American Provinces.* Vol. 2. Philadelphia, PA: John W. Moore.

Lanman, Charles. 1870. "Peter Pitchlynn, Chief of the Choctaws." *Atlantic Monthly*, pp. 486–97. [The article is not attributed, but parts of the article were previously published with Lanman's name.]

Lanman, Charles. 1906. "Indian Legends: The Origin of the Choctaws." *Magazine of History* 3(1):40–41.

Lévi-Strauss, Claude. 1963. "The Structural Study of Myth." In *Structural Anthropology*, vol. 1, pp. 206–31. New York: Basic Books.

Lincecum, Gideon. 1861. "Traditional History of the Chahta Nation." Unpublished manuscript housed in the University of Texas Library, Austin.

McKee, Jesse O., and Jon A. Schlenker. 1980. *The Choctaws: Cultural Evolution of a Native American Tribe.* Jackson: University Press of Mississippi.

Mould, Tom. 2002. "Prophetic Riddling: A Dialogue of Genres in Choctaw Performance." *Journal of American Folklore* 115(457/458):395–421.

Mould, Tom. 2003. *Choctaw Prophecy: A Legacy of the Future.* Tuscaloosa: University of Alabama Press.

"Mouse, Rooster, and Cat." 1987. *Choctaw Community News*, Choctaw Fair Edition, 17(5):10, July 6.

Nanih Waiya. 1974. "Viola Johnson Remembers." 1(2):15.

Nanih Waiya. 1975. "A Story by Wagner [Wagoner] Amos." 2(4):53.

Nanih Waiya, 1975. "Waggoner [Wagoner] Amos Tells Us a Story." 3(1):21–24.

Osburn, Katherine M. B. 2017. "Mississippi Choctaw Indian Federation." In *Mississippi Encyclopedia*, Center for Study of Southern Culture. Accessed on August 25, 2023. https://mississippiencyclopedia.org/entries/mississippi-choctaw-indian-federation/.

Peterson, John Holbrook, Jr. 1971. "The Mississippi Band of Choctaw Indians: Their Recent History and Current Social Relations." PhD dissertation. University of Georgia.

Roberts, Charles. 1986. "The Second Choctaw Removal, 1903." In *After Removal: The Choctaws in Mississippi*, ed. Samuel J. Wells and Roseanna Tubby, pp. 94–111. Jackson: University Press of Mississippi.

Romans, Bernard. 1962 [1775]. *A Concise Natural History of East and West Florida.* Vol. 1. Gainsville: University of Florida Press.

Schrempp, Gregory and William Hansen, eds. 2002. *Myth: A New Symposium.* Bloomington: Indiana University Press.

Spratt, R. D. 1938. "Choctaw Names of Places, Watercourses, etc. in the old Choctaw Country." Smithsonian Institution, National Anthropological Archives, Bureau of American Ethnology Manuscript Collection, 4129. John R. Swanton Collection. Washington, DC.

Stewart, Mary Ada. 1931. "Legends of Mississippi Indians in Prose and Poetry." Master's thesis. George Peabody College for Teachers, Nashville, Tennessee.

Swanton, John R. 1928a. "Sun Worship in the Southeast." *American Anthropologist* 30:206–13.

Swanton, John R. 1928b. "Choctaw Stories from Olman Comby, in English." Smithsonian Institution, National Anthropological Archives, Bureau of American Ethnology Manuscript Collection, 4132-b. Washington, DC.

Swanton, John R. 1929a. "Choctaw Myths from Simpson Tubby." Smithsonian Institution, National Anthropological Archives, Bureau of American Ethnology Manuscript Collection, 4128. Washington, DC.

Swanton, John R. 1929b. "Studies among the Choctaw of Mississippi and the Creeks of Oklahoma." In *Explorations and Field-Work of the Smithsonian Institution in 1929*. Washington, DC: Smithsonian Institution.

Swanton, John R. 1931. *Source Material for the Social and Ceremonial Life of the Choctaw Indians*. Bulletin 103. Bureau of American Ethnology. Washington, DC: Smithsonian Institution.

Tedlock, Dennis. 1983. *The Spoken Word and the Work of Interpretation*. Philadelphia: University of Pennsylvania Press.

Thomas, Gerald. 1996. "Tall Tale." In *American Folklore: An Encyclopedia*, edited by Jan Harold Brunvand, pp. 700–702. New York: Garland.

Thomas, Hazel. n.d. "Shokkata yat Nashóba alhíha haksicihh tók (How the Opposum Tricked the Wolves)." Department of Chahta Immi. Accessed July 25, 2023. https://choctawculturallegacy.com/wp-content/uploads/2020/03/SA-SB-Shokkata-yat-Nashoba-Alhiha-Haksichi-tok-How-the-Possum-Tricked-the-Wolves.pdf.

Thompson, Cynthia. 1979–80. "John Hunter Thompson on Things" [interview with John Hunter Thompson]. *Nanih Waiya* 7(1–2):25–31.

Thompson, Tok, and Gregory Schrempp. 2020. *The Truth of Myth: World Mythology in Theory and Everyday Life*. New York: Oxford University Press.

Tubby, Vernon. 1976. "Estelline Remembers." *Nanih Waiya* 4(1):114–18.

Tuggle, William Orrie. 1973. *Shem, Ham & Japeth: The Papers of W. O. Tuggle*. Edited by Eugene Current-Garcia with Dorothy B. Hatfield. Athens: University of Georgia Press.

Wallace, John G. 1977. ". . . A Dollar a Day" [interview with Annie Tubby]. *Nanih Waiya* 4(3):19–24.

Weill, Susan, Julia Williams, and Bob Ferguson. 1985. *Stories from the Red Clay Hills: Various Stories by Choctaw Elders*. Choctaw Video Production.

Whitman, Walt. 1875. "Chahta Wit and Humor." *New Orleans Bulletin*, August 6.

Willis, Hulon, Bradley Alex, Jimmy Ben, Rick Billy, and Johnny Osceola. 1975. "Baxter York Again." *Nanih Waiya* 2(1–2):11–18.

Wright, Alfred. 1828. "Choctaws: Religious Opinions, Traditions, &c." *Missionary Herald* 24:178–216.

INTERVIEWS

Alex, Bradley. Interviewed by Makaylin Alex and Tom Mould with Taylor Ben on June 30, 2021.

Alex, Lorena. Interviewed by Tom Mould, Taylor Ben, Lakylee Martin, and Jaeden Wesley on June 10, 2021.

Allen, Sally [with Judy Billie and Regina Shoemake]. Interviewed by Tom Mould and Curtis Willis on June 3, 1997.

Allen, Sally [with Regina Shoemake]. Interviewed by Tom Mould on January 10, 2000.

Amos, Billy. Interviewed by Tom Mould on June 19, 1997, and August 1, 1999.

Amos, Wagoner. Interviewed by staff of *Nanih Waiya* in 1975. Published in *Nanih Waiya* 2(4):53 and 3(1):21–24.

Anderson, Odie [with Jeffie Solomon]. Interviewed by Tom Mould, Glenda Williamson, Meriva Williamson on August 12, 1997.

Bell, Amanda. Interview with Tom Mould, Makaylin Alex, Taylor Ben, Lexi Flint and Lakylee Martin on July 1, 2021.

Bell, Howard. Interviewed by Tom Mould, Taylor Ben, and Lakylee Martin on June 30, 2021.

Bell, Howard. Interviewed by Tom Mould on June 6, 2023.

Ben, Terry. Interviewed by Roy Ketcher in November 1984.

Ben, Terry. Interviewed by Tom Mould and Rae Nell Vaughn on May 30, 1996.

Ben, Terry. Interviewed by Tom Mould on June 3, 1996.

Ben, Terry. Interviewed by Tom Mould with Lakylee Martin, Meka Willis, Taylor Ben, and Thomas Saunders on June 10, 2021.

Bigpond, Casey. Interviewed by Tom Mould with Thomas Saunders on June 24, 2021.

Billie, Brian. Interview with Lakylee Martin, Tom Mould, Makaylin Alex, Taylor Ben, Lexi Flint, and Jaeden Wesley on June 30, 2021.

Billie, Judy [with Sally Allen and Regina Shoemake]. Interviewed by Tom Mould and Curtis Willis on June 3, 1997.

Billy, Nellie. Storytelling session at Choctaw Language Immersion Camp recorded by Tom Mould and Liasha Alex on June 30, 1997.

Clegg, Cynthia. Storytelling session at Choctaw Language Immersion Camp recorded by Tom Mould and Liasha Alex on July 27, 1997.

Comby, Gus. Interviewed by Roy Ketcher on November 26, 1984.

Comby, Gus. Interviewed by Gregory Keyes and Ken Carleton on December 16, 1990.

Comby, Harold. Interviewed by Tom Mould and Liasha Alex on June 4, 1997.

Comby, Harold. Interviewed by Tom Mould on July 23, 1999.

Comby, Harold. Interviewed by Tom Mould on July 31, 2000.

Comby, Harold. Interviewed by Tom Mould on January 10, 2000.

Comby, Harold. Interviewed by Tom Mould, Lexi Flint, Jaeden Willis, Taylor Ben, and Eddie Johnson on June 1, 2021.

Comby, Harold. Interviewed by Josh Foreman on February 24, 2022. https://www.youtube.com/watch?v=FvX8NmVeF_E.

Cotton, Donald. Interviewed by Tom Mould on June 27, 2021.

Davis, Evaline. Interviewed by Tom Mould, Makaylin Alex, Taylor, Ben, and Lexi Flint on June 3, 2021.

Denson, Carmen. Interviewed by Tom Mould on January 12, 2000.

Denson, Charlie, and Carmen Denson. Interviewed by Tom Mould on March 12, 1996, and May 25, 1996.
Denson, Theron "Duke." Interviewed by Tom Mould on June 17, 2021.
Farve, Melford. Interviewed by Tom Mould on July 10, 14, 16, and 28, 1997.
Ferguson, Martha. Interview with Tom Mould and Jaeden Wesley on June 14, 2021.
Gibson, Eddie. Interviewed by Jaeden Wesley and Tom Mould with Lakylee Martin, Lexi Flint, and Taylor Ben on July 1, 2021.
Gibson, Esbie. Interviewed by Tom Mould, Glenda Williamson, Meriva Williamson, and Lionel "J. J." Dan on July 25, 1997.
Gibson, Lillie. Interviewed by Tom Mould, Glenda Williamson, and Meriva Williamson on August 5, 1997.
Henry, Frank. Interviewed by Tom Mould on July 23, 1997.
Henry, Inez. Interviewed by Geri Harm on February 20, 1986.
Henry, Inez. Interviewed by Geri Harm on October 28, 1988.
Isaac, Dan. Interviewed by Tom Mould, Makaylin Alex, Taylor Ben, Lexi Flint, and Lakylee Martin on June 23, 2021.
Jimmie, Leonard. Interview with Tom Mould on July 11, 2021.
Jimmie, Mack. Interviewed by Tom Mould on July 13, 2021. Not recorded.
Joe, Bobby. Interviewed by Tom Mould on July 30, 1999
Joe, Bobby. Interviewed by Tom Mould on January 6, 2000.
Joe, Frank Bell. Interviewed by Lonus D. Hucks on April 16, 1975.
John, Grady. Interviewed by Tom Mould on February 22, 1998.
John, Grady. Interviewed by Tom Mould on July 17, 1999.
John, Grady. Interviewed by Tom Mould on January 15, 2000.
Johnson, Eddie. Interviewed by Tom Mould on June 11, 2021.
Johnson, Katie Mae. Interviewed by Tom Mould, Glenda Williamson, and Meriva Williamson on August 12, 1997.
Martin, Lakylee. Interviewed by Eddie Gibson on July 25, 1997.
Miller, Jessica. Interviewed by Tom Mould and Eddie Johnson on April 11, 2024.
Patrick, Mark. Interview with Tom Mould on July 7, 2021.
Polk, Harry. Storytelling session at Choctaw Language Immersion Camp recorded by Tom Mould and Liasha Alex on July 1, 1997.
Polk, Harry. Interviewed by Tom Mould and Curtis Willis on July 8, 1997.
Shoemake, Regina [with Sally Allen and Judy Billie]. Interviewed by Tom Mould and Curtis Willis on June 3, 1997.
Shoemake, Regina [with Sally Allen]. Interviewed by Tom Mould on January 10, 2000.
Smith, Grace. Interviewed by Tom Mould and Glenda Williamson on July 30, 1999.
Smith, Mallie. Interviewed by Tom Mould and Glenda Williamson on July 30, 1999.
Solomon, Jeffie [with Odie Anderson]. Interviewed by Tom Mould, Glenda Williamson, and Meriva Williamson on August 12, 1997.
Solomon, Lela. Interview with Bill Brescia, Marian Isaac, and Carolyn Reeves in February 1982.
Steve, Rosalee. Interviewed by Tom Mould on February 21, 1998.
Thompson, John Hunter. Interviewed by Cynthia Thompson in 1979. Published in *Nanih Waiya* 7(1–2):25–31.
Tubby, Annie. Interviewed by John G. Wallace in 1977. Published in *Nanih Waiya* 4(3):19–24.
Tubby, Doyle. Interviewed by Tom Mould on July 2, 1997.

Tubby, Estelline. Interviewed by Vernon Tubby in 1976. Published in *Nanih Waiya* 4(1):114–18.
Tubby, Estelline. Interviewed by Tom Mould on May 31, 1996; August 5, 1997; July 19, 1999; and July 22, 1999.
Tubby, Nettie. Interview with Bill Brescia in March 1982.
Tubby, Tom. Interviewed by staff of *Nanih Waiya* in 1973. Unpublished interview housed at Neshoba County Library.
Vaughn, Harley. Interviewed by Tom Mould on May 31, 1997.
Vaughn, Rae Nell. Interview with Jack D. Elliott Jr. on May 22, 1993.
Vaughn, Rae Nell. Interviewed by Tom Mould on March 14, 1996.
Vaughn, Rae Nell. Oral history interview on December 14, 1999. Center for Oral History and Cultural Heritage of the University of Southern Mississippi. Audio available online: http://choctawculturallegacy.com/audio-resources/.
Vaughn, Rae Nell. Recorded by Rae Nell Vaughn on April 28, 2024.
Wesley, Hubert [with Gara Wesley]. Interviewed by Jack D. Elliott Jr. and Ken Carleton on December 18, 1992.
Wesley, Hubert. Interviewed by Jack D. Elliott Jr. on May 22, 1993.
Williams, Henderson. Interviewed by Tom Mould on July 25, 1997.
Williams, Henry. Interviewed by Tom Mould on June 24, 1997.
Williams, Linda. Interviewed by Tom Mould on June 15, 2021.
Willis, Gladys. Interviewed by Tom Mould and Rae Nell Vaughn on May 23, 1996.
Willis, Gladys. Interviewed by Tom Mould on August 6, 1997.
Willis, Hulon. Interviewed by Tom Mould on May 27, 1996.
Willis, Linda. Interviewed by Tom Mould on January 7, 2000.
Willis, Louise. Oral history interview with Dr. John K. Mahon, December 4, 1973. Samuel Proctor Oral History Program Collection, P. K. Yonge Library of Florida History, University of Florida
Willis, Travis. Interviewed by Tom Mould on June 14, 2021.
Wilson, Louise. Interviewed by Tom Mould and Danielle Dan on June 10, 1997.
Wilson, Louise. Interviewed by Tom Mould on July 29, 1999, and January 11, 2000.
York, Baxter. Interviewed by staff of *Nanih Waiya* on July 8, 1974.
York, Baxter. Interviewed by Hulon Willis, Bradley Alex, Jimmy Ben, Rick Billy, and Johnny Osceola in 1974. Published in *Nanih Waiya* 2(1–2);11–18.
York, Jake. Interviewed by Tom Mould and Liasha Alex on June 30, 1997.

INDEX

Ahojeobe (Emil John), 16, 24, 30, 51, 58, 136, 157–58
Alex, Bradley, 31, 216
Alex, Liasha, xxvi, 31, 76
Amos, Billy, xxvi, 32, 33, 94, 206–8
Amos, Wagoner, 33, 101–3
Anderson, Odie Mae, 34, 64, 87, 107, 208–9, 269–70
animal tales, 16–17, 80–84, 89, 231–58, 273–75
animals, in tales: alligators, 120–21, 222, 228, 238–39; bats, 232–33; bears, 105, 126–27, 134–35, 149; bees and wasps, 113; cows, 146, 159, 179, 203, 219; deer, 105, 116, 119–21, 126, 127, 129–32, 174, 175, 228, 229, 247; dogs, 112, 129–31, 146, 148, 159–62, 192–93, 226–27, 257; fish, 128, 138, 238–39; frogs, 112, 124–25, 209, 225, 239; horses, 134–35, 146, 163, 179, 181, 204, 221–22, 227, 229, 253; lizards, 244; pigs, 129, 163, 179; rabbits, 119, 122, 160–61, 174–75, 222; snakes, 9, 112–13, 132–34, 138, 146, 153, 216, 225, 227, 249; squirrels, 107–10, 111, 159–60, 229, 232–33, 239; turkeys, 82, 129, 163, 224; turtles (terrapins), 229, 233; wolves, 120. *See also* birds, in tales
animals and birds, as recurring characters: Bear, 5–6, 126–27, 134–35, 226, 236–38, 252, 255; Crane, 232, 235–36; Deer, 239; Hummingbird, 233–34; Monkey, 240; Mouse, 240, 257–58; Panther, 247, 255; Possum (Opossum), 80–81, 245–51, 255–57; Rabbit, 5–6, 9, 237–41, 251–57;

Raccoon (Coon), 80–81, 245–46, 255; Turkey, 241–43, 253; Turtle (Terrapin), 240–45, 255; Wildcat, 126–27, 251; Wolf, 221, 223, 248–49, 253, 255
Ashman, xxi, 72, 218, 222

Bartram, William, 13, 14, 16, 18
Ben, Jesse, xxvii, 95
Ben, Robert, xxvi, 201
Ben, Terry, 10, 23, 24, 35, 90, 92, 110, 137, 147, 152, 159–61, 163, 184–86, 189–91, 194–97
biblical references. *See* Christian influence: in tales; religion
Bigfoot. See *na losa chito*
Billie, Judy, 32, 36, 63, 161–62
Billy, Nellie, 38, 78, 150–51, 269
birds, in tales: buzzards, 115–16, 235; doves, 106, 117, 234; ducks, 111–12, 163; eagles, 126; geese, 111–12; guinea hens, 236; hawks, 105, 229; owls, 113, 126–27, 151, 164, 235. *See also* animals, in tales
Black people. *See* race relations: Choctaw and Black people
Boas, Franz, 18
bohpoli (Little People), 8, 10, 23–24, 86, 92, 97, 124, 151–62
Bushnell, David I., Jr., 16, 18, 22, 30, 51, 59, 110, 114, 120, 124, 126–27, 131
Byington, Cyrus, 16

casino, xviii, 3–4, 148
Catlin, George, 14, 18, 60

Celestine, Louise. *See* Heleema (Louise Celestine)
Chahta, legendary leader, 8, 103–4
Chickaway, Billy, 82
Chikasa, legendary leader, 8, 103–4
children: mythic, 116–18; as orphans, 107, 111; in peril, 124–25, 128–29, 143, 150, 169; as specially chosen, 157, 161, 212–13; as unwitting helpers, 126
Chitto, Maggie, 83, 95
Choctaw Indian Fair, xvii, 11, 25, 32, 68, 204, 208; Neshoba, 189, 199, 219
Choctaw Indian Princess, 25, 27
Choctaw Robin Goodfellow. *See bohpoli* (Little People)
Christian influence, 19, 96, 98, 170–71, 219; of recorders, 15–19, 64; of storytellers, 30, 33, 47, 69; in tales, 98, 100–102, 105–6, 124, 171, 181
clans. *See* social structure
Clegg, Cynthia, 38, 78, 87, 132–34
Comby, Gus, xix, xxi, xxviii, 39, 157, 163, 167, 237, 239–41, 252, 253
Comby, Harold, 40, 54, 84, 86, 107, 146, 169, 185, 190, 195, 205, 212, 217
Comby, Olman, 18, 24, 40–41, 69, 106, 112, 113, 168, 221, 229, 235, 238, 242, 251, 254–57
competitions, 232, 237; fights, 235; races, 233, 240–42
Copeland, C. C., 15, 115
courtship. *See* marriage
creation stories, xx–xxi, 11–16, 22, 85, 90, 96–121. *See also* origin stories
culture, Choctaw: balance with popular American culture, 3, 23–25, 202–3, 206–7; fear of deterioration, 202–5, 208–10; traditional, 205, 208, 214, 222, 224
Cushman, Horatio B., 15–18, 21–22, 46, 60

Dan, Danielle, xxvi, 76
Dan, Lionel, xxvi, 49, 76
Denson, Carmen, 42, 88, 153, 183, 213, 223
Denson, Charlie, xxvi, 42
Denson, Theron "Duke," 43, 148–50, 245

devil, 124–25
Dixon, Jim, 78, 83, 218, 227–29
doctors, Choctaw (medicine people/*hopaii*), 23, 92, 115, 123, 152, 154, 157–65, 239
du Pratz, Antoine Simon Le Page, 14, 16, 18

education, 20–22, 24–25, 88, 204. *See also* storytelling: education through
etiological endings, 110, 116–18, 124, 172, 233–35, 236–39, 242–49, 251

family. *See* social structure
Farve, Melford, xxvi, 13, 24, 44–45, 91–92, 122, 144, 164–66, 169
flood, 19, 58, 98, 105–7
Folsom, Israel, 46, 60, 105
Folsom, Peter, 47, 103
formulas. *See* stories: formulas in

ghost stories, 9, 38, 92, 122–23, 168–69
ghosts, 57, 143, 151, 168–69
Gibson, Eddie, 48, 198, 199
Gibson, Esbie, 49, 82, 139
Gibson, Lillie, 50, 219–20
Green Corn Ceremony, 25

Halbert, Henry S., xxvii, 17–19, 22, 47, 53, 59, 116, 127, 151, 233–35, 236, 239, 241, 244, 247, 252–53
Harm, Geri, xxvi–xxvii, 52, 95
Harm, Harry, xxvi–xxvii, 52, 95
Harris, Joel Chandler, 41, 232
hashok okwa hui'ga, 123, 166
Heleema (Louise Celestine), 16, 24, 30, 51, 58, 137–38
Henry, Inez, xxvii, 52, 180, 238, 244
Henry, Jack, 17
hero quest, 114–15
history: conveyed in tales, 20–23, 85, 90–91, 97, 170–201, 211–14; of the tribe, xv, xx–xxiii, 25–28
Hoentubbee, Charly, 18
Hopahkitubbe, 18
hopaii. *See* doctors, Choctaw

hopáki ikhana, xx, 85–93
humor, xx–xxi, 9–12, 80–85, 218–30. *See also* jokes
hunting: stories told during, 10, 122–23; in tales, 16–17, 91–92, 115–18, 120, 127, 129, 131–32, 134, 136–37, 155–56, 159–61, 172–76, 225–26, 229, 235

Ilaishtubbee, 18, 53, 111
Isaac, William "Dan," xix, 54, 155, 176–77, 199–200

Joe, Bobby, 55, 171, 205
John, Emil. *See* Ahojeobe (Emil John)
John, Grady, 56, 176–77, 204, 246
jokes, xxx, 41–44, 45, 47, 176–91. *See also* humor

Kashehotapalo, 136
Kashikanchak, 86, 91, 124, 127–29
kinship. *See* social structure
kwanokasha (*kowi anukasha*). See *bohpoli* (Little People)

land: changes to landscape, 203–5; destruction of, 215–16; infertility of, 205; loss of, 177–80
language, xx, 15–16, 197; danger of loss, 209–10; preservation, 37–38, 62, 78, 226; structures, 87–88. *See also* translation
Lanman, Charles, 14–16, 18, 60–61
legend. historical, 171–82; supernatural, 122–39, 140–43, 144, 147–48, 151–52, 157–58, 163, 164, 166, 169
lights, mysterious, 92, 144–45, 155–57, 165–67
Little People. See *bohpoli* (Little People)

marriage, 101, 116–19, 203, 205, 224, 229. *See also* social structure
Martin, Phillip, xv–xvi, xviii, 4, 77
McDonald, J. L., 128
medicine. *See* doctors, Choctaw
mermaid. See *okwa nahollo* (*oka nahollo*)
Miller, Jessica, 57, 135, 139–40, 153

missionaries, xxi, 15–18, 47–48, 51–52, 69, 98, 170
Morris, Caroline, xxii, xxviii, xxix, 11–12, 75, 122
murder, 193–94; trial of Cameron Wesley, xxi
myth, 12–14, 18–19, 22, 79, 90, 96–121

na losa chito, xx, 8, 10, 43, 124, 145–51
na losa falaya, 136
Nanih Waiya magazine, xxvii, 31, 52, 72, 73, 77
Nanih Waiya mound, xxi, xxv, 12–13, 33, 47, 57, 96–98, 101–5, 110, 152–53, 174, 177–78, 216. *See also* origin stories
Nickey, Roseanna, xxvi–xxvii, 82–83, 95
nishkin chafa, 8, 10, 63, 143–44

okwa nahollo (*oka nahollo*), 137–39
omens: death, 141–42; good, 104, 158–61
origin stories, 12–14, 19, 90, 96–98; of alcohol to Choctaws, 172; of bayous, 124; of corn, 110–11; emergence story, 13, 96–99, 100–101; migration story, 13–14, 17–18, 26–27, 96–98, 103–4; of races, 12, 101–3; of sewing, 116–17; of tribes, 98–100; of water, 111. *See also* etiological endings
orphans, 107, 111
owls. *See* birds, in tales

Paš Falaya, 141–43, 265–68
Pisatuntema (Emma), 16, 24, 58, 99–100, 111–13, 136, 166, 216, 243
Pistonatubbee, Isaac, 24, 59, 98
Pitchlynn, Peter P., 14–15, 60–61, 100, 118, 129
Polk, Harry, 62, 78, 81, 88, 134
prophecy, 90–91, 94, 202–17
Pushmataha, 8, 170, 175–77

race relations, 12, 101–3, 182–84, 189–90, 203, 205, 218–20, 232; Choctaw and Black people, 12, 164, 181–82, 203–5; Choctaw and other Indian tribes, 98, 100–104, 172; Choctaw and whites, 171–72, 175–81, 185–89, 190–201, 203–4, 206, 221, 228
races. *See* competitions: races

religion, 96, 181, 215, 218, 229. *See also* Christian influence
removal, xxi, 15, 17, 21–22, 30, 51, 52, 57, 67, 77, 90, 170, 177–79; third, xxv, 68, 202, 212–14
Romans, Bernard, 13–16, 18
Roquette, Adrien Emmanual, 16, 51, 58

Saunders, Summer, 25–27
shape-shifter, 92, 148, 164. *See also* doctors, Choctaw
Shoemake, Regina, 36, 63, 86, 144
shokhannǫpa, xx, 41, 75, 80–86, 91, 218–58
Smith, Pam, xxvi–xxvii, 95
snakes. *See* animals, in tales
social structure: addressed in tales, 101, 116–20, 126–27, 132–34, 173–74, 222, 228; of tribe, 6–12, 19–23, 173–74
Solomon, Jeffie, 34, 64–65, 87, 129, 138, 145, 234
sports, 164, 185, 232. *See also* competition, races; stickball
St. Tammany Parish, Louisiana, 16
Steve, Rosalee, 66, 125
stickball, 11, 17, 24–25, 40, 54, 67, 80, 140, 181, 208, 224
stories: attribution of, 86–89; creation of, 80–82; editing of, 14–20, 93–95; formulas in, 85–89, 231; recorders of, 13–24; style and structure, 13–24, 93, 231–32
storytellers, 3–7, 11–13, 29–78; appropriate, 84–86; changing, 19–24. *See also individual storyteller names*
storytelling: contemporary, xviii–xxi, 3–7, 11–13; education through, 20–25, 63, 122–24; generic system, xix–xx, 79–93; historical, 8–11, 13–19
structure, of stories. *See* stories: style and structure
sun, 97, 102, 105, 108–10, 114–16
supernatural beings, 8–11, 86–87, 91–93
supernatural stories, 122–69
Swanton, John R., 17–19, 41, 69

talk of the elders. *See hopáki ikhąna*
tall stories (tall tales), xx–xxi, 79, 83, 89, 218–30

technology: prophesied, 203–5, 206–8; in tales, 219–20, 221
Thompson, John Hunter, 67, 76, 104, 172–73, 203
Trail of Tears. *See* removal
transcription. *See* stories: editing of
translation, xxvii, 18, 80–81, 93–95
tricks (tricksters), 100, 112, 116–20, 124–29, 132–34, 136, 151, 166, 172, 177, 179–80, 237–43, 245–58. *See* animals and birds, as recurring characters: Rabbit; *bohpoli* (Little People)
Tubby, Alexander, 5–6
Tubby, Estelline, xxv, 12, 24, 28, 68, 69, 94, 158, 181, 212–14
Tubby, Marilyn, 6
Tubby, Simpson, 18–19, 24, 68, 69, 77, 232

Uncle Remus, 41, 232, 255–57

Vaughn, Breanna, xxii, xxix, 11–12
Vaughn, Harley, xxii–xxvii, xxix, 11–13, 28, 65, 122
Vaughn, Hillary Meagan, xxii, xxix, 11
Vaughn, Mahlih, xxii, xxix, 11–12
Vaughn, Rae Nell, 11–12, 35, 70, 107–8, 147

war stories, 171, 181–82, 184–86, 214
warriors, 21, 27, 118–20
Weaver, Sandra, 6
Wesley, Cameron, xxi, 8, 57, 74, 217
whites. *See* race relations: Choctaw and whites
Whitman, Walt, 16
Williams, Henry, xxvi, 71, 80–85, 224
Williamson, Glenda, xxvi, 34, 49, 64, 82
Williamson, Meriva, xxvi, 34, 49, 64
Willis, Curtis "Buck," xxvi, 32, 76
Willis, Gladys, xxii, xxvi, xxviii, xxix, 9, 24, 72, 75, 146–47, 220–21
Willis, Hulon, xxiii, xxvi, xxix, 3–7, 9, 24, 28, 31, 71–73, 75, 82, 85, 167
Willis, Linda, 74, 214, 217
Willis, Mary, 6
Willis, Travis, 75, 153–54, 167–70
will-o-the-wisp. *See hashok okwa hui'ga*

Wilson, Louise, 67, 76, 173, 211, 215
Wright, Alfred, 15–17, 21

Yellowman, 84
York, Baxter, 69, 77–78, 111, 171, 185
York, Emmett, 77
York, Jake, xix, 77–78, 83, 84, 155, 179–80, 226–29

ABOUT THE AUTHORS

Photo courtesy of the editor

Photo by Bradley Isaac

Tom Mould is professor of anthropology and folklore at Butler University. He is author of *Choctaw Prophecy: A Legacy of the Future*; *Choctaw Tales*; *Still, the Small Voice: Narrative, Personal Revelation, and the Mormon Folk Tradition*; and *Overthrowing the Queen: Telling Stories of Welfare in America*, which won the Brian McConnell Book Award and the Chicago Folklore Prize.

Rae Nell Vaughn is a member of the Mississippi Band of Choctaw Indians and has served as chief justice for the Choctaw Supreme Court, chief of staff for the tribal chief, chairwoman of the board of directors of a tribally owned business, and tribal archivist.

www.ingramcontent.com/pod-product-compliance
Lightning Source LLC
Chambersburg PA
CBHW031847220426
43663CB00006B/521